Y0-BQZ-825

troop convoys we had to stop for

Who Stole my FATHER?

I breathed a sigh of relief

impenetrable darkness

Russian Town Church of San Francisco

PETER SLONEK

Boots on the cobble stone marching instep

Cover Design by Tina Slonek-DeMattia (www.tinamft.com)

Cover and interior photographs
property of Slonek Family

Author Portrait by Dan Tong

"Who Stole My Father" by Peter Slonek. ISBN 978-1-62137-168-7.

Published 2013 by Virtualbookworm.com Publishing Inc., P.O. Box 9949, College Station, TX 77842, US. ©2013, Peter Slonek. All rights reserved. No part of this publication may be reproduced, stored in a retrieval system, or transmitted in any form or by any means, electronic, mechanical, recording or otherwise, without the prior written permission of Peter Slonek.

Manufactured in the United States of America.

to all children

who have missed

or

lost a father

To a fellow writer with best wishes!

Peter

Christmas 2015

Contents

INTRODUCTION 1

PROLOGUE 3

1. THE DREAM 15

    FLOWERING MEADOWS 17

    DANGEROUS PLAY 22

    SEARCH FOR PLAYMATES 27

    NEW NEIGHBORS 36

    ILL AT HOME 42

    A REAL VACATION 48

    NEW FAMILY MEMBER 52

    HALF A CAR FOR THE FAMILY 55

    FOUR OF US IN THE COUNTRY 66

    HARD TIMES—NEW JOB—NEW BABY 70

    THE NEW HOUSE 74

    HORSE APPLES, GYMNASTS AND PUPPETS 83

    PAPA IN THE DARKROOM 88

2. THE WAR 91

    FRIENDS AND FAMILY 91

    THE FATHERLAND IS CALLING 94

    FIRST LETTER FROM THE ARMY 104

    SOLITARY CONFINEMENT: SCARLET FEVER 107

    VACATION WITH COUSINS 116

    ON LEAVE FROM THE RUSSIAN FRONT 124

    HITLER YOUTH IS PLAYING WAR 135

    RECORDING THE WAR 143

    CHRISTMAS SURPRISE 149

    OUR FIRST PET: A RABBIT 167

    PROPAGANDA MARCH 169

    DID YOU KILL? 179

    EASTER PRESENTS—4/4/44 196

    A LONG WALK HOME 199

3. THE CHAOS 224

    SEPARATION 224

    DANCING WITH THE GIRLS 235

DESTROYING EVIDENCE 239
REFUGE WITH AUNT MARTHA 244
NEW QUARTERS AT THE LAKE 251
LOOKING FOR GOODIES 256
THE ENEMY IS HERE 268
MILKRUN BY BOAT 272
CLOSE CALLS 287
WHAT'S UP AT HOME? 309
4. THE RETURN 337
FROM THE LAKE BACK TO TOWN 337
LIFE WITH THE SCHREIBERS 344
NEW NEIGHBORS—ANOTHER NEW LIFE 354
FATHER'S BEST FRIEND 363
VISIT TO THE RUSSIAN ZONE 374
GOING TO THE MOVIES 387
TROUBLE IN SCHOOL 392
LIVING WITH THE OBERBAURATS 396
HOME FOR THE NEWS 399

INTRODUCTION

Every time I read or hear about soldiers or civilians being killed in a conflict or in a bombing raid, there are parts inside of me that start hurting and bring on the tears. Then follows a bout of anger. Will there always be war, must there always be killing? Why have we not learned yet? Will we ever learn?

One of the reasons that kept me working on this book all along was the fact that a story like mine happens every moment somewhere in the world. Most of them out there are a lot more dramatic and scarring than mine. But mine is another one, a real one from many years ago, nevertheless true and saddening. Do we really need to tolerate and perpetuate a world like that? I firmly believe that we can do much better.

So many outstanding people have tried and are trying to get the great majority to believe in peace. When will we reach the "tipping point?" Is it in the big plan to reach the tipping point? I do not believe the universe was designed to function the way it is functioning today. How do we get to a peaceful world without wars? I do not have the answer, I just have the burning desire that we might get there. For myself, for my children and for my grandchildren. For all people. Most of the time it does not look very promising and at other times there appears a glimmer of hope.

Many years ago I started to write down what I remembered from my family's life in Austria before, during and after World War II. The writing became a healing exercise for me. It also opened up many wounds I did not know were still festering in my psyche.

Why do I feel my story needs to be out there and read, along with all the innumerable other writings about war and loss? Maybe one more story about the insanity of war, about the sadness and loss that war brings upon us, might tip the scales for once and for all.

My story shall be like one of the little brass weights I used on my mother's kitchen scale weighing flour and sugar when baking cookies and cakes, one of those little weights that intrigued me by their shape and feel, that

1

taught me about the metric system and also about balance. Maybe those ten or twenty grams will finally tip the scales.

1920's Measuring Weights

PROLOGUE

As soon as the train left the station, it went into a small turn, enough to lose sight of the people waving their goodbyes from the platform. No matter how far I leaned out of the window, I could not see any one. I imagined my mother, brother and sister standing there waving their little white handkerchiefs as a sign of their sadness over my leaving them. But nobody had been there. I had gone to the station on the bus alone. At fourteen years of age, I was deemed old enough to take care of myself.

I had said my goodbyes individually. I had kissed and hugged my brother and my sister as always when I left the house. They were too young to realize that I was going so far away. My aunt, who was taking care of my siblings while my mother was off training to be a midwife, did not really know what to say.

My father's best friend and his family of three had stood at the bottom of the stairs to wish me well. They had become part of the household two years ago when my mother had taken them in because they had nowhere else to go. Aunt Helga, who knew that I had a premature crush on her, said that the best farewell present she could give me would be a big kiss, but she could not deliver that because she had a bad cold. *I will take the cold any time, for a kiss...,* I thought but did not speak... I had visited my mother at the hospital where she was now doing her internship. She had traced a little cross on my forehead with her thumb, something she had never done before, then gave me the traditional kisses, one on each cheek, and hugged me quickly. I always felt she did not want to hug me any longer than was necessary. But then, how long was absolutely necessary?

"Be good, work hard, don't embarrass Uncle Toni, and write to me, please! Tell me all about the school," she said. Her voice and her body were pleading. I felt she had given away control over me some time ago. She was my mother but she was no longer in the position of a parent.

"I will, Mama, I promise. It will be interesting."

I had a thousand thoughts running through my head. I was going to be cooped up in a Catholic boarding school

3

for all of the next school year, possibly for the next five school years. Nothing I had ever heard about Catholic boarding schools had been encouraging. My benefactor, Uncle Toni, who was married to my mother's oldest sister, was the most devout Catholic in several large families of devout Catholics. Two of his brothers were Jesuit priests, his two sisters were nuns. Only one brother other than him had remained in the lay world. This uncle had felt responsible to ease my mother's burden of bringing up three children all by herself after my father had been killed in action in the war. Uncle Toni had offered to put me into this boarding school and pay my tuition.

Speculations within the family as to the uncle's real motive varied widely; the first and most kind was to take me off my mother's worry list but after that, nobody was sure. Was it to get me out from the influence of the liberal, ex-Nazi uncle who had sponsored me the year before? Was it a concerned move to bring me back into the fold of the church? Was it a gentle push to maybe even make me into a servant of the church?

"Do not believe everything the *Padres* tell you. Think on your own!" was the liberal uncle's advice when I had said goodbye to him.

They managed to keep me out of the elite Nazi school, the NAPOLA, now I am committed to a monastery school. I had closed the window of my train compartment. The soot particles flying back from the steam engine puffing hard to gain speed had stung my face more than had been comfortable. I sat down on the wooden slat bench, next to the window looking out at the familiar stretch of town. How many times had I been up and down this road along the tracks, on foot, by bicycle, on the bus, on the local electric train? The train sped by the crossing where I had had to wait on my way to school. Nobody was waiting there today.

"*How long before I will be back?*" I thought. So far, every time when I had gone somewhere, there had been a return date in the plan. Not this time. *"Five more years till I graduate from the Realgymnasium—but I will be back for Christmas, it is only five or six hours on the train—FIVE or SIX HOURS? That is an awful long time to sit on this bench*

... I wonder what Auntie packed for provisions ..." I reached up into the overhead rack and pulled down my satchel and opened one of the two bags with food. Tomatoes from the garden, two slices of my favorite farmers' bread with butter, something blue at the bottom, a small chocolate bar! That was a nice surprise. I guessed correctly about the second bag: two apples, several slices of the pound cake she always made for the weekend, a package of dry cookies, my old canteen filled with water.

I bit into one of the sandwiches, savoring the full flavor of the grains and the butter mixing. It reminded me of the best farmers' bread I ever had, at my friend Werner's parents' farm. Werner had been one of three students who shared space with me in a household under the supervision of an older couple in town, where my liberal uncle had paid my way to keep me out of trouble. Werner and I became friends and made plans to climb the *Grosse Priel,* one of the minor peaks in the foothills of the Alps. I had ridden my bicycle a few hours to Werner's farm home. I stayed overnight and then had breakfast there before taking off for our mountain climb. This would be my first alpine tour alone, without adults. We rode our bikes loaded with big rucksacks on our carriers to the trailhead. I remembered the exhilarating feeling of having made it to the top, taking in the snow-capped peaks of the Alps on the horizon, and looking down on lush green meadows and forests, with a few small lakes in between.

The train was now moving through the countryside, winding along rivers and in between fields and grazing cattle. It was early September. Only some late barley was still pretending to be an ocean on dry land. All the other grains had been harvested.

I pulled out the book I had brought with me: James Fenimore Cooper's *"Lederstrumpf." "Fenimore is a real strange name. I wonder what it means,"* I thought and opened the book to the bookmark, which was a photograph of my brother and sister. Now I would see them only at Christmas and during summer vacation. Ever since they were born, five and eight years after myself, I had watched over them and played with them. Then, before we all moved out of town because of the constant air raids, I had been sent to a school in the country, alone. When my mother finally found temporary quarters close by we all lived in one room for a while and became very close. Back in our old house, I played with them a lot, but then I went to the *Oberbaurats*, the study den in town, and now I was on my way out of town, to Graz.

I had never been to Graz before. From what I had gleaned from adult conversations over the years, compared to Vienna, Linz was still socially acceptable, Graz was 'in the provinces,' or so they said. I did not know who the authority on that was, but this hierarchy was generally accepted. I remembered the discussions in the family, when my uncle was offered the position as head of the Dermatology Clinic within the *Landeskrankenhaus* in Graz, the largest and most prestigious hospital in the province of Styria, and a teaching position at the Medical Faculty at the University of Graz. They were wondering how he could move to the provinces when he could have a career in the capital city of Vienna, with its world-renowned medical schools and hospitals?

The conductor opened the door to the compartment, "*Jemand zugestiegen?*" "Anybody new here?" A woman had entered the compartment at the last stop. She was a countrywoman, with a big basket for luggage, its contents covered with a large checkered cloth. The basket sat by her side on the empty seat. She had draped one of her arms over it for protection.

"I am getting off in Hinterstoder, *Herr Schaffner*," she said as she handed him her ticket, "will you please tell me before the station, so I don't miss it?"

"Well, it is the second stop. The next stop is Steyrling, the one after that is Hinterstoder. But I'll come and get you. Don't worry. This young man is going all the way to Graz. He doesn't have to worry; he'll get off at the end of the line. Good day," he said, tipping his finger to his cap and closing the door behind him.

"You go to Graz? I have never been to Graz. Your parents live there?" the woman had turned to me.

"My mother lives in Linz. I am going to go to school in Graz. My uncle and aunt live there." I had learnt about train conversations on my trips to Vienna. The trains had always been packed. Full compartments, full hallways, people sitting on their suitcases in between the legs of the passengers in the compartments. Unpleasant, with no space to move, my long legs were always running out of room, always colliding with somebody else. This trip was luxurious. For now, it was just this woman and me.

"You live in Hinterstoder?" I asked.

"No, I am visiting my sister there. She married the miller down at the end of the town," the woman answered.

The miller, I smiled to himself. That was one of the professions the family council had considered for me when I had done badly in school.

A friend of the family, who had found that his job in the war bureaucracy had evaporated after coming home from a POW camp, ended up as an inspector for grain mills. He traveled all over the countryside checking up on the sanitary conditions at these old mills that had been owned and run by the same families for generations. His plot was to find a spot for me as an apprentice in a mill and then search out an eligible miller's daughter for an eventual match. Then I would inherit the mill and sit pretty. The family council forged many such plans over time, none with my input, but with great gusto and sense of accomplishment on the side of the adults.

I looked out the window contemplating my fate as a miller's apprentice at the other end of Hinterstoder, a town of about five hundred souls, counting the farmers in the surrounding hills. Heaving heavy sacks of grain and flour, feeding the grinding stones churning away twenty four hours a day during the season, trying to get the flour dust off my body and out of my hair at the end of a long day—a life without revengeful teachers, without homework, without "F's" to be signed off by my mother. A country life in the arms of a plump miller's daughter who probably knows that all the attention showered on her was really directed towards her father's mill. A righteous, simple, and rewarding life—maybe? I did not know. It sounded better than propagating tulip bulbs in Holland or learning to plant hundreds of them in wonderful patterns, so their blossoms would eventually form royal crests, the Tower of

London, or the Clock Tower in Graz. That had been another suggestion of the family council.

I had shown no great enthusiasm for any of these master plans. I was grateful to my uncle that I could be on my way to Graz today, to continue on my scholastic path. I did not know what to think of the Marianist brothers, who would provide supervision during all hours of my life when I was not in the public school in the same building.

"Do you know Hinterstoder?" the woman asked, pulling me out of my musings.

"Not really. My father took my brother and me on a bicycle trip once. We got off the train at the Hinterstoder station and then rode up along the river. It was raining cats and dogs, we did not get very far," I said. My voice was trailing off with the memory.

"The river is wild. I am afraid of it. Sometimes it floods. So you went with three bicycles, your father, you and your brother?"

"No, my brother is five years younger than me. It was a long time ago. Before my father had been drafted into the army. My brother was too little. He sat on my father's bike, on a little seat in front of my father," I answered. "We had been looking forward to this trip for a long time. My mother and my little sister did not get to go. It was only for the boys."

"Did you sleep in a barn, in the hay? When we went visiting when we were kids, we always slept in the hay. It smells so good. And it is warm." The woman wiggled in her seat with a big smile on her face. "Oh my, we are stopping..."

The train was slowing down, the brakes were squeaking and the whole car was shaking from side to side.

"It's *Steyrling*, the conductor said; you get off only at the next one." I leaned forward and looked through the window to spot the station sign. There it was. "*STEYRLING*" it said in big black block letters. "Yes, it is *Steyrling*, see?" I said to the woman. She looked out at the sign and sighed with relief.

"I am so nervous. I always think I will miss my stop. Never mind me. Thanks for checking for me. The conductor will tell me." She lifted the cover on the basket at one corner and reached in with her hand. "Here, you want a pear? It is from my tree, I have two pear trees. We had nice fruit this year."

"Oh, yes, thank you," I said, "are you sure you can spare it?" I liked fresh fruit and there never was enough. We had a few trees in our garden but they were young and small and did not bear much yet. In a good year, the neighbors would sell us or trade some of their crops. A few times, we had gone into the country and picked apples or plums at a farm: two, three rucksacks full at a time and they were heavy to carry home. What we did not eat right away, my mother had canned.

The pear was big and ripe; it looked juicy and smelled good. "Thank you very much!"

The door to the compartment opened and the conductor stuck in his head. "Next stop is *Hinterstoder*, about ten more minutes."

"Thank you, *Herr Schaffner*!" the woman said and bowed her head slightly.

The conductor nodded with a smile and closed the door.

After ten minutes or so, the train slowed down, squeaked again and stopped. The woman said goodbye to me and got off. I looked at the station sign leaning out of the open window. There was a fresh breeze under a clear fall sky. I remembered arriving with my father and brother. We had walked to the freight car, the first one behind the locomotive and coal tender, where my father presented our claim checks to the attendant in the navy blue railroad uniform. He handed the bicycles down from the car. Then we had mounted the big Rucksack with our provisions on my father's luggage carrier and a smaller pack with extra clothes on my carrier.

"Keep the raincoats on top, Peter, it looks like we might need them," my father had said. I had seen the dark clouds above us from the train, but I had ignored them.

We had set off across an old iron bridge and then climbed the road along the roaring river. The grade finally became so steep that we had gotten off and pushed the bikes. But not for long. We had walked through a tunnel and then it went flat and even downhill a little. The canyon narrowed and the sky had become darker. The wind was loud and fierce in the trees, the water in the river came tumbling down over big boulders, there were short tunnels blasted through the rocky canyon walls, we were on our trip. Adventure was ahead. I was excited and pedaled hard to keep up with my father. When the rain started suddenly, we had pulled over and put on our loden ponchos and our little loden hats. My father had an old rain hat he said he had saved from the time when he was a scoutmaster. We laughed at its odd shape.

"Let's just go for a while and see what happens. Maybe it will clear up, if not we will stay at the next Gasthaus," my father had said and we agreed. It was hard to ride with the poncho on because it caught the wind and the rainwater would form a puddle on the part that hung over the handlebars and make the load heavier than it was. I kept emptying the water out, but it rained so hard it filled quickly again. Water ran down my face and, in spite of the poncho, down my legs into my shoes. There was a short break in the heavy downpour and we could see a piece of blue sky. We all cheered and father said it would certainly clear up soon, so we could make headway. But the clouds closed up again, it was so dark it felt like late evening when it was only early afternoon. Dieter had started to cry when he saw the first lightning. The thunder echoed through the canyon as if somebody had shot off a cannon right in front of us.

"Next Gasthaus we turn in, that's it, boys!" father had said. "Let's go as fast as we can!" We were lucky. After a few turns in the road there was a big whitewashed Gasthaus. The owner's wife took pity on us. "Oh my, oh my!" she had said over and over again and then she told us to sit in the kitchen by the big ceramic stove to dry out while she built a fire in the pot belly stove in one of the guest rooms upstairs. We sat in the kitchen, watching the woman's helper wash pots and pans and put them away. The kitchen was huge, bigger than our whole downstairs at home.

The woman served us hot soup and sausages and sauerkraut in the dining room. It was cold in there and it smelled of stale beer and stale cigarette smoke. We were all alone with the massive wooden tables and chairs, heavy linen tablecloths and skimpy paper napkins. The food was wonderful. So were the big featherbeds and huge pillows on our beds. I watched the dancing spots of light on the wall that came from the fire in the stove. My brother was asleep already and breathing deeply. My father had talked quietly about the weather and about how nicely these people had received us.

I had been worried about the money. We had not planned to stay in an inn or eat in a restaurant. My father had told me not to worry, it was very reasonable. Tomorrow we would eat the food we had brought and we would find a barn to sleep in.

I recalled that when we woke up it was cold in the room. I went to the window and pulled the curtains aside. It was dark and gray outside and raining hard. "If this keeps up, we have to go back home," my father had said. I remembered feeling a knot in my stomach that normally had to do with school. That time it was disappointment. I had felt like crying. We had planned on three days. Giving up on the first morning was too much.

During breakfast, my father had consulted with the owners. "Can't tell ever, but when it is that gray and cold, I figure it will be hanging here in the valley for a day or two. That's the way it has been. It's not just a thunderstorm that moves through. It's settled in." The owner had offered us to "sit it out" here and use the bowling alley in the back for amusement.

I was awakened from my daydream by a few shouts from the stationmaster and the train starting up jerkily. I looked for the road we had taken then. I did not recognize any landmarks. The river looked like many a river I had seen in the meantime. The road probably had been widened or repaved. All was gone, done with. There were only patches of memory left. No repeats. No scoutmaster to lead.

Slowly I was overcome by sadness. I had tears in my eyes. Were they caused by the air rushing by the open window or were they from the memory of the trip that had ended before it started? I closed the window and sat down.

I bit into the pear the woman had given me. It was very sweet and tasty. I ate all but the stem. That's the way my father had liked us to eat apples and pears. He said it was good for the digestion to eat the seeds and the little green seedpods. As long as there were no worms, that was not a problem for me. But eating around worms and their traces could become a nuisance.

Too many worms in my life, I thought. My father dead, my mother not really healthy enough to get started in her new profession, the family split into three, the house, owned by the steel mill, maybe not ours for much longer, my father's friend wearing my father's clothes and having them altered as if they were his to keep, my father's art and design tools and supplies traded away, one by one, for food, for clothing or shoes. Friends coming by and borrowing books—art books, engineering books, architecture books—never to bring them back. My mother did not follow up on them—we don't need them, she said. Why didn't she consider that maybe I would like to do the same things Papa had done—working with the potter, with the weaver, with the furniture designer, building the house he had designed, completing all his projects and dreams because he had shared them with me, his oldest son?

There was another stop. Officially this train was called an *Eilzug*, which was somewhere between a local and an express, but there were very few stations along the way it did not stop at. This was the only train for the day, so it had to give every village a chance to get its mail and passengers.

I looked for the station's name. It was *Windischgarsten*, a famous old spa, where some of my older aunts and uncles had come for the waters and the baths.

There were vendors walking up and down the length of the train selling samples of the local healing waters as well as just plain drinking water by the glass. Their voices were loud and urgent. I opened the window and leaned out. I got a whiff of the fresh rolls with cold ham and hot mustard another vendor was offering. I was tempted to buy one but then I thought better of it. My spending money was rather limited and I was going to be on my own for a long time. The good smells had made me hungry now, so I opened my bag and started eating the second sandwich. It was good, the bread was good, but the sandwich was not the same as when my mother made it. I could not tell what the difference was, only that there was a difference.

What would they feed me at the boarding school? Food was still scarce, would there be enough? I would have to compete with all these other boys for my share.

The train had started up again. I closed the window halfway so that I still could feel the breeze, which was cooler now because the mountains were closer and higher. The train was puffing up towards the pass and the long tunnel going under it.

When I was finished with my bread, I ate an apple, again down to the stem. I wiped my hands and went back to my book. The wooden bench was uncomfortable. The slats kept pushing on my backbone. I tried different positions and finally settled on just leaning forward with the book on my knees.

America, the Wild West, the Prairies, the Indians, the trappers, buffalo, elk and moose—would I ever have a chance to see it? I often imagined myself traveling across the Great Plains until I could see the Rocky Mountains in the distance. I would have a faithful horse, tall, with a silky coat and intelligent eyes, with an exceptionally good sense of smell and direction. Just like the Indian Chief Winnetou I had read about. The noble prince of the red race.

But Africa still was my first choice. No return of the German colonies, though. They messed that one up good by losing the war. The Germans had lost their chance of regaining their colonies forever. Another one of my dreams shattered. Before anything else, I needed to finish school. Nobody knew how that would go. Boarding school. Marianists. Priests. How strict would they be? Catholic strict? I had no experience other than Aunt Martha who had gone to church every morning, and made us say grace before every meal. When she prayed she always closed her eyes and bowed her head forward for a long time. There was my grandfather in Vienna, who went to church every morning, and prayed before meals, by himself. Only on holidays, the family would join him.

I remembered my uncle in Graz only vaguely from a wedding and from another family gathering. My aunt and my cousins I knew from two vacations we had had together, when our mothers wanted to be close while their husbands were away in the war. I had good memories of playing, hiking and swimming with my three cousins.

I tried to figure out how many years had gone by since I had seen them. At least four, when we visited with them in Vienna. Well, I was almost a young man now, and girls forge ahead during these years, so my cousins must be very much into young ladyhood. I leaned back in my seat and imagined the three of them at the station greeting me. Would they be happy to see me? Would they look at me as the intruder who would take a share of their parents' money and attention? Or would it be a joyous reunion for plotting more pranks and adventures together? Would they be showing me off to their friends or would they deny any connection?

The train was approaching the highest stretch on this trip. The engine sounded as if it were running out of steam. It pulled its load through a curve with much squeaking and shaking. Because of the turn, I could see the entrance to the tunnel, the long famous tunnel that was carved into the Bosruk Mountains along the route of the *Phyrn Pass* road to make it easier for the trains to conquer this range. After the few obligatory hoots of the steam whistle, the train entered the tunnel. It would take twenty minutes to get through. There were no lights on the train. I sat in absolute darkness, which was interrupted only once or twice by a small ember flying by the window before ending its short life.

From here on, after the tunnel, it was downhill all the way for the train. I was crossing the watershed between my home in Linz and my exile in Graz. More or less on my own, I coasted into a new world, a new life.

1. THE DREAM

FLOWERING MEADOWS

"Peter, please do not run. Walk slowly. There are people living downstairs. They get very upset when we make noise. Please be a good boy and remember that," my mother said.

I was four years old and active. I did not understand what my mother said because I did not think running makes that much noise.

The house we had moved to was an absolutely square cube house with a roof that had an almost perfect forty-five degree pitch. The owners lived downstairs, and they were just as square and angled. That is how trouble began.

The landlords, the Hallers, were an odd couple. They were older than my parents were. But not as old as my grandparents in Vienna. Sort of in between. Hertha, their daughter was two years older than I was. In the backyard there was a swing on a high mount. It stood in the middle of a big lawn, which was surrounded by her mother's immaculate flowerbeds. Sometimes I was allowed to play with Hertha and to use the swing. I never figured out why I could not go downstairs and into the garden when I wanted to. My parents never gave me a direct answer to that question.

"Mama, can I go and ask if Hertha can play?"

"Frau Haller does not want Hertha to play with you. And we can go down into the garden by ourselves only when they are not at home at all."

"Why can I not play with Hertha? She is nice. She pushes me on the swing. We have fun. We went out of the garden and up into the meadow to pick marguerites for you. I brought them to you. Remember? I like the meadow with the many flowers. They are this high," I held my hand at my eye level.

15

"Yes, I almost could not see you when you were up there, the grass is so tall. Peter, there are things which grown-ups talk about, that children do not understand. I cannot explain why you are not allowed to play with Hertha. Maybe when you get older we can tell you." My mother sounded uncomfortable with this answer but she was the one who had to enforce the new rule.

"Did you talk to Peter about Hertha?" my father asked my mother that evening.

"Yes, Emil, I did, and he did not understand. He thinks everything is fine between him and Hertha."

"Well it is—and I wish the Hallers would not get the children all caught up in this mess—but that is what they elected to do. I tried to talk them out of it. They are such..."

"Emil, please do not get upset again. It is not worth it."

"I know it is not worth it, but—, how can we stay here if Herr Haller keeps bringing this up. Who does he think he is, anyway?"

"Do you think Frau Haller could convince him that this is not the time, to just let it go?"

"No, he is too stubborn, too involved, and too fanatical about the Party. They are all like that."

"Would you ever consider joining the Party? You once said they have good ideas, that they would change things that needed changing," she asked.

"The Nazi Party? Never! Yes, they do have some good ideas—all of the parties have good ideas until they are in power, then they do what they want. Look at the mess we have in Vienna! I just want to do my work. I am enjoying what I am doing, for the first time since the University. Why can't everybody just leave me alone?"

"I don't know, but I am sure there is a way to keep out of it, don't you think so? I better start getting dinner ready." She moved towards the kitchen.

"You should hear Herr Langer," he said, following her, spreading his arms wide, "he is livid about the ugly things happening in Germany with the Jews. It is a terrible shame. I hope the Nazis never make it here." He gave the doorframe a slap as he moved through it.

"Is Herr Langer afraid the Nazis might get more support in Austria?"

"He does not talk to me about it. He does not trust me. Somehow, he believes I am in favor of the Nazi politics—and he treats me accordingly. I wish I could convince him otherwise. It is a pain. And then I come home and this ass of a landlord is pushing his Nazi stuff in my face..."

"Emil, did they approve your ad?" she turned towards him, holding the empty salad bowl.

"Yes, they loved it! Even the Director—he thought the coffee beans spilling from the package were a great idea, and he liked the colors of the coffee. Herr Langer was happy for once, too." He beamed a big smile at her.

"Well, congratulations! How shall we celebrate?" she asked.

"I already took care of it, my dear," he said. His one eyebrow arched over a big smile.

"Did you stop by Gerhardinger?"

"No, one better: Jindrak."

"Oh, Emil, you didn't—the chocolate pyramids with the Parisian cream?"

"How did you guess?" He laughed and pulled her close and kissed her.

"Didn't you say 'No luxuries during the week?'" she asked as she pulled back from the embrace.

"This was such a surprise, it warrants a splurge, even if it is midweek. They have never accepted an ad layout of mine during the first presentation—this time they liked everything—the photography, the graphics, and the fonts. All mine! Everybody in the meeting was impressed."

"I am so happy for you! And I am proud of you!"

"I will show them what I can do. Just watch, I will run that advertising department—soon. I think we should drink to that. Let's have a glass of Vermouth."

Moving from Vienna, the Capital, to Linz, in the Provinces, had been my father's answer to avoid undue influences on his new little family by either his own parents or his wife's parents. Both these families had been deeply enmeshed in Vienna's society for as long as anybody could remember. On my mother's side, it was a dynasty of Burghers, built on cheese production and an upscale delicatessen, *Providers to the Court of His/Her Majesty* at the time. The family produced their own cheese, supported by herds of cows kept on pastures high up in the Alps. Aging of the cheeses took place in three stories of cellars under the family Burgher house and store in the center of Vienna. A not so cheesy uncle was breeding Lipizzaner horses for the Imperial Spanish Riding School.

My father's ancestors had established a paper and cardboard manufacturing plant on a large estate, near the Roman ruins in Petronell, a small village between Vienna and the Hungarian border. The plant hit its peak of production and profits during the First World War.

My grandfather was said to have been very talented in negotiating contracts with customers throughout the Monarchy and in Germany. Rumors have it that all this was accomplished over excellent meals and plenty of drink. He was not averse to a good cigar either. When he was not negotiating, he was out hunting on his estate and beyond, or participating in social events in the city of Vienna, where he kept his main office. One of my favorite old photographs from the estate shows a number of gentlemen, all dressed in proper hunting attire: knickers, vests and jackets, pocket watch chains showing, standing along a canal, which was feeding water into the plant, rifles at the ready, waiting for one of the abundant muskrats to show its head.

My grandmother enjoyed city life in Vienna more than being the country matron. One story being told about her, illustrating her character, was that she was riding in a carriage along the *Prater Allee*, the main promenade at the time, flirting with the young gentlemen and officers parading there for exactly that purpose, at a time when she was not only married but also a few weeks away from delivering her first child, my father.

At the time of my father's decision to separate his family from the combined family histories in Vienna, Austria had been in political turmoil for several years, Hitler was entrenched as Chancellor in Germany; the Austrian Prime Minister had just been assassinated in an attempted Coup d'Etat staged by Austrian Nazis. In the wake of the worldwide economic crisis, hundreds of thousands of Austrians were unemployed. I had been the tender age of three.

My mother's father, called the *Grosse Opapa*, the tall grandfather, was working in the family business, responsible for financial matters, with little or no respect shown to him by other family members, his partners in the firm. My first memories of him are that of a funny, caring grandfather, mixed with an image of a very nervous and cranky man, who was best served by feeding him what he wanted and by being quiet around him.

My mother was the second oldest of six living children, four girls and two boys. Two siblings had died at birth. The other six live births in quick succession had shrunk my grandmother to a very thin, always sickly looking woman, whose actual physical and moral strength surprised everybody. My mother was the first of the children to be married.

According to my father's view, her parents' household was in steady chaos. One of the main factors contributing to this image was that my grandmother was cooking different dishes for each of her children for almost every meal, since their individual tastes rarely coincided with that of their siblings. My grandfather's habit of eating every food item from a separate dish did not contribute to a harmonious family dinner atmosphere either: He went to the extreme where he would eat the noodles separately from the soup, and, of course, the spinach, the beef, and the potatoes had to be served on separate plates, at separate times, so they would all be hot off the stove.

On my father's side all that was left of the family estate at that time was an expensive flat in an exclusive neighborhood in the city, occupied by my grandparents. There was also a small office where my grandfather functioned as a sales representative for the old factory, which had changed hands shortly after the end of World War I. Why and how that transaction happened was never talked about. Even much later, after my grandfather had died, I never received an answer to my questions about the fate of the factory. The same was true for many other questions I had about the family. My grandmother told one story over and over again. On a whim, my grandfather had gone to visit the old factory grounds and had come back very upset because the current owners had cut down some trees next to the entrance.

My grandparents still owned several old apartment buildings in Vienna. The meager cash flow from these rent-controlled properties provided their income. They lived very frugally, my Oma forever chiding the "*Kleine Opapa*," the short grandfather, as I called him, for hanging on to his expensive pipe and cigar habit. She was the one who managed the money now, which lead me to the assumption that either my grandfather was to blame for the loss of the factory or that my grandmother was the one who had brought the apartment buildings into the marriage, or both.

My father had a younger brother, uncle Otto, who was enamored with motorcycles, automobiles, and women. He lived by himself in a flat outside of Vienna, working as a representative for one of the large oil companies, traveling around the countryside doing his work and arduously searching for a woman to marry.

I was the first grandchild in both families. Everybody had his or her ideas about how to bring me up, which translated mostly into how to spoil me. My father would have moved away as soon as I was born, if economic reality had not kept him from doing that. He had his own plan on how his son was to grow up.

That was why he finally decided to take his wife and son to another town where we could build a life according to his own ideas. First on the agenda was to find a job. Being new in the area, he would have to struggle to find enough clients for his own advertising business to make enough money to support the family. After some soul searching, he decided to go for a full-time job. He was hired by an international coffee importer, roaster and distributor as an assistant in the advertising department with promises of great advancement.

Next on the list was to find proper living quarters. It had to be a house, not an apartment, it had to have a garden, and it needed to be in a nice neighborhood. After much searching he rented the upper story of a small villa, located on Frog Mountain, *Am Froschberg* in German,

named for a series of large ponds close by which were full
with frogs, making quite a romantic racket every night
during frog season.

The green area containing the ponds was one level
above the actual city of Linz. Access to the residential area
also provided access to yet another level, the *Gugl*. There
was a Jesuit Monastery in a park-like setting and around
it, the rich had built their mansions. For many in the city,
it was a must to do their Sunday walk up there, maybe
just to rub elbows with the haves. I never liked to be there,
it was too dark under the old trees, and the big iron fences
and gates looked like they were made to lock children
either out or in. In addition, the Sunday walkers were a
rather boring lot, sullen and much wrapped up in their
Sunday best, not tolerating any noise, like running and
other low class behavior by children.

There was one exception to my dislike: an intriguing
house half way up the hill on the road that lead to all this.
It was the home of Mr. Wu, an internationally known
"Zopfrutscher"—an acrobat who slid down a long steel rope
reaching from under the eves of the circus tent way over to
the main entrance for the performers, supported only by a
little pulley wheel attached to the end of his long braided
hair. Later in my life, my "little" grandfather, who was very
much enamored with circus and variety shows, took me to
see the Zopfrutscher performing in a circus in Vienna.
Ever since then my friends and I would go by there,
staring at the nameplate in awe—nobody else in Linz had
a last name of "Wu" -, trying to catch a glimpse of the man
himself. Only once was I able to spot him briefly slipping
into a fancy black car, which of course added to my
imagined mystery reputation of this man.

The street Mr. Wu lived on has another significant
memory engraved on its asphalt: The prime method of
self-propelled transportation for kids of all ages at the time
was the scooter. It was a board with a wheel at each end,
the front wheel steered by an upright board, which ended
in a handlebar. Standing with one foot on the lower board,
holding on to the handlebars, one pushed with the other
foot for propulsion. Downhill, of course, no pushing was
necessary, both feet were on the lower board and off you

went. One day, on this very hill, where my friends and I played often because of its steepness, I was the passenger on my friend's scooter crouching right where the two boards met, holding on to the lower part of the upright board. We had a fast, exciting ride, almost to the bottom of the hill where there was a major street with some traffic. My friend messed up his breaking maneuver; the front wheel turned sideways and sent us tumbling: scooter, friend and me. Unfortunately, from my crouched position, I had very little choice on how to fall. I slid off the board and continued to slide, on my side, a few meters down the road, which had been resurfaced recently with tar and split. Those sharp little stones made an awful looking mess on my skin, from shoulder to shin. I was blackened, bleeding and hurting. However, my main concern was not the pain but fear. My father had strictly forbidden me to play and ride on that hill. What would I tell? The stones and the traces of tar were a dead give-away.

In order to get the wounds cleaned and bandaged, I had to make my way home. I found my mother in the kitchen, cleaning spinach in a big bowl of water in front of her. She was in total shock when she saw me. Later in the day, my father had a serious talk with me and doled out some consequences. The wounds healed. Mr. Wu's hill became really off limits for play from then on, which probably was a very good idea since there was more and more traffic on the bottom cross street and the intersection became increasingly hazardous.

DANGEROUS PLAY

My favorite presents from my fourth birthday were two *Schuco* cars. They had a windup motor and an odd shaped bumper that would not allow them to fall off the edge of a table. They would drive right up to the edge, turn around and continue. In an unexpected fall, one of them had broken apart into chassis and body. It still worked because the trick bumper was part of the chassis. The little motor was visible now and I was fascinated by all the different size cogwheels inside of it. The strong steel spring that provided the driving force shone with the colors of the rainbow.

"Come on, it is time for bed. It is late. Just because Papa is not home, you cannot stay up," my mother said and came to collect me from the living room.

"One more turn, please Mama!" I pleaded.

"Yes, you can wind the car up one more time, and let it run out. Then it's off to bed without a word, promise?"

"Promise," I said without looking at her. I wound up the car's motor. It purred on top of our round dining room table, going to the edge, turning around and going to the other edge, back and forth, until finally it went slower, slower, and stopped.

"Now—ready?" my mother asked.

"Yes, no more asking, I promised," I said with a smile.

I walked towards the bedroom in front of her. "You look so grown up in your little bathrobe," she said.

"Can I leave the light on five more minutes, please?"

"Peter, I told you, no more extensions, otherwise you won't be asleep when Papa comes home and then he will be very upset. It is late already. Please go to sleep. Tomorrow you can play all day again, yes?"

"Yes, Mama, good night." I pulled her head down with both my hands and gave her a big kiss. "Good night, sleep well!"

"Good night, you sleep well, too, my darling!" She always stroked my face gently before she turned off the light.

I had the car under my pillow. I found it quickly after my mother closed the bedroom door. I wound it up again. I held the big cogwheel with my thumb so the motor could not unwind.

By now, my eyes had adjusted to the darkness. The light coming in through the window from the street lantern out front was enough to see everything in the room. The big rubber plant in the corner of the room cast a weird shadow on the ceiling. I liked to make up figures and stories with the different shapes before going to sleep. Tonight I was going to play some more with the car.

The sharp teeth of the cogwheel moved a little bit over my thumb as soon as I let up with the pressure. For a while, I made noise patterns that way. Run, stop, run, stop. Now it did not pull as hard as with the fully wound spring. I let it run and let it move up my arm. It tickled. I ran it up and down my body, over my tummy and across my chest.

I rewound the spring and started the tickling trip again. Up the outside of the arm and down on the inside. Down one leg and up the other. Somehow, through the different movements my little penis had slipped out of my pajama shorts and presented itself as another target. Carefully I steered up—ouch—ouch, I screamed as the tender foreskin was pulled in between the two top cogs. The motor stopped from the obstruction. I panicked. I tried to turn the key backwards but nothing moved. I tried to pull, it hurt and I stopped.

Prompted by my scream, my mother came into the room and turned on the light.

"What on earth are you up to?"

"The motor got caught on my *Zipferl*," I said in a very low voice, "and it is hurting. I cannot get the car off."

My mother's thoughts raced back and forth from medical emergency to moral pangs. What can she do to free me from this painful appendage? What will she tell her husband? Will he think she did not take good care of the child and was negligent? Would he wonder why she let me play with my genitals? She stopped herself. First, she had to get this machine off this little penis. But how?

She bent down and tried to turn the wheels backwards. Nothing moved but I jerked and let out another ouch.

"Turn the key backwards," she said to me.

"I tried, it does not work. It is all stuck in there. Please get it off."

"I don't know how. Your father will not be home until very late, I am sure he would know what to do. Can you hold on that long?"

"No, Mama, the skin is turning blue around the wheels already. It has to come off soon."

She had a thought, but immediately pushed it away. It came back. She could ask the landlord. He is home, she heard his voice earlier. However, she could not possibly tell him what happened. She could describe the motor stuck on something else, and he could give her advice on how to get it off.

No, we are barely speaking since last week. Emil would kill her, if he found out. Not only the breach of silence but also the embarrassment—our son, playing with his penis.

But what else could she do? Should she call the doctor? It was not a medical emergency. It was mechanical. A little medical, perhaps. Delicately medical? But it would take the doctor about an hour to get here. That was too long. Something had to be done sooner. Right now.

It is my child's health, she said to herself. The closest help is downstairs. That is where I will go. She shut out the consequences, her husband's reaction, the discussion, the possible gossip and all her other unthinkable thoughts...

Herr Haller, who was tall and not very coordinated, came up immediately, and looked at the damage.

"What do we have here? How does that feel, Peter? Well, it does not look too complicated," he said, "Do you have a pair of pliers handy? I can get mine."

"No, I do have some, let me get them, what size do you want?" my mother asked.

"Oh, anything not too big will do. You don't have to be afraid," he said to me, "it'll snap right open."

He took the pliers and pushed the two metal plates, which held all the cogwheels in place, apart. The spring made a whirring sound and flew away as it unwound freely and the insides of the little motor tumbled all over my body and the bed.

I covered myself immediately, my mother blushed and said, "Thank you!" as she was handed the rescue instrument. "I could have thought of that," she said.

"With the surprise, the shock, one does not think very logically right away. It's fine now, just check that little thing for a wound, but I don't think there is anything, that motor was so little," Herr Haller reassured them.

"Thank you so much, sorry for interrupting your evening this late ..."

"Oh please, don't even mention it. It was nothing, I was glad I could help. That is what neighbors are for. Give my regards to your husband, please. I have been meaning to talk to him. Maybe we can get together this weekend. He is such a busy man. Always working, isn't he?"

"Yes, he is, he cannot say no, when they ask him for more."

"Well, Good night, good night Peter. You are feeling fine after this operation, yes?" he asked.

"Yes," I said with my head barely visible under the covers.

"Say 'Thank You' to Herrn Haller, for rescuing you!" my mother admonished.

"Thank you," I said. My voice was very little.

Herr Haller shook my mother's hand and turned to go. My mother accompanied him to the front door.

"Thank you, and good night!" she said into the stairwell after Herr Haller. Her voice sounded hollow and dry.

"*What will she tell my father?*" I did not want to think this one through.

"I cannot believe you really did that! What were you thinking?" my father said. "I thought we were very clear on 'no communications' with these people unless it was about business? And then you let him in on an embarrassing situation like that ...? I do not want these people in our apartment under any circumstances. They have no business knowing how we live."

I was still awake in my bed. I had heard the door when my father had come home. I could hear my parents talking but could not make out most of the words. My mother's voice was very low, my father's was louder and sounded angry. I raised my head to hear better but through the closed door the voices were not clear enough for me to understand. I panicked. If my father is that angry, what will my punishment be? I had better pretend to be asleep. Maybe by tomorrow my father would be less angry. I reached down towards my penis. I flinched. The spot where the cogwheel had bitten into the skin was very sore. I drifted off to sleep.

SEARCH FOR PLAYMATES

Since the situation with the built-in playmate at our new house had its problems, my parents decided they would go in search of others, less prone to politics and landlords' moods. Since they had seen no other children my age on our street, they were talking about finding a Kindergarten so I would meet other kids and develop my social skills.

The first opportunity presented itself soon after the decision had been made, at a playground in the neighborhood. Another mother with a son about the same age as I appeared and we started to talk and play in the sandbox almost instantly.

The other boy's mother came up and started a conversation. "Good Day!" she said, "Excuse me for asking, but does your son go to a Kindergarten? He really plays well with my son."

"No, but we have been talking about finding him one. We just moved here several months ago. Does your son attend one?"

"Yes, he does. I can recommend it highly. It is not too far and all the children there are very well behaved. They seem to come from good families. I can give you the address and the woman's name if you want to try."

"That would be very kind. My name is Slonek, Lisl Slonek." My mother stretched out a hand.

"I am Frances Baumer. I am pleased to meet you. Where do you live?"

"We live up on the Froschberg, the last house on the right. And you?"

"We are at the bottom of the hill from you, the first house on the right, when you turn into Wieseneder Strasse coming from town. It looks like a haunted castle, all overgrown with wild grapes and surrounded by trees. You must have noticed it."

"Oh, yes, we walk by there all the time. Actually, my husband commented on it the other day. He thought it was a quite romantic looking building. You live there alone?"

"No, we just have the upper floor, the one with the big balcony. There are two other couples living there, on the lower level, but we are the only ones using the garden. There is a narrow gardening area up behind the house. The front and the side parts you can see from the street are too steep to do anything there other than tend to the shrubs. Hans loves to play there."

"Oh, is that his name? My son's name is Peter! You seem to have an accent, where are you from, if I may ask?"

"I know, everybody tells me that, although I have been in Austria for many years. I was born and raised in Leipzig. I guess the Saxonian overtones might never go away." My husband though is Austrian.

"Well, it sounds very nice, it just does not sound like the local dialect, but I do not think you want to sound like a true Upper Austrian."

"No, I am having the hardest time to get Hans to speak properly. He imitates what he hears. It must be one or two of the children in the kindergarten. He must pay attention to them."

"Yes, we are concerned about the same problem. My husband is adamant about speaking proper German, he does not even call it 'Austrian.' He thinks the Viennese dialect is the worst of them all."

"I am not really familiar with that, but I have heard said that it is quite vulgar sounding." Frau Baumer reached into her purse and produced a little note pad. She wrote the name of the Kindergarten and that of the director on the first empty page, tore the page out and handed it to my mother. "They will be there again on Monday in the morning. I would recommend that you stop by and bring Peter with you."

I was standing in front of the two women and had overheard the last few sentences. "I do not want to go to a Kindergarten. I hate Kindergartens."

Frau Baumer looked at me in surprise. "Hans goes there and he likes it very much. You can play with him there. Then you will have a friend already."

"We can play here. It is nice here. I like it." I retorted.

My mother said, "We will go and look at it. I think you
will like it. Many children go to a kindergarten and they all
like it."

"Well, no harm in going there. I am sure he will
change his mind," Frau Baumer said. "We will have to go
now, I have to do some shopping for tonight. How about
meeting here again? Let us say Tuesday afternoon, if I do
not see you on Monday. Yes?"

"Tuesday would be fine. We will be here unless
something unforeseen happens. It was nice meeting you,
Frau Baumer and you, Hans. Auf Wiedersehen!"

"The pleasure was ours. Auf Wiedersehen, Frau
Slonek, and Peter. Good luck at the Kindergarten! See you
Tuesday! Adieu!" She used one of the many French words
Austrians love to sprinkle in with their German.

I won on the Kindergarten front, I did not know
whether it was my resistance or whether the fee was too
high, or if my mother felt it was inconvenient taking me
that far twice a week. Anyway, no Kindergarten, but Hans
stuck with me. Until we moved away from Froschberg, he
was my main playmate. The Baumers' house was located
conveniently on the way to town, Frau Baumer was happy
for Hans to have proper company, and the garden was a
paradise for both of us. On rainy days we would play
inside, Hans had a never-ending supply of toys and his
mother fed us wonderful snacks. Once in a while, she
would make a recipe from her homeland and some of that
I liked, too, but *Rote Grütze*, for example, I had a hard time
with. It was kind of a pudding—Germans must love
puddings—made of sago or grits, flavored with red currant
juice, hence the name. It did not taste like red currants,
which I loved, and it was not firm like other things we ate.
It shivered when you looked at it, and it trembled violently
when it was touched. The rule at my house was that I had
to eat everything that was served at the table. Therefore, I
ate the trembling mess out of fear of being reported. It was
really not all that bad, especially when we would get a
little treat of whipped cream with it.

"Why is your father always so serious?" I asked Hans.
"He sits down at his desk and looks at the papers from his

briefcase right after he comes home from work. Does he ever do anything else?"

"That's just how he is. He manages a big factory where they make sugar. Many people work there. He has lots to do to keep it running."

"How do they make sugar?"

They buy sugar beets from the farmers and cook the beets until they turn to sugar. I do not know how it works. My father took me once to see but I was very little then. Do you know what sugar beets look like?"

"My mother cooks beets, red beets. She makes salad with them. I like the taste. They do taste sweet. Are they like sugar beets?"

"Sugar beets are much bigger and not red. I think they are yellow inside. Let's ask my father." We went over into the living room where Herr Baumer's desk stood in a corner. He was bent over his papers.

"Excuse us, Vati, we have a question for you."

Herr Baumer turned towards them and smiled. "What is the question?"

Peter wants to know what sugar beets look like. He only knows red beets. I am not so sure either."

"Well, Peter, you never see sugar beets in the grocery store, so you would not know what to look for. Have you ever seen a train go by with lots of open freight cars loaded high with grayish-brownish clumps looking very much like a large potato or a very fat carrot with a little tail? Mostly they are rather dirty, still, and the greens are cut off."

Oh, I think I have seen them growing in a field. The big green leaves on top and half of the 'big potato' sticking out of the earth. Long rows of them, very green leaves, yes?"

"Very good, Peter, did your father point them out to you, maybe?"

"I think he did. He knows many plants and many animals. He grew up in the country next to his father's factory."

"Oh, what kind of factory? Where is it?"

"They made paper there and cardboard. I do not know where. My grandfather does not own it anymore."

"Well, that is sad. You never were able to visit there. Back to the sugar beets: What else did you want to know about them?"

"What color are they on the inside?" Hans asked.

"Do you remember when you came with me to the factory, when we looked at the cutting machine? The inside flesh is yellow/white/reddish—there are several kinds of sugar beets we are processing."

I thought it funny that Hans' father talked slightly through the nose, as if he was stuffed up. When he joined them for meals—sometimes I got to eat lunch or dinner there, as a treat, or because my parents had something planned and had asked if I could stay—Hans and his mother seemed to be in awe of him. He was always friendly, not smiling and laughing, but quiet and asking what we had been playing. He seemed to think always about his factory, even when he was talking to us. Rarely Hans would ask him to help us solve a problem, he just could not be that involved. This was strange to me because my father was always available to find something I was missing, or he had a suggestion on how I could do things easier or better.

Hans never came to play with me at my house. My parents were afraid we would make too much noise and get into trouble with the landlords. Hans' parents did not seem to mind, especially since we got along without fighting ever, and they were glad he had someone to play with at their own home.

Some habits in Hans' family were very different from ours. A certain amount of time after lunch, Hans had to go to the toilet. His mother would call him, if he did not remember by himself, and he had to sit there until he had produced results. I was allowed to go when I had to. That seemed a lot easier to me. Hans often made a face when he heard his mother's call, he looked like his father then, slightly tortured and sad. But there was no escape for him.

When Hans' mother deemed it necessary, he needed to put on a sweater. I could never understand that. Did she have a hidden thermometer on Hans that indicated when he was cold enough to need a sweater? Maybe she did go by the clock: 4:30 in the afternoon, it would be cool enough to wear a sweater. I never figured it out and it bothered me no end, because her calling Hans to put on a sweater never coincided with my getting cold. I was cold either before or after, never at the same time. The strictness in that household seemed to forbid asking questions about habits like that. I just knew, if I asked I would get into trouble. So I did not ask. Consulting my own parents about things like that, they always seemed to have an answer, which protected the perpetrators of such illogical acts, as I called them secretly in my head. I had to figure it out myself or never know the answer.

I loved the garden around Hans' house. Coming in from the street there were about a dozen steps leading to the level where the house stood, built into a steep hill, and three stories high. Next to the house, on the left, the steps went on all the way to the top where one was at eye level with Hans' flat's windows, but separated from them by a twelve foot "moat" which went down all the way to the basement level. The top rim was securely fenced, so nobody could fall into this big trap. The area, way down there in the moat, came in handy later when Hans received a BB gun for his birthday and we could safely shoot at a target mounted on the far wall in the moat.

Up on top Hans' mother had her garden. There were beds the whole length of the house, planted with strawberries, rhubarb, onions, tomatoes, different herbs, kohlrabi, cabbage and kraut. Only when we were a little older she asked us occasionally to help with the weeding or the watering. Hans' mother did most of the work by herself, quietly, her hands covered with gardening gloves in flowery patterns and colors. At the proper times she allowed us to pick a given number of ripe strawberries, or a cup full of red currants, which we then had to wash and eat, sitting down, from small glass bowls. Sometimes these fruits became part of an afternoon snack, as a topping for pudding, or just as a spot of color on a piece of coffee cake.

Playing with Hans never got wild. He was in good health, with the correct weight for his age and size, but he was not a fast mover. I always thought he moved like his father but I kept this observation to myself until much later. We never ran through the garden around the house, which was hard for me to understand since the paths all connected, and the incline up and then down behind the house would have been ideal for a little race. I could not remember a single time when we were admonished not to run. At Hans' house one did not run.

Somewhere along the way, we discovered loam about half way up the hill. It was beautiful ochre loam, as pure as we could imagine it. We must have heard about pottery and firing green ware, because we immediately launched into an all out production run of ashtrays although there were no smokers in either family. We had a big pit with water where we would mix the clay, we formed the ashtrays on a large old garden bench higher up on the hill. We dried our pieces in the hot Austrian summer sun, which did not make the pieces unbreakable, but firmed the clay up considerably so one could handle the ashtrays quite normally. Instead of glazes, I had brought my watercolors and we used those quite liberally. The dark green looked especially good on the light clay and we used it up rather quickly. The pieces took loads and loads of paint, because the dry clay absorbed incredible amounts of water with the watercolors.

After our artistic pottery period, we moved into a construction phase. We both had Matador sets—a must for any boy our age—which were a wooden version of the metal erector sets. By combining our sets, we had a great selection of wooden blocks in different lengths and thicknesses, also flat boards and wheels in different diameters. We built from instruction sheets but mostly created our own designs: cars, planes, tanks, streetcars— anything we could imagine. Hans' large set and my medium one provided enough pieces to build quite a collection of smaller items or several big ones. That was when we invented stability testing. I had built a big bus, Hans had built an equally large truck. At one end of Hans' living room was a French door leading out to a terrace again as large as the living room. It had a smooth floor and provided an ideal playing field for our cars, Hans' model railroad—and for stability tests.

We had decided we would crash our two vehicles into each other to see which one would break first. We took up positions at opposite ends of the terrace and on the agreed upon signal we shoved our vehicles with as much might as we could muster towards the other. The test cars crashed head on—if we aimed right—and on first impact lost a few outside parts, none that would hinder the basic function of rolling. Hans and I continued the crashes until one of the cars would snap apart totally, with most of the sticks holding it together broken, parts flying all over the terrace. The sound of wood on wood, the snapping of the little sticks (which we could replace for very little money), the flying roofs and wheels, all this created a spectacle we thoroughly enjoyed. Should one of the adults be close, we would tone down the speed and have "civil" crashes, which did not do much damage at all. We refined our designs over a period of time to withstand six or seven major hits before the vehicles started to loosen up and disintegrate. This was as wild as it ever got with Hans and me. However, after we broke a few of the larger and expensive block pieces we decided to abandon this game. We started to concentrate on especially elaborate cranes that could hoist toys off and on the terrace, all the way down to the garden, two stories below.

When we were in fifth and sixth grade, respectively, we did escalate our experiments to include gunpowder. Hans had discovered the simple formula in an old chemistry book. After a few purchases of the ingredients at the local drug store, the pharmacist became suspicious and stopped Hans' powder mixing quest. From then on, each of us went to different drug stores, bought only one ingredient at a time with a cover story of a school experiment we would need this particular chemical for. We had no more supply problems, even though we needed more and more powder since the explosions got more elaborate. Initially, we just blew up small pillboxes, then larger containers but these explosions would melt the asphalt on the terrace and leave black streaks on the walls. We had to get more sophisticated to be safer and have more fun.

Wartime rocketry inspired our best (and last) experiment. We decided to propel a model train car with a rocket. Hans had a zero-gauge model railroad. We laid a straight line of tracks across the terrace ending in a big curve all the way to the corner. We picked the coal tender as the carrier for our rocket motor.

In our search for a workable rocket, we had come upon a small grease gun that seemed ideal for this purpose. It had a solid steel mantle and a small opening at one end. To ensure a successful launch, we filled it with tightly packed powder. We used the best of our fuses, hemp string doused with some kind of solution that Hans had learned about in chemistry class. Then we laid it all out, coal tender at the end of the tracks, ready for take-off. We lit the fuse, we stepped back into the terrace door for protection and waited. The fuse burnt steadily and slowly. We could follow the little smoke trail with our eyes. When it disappeared into the nozzle we worried about it being smothered by the lack of oxygen.

A little streak of fire started hissing through the nozzle. Next thing, it had to start to push the car... we leaned forward in anticipation. The little hiss all of a sudden turned into a big hiss, the car did not move but turned into a fireball, followed by an awesome explosion, which scared us to death. We both jumped back through the door, much too late of course, the explosion was over. Hans looked at his knee: Blood trickled from a black spot and it hurt. When he carefully wiped over it, a small piece of metal fell to the ground. It was a piece of the grease gun. Since we did not notice any other injuries, we went to inspect the scene of the explosion. The poor little coal tender was nowhere to be seen. The piece of track where the explosion had occurred was demolished. We found the wheels of the car in different corners of the terrace, and, lodged into the mortar of the terrace wall, the stronger part of the grease gun. Much later, after we had extended our search to the garden below the terrace, we found the piece of sheet metal that had made up the coal tender. It was scorched and had lost all its paint. It was totally flattened out.

For some reason we were not able to assemble another test until much, much later, after the end of the war, when we had access to real gunpowder, extracted from machine gun ammunition or rifle shells left in the fields by fleeing German soldiers. We removed the actual bullets and then poured out the powder. A more hazardous way of mining the precious stuff was to pry the projectile off an anti-aircraft shell: The explosives inside looked like black spaghetti and were easier to handle than the powder.

Our last experiment was set up in my garden and was somewhat more successful. The train car moved at least ten feet along the track before the rocket exploded. The explosion again flattened the car and the tracks and laid open an underground anthill we had not known to exist. After that, we gave up on rocket experiments. We had learned about jet-propelled planes and we had seen drawings of the German rockets that had created horrible damage in many British cities. Our experiments had been fun and our guardian angels had watched over us well. Our parents had not been aware of how close we had been to losing life and limb, or at least an eye.

NEW NEIGHBORS

The house across the street from ours stood alone in a large field. An eight-foot high privet hedge backed the metal fence. Only the metal gate provided a peek at the entrance of the brick house, which was totally overgrown with ivy. I never saw any people coming or going at this green fortress. There were no lights in the windows after dark. I began to suspect that maybe this was a haunted house like the ones I had read about in fairy tales and ghost stories. Then one day a big moving truck appeared and men started carrying furniture and boxes into the house. After that, all went quiet and mysterious again.

Several days after the movers had come, people appeared. I observed the comings and goings of a father, a mother and two children; a girl close to my age, six or so, and a boy somewhat younger. I only got casual glances of them from behind our curtains because my father frowned on watching neighbors. Being nosey was not part of good behavior.

A week or so after the new family had shown itself, my mother went over there and introduced herself. After much pleading, she had allowed me to come along. A friendly woman greeted us and asked us in. She introduced herself as Frau Graf and her two children as Ingrid and Erich. She went to great lengths apologizing for the disorder in the house and for not being able to offer us something like lemonade or coffee and cake, which normally she would do.

"Oh, we will do that at our place, you have too much to do!" my mother said. "When could you come over?"

"Thank you, but not before next week, I really want to get all the things sorted out and put away before I start going out!"

"Well, how about Tuesday afternoon then, about three o'clock?"

"That is very kind of you, Frau Slonek, thank you so much. If anything comes up that would make it impossible to come, I will let you know. Would that be acceptable?"

"Certainly, I know how it goes with moving, we just barely got organized. It would be our pleasure to have you on Tuesday. If you cannot make it, we will schedule another time!"

"If Peter wants to come over and play with Ingrid and Erich, he is most welcome to do so. They would love to have a new friend! We have a sandbox in the back, and my husband is going to install the swing this weekend as long as the weather is good."

"We have a nice swing, it will go on the tree," Ingrid said. "Can Peter come into the garden with me, I'll show him where."

They went outside and Ingrid gave me a tour of the garden in the back of the house. It was nice and spacious. The overgrown hedge here consisted of various shrubs. A formal path lined with tree roses divided the garden in half. The swing would go on the big tree in the corner.

"My father will have to take care of them," Ingrid said and pointed at the roses. He really does not want to but he has to, the property owner said. We are not allowed to play in the garden in front of the house. That part is for the other people."

"Where are the other people?" I asked.

"They live upstairs."

"I have never seen anybody in this house before you came."

"I do not know, maybe they are hiding, but my Daddy talked to them when we arrived. They gave us the key to our apartment," Ingrid said, shaking her head.

Ingrid was shorter than I was. She had thin blond hair, very blond, almost white. It looked nice around her tanned little face. She wore a bluish gingham dress, with a white apron tied in front. I liked her. She moved quickly and talked rapidly. I liked that. I did not like to wait for people to talk. Her mother was a talker, too. She was rattling along with a nice guttural voice, full in tone and underlined by small gestures made with hands and arms. One had to keep listening because she always looked intensely at you while she was talking to you.

Ingrid appeared to me like an angel. Her blond hair, her angelic face, her fragile body, and her soft ways of playing, all intrigued me. I took to her very quickly after we started spending time together. The petite blonde-haired woman, with blue eyes and a gentle manner became an image that followed me throughout my life: from that time on, I always was attracted to this type. Strangely enough, I never fell in love with a woman with those features. A major reason was that I grew to be rather tall and petite women did not make a good physical match, which became an important factor mostly because I got involved in ballroom dancing where compatible height was of the essence. For a decisive period in my growing-up years, dancing was my topmost priority. My body craved movement with music. I was entranced by the elegance, the manners, and the interaction between partners and the general settings in which dancing happened. The ballrooms were splendid, the orchestras lively, and the women were beautiful. All my other dreams and wishes were relegated to a secondary level.

Many years later, when fate brought us together in another town, Ingrid's parents asked me to be her escort to a very special ball sponsored by her father's old student organization. I gladly accepted, she turned out to be a good dancer, we had a wonderful time at a very elegant ball, but for some reason I did not follow up. We talked about going out some more but never did. I was extremely "busy" at the time, through my dancing school and club, but also with all my friends' graduation balls and other invitations.

There was one possible block against a closer relationship in my mind, which for most other people probably would have worked the opposite way. It originated in our play years together. We mostly played in the sand box, and on hot days, Ingrid's mother put out a little play pool for us. We used the water to make lakes and streams in the sandbox, we baked wonderful sand cakes and built mud castles, we splashed each other and her little brother Erich, who always tagged along but never really got to play with us. He was too young for us— although we were admonished regularly to include him in our games and watch over him. Sometimes we did, mostly we did not.

One hot summer afternoon, when Erich was taking a nap, and my mother was sitting in the shade by the roses knitting, Ingrid and I were playing. We had a few hideouts in the bushes along the fence. There we would open grocery stores, make them into the residences of grand parents or friends to be visited, or into theater box offices and dressing rooms for the actors, and whatever else we could think of. On this afternoon, we were in one of them.

"I want to play doctor. You are the doctor and I am the patient. This is your office. I will come and see you in a little while." Ingrid said and left. New game, I thought and looked around for tools or something that I could use to make me more official. All I remembered from my own doctor visits were the tongue depressor and the stethoscope. I found a broken off handle of a sandbox shovel. That will have to do for both. My patient was at the door.

"Come in!" I said, holding aside a few of the branches blocking the entrance. She wore her little sandbox outfit, she had put on a hat and was carrying a purse." I like her looks," I thought, and sat back to settle into my role.

"Good Day, Mrs. Müller! How are you today?"

"Good Day, Doctor. I am..." she hesitated a moment, "fine. And how are you?"

"Good, thank you. It is a little hot today."

"I am here because I have this pain, Doctor."

"Well, let me see." I reached for my stick. "Can you open your mouth wide and say aah?"

"No" she said, "that's not where the pain is!"

"Oh, where is it?"

"Here!" she said, pointing to the front of her panties.

Before I had decided on my next move, she had put away her purse, had slipped the halters holding up her sundress off her shoulders and had pulled down her panties. There she stood in front of me, naked, with the dress around her feet and the hat still on her head.

"There it hurts!" she said and pointed at that little mound with the crease in it. She looked me straight in the eyes, with her expression clearly saying 'do something.'

She took me completely by surprise. I swallowed. I had never seen a naked girl before. I might have been curious what they look like, but I was not sure. Here I was sitting down and this—thing—stared me in the face.

"Well? It really hurts." Ingrid stated her case again.

I plucked one of the bigger leaves off a branch next to me. I carefully placed it over the 'sick' body part—maybe my subconscious remembered seeing a picture of Eve after the Fall—and tried to think of something that could hold it in place. Short of a major bandaging effort—which was out of the question, I could only think of folding the leaf slightly into that little crevice. That is what I did; apparently to the satisfaction of my patient because she did not complain any more.

"Leave this on, for a day or two, then come and see me again. It should take care of your pain," I said. Since I was in the lower position of the two of us, I started to pull up her dress, so she could reach it with her hands. I did not dare to breathe for fear the leaf might fall off and I would have to repeat the procedure. With all the excitement of the newness of this game, I had completely forgotten about my mother's presence. I now became aware of her. Glancing through the bushes over to where she sat, I could see that she had not changed her position. She was knitting away, obviously enjoying the fresh air and the quiet of the afternoon.

"Goodbye, Doctor, I'll see you tomorrow!" Ingrid had put everything back on, picked up her pocket book, and slipped out the 'door.'

I quickly calculated what 'tomorrow' would mean in playtime. It could not be very far away. Somehow, I was uneasy with my mother sitting there, a stone's throw away from us. After my embarrassing accident with the toy car and the unwelcome visit of the landlord, I was almost sure that what we were doing here would not be quite what our parents had in mind for us. But it was new and it felt exciting. Before I was finished dealing with my emerging moral conflict, the patient had appeared again at my door.

"Knock, knock—I want to see the doctor."

"Come in, please!"

Ingrid had left the hat off this time, but she still carried the purse. She stood in the center of our little hideaway, straight and challenging, as if waiting for me to say something.

"Did the pain go away? Are you feeling better?" I asked after a short pause.

"No, it is still there. You have to look at it again," she said and dropped her pocket book and her dress faster than I could come up with an answer.

I reached for another leaf to repeat the procedure from the first visit.

"What are you two doing in there? Why don't you come out here and play in the sun?" It was my mother's voice.

"But it is so hot out there; it is cool in the shade. We are fine." I said.

"No, I want you to come out, right now, please! The sandbox will be in the shade in a little while, anyway."

"No, I want to play doctor in here, it is fun!" Ingrid yelled.

41

I froze. Why did she say that? What will my mother say now? We are in trouble.

"Please do as I said, come out right now!" my mother's voice was as firm as it would get. I could tell, she wanted us out of the bushes right away. Ingrid looked at me questioning. I shook my head and started to put her clothes back on. Ingrid sensed from my panicky looks that something was wrong and we had to comply. She pulled her straps back over her shoulders and picked up her purse. "We were having fun playing doctor," she said as she went out in the open.

"You can play doctor out here, on the lawn or by the house. I loved to play nurse with my brother. He always was the wounded soldier and I had to put bandages on him. We had lots of fun. Do you have a nurse's kit, Ingrid?"

"No, I don't." Ingrid said in a sulking voice.

"Well, maybe we can get you onc for your birthday!"

"No, I want Peter to be the doctor; I don't want to be a nurse!"

"They have doctor kits as well. I am sure we can get one for Peter."

"But why can we not play in the office in there?" Ingrid pointed to our hideaway. She did not want to give up.

"I'd rather see what you are doing." My mother was back to her normal voice now, "I do not want you to get hurt. And I really cannot see you when you are in there."

I am glad you did not see us, I thought. I turned towards Ingrid. "Let's go and work in your little garden in the corner, we will be in the shade there."

"But I'll get to do the raking, yes?" Ingrid said, putting down her purse next to where the hat laid on the lawn and ran towards the small plot her mother had assigned to us kids to do our own gardening.

I followed Ingrid. I was glad we had avoided getting into trouble, but I was also sad, because I found Ingrid's nakedness exciting and now there was little chance that we would be playing doctor in the bushes again.

ILL AT HOME

"Mama, my throat hurts."

"Does it hurt real bad or just a little?"

"Real bad when I swallow."

"Well, let me look. Open your mouth very wide, say 'aah'!—- Oh, I cannot see anything. Let me get a spoon. You can close your mouth for now."

"Here, let's try again. Say 'aah'"

"AAAAAAAAAAAAAH"

"Very good. Oh, oh, your tonsils are red again. Let me feel your head. Could be a little fever, we will take your temperature, just to be sure."

"Peter has a fever again. Not much but it is elevated. His tonsils are red. I do not know why he gets sick so often. I think more than other children we know. We really watch over him, he does not get too hot, he does not get too cold, he barely sees any kids he could catch something from—and he does not look sickly ..." my mother said when my father came home.

"I think it's just the way children are. Some are more susceptible, others are hardier. Peter just has had bad luck. Maybe he'll get hardier once he starts school," father said.

"He'll probably pick up everything that floats in the air, the way he is now. I am afraid of that already."

My fever was higher the next day and the pain worse. My mother called the doctor. She came and examined me. "Nothing serious, make him a chest wrap and let's see if that will bring the fever down. If not, call me again, please."

Sweating was not my favorite treatment. I had done it before. At first, the wet towels wrapped tightly around my chest felt sort of cooling and supportive. After a while, they became very uncomfortable, every time I moved they shifted, and outside air would seep under the wrap and make my body feel cold. I fell asleep for a couple of hours. When I woke up everything around me in the bed was sopping wet. My mother unwrapped me carefully, toweled me dry, gave me dry pajamas, and put a new blanket over me. I then had to sit in an easy chair next to the bed while my mother was changing the bed linens. I felt very tired and weak. As soon as I was back in the fresh bed, I fell asleep again. I did not touch the fresh apple compote my mother had made especially for me.

The next morning, the fever was again higher than the night before. My mother was baffled. This had to be more serious than just infected tonsils. What else could it be? She had no idea but she began to worry. She called the doctor again. The doctor did not believe it could be anything serious. What would it be? Just the fever was higher than with a normal tonsillitis. Peter has had several, so maybe it affects him more intensely this time. Nevertheless, she said she would come by later, anyway.

I got weaker, and the pain in my throat got worse. I would not eat anything because it hurt me too much to swallow. My mother kept checking my throat. She had noticed grayish spots all the way up to the roof of the mouth. My breath smelled awful. During her days as a special nurse, my mother had acquired a few books on general medicine. She now looked for the one used for diagnosing. Her intuitive guesses about my illness were pointing towards diphtheria. She hoped she was wrong, but she wanted to check it out. Unfortunately, what she read confirmed her suspicions: the spots, the bad odor from the mouth, the difficulty in swallowing. As she read on and realized how dangerous this illness could be, and how fast it progresses, she panicked. She called the doctor again. She had left the office already, for her daily rounds of house calls. She would arrive here whenever it was our turn.

As soon as the doctor entered the door, mother told her of her suspicions and the reasons why she thought so. The doctor's face became serious, and she looked at my throat a few more times. Then she nodded.

"You are right, Frau Slonek, it sure looks like diphtheria. I am so glad you called me again after you saw what you saw. I am sorry I did not catch it yesterday already, but there are no other cases around, who would have thought... I will have to go to the pharmacy and get some vaccine. Peter will have to have that immediately."

She reached into the side pocket of her bag and pulled out the chart showing the pharmacies on night call.

"May I use your phone and make sure they do have what we need?"

"Of course, Frau Doctor, you know where it is—out there in the hall."

"I also have to call my other patients,—I have two more after Peter—that I will be late."

She returned from the hall a few minutes later and nodded: "They do have the vaccine we need, I will go right now and pick it up. I will be back as soon as I can. Unfortunately, the pharmacy on call tonight is way over by the Herrengasse. But I guess it could have been another one, much farther away."

"When I read about the way diphtheria develops, I really felt like panicking. So many things can go wrong, serious things ..."

"I know, but we caught it—you caught it—in time, if he gets the vaccine tonight and we take him to the hospital tomorrow ..."

"He has to go to the hospital?"

"Of course, it is a highly contagious disease, as you know, Frau Slonek, and that calls for a hospital. He'll be there for a while, four or five weeks. They won't let him go until the throat is totally clear."

"Can't I keep him at home? I can take care of him and we will keep my husband locked out of the sick ward?"

"I do not know exactly what the rules are, but I seem to remember that as long as there are no other children in the household, and the husband does not work with or near children, let's say as a school teacher, then the Health Department can make an exception. We will check that out tomorrow. I better run along now for the vaccine."

The doctor left. Mother sat down next to my bed. She finally let go of some of the tension. We know what it is; the serum is on the way, good.

"Well, did you hear what Dr. Thier said?"

"No, something about dipped ..."

"Diphtheria is what you have. It is a very contagious disease. You cannot see anybody but me until you are done with it! Frau Dr. Thier even said you have to go to the hospital ..."

"No, Mama, I don't want to go to the hospital! I want to stay here."

"The Health Department makes the rules, I don't. But the Doctor said she is going to check it out tomorrow and let us know. I told her I want to take care of you here, if it is at all possible." She grabbed my hot little hand by the blanket. "I'd rather have you here!"

"Is the Frau Doctor coming back? What for?"

"Yes, you will have to get a shot. She has to do it tonight, so you don't get worse."

"With the long needle?"

"Yes, I am afraid so. But she is very gentle, she has given me shots and they did not hurt."

"I do not want to be hurting, Mama, my throat hurts so much already!"

"Well, the little hurt will take the big hurt away. And you will get better much sooner."

"Better not kiss him—he has Diphtheria! Very contagious!"

"What? When did you find out?" my father said.

"I had an inkling—so I checked it out in the book. Dr. Thier was here just now and confirmed it. She will be back to give him the vaccine. We caught it just in time. I am still worried whether it is soon enough. If not it affects the esophagus and the Adams apple—if you do not inject the vaccine, the patient might suffocate."

"Does Peter know?"

"He knows he has diphtheria, and that it is contagious and that he might have to go to the hospital—and that he is going to get a shot—other than that—NO. Dr. Thier was concerned but she said we are in time ..."

"We better be in time, she ought to have known what it was, last night, fine doctor she is—and you already said it did not look like a normal tonsillitis. Oh, my love, my little doctor and nurse, what would we do without you?"

"Emil, I just had a hunch, nothing but—luckily I was right on and she confirmed it."

"So, what about the hospital? Are you sure, you want to handle it at home? Would he not be better off with professional care?"

"First I am not sure if they will let me keep him. Second, he has never been with anybody else but us, it would be a big shock for him, and thirdly, I would be giving him professional care, the best. You know that, don't you?"

"Yes, my dear, I do know that. But it will be complicated."

"We will have to let Frau Dr. Thier or someone from the Health Department explain all that to us, I am not familiar with diphtheria. I do know though that nurses working with contagious patients get to go home and have a normal life ... "

"Don't let them put up a sign on the front door, the Hallers will never let us live this down ... they'll probably take Peter to the hospital themselves. The Health people can put the 'contagious' sign up on our door upstairs. That should be good enough. The Hallers rarely come up here, anyway, except when you call them for emergencies ..."

"I knew I would hear about that again, in due time. Please Emil, we agreed, no more of it."

I remember six endless weeks in bed, regular doctor's calls, brushes with foul smelling medications stuck down my throat, the threat that everything I had touched during the weeks of quarantine would have to be burnt as a measure of disinfection, which I could not understand, since the bed and the room did not have to be burnt—why could my things not be disinfected the way the room was? With a spray?

I remember my mother looking angelic next to our large houseplants—a picture my father later on immortalized with an award-winning photo. I remember her patience with me, reading to me, showing me handicrafts for little boys (and girls) because there was so little to do without exerting myself. We played games and she cooked the things I wanted because with the throat and the medications most food tasted awful.

I recall glass bowls filled with wonderful cold apple compote, spiced with cinnamon and cloves, an occasional treat of a wine chaudeau, a warm wine sauce with beaten eggs supposed to help with recovery, and several other goodies otherwise not served in the household.

I remember being left alone and being afraid, just afraid of nothing in particular but being alone, anxiously waiting for my mother to return home and insisting that she spend most of her time with me, entertaining me.

I remember missing my father, who could only peek through the door and wave at me when he came home at night. I was used to sitting close to him and listening to his stories from work, or about our plans for the future. He always talked about the house we would build, with a big garden and I would have my own plot of land to do with as I pleased. I could dig in it, I could plant things, and I could put big stones on it or wooden poles. All this was on hold because through a partly open door, none of it could be discussed, and sitting close to him was an important part of the communication.

Finally, the day came when Frau Dr. Thier had her last look down my throat and declared me healed, no longer contagious, and free again. The next day the men from the Health Department came with a big sprayer and disinfected my room. Mother talked them into also spraying my good toys and books instead of taking them away for burning. Ever since that illness I do not like when somebody mentions a time period of six weeks—it reminds me of six weeks of isolation and leaves me with a bad taste in my mouth.

A REAL VACATION

"We are going on vacation to Tyrol." I had heard this sentence several times and really had no concept of what it meant. We will be going away and staying somewhere other than our house. It will not be at Aunt Martha's or the Grandparents in Vienna. There would be mountains and a lake. My parents were excited and seemed happy in the bargain. Suitcases came out and my mother folded clothes into them. Beach towels and bathing suits, Lederhosen, wool socks, hats, my mother's Dirndl dresses, a couple of Rucksacks and hiking boots for both my mother and my father.

"When are we leaving?" I asked.

"We will sleep three more times and then we will take the train to Tyrol."

"How long will we be on the train?"

"Much longer than it takes to get to the grandparents in Vienna."

"Can I sit by the window?"

"Yes, if we can find a window seat, you can sit there."

The train trip took a lot longer than the one to Vienna. We had to change trains once and then we changed to a bus which was waiting outside of the railway station. I was proud of my father to have figured all that out. I was sure it could not have been easy.

After a short ride through woods and fields and past big farm houses and grazing cows the bus dropped us off in front of an inn. There were mountains all around us.

"Where are we staying? Here?" I asked.

"One more little trip," my father said and disappeared into the inn. When he came back out, he told us that 'our place' would send a horse buggy to pick us up. They would be here in a few minutes.

A solid wood buggy with two benches on top, pulled by two nice looking horses appeared around the corner. The man who had held the reins jumped off and greeted us with a warm handshake.

"Welcome, Herr Slonek and Frau Slonek, and—he looked at me ..."

"Peter," my mother said.

"Mr. Peter, you will like it with us. Lots of animals, nice lake, nice trails ... and good food from the farm!"

"These yours?" he pointed to our suitcases sitting in front of the inn.

"Yes," my father said and headed for them.

"No, no, let me do that," the man said and heaved them up onto the back of the buggy. He motioned us to get on to the buggy and helped us to our seats.

"Let's go, it will be dinner time soon! You've been on the train a long time from Linz—that's where you come from, no?"

"Yes, we started in Linz this morning," my father answered as he settled in his seat. I was sitting between my parents, the driver now took his seat in front of me and flipped the reigns lightly. The horses responded immediately and settled into a light trot. They knew where we were headed.

We stopped by the side of a small inn, built in front of a large farm house. Our room was on the second floor and had a balcony looking out over the valley and towards the mountains across it. Another mountain range started right behind our buildings.

Over the next few days we explored the farm house with its out buildings and stables, now nearly empty except for the horses that had brought us here and a couple of cows kept close for milk. The rest of the cows were out on the pasture in the mountains. We also heard of sheep and goats grazing somewhere. Chickens were roaming everywhere. Loud noises directed us to the pig pens, where two huge mother sows were surrounded by sweet pink piglets.

Except for a few short looks into stables on hikes I had never been that close to farm animals. I stood there in awe. Swallows were flying in and out, their mud nests plastered to the beams in the barn. The cries of their young for food were almost as loud as the piglets in search of their mothers' tits.

Even with most of the cows gone and their stables clean there was the strong smell of their bodies and excrement, hovering in the low-ceiling chalk walled stable. The horses were out most of the day pulling some thing or another or grazing nearby. I paid close attention of how they were hitched to the different implements, my father having a hard time keeping up with my questions.

The farmer himself was an old white-haired friendly man who was happy to indulge my curiosity. I felt very adult stomping around in the stables and barns, carefully avoiding the droppings of the various animals. The smells around me impressed me very much and stayed with me throughout my life. They bring up an undefined longing and sense of being at home and part of nature. The same with fresh mown grass, a pine forest in the noon heat, or the moist electric, sulfurous smell of a thunderstorm after it has gone through and cleaned the air.

After a few days we started to go on longer hikes, up in the hills where there were berries and mushrooms to be found, sticks to be cut and carved, ant trails to be observed, cow pastures to be crossed with a little uneasy feeling about the huge eyes of the animals following us, while calmly re-chewing their mornings fodder.

"I am very tired," was the signal for my parents to either settle down for a rest or to think about returning to our quarters. My father used to be a good sport and carry me over long stretches when I pooped out but this was no longer an option since I had grown taller and heavier. Jokingly he called me "an old donkey" and I would tease back by requesting that he carry the "old donkey." Much later I found out that the expression came from an old Arabic fable where the owner and rider of the donkey ends up having to carry "his old donkey." By the time the issue was laughed at and turned around several times I had forgotten about my tiredness and marched on bravely.

After one very long hike I experienced for the first time the exhilarating feeling of standing on the top of a mountain, caressed by the wind and rewarded for the effort of getting there with an incredible view of valleys, woods, streams below and clouds and sky above. My parents and I would sit there for a long while and drink in all these miracles with all our senses.

The breakfasts and dinners with my parents, served to us at the inn, weather allowing out on a terrace, were a special treat for me I'll never forget. Although my parents ordered for me, I got to try many things I had never had at home. The farmer's wife was the cook. She knew how to make things tasty and talk them up to us. The times spent around the table without my mother having to run back and forth to the kitchen were precious for all of us. It was a real vacation. Now I knew what that meant. Throughout my life I have tried to follow this ideal. Many times it worked out just like that and other times I had to do with a lot less. My children grew up with this tradition and I hope they will pass some of it on to their offspring.

NEW FAMILY MEMBER

During our third year in Linz, my parents told me that I would be joined by a brother or sister. The baby would grow inside of my mother's tummy. It was put there by their love. How and when, I was not able to find out. It was exciting to watch my mother's tummy grow bigger. I was allowed to put my hands there and feel the baby move around. When it was quiet around the house, I put my ear there and listened for the baby's heartbeat. My mother's tummy felt soft and warm. I loved that baby even before it came out into the light.

My mother took me with her on her regular visits to the doctor. I had to sit in the waiting room with all the other women with big tummies. Every time before we left, the doctor called me into his office and told me that my mother and the baby were doing fine and that I was doing a good job helping my mother taking care of herself and the baby. He told me that she was not allowed to lift heavy things and to bend down too far. I started carrying groceries and moving chairs for her, much to the amusement of family and friends. My Omi came from Vienna just before the baby was due, to take care of me while my mother was in the hospital.

My brother was born exactly two months after my fifth birthday. He was beautiful with big dark brown eyes and lots of black hair. My father was happy about the date: November 16. My parents had been married on the 16th of August, and I was born on the 16th of September. My Omi was happy because my brother had the same color eyes and hair as her other son, Uncle Otto.

My parents had been searching for suitable boys and girls names for months. My father insisted that it had to be a name that was not common, it had to have two syllables like Pe-ter, so it would sound good when they called both of us, "Peter and *ba ba*." For a boy they had liked Dieter the best from the beginning, although for my father that sounded too Germanic. The Nazis in Germany and the people sympathetic to the Nazi movement in Austria had started using Germanic names for their children, instead of the conventional names of the Catholic Saints. My father did not want to be associated with either of these groups. Since *Dieter* did not sound quite like *Siegfried, Hedda, or Thor*—and it was a name just more common in Germany than in Austria but not really from one of the Germanic Sagas—he considered it. My Omi protested because Dieter would not have a "name day," celebrating his patron saint's day on the Catholic calendar, which to some Catholics is more important than celebrating the actual birthday. After much back and forth, it was finally decided: my brother's name was going to be Dieter. As a compromise, he would have Robert as his middle name, in honor of Saint Robert and Uncle Robert, a Jesuit priest, who had baptized me and would do the same thing for my little brother. During all these discussions about names I found out that I had two middle names, Maria and Dominik, after my grandparents on my mother's side. Having a girl's name, even as a hidden middle name, was very embarrassing to me. I could not understand how my parents could have done that to me.

"Well, it was customary at the time, and it only shows in your birth certificate," my mother said when I asked her. My father was occupied with creating a birth announcement, which had to be unique, artistic, and would be talked about for years to come. He never chose easy tasks.

Life was different now. I had to be very quiet when the baby was sleeping and when my mother was feeding him. I loved to watch my little brother snuggle his tiny crumpled nose up against my mother's breast and suckle with all his might, making funny noises. Dieter was always hungry and drank a lot. He did not cry much and everybody was happy about that.

My Omi had come from Vienna as planned to help until my mother had recuperated and was used to dealing with the additional being in the household. Since Omi had grown up and lived most of her life with servants taking care of the household chores, she was not much help to my mother other than spending time with me and taking me out of the house, providing quiet time for my mother and her baby. Omi and I went to town by bus and then by streetcar over the big bridge across the Danube. At the foot of the *Pöstlingberg* there was a little train station from where the Pöstlingbergbahn took us to the top of this small mountain. The cogwheel train climbed very steeply and soon we could see the Danube below us. I loved to look out over the gardens and woods from the open carriage. From the lookout at the final stop Omi took a long time to get her bearings but then she pointed way over to the horizon.

"Over there is your house, far away in the distance. That's where you live."

I rose on my toes to see better over the stonewall in front of us.

"Over there?" I pointed.

"Yes, right in front of the big green spot, where the woods begin."

"I will tell Mama that we saw the house!"

"Would you like to go and ride on the *Grottenbahn?*" Omi asked.

"Is that the little train through the scary tunnels in the castle?"

"Yes, we went on it last year and you were a little frightened at first but then you liked it."

"Is that where Snow White and the Seven Dwarfs are?"

"Yes, and also Hansel und Gretel, Little Red Riding Hood, and the Princess and the Frog."

"I want to go, please. I promise I will not be scared!"

"First let's go and have something to eat."

We went and sat in the wood-paneled dining room in the Gasthaus. Omi ordered pairs of Frankfurters with mustard and rolls for us. I had a lemonade and Omi drank mineral water.

My grandmother and I talked about my next visit to Vienna.

"Omi can we go to the Zoo again, please?"

"Of course, we will go to the Zoo in Schönbrunn. I know how much you like it there!" she promised.

Then there was a day when Omi treated me to a children's movie matinee in town. On the way, we would stop at the city park and feed the ducks with some old bread Omi had brought in her purse. We even sat on the chairs in the park where you had to pay to sit.

Although Omi was quite different from my parents, I loved her and enjoyed the time with her immensely. Unfortunately, after a few weeks of being spoilt, I had to let her go back to Vienna, to take care of Opapa who had been left to his own devices all this time.

HALF A CAR FOR THE FAMILY

My parents discussed important things like money matters, family affairs, major political issues and the like only after I had gone to bed. Since I had to go to bed rather early, most of the time, it took me a while to go to sleep. When I was lying there awake I would understand a word here and there, or a sentence spoken a little louder than other words, but mostly I heard just general noises that meant they were talking but I could not understand what they were saying. Eventually I would fall asleep with these sounds hovering around. At other times, I would hear a word over and over and become interested and start to listen closer if I could make any sense of what I was hearing.

One of these words was "car." I had heard it repeatedly, and I thought I had heard a tone of protest in my mother's answers to my father. Money had always been an issue in their life. Both of my parents had grown up with plenty, but before they became adults, their parents' fortunes changed and they had begun to struggle. They were forced to live frugally with what they had left. My parents now had to fend for themselves in the new life of theirs. My mother's dowry had consisted of some nice linens and silver, already accumulated during better times, and they had been given practical things for the wedding. Everything else had to come out of their savings and my father's current income. We did not lack anything, as far as I was concerned, but I guessed from the conversations overheard that my father wanted a car. His brother had always had one, he needed it for his job, and my father had always had a motorcycle, which in his younger years he had ridden on rallies and other motor sports contests. He had given up that part of his life when he got married. Whether voluntarily or upon my mother's request I did not know. Now it sounded as if my father was eager to own his own wheels again.

My father found a partner in his office who was willing to share the purchase and use of a car with him. Therefore, we would own half a car. We would be able to use it every other weekend. There would be special arrangements made for longer holiday use. My friend Hans' parents owned a *"Steyr Baby,"* officially called a *Steyr 50*. It was designed and made in Austria, and had a good reputation. They had invited us on a few weekend outings in it. I particularly enjoyed sticking my head and arms out through the sunroof, while my father was more interested in the power loss when driving uphill with four adults and two boys. Still, it was a relatively expensive car. We finally ended up with a DKW, short for *Deutscher Kraftwagen,* made in Germany by Auto Union. Its logo was the Olympic Rings displayed on the front grill. It was propelled by a two-stroke engine with thrifty gasoline consumption, had four doors, a canvas roll-up sun-roof, a unique push-pull gear shift lever coming out of the dash, and looked pretty snazzy, considering the times. My father was in seventh heaven. He wanted my mother to get her drivers' license right away. She did not agree. She had mastered riding a bicycle just recently and she was not yet ready for another technical challenge.

The half ownership became one of our family secrets. Nobody owned just half a car. My father instructed me never to mention this arrangement to anybody. It was "our" car, period. I never met the owner of the other half. My parents never mentioned his name. We announced travel plans only after my father had cleared the mutual schedule. I was aware of the tensions created by this situation in our household. I had to carry my portion of it. I thought my father was clever having found a way to provide us with this luxury. I wanted to share this accomplishment with my friends. Of course, I was not allowed to. There was a contradiction in the air and one more thing I could not figure out.

Our first major family excursion was to Vienna. Whether it really was a necessary visit or just served to show off our new life style, I did not know. One of the photographs taken on the way back shows the car from above, framed by branches full of blossoms, with the top down, and the happy riders—mother, Omi, my brother and myself—looking up and smiling. All I remember is my Omi having fits of *angst*, concerning speed, oncoming traffic, and other assorted driving sins she pinned on her son. My father took it in stride and we had a good trip.

From Vienna, we made an excursion to one of the old family compounds in Payerbach, south of Vienna, close to the well-known vacation area of the Semmering Mountains. My parents had been married there, upon invitation of my mother's Uncle Ernst, who had built a large summer residence for the family there. The place also had one of the first swimming pools that my Great Uncle had built against the recommendations of everybody around. In order to keep the water fresh, he let part of the local stream, which formed one of the borders of his property, run right through it. This did result in some very refreshing swims and during the hot summers a welcome way of cooling off. Years after our visit with the car, relatives still pointed out a crack in the right pillar of the entry gate, which my father had backed into, pushing the top part of the pillar slightly off center. Like all other stories around this family gathering place, it was embellished over the years and my father's driving skill reputation went up or down, depending upon who told the story. It was always good for a laugh, though.

Another excursion by car from our home in Linz was Aunt Martha's house—we always called it "Aunt Martha's" house although it was built by Uncle Franz, her husband, a well-known physician, who mostly remained invisible for reasons unknown to me. The house's driveway had a gate with brick pillars too, so there was much joking going on about my father clearing them with the car without damaging them. He did fine and left them unharmed.

The house was situated right on the shores of beautiful Lake Attersee. It was a "paradise lost" for me, because of all the rules surrounding it, strictly enforced by

Aunt Martha. I had to be on extra good behavior, I had to sit quietly, not touching anything, be polite and not ask for anything that was not offered. Even on the dock to the boathouse there was no running allowed, no bending down to the water, no throwing stones. Thus, I took in the *paradise* with my senses only, the shore, the lake, the dock, the boat, the big old fruit trees in the garden—but I could not live out my physical presence there. It was as if I was flying over it all but had no permission to land. I felt shortchanged by the lack of personal connection to my great aunt and her children and by the restriction of my movements on the property. How this came all about I could not figure out. Aunt Martha was very stiff and formal. She was a very devout Catholic, reminding me of the nuns I had met in other parts of the family, except that she always wore colorful local dirndls instead of any kind of a nun's habit.

We always left her house generously gifted with bags full of fruit from the garden, and a glass or two of home-made jam, plus a few other goodies like a chocolate bar, a piece of cake or some freshly baked cookies for me. While there, Aunt Martha would always serve an appropriate snack for the time of the visit: around lunchtime, it was fancy cold cuts and an assortment of cheeses with wonderful local bread, served on a wooden plate, and in the afternoon, it was coffee, milk or cocoa with a freshly baked cake topped with fresh fruit from the garden.

My favorite excursions with the car were when we just took off on the weekends when it was our turn to use it. We headed somewhere in the woods or hills around Linz. My mother would pack sandwiches, fruit, and a dessert, which we ate on a blanket surrounded by grasses, flowers, bird noises, and an occasional wild hare or a deer. There the fear of spilling, dropping crumbs, or chewing the wrong way was greatly reduced. Dropping a few crumbs on the blanket or into the grass was not considered the crime it would have been at Aunt Martha's. We picked berries, found wild mushrooms, and climbed up the hunters' perches from which they watched the deer before they shot it during hunting season. I saw my father in a different light in this environment: free and happy, laughing and showing me all kinds of things and tricks he had learned as a boy growing up in the woods around his parents' estate and during his time with the Boy Scouts. My mother was mostly observing, smiling happily, and taking care of my brother. The only time she seemed uncomfortable was when my father started to pose us for his *family portraits*. We had to look "natural" but he wanted certain compositions, which did not come naturally to us and therefore lead to tensions when the instructions on how to sit, stand, smile or look, took too long. In the end, he mostly came away with a few excellent shots, which then would be "perfected" in the darkroom, sent out as postcards to the grand-parents and other important relatives. The best ones were enlarged and mounted for the next photo contest.

Shortly after Germany's invasion of Poland, which started the big war, gasoline was rationed to a point where any meaningful excursions became impossible. The car remained in the garage most of the time. Within a year, my father received a notice from the local *Wehrmachts-Dienststelle* saying that the German Army requisitioned the car for military duty. The notice stated a date and place when and where we had to deliver it to the authorities. My father and his partner were "compensated" by a receipt, which entitled them to an amount equivalent to the car's present value, payable as a share towards the postwar "Volkswagen," in case the original car would not be returned in usable condition.

Needless to say, we never heard anything about "our" car ever again, nor did we get to use the "coupon" towards a new Beetle, although one of our neighbors who had opened a special Volkswagen savings account did get preferential treatment and a rebate when the first Beetles were finally produced.

The trademark showing the Olympic rings stayed with me, though. When I bought my first brand new car many eons later, I remembered the Olympic Rings and ended up with an Audi.

The memories of my first school day are not very pleasant. My parents, family and friends had built up this event as some wonderful turning point when I would start my formal learning under expert tutelage. I was six years old, I already knew my alphabet and my numbers, I could write all the letters, all the numbers, my name and a few other words. My father had been good at teaching me to draw and paint. I really was looking forward to speeding up the pace of learning, but I had a big knot in my stomach about how all that would happen.

Can you come in with me, please?" I begged when my father stopped the car in front of the *Figuli* School, as it was called after a prominent Austrian educator.   "I do have to be in the office very soon, but I can take you to your class room, let's go." He parked the car and led me by the hand through the enormous entrance. After some searching, we found the classroom for *die erste Klasse*, first grade, where I belonged. My father looked around once, wished me luck, and then said goodbye and left. The room breathed oppressive darkness, mirroring the feeling in my stomach. Although there were huge windows, reaching almost all the way up to the very high ceiling, the paneling around them and in the gigantic window wells was dark brown. The floor was black from years of being treated with oil; a wide brown board ran along two walls, which held the hooks for coats and hats. In the rear of the room there was an imposing black cast iron stove with its pipe running the width of the room. The center part of the front wall behind the teacher's desk held a large blackboard. It all added up to a lot of darkness.

I sat down in the last row, which was still empty. I looked at the other boys in front of me. Most of them were chatting with each other as if they had known each other before. I did not recognize anybody. Hans went to the same school but he was already starting second grade. I had not seen him this morning. A few parents were still standing in the back of the room, occasionally making supportive eye contact with their offspring. I felt very alone. I was longing for my father or my mother to be there with me. However, Papa had that meeting in the office and Mama was home with my baby brother Dieter.

A very loud bell rang throughout the building. Seconds later a tall, thin, gray-haired man appeared in the door. He was wearing a black smock over dark grey striped trousers and a white shirt with a stiff collar and a black tie. He stood there until the class noticed him. Then he asked us to stand and walked to the podium. From there he looked the class over with a stern glance before he told us to sit. "My name is *Herr Oberlehrer Veith*, I will be your teacher for this your first year in school. When you speak to me, I will be addressed as *Herr Oberlehrer* at all times."

Raising his head and eyes a little towards the parents in the rear, he said "Thank you for coming. You may now leave the classroom. School will be out at 12:00 noon, in case you want to pick up your son. If you want to speak with me for any reason, please make an appointment with the school clerk. If I need to speak with you about your son, I will send you a note. Thank you." He waited for the parents to file out before he addressed the class again. This is a very difficult time for you boys. You will have to sit still, you will have to be quiet—you will have to learn discipline before you learn anything else. I know this is hard for boys but it has to be that way. I do not tolerate talking during class other than when being asked by me. You will raise your right hand when you have a question or need to say something. We go to the bathroom only during breaks. There will be one ten minute break every hour signaled by a bell. At the end of the break I want you to be in your seats and quiet before the bell has stopped ringing."

The *Herr Oberlehrer* moved a few obviously shorter boys to the front and a few taller ones to the back. One boy, about as tall as I, ended up in the last row but on the other side. So now there was one tall pupil on each side of the aisle. The other boy looked over and made a face at me. I had spotted him in the classroom earlier and had decided that I did not like his looks. The teacher made a chart of the seat assignments, asking each boy for his name, which he then checked off on his enrollment list. There was spontaneous laughter when one of the boys said his name was Bayerlein, which could be taken for *Bäuerlein* meaning 'little farmer.' Herr Veith stood up and said rather sharply "We will not have any comments here, not spoken and not with laughter. Is that understood?" Everybody shrank an inch or so, mumbling *"Ja, Herr Oberlehrer!"* already afraid of being singled out for bad behavior.

There were more directives about discipline and the teacher handed us a list of supplies we had to bring the next day. Herr Veith handed out the books we would be studying from with a serious admonishment on how to treat these books—no writing on or in them, no bent pages, and no dirt marks, best would be to have the parents wrap them and put their son's name on the wrap. He told us what we had to wear for gym on Thursdays and what the consequences would be if we did not. After the first break, he held up the different books one by one and explained what we would be learning from them. Another question he had to settle was the matter of religious instruction. A show of hands established that all but two in the class were Catholic. The two others were Lutherans. It took a while to explain to them where they would find the proper instruction when the Catholics had their lessons in the classroom, where the Lutherans were not welcome. I felt sorry for them. I thought they were treated like outcasts, because they would have to leave the classroom and find another instructor while the rest of the class would be instructed in "Religion"—not even called *Catholic* religion. So what were they teaching differently? As far as I knew, *Lutheran* was a religion, too. I was going to ask my father about that.

After so many admonishments, the noon bell announcing the end of the first day came none too soon. I stuffed my books into my S*chultasche*, made out of black leather, weighing a ton, and held to my back with two shoulder straps. It was a nice one, compared to others I saw in the classroom. Mine was a gift from my Omi.

Many other parents were waiting outside the school already. As soon as they connected with their sons, they bombarded them with questions. In a way I was glad I did not have to answer any—yet. I traipsed off in the direction of home. My mother had said she might come to meet me close to our house where she was walking with the baby carriage.

"*Servas Slonek*" a voice interrupted my contemplation. "Remember my name?"

"*Yours starts with an 'S' too, doesn't it?*" I answered, but I did not remember the full name of the other boy.

"*I bin der Sternad, Alfons,*" he told me. "Where do you live?"

"Am Froschberg, the last house on the right hand side, up the hill."

"Hey, that's good; I live at the bottom of your hill, where the street comes down from the Gugl. We can walk together, that will be fun."

"Yes, I would like that. When do you leave in the morning?"

"My parents want me out of the house by 7:30. It's downhill to school, we'll get there in plenty of time for Herr Oberlehrer! Do you like him?"

"I don't think so; he is too stuffy and too serious. And all those black clothes. How about you?"

"I think I am in trouble, I don't like him at all. He already looked at me a couple of times today—I didn't do nothing ..."

Alfons became my way-to-school friend. He had been around this neighborhood for a couple of years and he knew more things about it than I did. He took me up to a meadow bordering Hans' house where we could walk along the wall surrounding a big park, looking down at the street, throwing things or trying to push each other down the hill. It was always fun. On the other side of the street Alfons showed me a path through the meadows and along the frog ponds, but that was trickier because it was private property and we were not supposed to walk there. We did anyway. Only once we were chased off. Walking with Alfons was fun. Until...

My father had been adamant about me not picking up the Upper Austrian dialect that was spoken around Linz. He thought it was vulgar, not as vulgar as the Viennese dialect but also bad. At home, we spoke 'high' Austrian, so to speak. It pronounces words meandering between the extremes of the local dialects, not quite as clean as in the High German spoken in certain parts of Germany, but distinctly cleaner than the Austrian dialects. This diction was at home nowhere geographically, it was a class thing, and mostly imagined. If you pronounced your a's "cleaner," without the inflection, you were thought a better person. If you let it slip and added those 'dirty' overtones, you yourself slipped down the social ladder, you let on that you came from the vulgar side and were uneducated. At least that is the story I got from my father.

Therefore, when father met Alfons and heard him talk, he issued an immediate absolute order: No more contact with Alfons.

"This boy speaks a vulgar dialect, has bad grammar, and is probably from a family we do not want to have anything to do with."

End of discussion.

I was crushed. First Hertha, now Alfons. I was glad Ingrid and family across the street spoke well enough to allow continued social contact. I was not so sure about another family with several children who had shown up at the construction site across from us where a big new house was in the making. They looked friendly and I was hoping that they spoke clean enough for my father's standards, because the children looked like interesting playmates. Just across the street, I could hop in and out, and the area around the new house was full of treasures, some of which, I hoped, would remain even after the construction workers had cleaned up the site: bricks, boards, mounds of sand and dirt, a few ditches and dug up old trees, not yet cut up.

That fantasy came true because I spent many happy hours with the children across the street. There were two boys who were a little older and a girl that was younger than I was. The boys took me under their wings. We built all kinds of forts and bridges, waged war in the wilds of the garden, climbed the fallen trees, and held family gatherings with the girl as the mother. Our parents never got beyond a superficial speaking acquaintance. I never became privy to my father's objections to them, but I could sense a difference in his behavior. He was not as open and outgoing with them as he was with people he liked. As long as it did not interfere with my friendship with these playmates, I was content. When we finally moved away, I was very sad to lose these fun friends.

Before that move actually happened, there was school to cope with. School had become a nightmare. I was the tallest in my class and also rather thin. That was enough to make me the target of continuous teasing. They called me any name that could mean something long like broomstick or beanstalk. I also had a long neck, which prompted my schoolmates to call me a *giraffe*. On top of that, my mother insisted on a style of dress that was fashionable in Vienna but had not penetrated the provinces yet, and never would, because it was too ridiculous. I had to wear a beret whenever there was wind or rain in the offing, accompanied by a black umbrella, child size, which earned me another nickname, Chamberlain, referring to the umbrella-carrying British Prime Minister. In the summer, I sometimes had to wear a two-piece suit, shorts with a top buttoned to them, made out of black shiny material, which I called the *priest outfit*, and made my classmates call me the *preacher*. As if that was not enough, the outfit came with long cotton stockings, held up by a sort of girdle/suspender construction. I was in special agony on gym days, when I had to take all this off to put on gym shorts and shoes. I dreaded all the looks and funny remarks coming my way. One day, when my father had promised to pick me up after school, I was struggling after gym class to put my gear back on but for the life of me, I could not get it right, no matter how hard I tried. When somebody told me *"Your father is outside, waiting for you ..."* I was so frustrated already, that I snatched up all the parts of my outfit with one hand, grabbed my *Schultasche* with the other and ran, half dressed out to where my father was waiting, dragging suspenders, stockings, and shirt behind me. I burst into tears with shame. When my father saw me, he started to laugh, which made me cry even harder.

There was a family council after that, and after much pleading from me, I was granted relief: I did no longer have to wear or carry certain objectionable and in this school uncommon items of dress or paraphernalia. However, this agreement was valid for school only, not for visits with family and friends. There I still had to be dressed in good taste. I protested but to no avail. My parents insisted on having to show our *class*. They came from Vienna, they knew what was in style, they refused to buckle and become *provincial*. What all that meant to them other than the clothes I did not like, I never could figure out.

FOUR OF US IN THE COUNTRY

"Like on our first vacation there will be a lake and several creeks, these will come in handy" my father said and handed me two toy barges he had brought home from a last minute shopping trip the day before we were leaving on vacation. I looked at the little boats in amazement.

"They are beautiful! Thank you, Papa!" I stretched and gave my father a big kiss and a hug. "Look how smooth they are. And yellow on the inside."

I let my fingers glide over the smooth metal. I kept looking at the boats. The paint felt like my mother's skin. They are as beautiful as a flower, look at the red decks!" I said in awe. The colors complemented the shape: the outside of the hull was a medium gray, the inside a very mild yellow. There was a deck running around the cargo compartment, which was painted a dark red.

"Look, there is a little chain in the front to hook them to the tugboat or to another barge," I held up the tiny chain.

The barges were very similar to the real ones I had seen on the Danube when my father had taken me to the freight harbor down by the big bridge.

I ran into the kitchen to find my mother. "Mama, look what Papa brought me! Aren't they beautiful! Can I try them out in the sink?" I was holding a barge in each hand and held them up for my mother to see.

"Papa says I can let them swim in the lake and in the streams on our vacation."

My father was standing in the kitchen door. He was happy that his gift had triggered such an enthusiastic reaction. He was proud of his son's way of looking at things: he had admired shapes and colors first. He was a little artist already.

"These are very beautiful boats. Did you say 'Thank you' to Papa?"

"Yes I did!"—"Yes, of course he did!" my father and I answered simultaneously.

This vacation was a special treat for the four of us. My brother was now old enough to tag along with us and still small enough to be carried on longer walks. Two weeks in an old Tyrolean farm house, right in the middle of a valley surrounded by a picturesque group of mountains. A friend had recommended the place to my father who then had corresponded with the farmer to check everything out. There was a boy my age and two girls that were older. The house was within walking distance of a small mountain lake with clear water, and a couple of streams flowing down from the surrounding mountains and ending up in the lush meadows of the valley. The small railroad station was at the other end of the valley. The farmer picked us up with his horse wagon as he had promised.

There were hiking trails going off in all directions, some low, some leading to the peaks where there were still patches of snow. High up here in the Alps the summer was late; the wildflowers were still in bloom. Every day we discovered a new soft carpet full of surprises.

I chased butterflies and found antler beetles. I again watched the huge forest ants scuttling around their mounds made of pine needles and dirt. My brother was also interested in all the creeping crawling life around us. He was not so pleased with the long hikes up into the mountains where the cattle were grazing on the spicy alpine grasses. I hid behind my father when we crossed a meadow full of young bulls that looked at us with glassy eyes. I remembered the exhilarating feeling of standing in the cooling wind on a mountaintop after an exhausting hike with a breathtaking view spreading out before us.

My parents cherished our delight with the surroundings. We were their joy and blessing in this adventure. I was full of admiration and curiosity about all of nature and, without guidance, gentle with plants and animals. My father captured it all in romantic photographs to remember for ourselves and for my grandparents.

I immediately liked Joseph, the farmer's son, who was about my age. We got along well. He took me to feed the cows and pigs, the horses and the goats, we chased the chickens and the ducks through the yard, and I even made uneasy friends with the dog after a period of fear, doubt and mutual sniffing out.

The lake was a dream. The shore was very shallow. One could see every pebble and every grain of sand under the surface of the water, even through the riffles made by the afternoon breeze. We played in the water, my father swam, I built endless canals for my barges, which transported logs and gravel, hay and bugs up and down these canals, to and from the lake. It was not easy to keep my brother from unknowingly trampling the canals which I had built so carefully. Some of the days, Joseph could join us and I gave him one of the barges to play with.

At the farm, Joseph and I played mostly in the inner court. Our favorite game was flying the planes that I had brought with me. They were a recent present from my grandmother. They were made out of silvery metal, and fit nicely into our little hands. They looked very real, with small propellers on each wing, which actually turned when we blew on them. The planes had a marvelous extra feature: We could load a cap into the nose of the plane. When it hit the ground or a wall, the cap exploded with a loud bang. Joseph's father, the farmer, was not too keen on this feature. The chickens and the ducks in the courtyard and the cows and horses in the stables did not take well to the new noise. Nevertheless, Joseph and I kept arming our little airplanes and simulated all kinds of aerial combat and bombing missions until we ran out of caps. Then my Papa, after much begging and cajoling, went to the local store and bought another container full of those little round boxes that held the caps on a long red paper ribbon.

The planes and the barges were very dear to me. They were new, beautiful, functional, and fun to play with and had a special air of quality to them. I cleaned them painstakingly every evening before dinner and put them on the nightstand next to my bed. From there they radiated a warm feeling of a prized possession until the next morning. I kept glancing at them until I went to sleep and looked at them first thing in the morning when I woke up.

When my father had told me about this vacation, he had promised me a special surprise: He would build me a small water wheel we could put into the stream next to the house. As a young man, when he was a scoutmaster he had learned how to build a water wheel. He had actually put one up at his parents' property when he was still living there. We had collected some wood for the project, my father had been shown the farmer's tools but so far, the wheel had not been constructed.

In my mind, this project had taken on gigantic proportions. It was a feat of engineering and a piece of art. With the exception that it had not been built. I reminded my father of his promise as I had done all along.

"Papa, we are leaving the day after tomorrow and you have all this wood and we know where to put it in the creek—can you still do it, please?"

The sadness and disappointment in my voice came through and my father decided to make a last effort to save face.

"I'll put some of it together tonight in the barn. If we get up early tomorrow morning we will have time to finish it and put it into the stream."

By noon the next day the elaborate water wheel was turning furiously, driven by the fast waters of the little creek running by the farmhouse. The white wood contrasted with the green grasses and the blue water around it. I stood there for a long time, getting dizzy from staring at the paddles rising from the water, dripping, turning over and dipping into the water again, where the stream would push them with force, one after another, without pause.

On the day before our departure I was very sad. I did not want to leave this paradise. As if that were not enough, my father had asked me to give one of each of the toys, one plane and one barge, to Joseph, since he had been so nice to me and enjoyed them so much. I really wanted to share and normally never had a problem with it. This time it seemed very difficult. We could give Joseph one of my older toys, a truck or one of the little race cars ... the barges and the bombers were still too precious. They were so new, so smooth to hold, so fast in the water and in the air. A whole world collapsed for me. Nevertheless, after much coaching, I reluctantly agreed and Joseph was dancing with joy and very grateful. When I saw Joseph's reaction I had a short period of feeling better for having done good, but when the loss hit me later on the train, holding only one of each of my favorite toys in my hands, the pain pushed out a few tears and I started to sob. My parents did not notice, my brother was asleep. The pain over the loss went unacknowledged.

When we got ready to leave for our train, I experienced another wave of sadness. My father had insisted that the water wheel was too big to take with us. It had to stay. No matter how vividly I imagined myself on the train with the dripping structure, Joseph was the one to keep it and watch over it. My father suggested that Joseph could connect a flywheel or something to it that would drive another gadget. For a long time the wheel appeared in my daydreams as the never tiring motor for my fantasy inventions.

Sitting in the train, my head was turned to the window, I watched the mountains disappear as the train entered a tunnel, I looked at a few more streams and lakes going by and then I fell asleep. I dreamt about living in the mountains, surrounded by lush meadows, in harmony with my parents and the powers of nature, close to the water, animals, flowers and trees.

When I awoke at the end of the journey, I awoke full with the promise of a harmonious life. The sadness that had come with having to part with a barge, a plane and the water wheel painted the picture one slight shade darker but did not take away any of the overwhelming beauty of the dream.

HARD TIMES—NEW JOB—NEW BABY

Something unusual was going on between my parents but I did not know what it was. My father was more withdrawn, more nervous and jumpy; my mother was quieter, her face full of worry. My parents' evening discussions had taken on a new intensity. The words I picked up at night when I was already in bed and they were talking were the name of my father's boss, the name of the company where my father worked, something about a party, money, and a baby. Something was not going well at my father's job, which had to do with his boss, who was Jewish and was in charge of the advertising department. All I was told in due time was that my father would leave his present job, and that the Nazis taking over Austria were to blame for it.

The job loss created quite an upheaval. Aside from sending out resumes and portfolios my father took on odd jobs such as using his calligraphy skills to put the names of recently graduated chimney sweeps on the diplomas they would be handed at a ceremony. The diplomas were oversize, printed in beautiful Gothic script, and had a golden seal at the bottom next to a number of ornate signatures affixed by the members of the Examining Board. There was a big stack of these papers. I asked my father where all these chimney sweeps would sweep chimneys. You rarely saw one in the street, and if you did see one, my grandmother had told me, twisting a button on your clothes while looking at him would bring good luck. Touching a chimney sweep in person was even better luck.

My father was not in the mood for silly questions and asked to be left alone. I could not even walk near him because that would create vibrations, which would make his writing uneven. The lettering my father did matched the font on the diplomas. After the ink on the names was dry, no one could tell the difference between the original printing and the inserted names. Whether the effort was worth the pay, I did not know. For me, any sum of money could not cancel the disturbances this job had inflicted at home. I lived in constant fear of creating too many vibrations, of getting any kind of liquid on the diplomas laid out to dry, of falling on one of them and permanently ruining it, of creating too much dust so it would lodge itself on the wet ink—there were too many traps and serious consequences for falling into them.

Shortly after completing this job, my father received a contract to put together a large exhibit showing plans and progress for a major revitalization project sponsored by the City of Linz. He did some of the conceptual work at home, which meant more quiet time for me, and less time for contact and questions, but once the work started on the actual exhibit, my father spent most of his time there—a big relief for me. The exhibit was well received by its sponsors as well as by the public. My father was very proud of it. It was the type of work he ideally would have liked to do all the time: elaborating on a complex subject by showing more in pictures and graphics than in words, setting the exhibit up in such a way that people would be pulled through it, seeing and understanding it all.

Probably through this exhibit, my father connected with the newly established *Hermann Göring Werk*, a big steel works under construction on the outskirts of Linz, where he was hired as Public Relations Manager, responsible for reporting on progress and accomplishments during the construction phase, in pictures and in words. From my father's behavior at home, I could tell that he was happy with this new position. The ogre of unemployment had gone away. Topping it all off, we were offered a company-owned house, under construction, in a newly built up area at the edge of town, where the people who had lived on the current site of the steel works had been resettled.

With the financial pressure gone, I was taken into confidence on the other good news: there would be another baby, to be born a couple of months before the new house would be ready. I was happy about the prospect of another sibling; my little brother had been lots of fun. Not so much lately because he had gone through a series of ear infections, which must have hurt him very much because they made him scream through many nights. Dieter was sleeping in my parents' room so they could take better care of him at night, but I still heard the crying and the movements of one of my parents carrying my brother through the flat to calm him down. I felt very sorry for him and felt badly that I could not help him at all, other than rocking him during the day when my mother was busy with cleaning, shopping or cooking. Another little one would certainly add more work and more confusion. I would be asked to keep an eye on them both, and my parents would have less time to spend with me. Luckily, my Omi from Vienna, who still came to visit us regularly, was always on the lookout for things to do with me. When the circus came to town we went to see it, and she found out about a special children's matinee in the local theater.

When the time neared for the baby to be born, my mother told me that she would go to a hospital in Wels, rather than in Linz, because the doctor who had helped to bring my brother into the world had moved to the hospital there. She had felt well taken care of and trusted this doctor so she wanted him around for her new baby's birth.

I thought this was exciting news. I was born in Vienna, my brother was born in Linz, and the third one would be born in Wels. There would be no such thing as a boring family where everybody was born in the same place. We were different. I could not wait to tell my friends at school. It came as a big surprise to me that my father had a very different opinion. He thought that this variety of birthplaces would cast a bad shadow on our family and therefore was something to be known only to us in this little band. It would become our secret and nobody else's business. When he found out that I had freely shared this with my school friends, especially including the one boy I was forbidden even to talk to, he had a terrible fit. I could not remember having experienced my father this irate with me. He yelled at me for a long time, he went on and on about this "family secret" business, which I did not understand because already in school I had to put down my birthplace several times—nobody ever had taken notice that I had been born in Vienna and not in Linz! I felt hurt and betrayed. If they wanted things to be secret, they had to say that in the beginning. Moreover, I argued in my mind, things that are easy to see and figure out could not be kept secret long—like my mother leaving for

Wels and returning with a baby. I could think of many secrets people would want to take to their graves without telling anybody. I had read about them in my books. The birthplace secret did not make sense. Somehow though, I had to accept that it is the parents who make the rules. Nevertheless, I decided to maintain my own rules from now on, and I would keep them a secret from my parents.

THE NEW HOUSE

After we had heard the good news about the new house we were to move into, my parents planned an excursion there for the following weekend. Good luck would have it that we were scheduled to have use of the car. My mother prepared our favorite picnic: smoked ham sandwiches, hard-boiled eggs, potato salad, fresh cucumbers and tomatoes. The whole family set out to explore the new home site. The area under development was called the *"Käferfeld Siedlung"*–the settlement on the 'field of beetles.' But the name also was spelled with an 'e' instead of an 'ä'—*"Keferfeld"*–it was said to be named after the *'Kefer Bauer,'* the farmer who had owned all the land. We did not find out how he spelled his name or which version was the correct one. It mattered because our address would be spelled either with an 'ä' or with an 'e,' so every time we wrote down where we would live, we had to make a decision. The 'Kefer' version eventually made it on the street signs and maps. It was the proper name of the farmer.

Our property was at the end of a cul-de-sac. There was a big square for cars to turn around, then a big square lawn with a few newly planted trees. Away from the street, bordering two sides of the lawn there was a big L-shaped building, three stories high, with one-bedroom apartments for single, white-collar workers from the steel factory. Four row houses, attached single-family dwellings, occupied the third side of the lawn square. My father pointed to the house at the open end, away from the apartments, the one with only one side attached to a neighbor. We were lucky to have that one because on the

74

open side there was lots of extra garden space between us and the other neighbor.

We had stopped in the big turnaround. Our top was down and we could get a good look at our new surroundings before we even got out of the car. The apartment building was finished. My mother noticed curtains in some of the windows and concluded that some people must have moved in already. The row houses were standing there in the raw. All the walls were up, bricks only, the rafters were up and the roof tiles stacked up underneath them. The windows and doors were still missing. My father, who routinely ignored 'No Trespassing' signs, got out of the car and motioned me to follow him into the house. Mother was not too keen on that idea and decided to stay in the car with Dieter.

My father carried with him a copy of the house plans. He explained the layout to me. Upstairs there were three bedrooms and a full bathroom, downstairs there was an entry hallway with a mudroom, a living room with French doors opening to the garden in the back, a formal dining room, a kitchen, and a half bath. Having an extra bathroom downstairs was a great luxury. My mother was relieved that we could use it rather than having to run upstairs every time anybody came in from the garden to wash their hands.

"Be careful and do not touch anything," my father said, "watch out for these low supports."

We checked out the ground floor. I had never been in a house under construction. I was excited to see where we would cook and eat. I took in the smell of bricks and mortar and dirt.

"The bedrooms are upstairs?" I asked.

"Yes, but that chicken ladder here is too dangerous for you to climb. I'll go and look. Wait here!"

Carefully my father worked his way up the bouncing board which had little strips of wood nailed to it to prevent the workers from slipping when they carried building materials upstairs.

"Nice view of the garden from your room up here, Petz!"

"Is Dieter going to sleep in the same room with me?"

"I think so; we have not figured everything out yet, but I think you boys need to be together. It will be fun."

He came bouncing back down.

"Why can't I go up, Dad?"

"There is no railing to hold on to and the board is really bouncy. It is too dangerous for you. Maybe next time we come out we will have more sturdy stairs. Then you will be able to go. Very soon we will be living here!"

"How soon, Papa?"

"They said it will be ready in late summer."

"When is 'late summer'?"

"I would say, middle of August, end of August ... before your birthday!"

They went back outside to report to mother. She had taken Dieter for a little stroll along the houses. Now she was headed towards what would become part of our garden.

"Where shall we have our picnic?" she asked, "I am getting pretty hungry."

"Eat." Dieter said.

"Let's take a look in the back. There we will be sheltered from the street."

We carefully stepped over broken bricks and remainders of scaffolding. Mother looked in through the windows we passed.

"This must be the living room here!" She pointed into the window.

"Yes, that's it. Look, here is the door from the living room into the garden! I always wanted to be able to step from the living room into the garden!"

"It is a pretty high step," my mother said with a smile. The opening for the door was almost two feet off the ground. The steps were not in place yet. Next to the "door," there were boards and tools stacked up against the back of the house.

"Let's eat here!" my mother said, pointing at two boards on the ground. "We can put some of those bricks under each end. Then we will have a bench to sit on. Will you help me Peter, please?"

"Eat," Dieter said again. He was moving across this challenging territory slowly but with a big smile on his face.

"Be careful, Dietz, don't fall and get hurt. No owies! Emil, can you get the baskets from the car, please?"

"Yes, I will; Petz, please come and help me carry the little things when you are done with the bench."

We sat in the weak sun of the spring afternoon and enjoyed our food. The ham sandwiches were made with crusty, dark farmer's bread, which went well with the hard-boiled eggs and the potato salad. My father drank apple cider; my mother and we boys had buttermilk.

We looked at the garden area in front of us. The ground was full of debris and rocks. A few meters from the house, the terrain started to slope down a bit.

"I wonder how far our lot goes. All the way down there, you think?"

Papa pulled out the overall plan he had been given. He studied it and turned it so it would line up with the foundation of the house.

"About sixty meters down from the edge of the house," he said.

"Oh Emil, you know I cannot imagine how far that would be. Where the shrubs are, down there?"

"No, I don't think quite as far. That little bunch of weeds you see there" he pointed, "I think that could be it, approximately. Don't take my word for it. When they are further along, we will see. I imagine they'll put in the fences last."

"Will they take the tracks and the little lorries?" I asked.

"Of course, Peter. They take them from one construction site to the next. It helps them move all the dirt and some of the bricks and mortar."

"I would like to play with those cars; it would be fun to ride them down the hill."

"You better don't even think of that!" my mother said. "That is dangerous, how would you stop!"

"Look Mama, the tracks go uphill on the other side, the car would just stop by itself. The workers must know how to stop, too."

"When there is no engine pulling them, they use big branches or boards as brakes. They wedge them between the struts holding the lorry and force them against the wheels," Papa explained.

"Can I try?" I asked right away.

"No, but we can go look at it together when we are done with our food."

Mother and Father talked about what the garden would look like, how the inside of the house would look once we were moved in, and they shuddered at the amount of work that will come their way before even the most rudimentary things would be done.

"We'll take it slowly. There is no rush. You had better take it easy in your condition! How are you feeling?"

"Oh, rather well most of the time, thank you. I get dizzy sometimes, and a little nauseated. It is bearable. The whole pregnancy has felt a little different than the first two, specially the one with Dietzi. I cannot describe how, but it is different."

"Do you think we might get lucky and have a little girl this time?"

"I sure would love to have a little girl, but what ever it will be it will be, as long as it is healthy. We will love it the same."

"Have you come up with a girl's name yet, one you really like?"

"No others than the ones we already considered, I am afraid."

"*Ina* still sounds the best to me and it fits with the boys' names, they sound nice together: Peter, Dieter, Ina … don't you think so?"

"Yes, I like the sound of it. I still think *Ina* is so cold and short. We'll see. What about a boy?"

Oh, I don't know, we've been through that too many times. I am waiting for an inspiration."

"I am getting cool, shall we think about packing up?"

"Yes, I think it is time. I have to get the car back to the garage tonight, too. He needs the car tomorrow. Wait for us, Petz and I will check out the lorry brakes for a minute. Then we will carry the baskets and all back to the car. Is that fine with you, Lisl?"

"Yes, just don't take too long. I'll walk a little while you do that. Please be careful and keep your eyes on Dieter!"

There were many more visits at all stages of completion of house and garden. The house plans were final. My father was able to modify the landscaping plans somewhat. He extended the concrete patio by one meter, he would not let them put in a bed of roses right in front of it because he wanted us to be able to step into the grass anywhere off the patio. He extended the lawn area and he worked with the laborers to install a natural stone retaining wall where the grass ended and the vegetable garden would begin. There were other small changes but I was not aware of them.

My mother went off to Wels and returned with a baby girl: blonde and blue-eyed. My parents' dream had come true. I did not notice much of a difference from when my brother had arrived, except that she cried a lot more than my brother did. I wondered if that had anything to do with her being female.

The space we were in was now crowded. I counted the days until we would be able to move to the new house. My brother and I would have our own room upstairs. I made all kinds of plans on how we could divide the space. There was plenty of it. We had a cozy corner under the dormer. There would be a big play area between our two beds up against the wall. It could even be enlarged by folding Dieter's bed up into a kind of cabinet, another one of my father's special designs. He had shown me how to draw a room layout and furniture to scale. I cut out the furniture and moved it around in the rooms. My mother and I had lots of fun furnishing all the rooms that way. The grandparents in Vienna had promised us a load of old family furniture, which would help us to fill all the extra space. It was delivered a few days after we actually moved.

I had absorbed the inside of the house from all our visits and all our planning. The "garden" had changed every time we went for another visit. The first thing I did after we moved in was to check all the surrounding areas, to see what the construction people had left. There was a small stack of bricks and many loose ones lying around throughout. I collected them and stacked them with the others. I made a pile of all the broken ones. As I was working, I already made plans on what to do with all those bricks. I tried to figure how long and high a wall I could build if I would use the bricks in single file. There were a couple of irregularly shaped sheets of steel, which looked like they had been used to mix small amounts of mortar on them. They would make a good wall or even a roof, I thought. They were heavy but with a little help from my brother, I could move them. The more I scavenged around the area, the more I could envision all kinds of fortresses and houses I could create with these scraps.

On the playmate side, it looked grim. The apartment buildings allowed only adults. On the open side of our house, there lived a girl named Helga, who seemed a little older than me. I had met her on one of our earlier visits. She was friendly and waved at me every time she saw me. She lived with her parents and her very old grandparents. Whenever I had been looking over there, her grandpa had been outside chopping wood next to a small lean-to stable in their backyard where the grandma took care of chickens, rabbits, and a goat. My father had not allowed me to go over there yet because he was not sure whether these people were up to our class standards. I was dying to check out the animals and the grandparents who looked as gnarly as the big tree-roots the grandpa was chopping into pieces small enough for a fireplace. Helga's mother was rarely outside, and I had never seen a trace of a father. The two row houses next to ours were still empty. An older couple without children had moved into the one at the far end, a few days ahead of us. They spoke with a German accent—as opposed to 'clean' Austrian. Mr. Metzger rode to work on the bus, which picked up all the other men from the "barracks," as my parents called the apartments. The bus came early in the morning and returned the men in the evening. After my father had made arrangements at work, he also used the bus to go to and from work every day. Mostly, though, his work hours were different from those of the others and he had to use regular public transportation, which was not quite as convenient.

WHO STOLE MY FATHER

I had started second grade at my old school in town before we moved. My father had talked with the teacher, still Herr Oberlehrer Veith, who had survived the purges after the Nazi takeover much against my hopes, and we had agreed it would be best for my academic well-being if I would finish out that grade with the same teacher and with the same classmates. There was only one slight problem: There was no bus connection from anywhere near our house to the school. My only option was to walk all the way to school every morning, and then walk home the same way in the afternoon. That took about forty-five minutes each way. My parents pointed out that my Kleine Opapa, who was almost 70 years old and still extremely fit had walked this stretch repeatedly already. On his first visit to our new house he had walked all the way to town to pick up some fresh apple cider from a wine cellar close to my school. He was healthy—so I was told—because he had been an avid walker all his life. He had no problem carrying a *rucksack* with several full cider bottles all the way. If he could do that, I could certainly walk to school for a few weeks.

My father walked with me the first day and showed me which streets to take, what to look out for, and where to be extra careful. My mother was a little nervous about the idea; she was worried about all the unknown dangers lurking along the way. So was I. Only I already had some concrete idea about those dangers: First and foremost was the bulldog I had to pass a few houses down from my own house. The dog was behind a fence barking ferociously at everyone walking by. I was afraid that someday the gate would be open or it would jump the fence altogether. There was another dog further down the street, but it was more docile. Still, it was a danger to me if it was not locked up. The rest of the way I did not know much about. It went on through the development, down a little hill next to the Kefer-Farmer's big farmhouse, along a big hedge towards the main street connecting us to town. There I had to cross the railroad tracks, four of them, shielded by a big gate operated by the guard living in the little house right next to the tracks. Then I walked on along the tracks, which continued flat towards the main station, but the road climbed slightly before it reached the town. By the time I arrived at the point where my old street from the old house came down—right at the corner where Hans lived—I could look down on the main railroad station. From here on out I followed my old school route, down the hill, through a passageway under the big building where our doctor, Dr. Thier, had her office. From there it was only a few more blocks to my school. At an even pace, without allowing for long trains at the crossing or anything interesting to watch along the way, it took me forty-five minutes. Other than on the last stretch through town, I rarely encountered anybody other than a few people on bicycles, an occasional pushcart on the way back from the market, sometimes pulled by a farmers' big dog, and very rarely a motorcycle or a truck. On the other side of the road there were small garden plots with little tool sheds where sometimes I could see people working on their vegetable beds, their berry bushes and their fruit trees. The stretch of road along the tracks was wide open to the elements. When the wind was blowing or the rain was coming down in sheets, it was not an easy walk.

I used my walking time to add characters and new adventures to the world of my stories. I planned my scrap buildings in the garden, and designed new sturdy trucks out of my Matador blocks. I was not the neatest looking kid after arrival either at school or at home, but that was mostly a function of the weather and my mode of dress. I refused to take the umbrella my mother still wanted me to carry. My beret, also not the most popular local headgear, was blown into the dirt by the wind, and was taken off and stuffed into my satchel when it was too hot. Carrying that satchel on my back was not an easy task either. It was heavy with books, notebooks, and my two sandwiches for the midmorning break. The straps cut into my shoulders and in the summer, the leather would make my back hot and sweaty. We were required to bring our books every day, and take them home for the homework assignments. Therefore, there was no way to lighten the load.

Some days I wished I was back on Frog Mountain—with an easy fifteen to twenty minutes walk all the way downhill to school. For the next school year, I would switch to the new school out on the *Keferfeld*, only ten minutes away from my house. It was still a country school and had boys and girls mixed in every class. I was not sure if I would like that. It would be more embarrassing not to know the answers in front of girls than in front of just boys. Now I still had to face Herr Oberlehrer Veith in his black and dark gray clothes.

HORSE APPLES, GYMNASTS AND PUPPETS

After all the garden rule restrictions on Frog Mountain, having our own backyard was certainly a step up. Here we ruled. My father laid out the garden and did the spading, weeding and raking, my mother planted and tended, I did most of the watering and whatever my father put on my list in the morning.

One day, as my father had predicted, a horse-drawn wagon appeared and unloaded all of its contents over our fence. When it was done there was a huge pile of steaming horse manure sitting on our lawn, emitting not-so-wonderful smells. The next day on my list appeared the task to move this pile by wheelbarrow down to where all the vegetable beds were waiting to be fertilized.

The wheelbarrow was made of solid wood, including the little wagon wheel, held together by a heavy band of iron. It was not exactly lightweight, but as a tall eight-year-old, I could manage. I experimented with different loading schemes. First, I needed to minimize the travel of the pitchfork from pick-up of the manure to the wheelbarrow, the distance as well as the height of lifting. A pitchfork full, picked up right next to the wheelbarrow, was ideal because it could just be slid over and emptied. This again meant careful placement of the wheelbarrow for loading was very important. Distribution of the load was also of paramount importance. The closer the load ended up towards the wheel rather than by the handle end, the easier the wheelbarrow was to lift. This made maneuvering a little more tricky because the heavy front would tend to tilt right or left, and in the worst case, fall over if the wheel ran into even the smallest obstacle. I dropped a couple of loads prematurely before I figured out the ideal pile.

With all these calculations and observations, I was able to keep my thoughts off my aching back and the blisters on both hands. Still, after working for two hours, the dent I had made in the pile was hardly noticeable. Had I not had the neatly arranged piles all over the beds down in the vegetable garden as witnesses of my labor, one would have thought I had loafed all afternoon. My father was pleased with my work when he came home, but stressed the fact that we really needed all of the manure down in the garden. He granted me a few little piles closer to the source, along the fence around the red currant bushes, and around the small fruit trees we had planted already. Another two days and another layer of blisters accomplished the feat. For years to come I took the credit for bumper crops harvested from the beds I had fertilized with so much effort.

Now, every time I see a pile of something like coal, firewood, gravel, sand, woodchips, I remember those blistered hands and I feel sorry for the person who is responsible for the transport of these piles.

By the first full summer after we moved in, my siblings and I had quite a crowd of regular playmates in our yard coming to play with us. They were mostly the age of my siblings, but there were a few younger and a few older ones tagging along. Since I was supposed to watch over my brother and sister, this extended family became sort of my charge, too. At times, I took it on myself to entertain them. My first effort was to teach them gymnastics. I did not remember where I had picked up the individual exercises, because gym instruction at school was mostly boring. All we ever did was play *Völkerball*, a game I did not care for because it involved two teams trying to hit each other into an "out" zone. If you did not catch the ball thrown at you, you had to go "out." In order to come back in you had to shoot somebody from the other team. I was neither a good catcher nor a good shooter and the whole idea of hitting someone close up with the ball as hard as you could was not appealing to me.

The elegance of gymnastics must have made an impression on me somewhere, in the movies or in some book with pictures. I started my neighborhood team on somersaults, forwards and backwards. The older ones I encouraged to try Judo rolls with a running start. Right from the beginning, there was serious competition within the group. The kids that fell over sideways when doing their rolls kept practicing and practicing until they too, could roll straight and all the way. Cartwheels were next. We worked on them a long time, to get everybody's legs up in the air and doing a full turn, touching the ground with both hands and both legs. There were collisions and crying in the process but after a while most of my students looked good. For the little ones I did 'carousels'— holding them by the hands, then by one hand and one foot, finally by both feet—and twirling them around. I had so many requests for repeats I was very dizzy even with changing directions all the time. The little ones I could also lift on my shoulders, stand them up holding on to their hands, and then let roll them down. They all wanted to do that over and over again. We tried a Roman chariot, one kid standing up in front, two behind him, bent down, holding on to the hips of the front man and then a little rider, standing on the backs, holding on to the arms held up by the front man. This whole configuration never went very far, because with all the laughter, one or the other part let go and the rider usually ended up in the grass. We jumped off stools, climbed ladders, raced around the garden and had lots of fun.

One of the parents, impressed by her child's nimbleness suggested we put together a show for all the parents. I went to work and choreographed a whole sequence, giving everybody a chance to show off his or her best. We rehearsed for days and finally set up a date for the performance. I made little invitations and sent them home with the kids. We put up a row of garden chairs, our own and some borrowed from the neighbors, and waited for the audience to appear. We had eight parents show up, full of expectations. The gathering place for the athletes was behind the big stepladder, which I had draped with a big sheet. We even used chaise pillows and folded blankets for mats to make it look professional. Everybody did a super job and we received lots of applause. The parents were very proud of the whole team and encouraged us to keep practicing and trying out new exercises.

All the kids liked the idea of performing. Somebody mentioned we should have charged admission. It was too late for the first performance and we could not repeat it right away. Then I remembered the puppets I had made during the winter. I had found instructions on how to make paper-mâché heads out of newspapers torn in little pieces, soaked in water and glue made of flour. I had gone to work immediately and never stopped until I had a *Kasperl*, the jester as the central figure of the puppet show, a Queen, a King, a witch, and something that was supposed to be a crocodile. Those were the main characters in every *Kasperltheater* I had ever seen. The instructions also included how to make the clothes for these puppets. My mother had a big box of remnants, which we had used for dress-up games in the winter.

I looked there for materials in appropriate colors and patterns for each of the heads: Green cloth for the *Kasperl*, a beautiful piece of red corduroy for the King, white lace for the Queen, dark blue flowery linen for the witch, and a wilder flower pattern for the body of the animal.

The patterns looked simple enough. I cut two equal pieces and started sewing them at the edges with my mother's sewing machine. She had shown me how to use the sewing machine some time ago, when I had just wanted to see how it works. The dress went together with a few derailments of the needle and thread, but overall I stayed pretty close to the edge of the material. Only when I reversed the garment, putting the seams inside, I found out that there was no way I could put my big boy's hand into the opening. The pattern was designed for a little child's hand, and not for the paws of a fast growing nine-year-old. I went through a few more prototypes before I got it right. In the meantime, I was getting better with sewing, so the Queen and the King, which I did last, looked quite regal in their outfits. My mother helped me to sew on some buttons and to put a little fur collar on the King's robe and some silver ribbons on the Queen's dress. The heads had been drying in the meantime and smelled rather sour. The flour and water must have gone rancid or something. For years, I always knew where those puppets were because I could track them by their smell.

While dressing and painting them I had been thinking about what kind of actions I could make up for them. I put all the puppets out and tried to remember my stories as I started to rehearse in front of the little kids. By their reactions, I could tell if the drama was good or bad. In the toy store, I had seen a fancy folding stage for puppet shows. I knew my parents would not spend money on something so frivolous, so I never asked. I had to improvise. Luckily, we had this little heirloom white desk-and-chair combination, all in one piece, made out of bentwood, held together by two floor railings. Standing it on end, with the desk facing the audience, and a little draping on the sides, I could hide behind the whole contraption and have the puppets act above the desktop.

Now I had to get ready for the performance. If I wanted to charge admission, I had to have tickets. I wanted them to look like the perforated ones they were using in the movie theaters. I had no trouble drawing up a whole sheet of them. The question now was how to get them perforated? What about the sewing machine? I took out the threads and started sewing up and down those lines. The tickets separated perfectly. The performance went well, and I collected enough admission money to buy myself a small bag of candy. My mother was not so sure about my asking for admission, she thought it was unfair to ask these little neighbor kids for money. I told her that the suggestion had come from the kids' parents. Kids with no money were admitted just the same.

For the wilder side of our play, one of our favorite toys was the remains of an old baby buggy. All that was left was the chassis, two axles welded to two springs, with four spoke wheels. I had all kinds of ideas for improvement, such as making it steerable or put a little engine on it, but they never came to fruition. We either used it to coast down the garden path or down the hill behind the last house in the row, or I let myself be pulled around, using my brother and sister as my horses. My parents did not like that game because it exploited my siblings rather than give them a pleasant play experience. After a while, we took turns on who was to sit on the buggy and who were the horses. The buggy was much in demand amongst all of our friends; it was always in use. We transported big loads with it, we raced and fell and got hurt, we made a jump for it, and finally it broke and there was no way to fix it. We were all very sad and hoped for another baby carriage to be dismantled in the neighborhood soon, but it never happened. The war made them a rarity, so they were refurbished with new linings and passed on from new mother to new mother.

PAPA IN THE DARKROOM

My father took great care in planning and taking photographs with his Rolleicord camera, which was his pride and joy. He had started this hobby as a young man and later used it professionally in different jobs, taking photographs of products and scenes, of items for catalogs as well as documenting construction progress of the big steel mill. His real affection though was for people and landscapes, which he captured with great love and sensitivity. He always went for a "natural" look but he went to great lengths in composing and posing to achieve it.

He did much of his own processing. At home, he would feed the exposed film into a black developing container, working under a big blanket in a darkened room. He then mixed the developer and poured it into the container, twirled the film around for the appropriate time, then fixed and rinsed it. After wiping all the water drops off with a suede glove, he would hang the film in the bathroom, attached to a clothesline with a wooden clothespin. I was always curious if I could make out any images on the film. Touching, of course was not allowed. The negatives from the 120 film used in the Rolleicord were much larger than the ones from a regular 35mm film so many times I was able to make out at least part of an image.

My father belonged to a photo club, which provided him with access to a studio and a darkroom, where he did all his printing and where he could work on his larger projects. It was in *Urfahr*, a part of the city of Linz located across the Danube. Sometimes I was allowed to accompany him there. I always enjoyed the tram ride over the long bridge spanning the Danube.

At the studio I would help with mixing the developer and the fixing baths in big flat glass containers. I loved the smell of the chemicals and the strange little lamp with a movable shade, which could make the light shine red, green or dark yellow. Mostly we used the dark red light because that did not expose the photographic paper. When the solutions were ready, my father would slip the negative he wanted to print into the enlarger, chose the size of the print and checked the enlarged image for sharpness and angle. He cut a small strip of photo paper, put it at the exposure level and pushed the button for the exposure light to come on, while counting slowly "twenty one, twenty two, twenty three ..." each number taking approximately one second. Then the strip would go into the developer, and then into the fixer, and when it came out sharp and with good contrasts he would print the same negative on to a full size piece of paper. I was allowed to rock the exposed papers gently in the magic fluid, as I watched each one intently until the outlines became clearer, the very dark ones first, then filling in the grays until the whole picture appeared, magically and magnificently. My father picked them up with wooden tongues, rinsed them in the fixer and then in water. The last step in the process was wiping the prints off carefully and then hanging them up to dry.

We took the dried prints home with us. They did not dry flat, even after being pressed in a book or in a special press. My father would hold a print by opposing corners and pull it back and forth over the smooth edge of the dining room table to flatten them out. Some needed cropping, some of the bigger enlargements needed retouching of the tiny dots of white caused by specks of dust on the lens, either of the camera or of the enlarger. He had a special watercolor set with all the shades of gray and brown with the tiniest little brushes I had ever seen. He used them to cover those almost invisible blemishes on his works of art. When they were done and dry they would be mounted and matted for photo contests, or sent to relatives and friends as postcard mementos of their visits, or they ended up in the family collection. He never put any of his photos in albums. My father did not believe in albums. I did not know why. I had never thought to ask him, I just accepted his belief.

In 1942 when my father was drafted, he left the Rolleicord at home and took an older 35mm camera with him. He begged my mother to take as many pictures as necessary to document our growing up. He also wanted pictures of our activities. In light of my father's artistry and professional perfectionism, my mother felt intimidated and ended up taking very few pictures. Most of them were–as per my father's evaluation either over- or under-exposed, had unsuitable backgrounds, or were taken at the wrong angle or from the wrong distance. I tried my luck a few times but did not fare much better. There would be no more real pictures taken at home until my father came back.

While in Russia with the army, my father filled innumerable rolls of 35mm film with photographs of people at the local markets, of the unusual arched hitches on Russian horse buggies, of churches and buildings. Most of all he captured the mood of the Russian flatlands and steppes. When on leave, he would develop the films feverishly and if there was extra time, he would make a few proof sheets. Most of them never were printed, the rolls of negative films ended up in airtight Dutch tobacco tins for an unearthing "after the war."

2. THE WAR

FRIENDS AND FAMILY

One evening, long after the remaining work crew had left the area around our new house, I heard the rumbling of one of the lorries on the tracks still left, way over beyond the houses. After the rumbling, I heard some loud squeaking noises. The pattern repeated. I also thought I heard some kids' voices.

"Can I go and play out front for a while?"

"Are you finished with the chores Papa gave you this morning?"

"Yes, I am."

"Who is out there?"

"Some of the kids down the street. I want to see what they are doing."

"Yes, you can go. Papa will be home pretty soon now, check back in about half an hour."

"Thank you, Mama; I'll be back in half an hour."

I ran along the houses and turned right towards the area where during the day the workers were still moving earth with the lorries. A group of boys and girls I had seen around but not talked to had unhooked the last car from the little train and were pushing it up the other side of the hill.

"Can I help?"

"Sure, just push uphill."

When the car was clear up on the top, one of the older boys put a big piece of lumber across the tracks in front of the wheels so the car could not roll back down.

"Who's going to ride this time?" the big boy asked. "We need a brakeman and two riders."

"I'll be the brakeman again," one of the boys said.

"We'll ride!" Two older girls stepped forward and took their places on the front of the car.

The big boy climbed aboard in the rear. He was carrying a long heavy piece of wood looking like a fence post. He wedged it behind the wheel just as my father had explained at our first visit here.

"You take that side again, hold it real tight! Are we ready? August, you take the block away.

The boy I had talked to came forward, took a look at the girls sitting on the front railing, holding on to the lorry itself.

"Are you girls ready? Hold on tight, if you start slipping, jump off to the side so the car won't hit you. Do you understand?"

He pulled the piece of wood. The two boys in back loosened their braking poles a little bit. The wood scraped against the steel wheels as they started turning. The car slowly gained momentum. I was afraid to look because this could go very wrong.

"I don't think I'll ride here tonight," I thought.

The brakemen did a good job of controlling the speed. They let go and then they tightened up when the car started moving too fast. Close to the bottom of the hill they let go altogether. The car went faster, the girls screamed with excitement. After a few meters the tracks started uphill again. The car lost momentum and just before it came to a full stop the brakemen jumped off and put their poles behind the wheels.

"Good ride!" everybody clapped and shouted.

"You want to try?" the big boy said to me and held out another pole. "What is your name?"

"Peter" I said and asked "Is it hard to brake right?"

"No, not really. I am Fredi. We have been doing it for two days now and we stopped every time we wanted to. I have been watching the workers during the day. Sometimes when they have an empty car alone without an engine they manage it with a braking pole. I've seen them go pretty fast with a full load, but I have also seen one of these lorries jump off the rails. That's a bugger to put it back up on the tracks, they are heavy, all steel."

"Where do we start from on this side?"

"We'll push it up to the train that is parked up there. That is as far as we can go. Come on, everybody push."

The whole crew rushed up and shoved the car up the hill towards the train. I looked back at the incline and got scared. This side was steeper and longer.

"*Maybe I should not do this.*" I thought. "Can I go from here rather than all the way?" I asked out loud.

"Sure, we won't have to push so hard—hey—put some blocks under the wheels. Thanks."

I got into position with the same brake partner as the big boy. Fredi checked the way I had put the pole by the wheel.

"Good," he said, "you'll have no problem. You are ready to go. I'll ride this time—who's with me?"

"August, will you do the blocks again, please?"

He looked at me and then nodded. "Sure!"

I glanced over at my brake partner.

"I am Walter!" he said, and gave me a smile and a nod.

We were rolling already. I leaned on the pole and we slowed down immediately. I played with a little pressure and more pressure, varying the speed. Walter went along with me.

"Let her roar..." Fredi shouted from the front.

I looked at Walter and nodded. He smiled and lifted his pole. The car picked up speed and made a horribly hollow noise as it rumbled down into the pit and up on the other side. I felt scared by the loud rattling and the noise. We stayed on the tracks and everybody clapped again.

"Again!" somebody said.

"My father is home, I have to go for dinner," I said, "I'll see you tomorrow?"

"Why don't you come over after dinner, we'll be here till dark!"

"I'd love to but I don't think they'll let me go again tonight. Thanks anyway. Bye. It was fun."

At home I never told what I had been doing. But I sneaked away as often as I could to play with that group. August became my best friend, Fredi moved away, but the others stayed and we formed a little family, even after the construction crew took the tracks and the cars away. We met almost every afternoon at that hill with the wild memories. There were a few big square holes in the ground left over from the earthmovers' work. Our family of friends took over the coziest one as our "home." It was surrounded by waste-high weeds, which made it even more private and homey. We put some good boards inside as benches. The older girls would sit there and knit until the light would be too weak. We picked wildflowers and weeds and decorated the inside. We told stories and made plans for rabbit hunts in the fields right next to us. August told of little lakes that would form after the snow melted, over there in these low areas between the fields. Last spring he had gone over there with some friends and they had built a raft to play on the water. It sounded like fun. One day somebody brought a kite and we let it fly until it broke. Then we built a few new ones from scratch, using different patterns, copied from craft books. The girls were laughing and teasing us when the kites came tumbling down. We threw small dirt clods at them to make them stop.

When the builders finally started to landscape that hill, we could not find another spot like it. The group fell apart and for a long time I was very sad for not having my family there anymore. Only August stayed with me as a faithful friend, and when I visited him at home I would see his older sister, who had been one of the knitting girls. We always had a nice chat about our good times together. But those good times never happened again.

THE FATHERLAND IS CALLING

I put down my book. I was sitting on my favorite perch in my room, right under the attic window where I had been reading since breakfast. I could not see the garden below because the windows were all covered with frost. The ice had painted delicate bouquets of flowers on the glass panes. I cleared a little peephole with my fingernail. The outside looked cold and dull this morning. There was no new snow.

It had been very cold for weeks. The newspaper had said 1942 had the coldest February in years with record snowfalls. I was still hoping for so much snow to fall in one day, that I would not have to go to school. Right now school was closed for a 'coal holiday.' They had run out of coal because of the war. I would have been home today for another reason. My father had to leave to become a soldier in the war.

The doorbell rang downstairs, I heard my mother going from the kitchen to answer it.

"Good morning, Frau Slonek. Can Peter come and sled with us?" It was my friend.

"Good morning, August. I guess so, if he wants to, but only for a little while. Let me call him. Oh, there you are!"

I had come downstairs and come up behind her. "May I go, Mama?"

"You have to be back before lunch, you know we are leaving with Papa right after."

"Yes. I'll be back in time. At noon?" I looked at my mother.

"At noon is fine," she said. "Don't get all snowy, though, please." My mother went back to the kitchen.

"Wait, I'll be out in a minute," I called to my friend, "I have to put on my boots." I took my dark blue winter sweat suit off the hanger in the hall, pulled it on, then slipped into my heavy boots, laced them up, put on the cap and the mittens my mother had knitted for me as a Christmas present and went for the sleigh.

"Let's go!" I said to August. "Who else is over there?"

"I haven't been there yet, but I heard voices."

We pulled our sleds across the square in front of my house. We headed for the little passageway between the apartment building and the next house. It had not snowed in a few days. The trail was a deep rut in between snow banks. It lead through the apartment gardens where some of the evergreen shrubs were wearing big white caps. There were no shadows this morning and no clouds. The sky hung low and tied everything together. Everything looked white and gray and cold.

Once out of the shrubs we could see the field in front of us. It sloped down gently into a little valley. There was another slope coming down on the opposite side, which was a little steeper than ours. Way up on the horizon there were houses again. I loved this wide-open space so close to my own house. It gave me a feeling of freedom and a chance to roam. In the summer the area was planted in wheat but in the wintertime its gentle slope made it a nice hill for easy skiing and some decent sledding. The field ended at the bottom of the valley with a sudden steeper drop. The kids had built a little jump there for an exciting finale of our run.

"Hey Peter, hey August, it's about time. The snow is fast this morning, come try the jump, we built it up a little bit. Joseph did almost one meter, would you believe that?"

There were four other kids with three sleds, two boys and two girls, all around ten years old, the same age as I was.

"Do you start from right here?" I pointed to our usual starting spot.

"Yes," one of the boys said. "Do a running start, it's worth it today."

My sled was a family heirloom. It was made of solid oak, even the slats of the seat were thin oak boards polished smooth by generations of riders. It had a nice, heavy hemp rope attached to brass eyelet screws on the top end of the runners. The steel runners were all shiny and showed no signs of wear after many years of use.

"Let's do it!" I said to August. I threw the cord on top of the sleigh, bent down, grabbed the sides of the sleigh with my hands and started pushing it down the hill. When I had enough speed I jumped onto it, sat down and leaned back as far as I could. I flew over the jump and hit hard after being airborne for a tiny bit. I dug my right heel into the hard snow, made a wide turn, slowed down and stopped.

I turned around to watch August coming down the hill. August waved to me just before hitting the jump, which made his sled turn enough to miss the jump with one runner. The sled turned over and August tumbled a few times before he stopped. His sled was upside down a few feet from him. August got up and laughed. He brushed the snow off his clothes, put his cap back on, yanked his sled upright and headed for me.

"Great jump, don't you think so?" August said. He was laughing.

We headed back up the hill, side by side, pulling our sleds behind us.

"Good snow," I said. "I am glad you got me out."

"I am glad you came, too—look at Hans," August said and stopped. "He's got some speed!"

We watched Hans going over the jump, coming down to a rocky landing, almost crashing.

"Let's ride together this time," I suggested, "we'll be a lot faster."

"No, I want to try the jump again, straight this time."

The snow was really icy. It sang out under our boots with every step as we continued to the top of the hill. We took off at the same time, side by side, August headed for the jump, I was right next to him.

"Don't miss it!" I yelled. He rocked his body back and forth to gain more speed.

We all gathered at the bottom. "Looked like a good jump, August," somebody said.

"Let's see who can jump the farthest, I'll stay here and measure, first one down can take over from me," August said. "Singles only, somebody can borrow my sled."

One of the girls took August's sled and everybody scrambled back up the hill.

With my long legs I beat the others to the top. I was the tallest in the group. Even in my sweat suit, I looked thin. "Who goes first?"

"I will, then August can have my sled back," the girl said. She did not wait for a response and took off.

One by one they took off, jumped, and went to check how far they had gone. They were all standing by the jump now.

"I am coming down, watch me!" I yelled.

I took a running start and crouched down while gathering speed down the hill so I would have less air resistance. Approaching the jump I sat up, grabbed the front end of the sleigh and yanked it up just before my weight went over the edge. I hit hard, the sled wobbled a bit when it landed, but I did not crash.

"You win, you win!" August yelled. "You went two centimeters more than I did! But look what you did to the jump; you carved it up with your ski-jump take-off!"

Everybody laughed and started back up the hill. "We will have to put some water on the jump so it will freeze solid, it is too cut up right now," somebody said.

August walked next to me. "How come your father is home today, where do you have to go?" he asked me.

"He got drafted. He has to report today."

"Oh, I forgot. It's today? But your father, isn't he too old ...? I mean the army is for young guys like Herman down the street, with no family"

August said.

"Not any more, my father is almost forty."

"My father said the war should be over soon, the Germans have better tanks and better planes—he said the noisy planes we have been hearing are rocket planes they are testing—when they are ready, they are going to win," August said.

"After they win, when they get the colonies back, I will go to Africa. German Southwest Africa. I'll raise sheep. My father gave me a book for Christmas—you saw it, 'Africa is Waiting' Papa keeps teasing me, saying 'Africa is waiting for Peter.' You should come with me that would be fun! See you!"

I wrapped the end of the sleigh cord around my mitten and waved 'bye' to the others on the hill. "Tomorrow with skis?"

"Yeah, with skis, we'll go over to the steeper hill, good."

I walked up towards the apartments. *"Papa was very quiet this morning,"* I thought. I do not like these low, gray skies. There is not enough room to breathe and move under them.

"You are home early, good!" my mother said. "Can you help me in the kitchen, please?"

"What do you want me to do, Mama?"

"You can set the table. We are having vegetable soup with bread. You can ask Dieter to help you."

My brother was a little over four years old. At times I thought him a nuisance, because he wanted to go along everywhere and slowed things down. But on the whole we got along fine.

"Dieter, can you take five napkins from over there. The white ones. Take them ups' them on the table, please," I said.

I took out the big serving tray, put the good plates on it, the soupspoons and the breadbasket with the rye bread my mother had cut up already.

"These napkins?" my brother asked, holding up a bundle of white ones.

"Yes. Did you count them?"

"Five," my bother said.

"Good, can you take the salt shaker in the other hand?" I asked him.

"Yes, give it to me." Dieter smiled and maneuvered up the wooden staircase opposite the kitchen door.

"Do you have the ladle or shall I take it?" I asked my mother.

"Take it on the tray, thank you."

I carried the tray and my mother followed with the soup tureen.

We were eating—and living—in the big bedroom upstairs because it was the easiest to keep heated. Coal was rationed and hard to come by after two and a half years of war. The large ceramic tile stove heated two rooms. We had a fire burning around the clock. Every morning we lit the kindling with the embers of last night's coals.

"Lunch is ready! Emil, can you bring Ina, please."

My father arrived at the table last, he sat Ina down on the edge of the sofa bed. My mother and my sister always sat on the big sofa bed. We took our places around the rest of the round table. My father, my brother and I sat on chairs.

The draft notice had arrived only two weeks ago. My father had to report with a specified list of belongings today at two p.m. at the Niederer barracks to be enlisted in the German Army.

This felt like the Last Supper, although it was lunch.

Mother started to ladle out the vegetable soup, my father's favorite, because it was made entirely from vegetables grown in our own garden. We still had canned kohlrabi and peas; carrots, potatoes and rutabagas were kept fresh in a sandbox in the cellar.

"I am not hungry," Ina said, with her head slightly leaning to one side. She was the only one in the family who did not have a ravenous appetite ever.

"These are the last of the carrots we kept in the sand in the cellar," my mother said, "they are all gone now."

Suddenly my father coughed several times, his spoon dropped into the soup. He bent forward and started to sob. His whole body went into convulsions.

"I don't want to go ... I don't want to leave you ..., I don't want anything to do with this war ..." he cried and reached for his napkin.

My mother choked, I stared at my father in bewilderment until my eyes filled with tears, too. My brother froze and held his full spoon in mid-air without spilling any soup. My sister looked from face to face, puzzled, and did not grasp what was going on.

My tears were running down over my cheeks into the soup. My head was spinning. *When will I see him again? How will we get along without him? My father, who masters all situations, is crying? No more trips to the photo lab to develop and print my many rolls of film, no more watching him lettering diplomas in beautiful calligraphy for extra money, no more assignments for me in the garden—will mother take over telling me which plots to spade, what beds to weed, and when to pick the caterpillars off the cabbage plants?*

"I am sorry, I cannot eat anymore ..." my father said after a while.

Everybody looked at him. Nobody spoke.

"Let's go!" my father said, breaking the silence.

We all got up, went downstairs and put on our overcoats.

"Don't forget your mittens and hats, it is very cold outside," my mother said.

It was a twenty-minute walk to the bus stop. My father carried my sister, holding her closely to his body to keep her warm. We walked in between the small houses flanking the street coming from our cul-de-sac.

We passed the house with the big bulldog. With my father next to me I felt perfectly safe. *There would be no more protection, at least for a while.*

"When will you be back, Papa?"

"I don't know. I should get some leave after basic training," my father answered in a strange voice.

"What is basic training?" I asked.

"That is where they teach me how to be a soldier."

"Where will you be? In one of the barracks here in town?" I said, with hope in my voice.

"I doubt it." After a pause my father continued. "It could be anywhere: Germany, Czechoslovakia, one hour or days away." He shifted Ina a little higher against his body to get a firmer hold on her. She tried to put her arm around his neck, but she couldn't because of her heavy coat.

The bus was on time and empty. It would take us half an hour to get to town. We all looked out the window at the piles of dirty snow along the road, and at the few people out on foot.

I was drawing flowers on the window with my finger, trying to imitate the frosty ones I had seen this morning. I felt my tears coming up again. My stomach felt like it did before a big test in school. *My father had cried. I had never seen him cry before, ever.*

When I glanced up from my doodling, I saw my father looking at my mother who sat across from him, stiffly, with eyes staring into space. I blinked and a few tears came rolling down. *Mother is losing her mate today. She would be alone with us, alone with the daily decisions, with no husband to share the burden. My father's look was full of tenderness and pain. And maybe confusion. But that could have been my confusion.*

I knew many of my father's looks. When he took photographs, he could look upset when the children were moving about rather than sitting still. I knew his look when he came home from work and walked through the garden to see how I had done with the chores. I knew the look of impatience when my father explained a modification to the drawings of our house-to-be and mother did not quite understand what he had drawn. I

101

knew his look of frustration when things had not gone well at work. This was a different look now. It was much more serious and very sad.

We got off the bus and walked the three blocks to the barracks. Here in town the snow was heaped high along the sidewalks, and it was so dirty it was offensive looking. I hated dirty snow. It was useless. Who would want to touch it and make snowballs? Or jump into it and enjoy that sinking feeling? You could not ski on it or sleigh on it. The dirt would scratch your skis or slow down your sleigh.

We went through the big wrought iron gate. Two big flags were hanging down limp in the quiet winter air. I could remember the Austrian flags, with red-white-red bands and a black two-headed eagle in the center. They were illegal now. When the Germans marched in, they brought their red flags with the black swastika in the white round spot in the middle. Somehow this flag did not look friendly to me. It had a cold, official look to it.

Inside the courtyard many families were standing around in clusters with their recruits in the middle. The men who had registered already wore big silver oak leaves in the lapels of their overcoats. Several of the groups were loud and boisterous.

I could not understand how anyone could even fake joy at this occasion. I looked at the loud ones in disbelief. *"My dad is going away. I don't know when I will see him again. I will miss him. We all will miss him."* I felt angry towards these insensitive people.

My father entered the building, which was decorated with a banner and more swastika flags. The banner said *"Ein Volk, ein Reich, ein Führer!"* proclaiming unification for all Germans in one country, under one leader.

"Where would he have to go and fight? Fight whom? The Russians? The English in Africa? The Greeks? The French? Germany was fighting the whole world."

When my father came back he had the silly silver leaves on his lapel. He looked serious and resigned.

"They said the bus will be leaving in half an hour."

"Most probably I will not be allowed to write to you where I am. In my first letter I will underline single letters and when you read them all together you will know the name of the town I am closest to. Do you understand what I mean?"

"Yes," I said, "I'll decipher it, sure!"

All around us people were getting ready to say their final farewells. Handkerchiefs were out and loud sobbing could be heard everywhere. Even the laughers were quiet now. Wherever I looked I saw red eyes, people embracing and holding hands. All these families were being torn apart because of the war. I did not understand war. I did not like war.

"Watch over your mother, you are the man in the house now!" my father said to me. I held him tightly and I could feel the salty teardrops falling down on my face. My body tensed up with the responsibility that had just been bestowed on me. I had not even turned ten yet. I turned away to hide my own tears and kicked the dirty snow.

After hugging and kissing us all once more my father started walking towards the building. He walked slowly, turning back every few steps and waving at us until he disappeared in the big black hole that was the door. The busses were waiting on the other side. Dieter started crying "I want my daddy!" with one arm wrapped around my mother's waist and the other stretched out towards the door, and Ina cried because she saw everybody else crying.

When we arrived back home it was dark.

"Let's put some apples in the oven and bake them," my mother said.

Soon the hissing sound of the juices and the smell of sugar turning to caramel filled the room that was so empty without Daddy.

We all slept in the big bedroom that night. Mother and Ina in the big bed, Dieter in Ina's bed, and I brought my mattress from the other bedroom and put it down next to my mother's bed for comfort.

I was awake for a long time. I listened to all the small noises in the house and outside. When I finally went to sleep I dreamt about tanks rolling through our garden and destroying all the orderly beds of vegetables and flowers and strawberries and crushing all the red currant bushes and the small fruit trees we had planted last spring. I was in charge of the garden and I had to get it all in order again before my father would return home.

FIRST LETTER FROM THE ARMY

"We have a letter from Daddy!" Mother gave it to me to read. The first thing I looked for was the underlined letters—where was Papa at?

k-r-u-m-m-a-u-m-o-r-a-v-i-a

"Where is that?" I asked my mother.

"It sounds like Czechoslovakia to me" she said.

"Let's look it up on the map." I went for my school Atlas.

"I already tried, I cannot find it," my mother said.

I went to the page for Czechoslovakia and looked carefully for a long time. I found the province of Moravia first, then the town of Krummau.

"Here it is. Just across the border. It is on the river Moldava." I was excited. I stared at the spot on the map as if it would yield a picture if I would only stare long enough. There was some green around it and some light brown. So it must be hilly, not just flat. A red line ran through it continuing all the way to Prague. The railroad. The other end of the line went to Vienna.

"Can we go and visit him?" I asked. It cannot be more than a day away, even if we have to change trains.

"Not unless he has a pass." My mother's face indicated that there might be a problem.

"What is a pass?"

"It is a paper that allows soldiers to leave the barracks."

"You mean they are locked in the rest of the time?" I had a hard time believing that grown men—even as soldiers—could not just leave when they were done with whatever they do.

"Well, yes. They are in the Army. That's it." My mother shrugged her shoulders.

"What do they do, all day locked up?" my voice had gotten louder. I did not like the idea of my father being locked up like that.

"I don't know. I guess they march, sing songs, learn how to shoot, drive a tank ..."

"Can I ride on the tank?" Dieter said, his face lighting up.

"No, I don't think so, Dietz, they will be all locked up in the garage." Mother gave him a kiss.

A few weeks later the next letter announced that Papa will be off for a weekend. He asked my mother to join him.

"I am going to visit Papa," my mother said, "I will be leaving on the train tomorrow afternoon. I'll be back Monday morning."

"Can we come? We want to see Papa, too!" Dieter was the first to respond. I had a notion in the back of my mind that this was something private between my parents, a time they needed to themselves without having to care for the children.

"I am afraid that's not possible—there is no room there for you to stay in," my mother said, "Papa only has one small place for me. And we have things to talk about. He has been gone so long already and we cannot discuss house things and garden things in the letters. It takes too much time." Her voice was weak and trailing off. "Next time he gets a pass, it will be a leave so he can come home and visit all of us!"

Dieter started to cry and Ina joined in right away. "I want my Daddy!" came from both of them, over and over again.

"Who is going to take care of us?" I asked.

"You'll be fine with Erna, and I will ask Frau Horn to look in on you."

Erna was our household helper from Romania, brought to Austria by the German government to help out mothers with three or more children while their husbands were away doing military duty for the *Vaterland*. She was cheerful and looked cheerful with her crown of braided blond hair, she spoke the natural German dialect from her homeland, cooked well and fit well into the family. She treated us children warmly and with respect.

Frau Horn was a neighbor with an engineer husband and a son Ina's age, probably closest to our way of life and upbringing, and therefore accepted and trusted by my father. She was my favorite of the three women living in the houses next to us. She was natural, had a good sense of humor, supported my efforts as a gymnastics coach and puppeteer, and–above all- she represented the 'dark woman'—the mystical female with her lean and tan body, pitch black hair and fiery eyes to match them. I felt an unexplainable affinity and attraction to the female in her.

Mother's being away from us for a whole weekend on her visit to Papa was a new and traumatic experience. The little ones were crying at every opportunity, I felt left out and put in charge, responsible for calming the misery of my siblings and at the same time resenting their incessant expression of missing their Mama and their Papa, which was just as nagging on me as on them, but I could not let that show.

It must have been close to evening when my father had taken the picture, in the harsh late light my mother did not look as happy as I had expected her to be. Was she thinking about having to leave her husband behind soon, or about his impending assignment to one of the many fronts in the war?

There was great hugging and kissing when Mama came back. Both Dieter and Ina hung on her for the rest of the day. I watched from a distance, going about my business, wondering quietly what kind of life lay ahead for us all.

2/3/1942 PAPA in KRUMMAU to Peter IN LINZ

Dear Peter!

A big kiss for your beautiful letter. If you behave you will be allowed to come and visit me with Mama. Then I will tell you about all the things soldiers have to learn. Do you have beautiful winter weather the way we do here? It is ideal for ice-skating. Why don't you try it again. Just have Mamsi go with you. I received a parcel from Omi, too. But you don't have to send me anything. Keep watching your brother and sister and yourself as well as you have been, then I will be pleased,

Your Papsi

SOLITARY CONFINEMENT: SCARLET FEV.

"DO NOT ENTER, CONTAGIOUS DISEASE," said the bright red sticker on the outside of the door. I was quarantined again, this time with Scarlet Fever, in my father's study, rearranged into a sick room for the long haul until I was declared safe again.

Just as she had done when I had had diphtheria several years before, my mother had decided to keep me at home and nurse me herself rather than to turn me over to the hospital, which was far away at the other end of town. I had never been away from home.

Also, I had not quite digested my father's sudden involuntary departure for the army and the ensuing changes in the household.

I had been locked away for two weeks already. Every detail in the room was etched in my mind, even with my eyes closed: The small Cuckoo clock my father had sent me as a present from basic training was ticking away right above my bed. A big world map hung on the wall across from my bed. The bold letters across the top said HAPAG LLOYD, advertising the German steamship company. In my feverish half-sleep, I had traveled many of the red and blue lines across the oceans, to Johannesburg, Rio de Janeiro, New York, Sidney, Auckland, and many other places, taking long journeys into jungles, the Wild West, deserts and steppes. The map also showed some white areas, not only around the polar caps but further into the continents, 'unexplored' it said in the legend.

This particular projection of the world's continents and oceans became a living picture to me: Europe and Africa represented a sitting woman, with Sweden her face, Norway and Finland her hair, Central Europe and Spain forming her body, the British Isles a hand with a pointing finger, Africa the lower body in a sitting position. Then there was the 'bear' of North America, with a twisted head and an outstretched tongue—the Aleutian Islands, and Central America its tail. Australia was a British soldier's head with a Tommy helmet strapped on, and New Guinea an Aborigine floating in the sea above it.

My immediate world could be contacted through the only window at the far end of the room, flanked by off-white net curtains and open every morning for airing out the bed, and after that whenever the weather permitted. It looked out over the side part of our garden, at our neighbor's house and into their yard.

The pale green ceramic tile stove from my parents' bedroom stuck its back end through the wall right next to the window. The corner opposite the stove was taken by a big wardrobe. My father's desk with an elegant dark blue leather top filled the space next to it. This desk had a special attraction for me. It was made out of fine hardwoods. The handles on the drawers looked and felt like amber but were made out of some new quality man-made material. The drawers were fitted perfectly and slid out and in without a sound. My favorite was the "pencil" drawer. It was just high enough to hold oblong compartments for pencils and pens. A second one, just as slim, held rulers and other drawing aides. I liked to just pull them open and look at the treasures inside. My father's tools of the trade were an awe-inspiring sight. But they were "off limits" to me. I myself owned a box full of pencils, a set of colored pencils and a watercolor set with an assortment of brushes my father had given me. He had also instructed me in the care of these utensils.

Two bentwood chairs moved about in the remaining space, left wherever they were needed last: by the bed where my mother sat and by the desk where the doctor wrote her notes and prescriptions.

The doctor and my mother were the only persons who could enter this room. The doctor stopped by once a week. My mother came with meals and for a stretch in the afternoon when my brother and sister were napping. For emergencies I had a small ornate table bell, a survivor from earlier, better days, when there were still maids in my grandparents' house answering bells. If I rang it loud enough, my mother could hear it, even in the garden when the window was open, and come to inquire about my wishes. I used it rarely because I did not want to place extra demands on my mother. I was most grateful for being allowed to stay at home under the circumstances.

The first two weeks had passed fairly fast. The persistent fevers had made me weak and sleepy most of the time. I did not have much of an appetite and when I read my eyes got tired and achy very quickly.

"Mama, I need some more books. I am all done."

"Did you do all the crossword puzzles in the magazines, too?" my mother asked.

"Yes, they were too easy."

"Oma said she would send you more, she knows where to get the difficult ones, and they will take you a little longer than just filling them in. Tomorrow Frau Dr. Thier is coming again, do you remember?"

"Yes, but what does she come for? She does not do anything. We already know it will take six weeks at least."

"She has to watch out for signs of complications. Scarlet fever is very dangerous, not by itself but because of what it can do to the organs in your body. She wants to make sure you will not contract anything else. I have time for a game. Anything you want to play?"

"Let's start with the chess," I said right away.

"Oh, that will take too long. We do not know how to play that. We would have to read the instructions."

My mother was not enthused about that game. We had been using her family's old game chest, a beautiful wooden box lined with dark red velvet on the inside, which contained several wood inlaid board games with beautifully carved pieces. The delicate chess figures were turned from expensive hardwoods. So far we had only identified who was who. From Pawn to King and Queen. I knew where they took their positions on the board and how they moved. But we had not started a game and not gotten into the strategy of it.

"Please, Mama, we will go as long as you have time, then we just save it for later, yes?" I pleaded.

"Good, as long as we can stop when I have to go, it is fine with me."

I had pulled out the checkered board already and had started to set up the figures. "You get white and I get black, which means you get to make the first move. Let's read. You read, please, and I move the figures."

"Where does it start? Oh, here ..." my mother said. "Standard Openings, looks like we are starting with that."

"Yes. The pawn in front of the queen, white, moves out first. He can move two fields straight out on the first move."

"Just on the first move?" my mother asked.

"No, all pawns can move two places from their home position, but they do not have to," I said, "they can also move just one."

"That sounds complicated to me, one way or the other would be easier for me to remember."

"But it is not an easy game, Mama, it is for people who can think, for the masters." I had read the whole introduction and after that I really wanted to learn to play the game well. I had to get my mother interested; she was the only partner I would have available for a while.

"That wasn't so bad," I said after we had played through the first of the standard opening sequences in the book.

"Yes, that was fun, but I have to go now."

"Can we leave the chessmen standing where we are? Then we can go on from here, please?"

My mother balanced the board over to my father's desk.

"Can you get me more books, please, I have read everything you brought me."

"You have to go slower on these books, you know, they all will have to be burned when you are done. There is too much danger of infection. We do not want Ina or Dieter, or anybody else, to get this. They are too little, it could really hurt them."

"There we go again, didn't we discuss this when I had diphtheria?"

"Yes, we did and we were lucky that you were able to keep some of your belongings after they were disinfected."

Well, why can't we do it the same way this time?

"Let's discuss this another time, please, I really have to go now."

She blew me a kiss and left the room. I heard her going into the bathroom right next to the sickroom, I imagined her taking off her white coat, and then I heard

the water running when she washed up. She always
changed into her regular clothes before going downstairs
to join the others. I wondered if this took her back to her
days as a special nurse, taking radiation treatments to
private patients at home. She had told me that she was
constantly afraid of being robbed of the radium, which
was very expensive. Her biggest fear now was to take the
infection to her two little ones. But the doctor had told her
that by being extra careful the chances of spreading the
scarlet fever were very slim.

"Look, what the mailman just brought! A whole box of
magazines from Musch-Omi. How dear of her to send
them to you!"

"Let me see, what are they? They look old!" I had
taken the box on my bed and pulled out the first
magazine. The cover page looked like it was printed in
sepia ink.

"This looks like Opa's old photographs, you know,
when you were a little girl, and Opa in his Hussar's
uniform. This girl looks like your sister. Is this supposed
to be a school uniform?" I asked.

"No. That's just the way young girls dressed at that
time. We read these magazines with a passion, my sisters
and I, Aunt Mimi and Aunt Martha. My mother must have
saved them. They were very popular then."

"Girls' magazines? What am I supposed to read in
them?"

"Look first and then complain. I am sure there are
some stories that will interest you ...and don't make that
face, please!"

"But Mama, they were printed in 1925, seven years
before I was born!"

"Well, that's all you have for now, maybe you can use
them for a lesson in history. What do you know about the
year 1925?"

"Nothing," I said. "We haven't even covered the World
War. Do you remember anything about the World War?
Was it really the whole world fighting?" I asked. I had my
right hand on top of the stack of magazines as if to keep
them from jumping out of the box.

"I was too little, I was only four when it started, and eight when it finally ended. My brother, your Uncle Niki, played the wounded soldier and I was his nurse."

My mother laughed a short little laugh. "I guess, I have been a nurse all my life, off and on. I had a real nurse's uniform with a cap and the Red Cross on it. It was a Christmas present one year. I had a little nurse's bag and a box of bandages. I would bandage him all up, make him crutches, and then he would get better but he always got wounded again. We had lots of fun, actually."

I had heard her tell the story before, it was one of her favorites. It always made her sad, because now she did not get to see her brother very often. First we had moved away from Vienna, and now he was in the Army.

"Where is Uncle Niki now, do you know?" I asked.

"I think he went down to Serbia or Croatia, I hope he is all right."

"That is on the way to Greece. Do you think he will go all the way to Greece?" I said and pointed to the map on the opposite wall. "Can you show me where you think he is, please?"

My mother got up and stepped over to the map. "It is too tiny on here," she said. "But look, here is the 'boot' that is Italy, next to it is the Adriatic, the blue here, and this," she said pointing at a small spit of land losing itself into the sea in many little dots, "is Greece, and above it somewhere there is Serbia and Croatia and Albania and Bosnia-Herzegovina—it all belonged to the Austro-Hungarian Monarchy before the World War."

"How do you know all these names?" I said.

"Well, we learned about them in school. In history. And in geography. The Austrian Archduke was assassinated in Sarajevo, the capital of Bosnia, that's what started the war, they said."

"Aren't we having a world war now? The Germans are fighting everyone around them, don't they?'

"It certainly seems so, look at Russia, how big it is on the map in comparison to Germany," my mother said, staring at the map. She traced the outline of the Soviet Union all the way to where just a small strip of water divided it from the northern tip of North America.

"What about the white areas?"

"You mean the North Pole and the South Pole?" my mother said.

"Yes, them too, but I mean the white areas on bigger maps, the areas where nobody has been yet. I want to go there. I want to be an explorer," I said.

Wouldn't you be afraid to go somewhere where nobody has been before?"

"I would go with friends and I would have a rifle to protect myself. Papa has to teach me how to shoot. He had guns when he grew up. He knows all about guns. They did a lot of hunting, he told me. Do you know anything about that? Did he tell you?"

"Yes, he told me many stories. Did he ever show you his scar where the squirrel bit his wrist?"

"No, he didn't. Where is it? What happened?"

"They were hunting squirrels. He shot one and it fell out of the tree. He went to pick it up, he thought it was dead. But it was only wounded. When he reached for it, it bit him in his left arm, just by the wrist. He was more careful after that, he said." My mother smiled.

"When I am done with this sickness I want to look at all the photos from when Papa was young. The place he grew up in looks pretty neat," I said.

"Do you mean Schwarzau, where they had the factory?"

"Yes, their property was so big, Papa told me they went camping far away from the house, he and his brother, and the parents did not know where they had pitched their tent. Will we go camping when Papa comes back from the army?"

"Sure, Papa has even discovered a small camping trailer we can tow with our DKW. It is big enough so we can sleep in it. I don't like to sleep in a tent," my mother shook her head.

"Oh, but I do. Can we put up the tent in the garden when I am well again, and I'll ask some friends to stay overnight?"

"Well, we'll see about that. If you promise not to make too much noise so the neighbors will not be disturbed, it will be fine. You could even have a camp fire. Now look at

113

the magazines, I have to go and start dinner. Anything you need until I bring you dinner?"

"Can I have something to drink, please."

"I'll get you some fresh water and some apple sauce that will be good for your thirst."

"The magazines weren't so bad after all, were they? It looks like you have been through the whole stack," my mother said.

"Yes, I found a serial, it is like a book, an adventure story. This girl is going on a treasure hunt with her father to Africa, looking for a small oasis in the Libyan desert. They are not there yet. It is pretty exciting. But there are a few issues missing in the middle, I really want to know what went on there. Do you think Oma has the rest of them still at home?"

"I can ask her, but I think she sent all of them. Why should she keep some back?"

"Well, I can make up most of it. I checked the last few issues, I do have all of them. I'll know the end of the story. They are running into all kinds of problems along the way. Some of the natives, they are called Bedouins, know about the treasure too. They want to steal their map. But they have a very clever Bedouin as the leader of their caravan, he protects them well."

"Are they walking through the desert? How far do they have to go?" my mother said.

"They started in Egypt, in Cairo. They went by boat up the Nile to Luxor. There they put together the caravan. The leader got them some purebred camels, which can outrun and outlast most others. So they have an advantage from the beginning. But they did not know that they were being followed until later."

"Is it just the father and the girl with the Bedouins?" my mother asked.

"No, there is a doctor with them. He is the one who deciphered the map to the treasure. He studies ancient people and ancient sites, an enteropologist?"

"You mean an anthropologist?"

"Yes, that's it. An anthro-po-lo-gist, I can never say that word."

"It sounded right to me, now," mother said.

114

"He is really funny. He can speak some Arabic, but he confuses the words and then the Bedouins do not understand what he wants to say. He is learning though, and he becomes very good at speaking their language."

"So you think a girls' magazine can be read by boys?" my mother asked with a little smile.

"The rest of it is pretty girlish, songs and games, crafts and short little cute stories. I lucked out finding this good one," I said. "I wonder if our magazines will look as old and strange as this one does twenty years from now."

"Probably. Fashion changes the most. The hats I wore two years ago look funny now. Remember the brown one with the bent brim and the big feather ornament on the side?" my mother asked.

"Yes I do. It looked funny when you wore it. It always looked funny," I laughed.

"Yes, but it was in fashion and all the women wore hats like that."

"I know. You all looked sort of weird."

"How are you feeling?"

"I am sore from being in bed all the time. When will I be able to get up?"

"Frau Doktor Thier said maybe next week, if everything checks out well. But just for a little bit every day. You will have to take it easy to the end of the six weeks."

"What is she checking for anyway? Still the albumen? That is when she looks at my urine after putting her drops in?"

"Yes, that is checking for the most dangerous after-effect. The bacteria could damage your kidneys for life."

"I still wonder where I got it from. Nobody at school had it. None of my friends here on our street, nobody. Why always me? Also the diphtheria. That was six weeks, too. But worse. Was it worse? I don't remember much of that, only staying in bed forever and you made me apple sauce a lot."

"Oh, it was much worse, we caught it just in time. I was very worried about you. You could have died. It came so fast. And the doctor said it was just a cold.

Letter from Papa in Krummau to Peter in Linz

March 16,1942

My poor, dear Peter!

You had to catch another one, didn't you! It is about time that you go through a period of great strengthening so that you will become strong enough that not every sickness gets hold of you ...

Don't make Mama's already difficult work even more difficult. Your being sick really plays havoc with our plans. I do not know now whether I should come to Linz. You can imagine how much I was looking forward to that trip ...

For now, do not read too much and rest. After the fever has gone down you will have enough time to read and play.

Most of all I would like to take care of you myself, hold you, talk with you, and stay with you all the time. Then we would have time, finally, to do projects together, to paint together, and do a thousand other things. That is still going to happen, sometime in the future.

I wish you a speedy recovery, Peter, I think about you all the time. Sending you many kisses,

Your Papsi

VACATION WITH COUSINS

Our whole gang was assembled, just like a year ago: My mother's older sister, Aunt Mimi, her four daughters Mirli, Martha, Hanni and Lisi, and the four of us, Mother, Dieter, Ina and myself.

"Do we have everything packed? Let me see, Mirli, you have the beach towels and the extra bathing suits,

Martha, you have ... what do you have in there?" Aunt Mimi asked her daughter, shaking her head.

"Lisi's diapers and bottle and everything else for her," Martha answered holding up her bag.

"That's it, thank you. Hanni? You have the fruit and the bread, anything else?

"The cups, Peter is carrying the lemonade in his rucksack," Hanni said.

We were all standing there, almost military style, waiting to be checked off. We were impatient to get going. It was our first day down to the lake this year.

"Did anybody tell the waitress we will be back for lunch?" Aunt Mimi asked looking around.

"I did," my mother said, "they'll be expecting us."

"I'll put Lisi into the carriage. Peter, can you help me get the carriage to the lake, please?" Aunt Mimi was quite the organizer this morning. She was the one who always worried about things being forgotten or not being taken care of. She carried the weight. She was heavier than her sister Lisl, who had joined her for these three weeks by the little lake in Carinthia, off the beaten path, peaceful and quiet. And reasonably priced.

I liked it here in the country, similar to the mountains we had spent our first vacations with Papa. I had asked my mother to come again this summer. I had had such a good time last year. Mother had been easy to convince. She still was not adjusted to living alone in Linz and having all her family back in Vienna. Although it was only a two-hour train ride away, visits were cumbersome and therefore rare. My father was glad that we had our own territory without the constant family influence. My mother liked to take every opportunity to be with her sisters or brothers. The six of them always had been close. My mother was the first one to get married. Aunt Mimi, the oldest, had not been far behind.

The last part of the walk was the hottest. The narrow path went across a large marshy meadow straight to the swimming area. We walked in single file, all except for Dieter who was next to my mother, holding on to her hand. I was pushing the carriage with Lisi right behind the girls. Lisi had been good this morning. She was making happy noises, kicking her feet and throwing her arms around. She was almost too big for the buggy. She was heavy and way past the age for being pushed in a baby carriage but she was not a normal baby. She had had meningitis as an infant, which had damaged her brain. She was a beautiful girl with long blonde hair and shinier, bluer eyes than I had ever seen. She would never be like her sisters. Aunt Mimi and her husband had considered putting her into a home with other children with similar afflictions. Aunt Mimi was at her limit in lifting Lisi up and carrying her around, soothing her whenever she developed one of her crying spells.

I remembered from last year. I had been out in the garden of the hotel by myself, watching Lisi. All of a sudden she had started to cry, loudly, and the sounds coming out of her mouth were not those of a baby, not of a child, we were throaty and desperate, animal like, so in contrast to the angelic beauty of her face and her body. I was scared. I could not calm her so I ran for help. Aunt Mimi took her up and carried her around until she stopped crying. But last year she was lighter. This year it would be much harder to lift her. Aunt Mimi still did.

The home was out of the question, my mother had told me. There was something about the *Master Race* and the *Third Reich*. Cripples were non-productive for the Fatherland and could not be tolerated. They must not be allowed to have children. There were rumors that in these institutions people would die without being sick, suddenly. It was suspected that they were killed. Euthanasia was the word for it. I could not believe that murder could be legal. It was murder.

Although I was terrified of her screams, I helped with taking care of Lisi whenever I could. But I felt sorry for my aunt who had carried this burden for several years already.

The facilities at the swimming area were rather primitive but functional. They were surrounded by a weathered wooden fence. At the entrance my mother and Aunt Mimi negotiated for a vacation pass for all of us because we would be coming here almost every day as long as the weather was good. They received our passes and with it a large key with a little copper disk bearing our family locker number. It was number ten.

The change cabins were in a long row to the right, facing the lake. Ours was about in the middle of the first row. My mother unlocked the door and everybody moved in and put down their bags.

"Ladies first," Aunt Mimi said. She, my mother and my cousins went into the cabin.

"Come on Dietz," I said to my brother and took his hand. "We will wait outside."

"I want to stay with my Mami!" Dieter started to whine at the door.

"It's fine, Dietz, she will be out in a minute."

Dieter burst into tears and let out a most piercing scream. My mother appeared.

"Come on Dietz, I am right here. You don't have to cry, I'll put on my bathing suit and I'll be out right away."

Dieter squeezed into the door and he would not let her go. She finally succumbed and came out without having changed.

"When is he going to stop that crying business?" I asked her.

"I hope soon, because I do not like it." She crouched down by Dieter's side and put her arm around him and turned him to face her: "Dietz, Peter is with you, we are all here together, some in there and some out here, and nobody is running away! Can't you be here with your brother for a minute without crying? You are a big boy now. Mama cannot be with you every minute of the day, do you understand?"

"No, I want you here," Dieter said. His head was lowered, his big brown eyes were sparkling with tears and his mouth was puckered with stubbornness.

"First one out, first one in the water," Hanni had come out through the door.

"No, you will wait until we are all ready, please!" Aunt Mimi's voice rang loud through the wooden wall.

"*Oh Mutti*," Hanni said, "you know I can swim."

"That does not make any difference, I want you to wait," Aunt Mimi said.

"Yes, I will wait. But Peter has not even changed yet," Hanni said.

"I'll be fast, I am wearing my swim trunks under my Lederhosen," I said, pulling my pants away from my tummy so she could see.

"What are you doing?" my mother said and shook her head.

"I am showing Hanni my swim trunks."

"She'll see them when you take your pants off."

Dieter was happy now, his tears had dried up. He was holding my mother's hand and looking out at the water.

"Hanni, was it hard to learn how to swim?" I asked.

"You can't swim? You are three years older than I am."

"Mirli can't swim, and she is older than you, too!" I retorted.

"I can swim with a cork belt." Mirli's voice came from the change room.

"It is easy, just like a frog, see," Hanni said and balancing on her left foot she pushed her hands up in the air and her right foot out to the side, "One," then she brought her arms around in a circle down alongside her body while she lifted her knee up, "Two," and now she pushed the arms and the leg out again "Three." With the suddenness of the movement she had lost her balance and caught herself just before falling over. We all laughed.

"I'll show you in the water."

"I know the movements but I go under, my mouth is under water, I cannot breathe," I said.

"You're next," Mirli said as she appeared in the cabin door.

Her mother and her sister were right behind her. Aunt Mimi was wearing a black bathing suit with little ruffles on the front and a skirt around her midriff. Her skin was snow white and made her look bulkier than she was. She looked awkward, bent over, a beach towel over her arm and a straw hat in the other. "She looks older than my mother," I thought.

"You want to go first with Dieter?" I asked my mother.

"No, you go ahead, so you all can go, and I'll come in a minute, you don't have to wait for us."

I was done in a flash. "Can we go?"

"Yes," Aunt Mimi said, "let's put all our towels and the sun lotions over there on one of the chaises. I'll be sitting there and watch you."

We all ran over and dropped our towels and then ran down to the water.

"Oh, it is cold," Mirli said. She had put her foot into the shallow water.

"No, it is not," Hanni said. She was in up to her knees already. She turned and waded on into the lake and then took off swimming. Her movements were very fast and hectic but she stayed afloat and moved right along.

I was standing there watching with envy. I felt embarrassed in front of my girl cousins. Not enough embarrassed though, to overcome my fear of letting my body float in the deeper water. I was determined to learn how to swim this summer. I would practice with the help of a cork ring and then without it.

"Peter, come on the raft with us, it is fun. Bring an oar," Mirli called to the shore. "We will pick you up over there by the boat house."

They were using an old wooden barn door as a raft and an old oar to push it around in the shallow water inside the swimming area. I ran along the shore over to the boathouse. I found another oar and waited on the dock between boathouse and shore. The girls were drifting back and forth; the raft had its own mind. They were having a hard time making it over to the dock. When they came close, the floating door hit one of the pilings and Mirli almost fell overboard.

While Martha was holding on to my oar, I let myself down onto the raft carefully. Now the four of us were standing on the raft, up to our ankles in water. Hanni and I were so tall, we looked like masts. I pushed us away from the pilings. We had a hard time keeping our balance, the raft was so unstable. Every time somebody moved, the whole thing started to rock.

"Hanni and Martha, you sit down, then we won't rock so much," I said, "Mirli and I will push us across to the other dock."

"No, I want to row, push," Hanni said.

"All right, go ahead, I don't want to any more anyway," Mirli said, and sat down. "Let's go!"

We waved to our mothers who were sitting on their wooden chaises talking. They waved back. Dieter was playing at the edge of the water with his toy sailboat.

We finally arrived at the other dock at the other side of the swimming area. The girls got off, leaving me alone on the raft. I immediately started on my way back. The raft was much easier to maneuver with only one person on it. I had fun drifting in circles and then moving ahead with a forceful push.

I, the proud captain, stood on my raft and surveyed the scene. My cousins were gathered around their mother, putting more lotion on their faces and backs. There were not too many people on the beach. Many of the chaises were empty. I loved the musty smell of the lake. The water was clear with a little brownish tint in it. There was a marsh at the other end of the lake and a peat-mossy bottom. People said it was healing to swim in this water.

When I turned around to look out at the lake I found myself close to the rope that marked the boundary of the swimming area. I had never been out that far. Carefully I lowered my oar into the water to push myself back. The oar turned up towards the surface, it wanted to swim. I could not touch bottom with the oar. I panicked and jumped into the water. I went in over my head without touching bottom. Full of fear I pulled myself back onto the floating door, crouched down on all fours, coughing out the water I had swallowed.

Now I was trapped way out here, in the deep. How could I make it back? There was no other way than to swim. That was not an option. I tried to use the oar as an oar. The raft just turned and floated closer to the rope, where the water was even deeper. I was scared. I looked for help. They must see me and come and rescue me. All of a sudden the people on shore looked very small. "God, I am so far out ... HELP!" I yelled. "Help, somebody help me!" my voice broke, I had yelled so loud.

There were no swimmers around me. The raft was in between the two docks, they were as far from me as the beach.

I started to cry. I imagined my waterlogged body, all swollen up, drifting through the reeds. The oar had slipped off the raft and was drifting away.

"Help, please help me!" I shouted again. I was standing up now and waving.

Somebody must have heard me. My cousins turned around and saw me. They all started laughing. They were bending over with laughter. My mother got up. She waved at me. My cousins pointed at me and continued to laugh even more.

I wanted to disappear. I even thought about drowning myself. I felt so shamed. I was in danger and they were laughing. Why didn't somebody swim out here and push me in?

Then I felt anger rising over my fear. *"I'll show them! Stupid girls!"* I thought. I stuck out my tongue, shook my head wildly and screamed as loud as I could. I crouched down again, moved carefully to the lakeside end of the raft. I lay down on my belly facing the beach, and pushed myself backwards until my legs were in the water. I started kicking furiously letting all my fear and anger come out. The raft started moving slowly towards the shore. My cousins were clapping and shouting "Bravo, bravo, Peter!" A few other bathers had gathered and had been watching the drama. Now they were laughing and clapping, too.

I finally made it into shallow water. I slipped off the raft, pushed it away from myself and started walking, running towards the beach. I slapped the water with my hands and when I reached solid ground I started clapping and shouted "Bravo" with the rest of them.

"Would you please learn how to swim," my mother said. "How about starting this afternoon? Mirli or Hanni will help you, I'm sure."

On rainy days we played around the farmhouse that was part of the Pension we were staying in. There was a big barn with all kinds of wagons and farm equipment. We climbed all over them and maneuvered the wagons around. We were also allowed to use the outdoor bowling alley, which had a roof over it and a loam alley with a wooden board for a runway for the ball.

Once or twice a week we would go for a long hike up into the mountains where the cattle was grazing and where we found gigantic mushrooms in the sparse stands of trees and shrubs. Back in our rooms we had to help our mothers cleaning the mushrooms, and cutting them into thin slices. Then we would string them on a long piece of yarn, which was stretched between the window frames so the mushrooms would dry in the sun. Later in the summer there were blueberries, wild raspberries and blackberries to pick and eat. I fell in love with the softly matted mountain meadows full of wild flowers, with the taste of wild berries, with the excitement of finding a perfect mushroom or walking through a cattle pasture full of young bulls, with my cousins.

Hanni, the youngest, was tall and thin and sort of stand-offish, Martha the middle one had very black hair and the eyes and the temperament to match—she was my favorite—and Mirli, although a year younger than myself, was more mature and sort of superior which I did not care for. She had blonde hair, the face of a Madonna and child rolled into one, and occasionally, was really attentive to me. I loved that but when she was not, I was crushed.

ON LEAVE FROM THE RUSSIAN FRONT

"Mama, Dad is ..."

"What is the matter—oh, my God ..." Mother's response to my alarm was swift. She had heard my voice, and had followed my frozen glance into the garden. She ran out the open back door.

My father was lying in a heap on the garden path just where it starts to slope down.

I ran after my mother. She was kneeling besides Papa.

"Emil, please, what is the matter? Is it a relapse? Come in the house, please! Can you get up?"

My father shook his head. His teeth were chattering so badly, he could not even utter an understandable word.

I remembered that my father had prepared us for these attacks. They come out of nowhere, without warning, look awful and are fairly harmless. Once you have had malaria, they are with you for the rest of your life. Looking at my father now, I had a hard time believing that it was a harmless attack.

"Let us take him in, can you help me—we will drag him backwards, yes? You take one arm, under the shoulder ..."

I hooked my arm under my father's and we turned him around so that his head faced the house. We began to pull. After a few steps we had to rest. My father was totally limp. He was very heavy and unable to help us in any way. His body felt hot with fever and he was shaking with violent cramps every so often. His teeth were still chattering. His face had lost all its color and yet, sweat was dripping off him continuously. The whiteness against his thinning black hair looked ghastly. I was shocked at the change. This morning my father had looked like my father. Now he looked like a very thin and very sick man.

The first thing that had come to my mind when I heard about my father having malaria was the film I had seen about Dr. Koch, a German bacteriologist working in Africa who had discovered that sleeping sickness was spread to humans by the tsetse fly—a kind of mosquito. Above all I remembered the images of the bodies of the sick natives, emaciated down to skin and bones, as I helped dragging my father's almost lifeless body through the living room to the couch.

"Do we have to call Dr. Thier?" I asked my mother.

"No, Papa has instructions with him; he has had attacks like this before, when he was still at the hospital."

"But he took his quinine pills, didn't he? He looks so funny when he does, the way he throws the pills in his mouth from way out..."

"Papa always has had problems swallowing pills, he still does, even these tiny ones..."

"W-w-w-water, p-p-p-please!" my father said. His voice was barely audible and his teeth were chattering while he formulated the words.

My mother reached for the glass and held my father's head up slightly while she was tipping the glass slowly towards his lips. I stood there watching. I felt my own body trembling. Was it from the exertion or was it from

125

my father weak and helpless? I did not know. But I felt tears coming up, tears of sorrow, tears of pain, tears of anger—they had taken him away, and now they had made him sick, very sick and weak. And still, he had to go back, back to the army, to some convalescence unit, until he would regain his strength, and who knows what then. Right now, he was a sad sight. Shivering under a pile of blankets, barely controlling his chattering teeth, fingers cramped around the edge of the blanket, his eyes staring at the ceiling without expression.

"Let's leave him alone for a while, he needs to rest. I'll check on him; we'll get him through this," my mother said.

I took another look at my father before I left. Then I went upstairs to my room and picked up the latest *Adler* magazine. I climbed up on the dresser under the window and started to leaf through the pages. I liked this magazine called the "Eagle." It was written for boys and had stories about the newest planes, air combat, fighter pilot aces and lots more. I liked to draw airplanes and so I was mostly interested in the shapes of all the aircraft involved in the war. I could draw the big boxy shape of the Junkers 142 that was used to transport troops and small vehicles. Its fuselage was made of corrugated aluminum that gave it a boxcar look. Another favorite for me to draw was the *Stuka* -the *Sturzkampfbomber*- the scary dive-bomber that delivered its bombs very accurately after a fast and noisy dive at the target. When I drew one of them, struggling to get the perspective on the bent wings right, I always imagined the howling sound these planes made during their deadly dive, the way I had heard it in the newsreels. The Messerschmitt fighter planes had elegant body shapes just like the British Spitfire.

I started to read an article about the *Flieger HJ*—the *Hitler Youth* branch that taught flying. There were photographs of boys pulling a glider into position on top of a hill and of a take-off sequence using a towrope. There was a boy in the cockpit with his instructor seated behind him, high above the training center in the foothills of the Alps. I had always wanted to fly.

After a whole bundle of long thin slats were delivered with a load of firewood my father had ordered I had drawn up detailed plans for a glider, which I was going to build using those slats. The fuselage I would cover with heavy tracing paper my father kept in big rolls for his drafting work. The plans were fashioned after a model glider my friend Joe had built just recently.

I had two more years before would turn fourteen when I had to decide between flying planes or riding horses. I had narrowed my choice to those two branches. Did I want to learn all about aerodynamics, the weather, how planes are built and piloted and then go off to glider camp, or would I rather stay with nature, learning to become one with another living creature, the horse, riding through the meadows and forests, over the mountains, jumping over fences and streams. I wanted to do both. I was allowed only one choice. No switching was permitted after you had made a decision. I tended towards the flying because my father had promised to teach me how to ride later, anyway. With him I would not be on my own, spending weeks at a time with the horse, which was the way the Hitler Youth did it. I kept imagining how both paths would play out and decided to keep an open mind towards both opportunities.

I looked up from the magazine and out the window into our garden. This was my favorite view. Above the red brick roof that sloped steeply away from my window sill there was the gravel path on the left where my father had collapsed. It sloped down just where the lawn ended in the little stonewall my father had designed, which now was covered with moss, different blooming cushions, and alpine flowers. There were little green lizards catching the sun on the stones, disappearing into the cracks at nighttime. At the other end of the stone wall there was a group of flowering shrubs. There were lots of hiding places inside this little jungle and right below it I had dug a manhole in the area designated as my own personal gardening spot. Digging I had discovered a layer of pure ocher loam which my friends and I had used to make clay bowls and ashtrays for presents, just like I had done with Hans.

From there on to the end of the property my father had planted six large red currant bushes. Below the stone wall there were two beds of strawberries with a few clumps of wild strawberries growing in between. My eyes scanned over the next beds. There were the tender greens of carrots, little plants growing into cabbage, cauliflower, radishes, kohlrabi, Brussels sprouts, and white little flowers on the potato greens. There was a trellis with sweet peas, and another one with pole beans. Off to the side there was a patch of herbs with parsley, thyme and others. Next to the concrete watering basin there were the large red leaves of two big rhubarb plants, showing off to anyone coming down the path.

Where the beds ended there was another area of lawn with a wooden clothes horse at each end where my mother dried her laundry on five long lines stretched between them. My friend August and I used the clotheshorses to sit on, high up in the air, undisturbed by the younger children playing in the garden. There we could talk about our secret plans, above all the others, and away from the house.

Beyond that grassy area there was a compost pile and right next to it was a patch of raspberry plants extending all the way to the fence on the right.

Looking at all this I realized how much work I had put into these beds: I had spaded them, planted them, weeded them, watered them—sometimes willingly and sometimes only under the threat of some consequences. After my father had been drafted, I was eager to help my mother but the enthusiasm for the nobility of my action had worn thin very quickly with the hot sun and friends calling for me to join them in play.

"Peter, dinner is ready, wash your hands and come down, please!"

I washed my hands in the upstairs bathroom, went downstairs and stopped in the kitchen. "How is Papa doing?"

"He stopped shaking and he slept for a while. I think his fever is down, he seems to be cooler. I am glad. It looked so awful when he was down. I don't want him to go back. I wish we could hide him somewhere and keep him ..."

I helped my mother carry dishes and food for dinner into the living room. My father lay on the couch in the corner. Turned on his side he watched us come in.

"I am better now. Sorry for scaring you. But I had warned you. The first time I saw an attack in the hospital, I thought the man was going to die." My father's voice was low and unsteady, with an unfamiliar tremble in it.

"Do you feel like eating something? You wrote from the hospital that you never could get enough!" mother said.

"Oh, yes, please—what are we having?"

"Kohlrabi sautéed in butter with new potatoes. Frau Meier brought the Kohlrabi, she grew them in her hothouse, they cut like butter, and they are so soft. Ours are just starting to form the bulbs." Mother put a portion on a plate for my father.

Dieter and Ina were sitting at the table quietly. They had been out playing two houses down. Their faces were red from the sun and the running around.

"Peter, can you put the pillow behind Papa's back while I hold him up?" my mother asked.

I went to the bed and held the pillow against the wall so my father could lean against it. He still appeared very weak. It was hard for him to keep his head up on the pillow. His arms functioned normally. My mother put the plate on a serving tray and puffed up the blankets so they would create a level surface for it.

"Daddy is sick," Ina said watching the whole procedure with interest. "He can eat by himself."

"Why is Papa sick?" Dieter asked. His voice sounded as if he was going to burst into tears any moment.

"Papa has a sickness that goes away and comes back sometimes. It came back this afternoon. He will be much better tomorrow if we let him rest."

"Shall I feed you?" I asked my father when I noticed how difficult it was for him to keep the food on the fork and bring it up to his mouth.

"Let me try a little longer, maybe I can manage—but thank you for asking!" my father smiled.

I sat down at the table and we all started eating. We missed our father at the table. Everybody looked over at him between bites and watched him struggle with his trembling hand.

"Tomorrow I will be better again, and I will sit with you. It goes away fast," he said.

MIDNIGHT RAID

The air raid sirens where still whining away when I heard my mother's voice from the other bedroom. "Get up and get dressed, Peter. Help Dieter, please. I'll get the rest. Don't forget your featherbeds and the blankets, and the pillow. We do not know how long it will be."

I hated the sound of the sirens cutting through the middle of the night. It was cold. It was dark. I was groping for my pile of clothes. I always piled everything I took off on the one chair next to my bed. I pulled my pants over my pajama pants, and put the shirt on top of the pajama jacket. Even in the summer it was cold down in the cellar.

"Dieter are you up yet?" There was no answer.

"Peter, please get him up and dressed. I want us all to be down fast. Remember the other day at lunch? How quickly the planes appeared?"

"Somebody goofed. The alarm should have been on a lot earlier."

By now my eyes had adjusted to the darkness. I moved cautiously along the wall towards my brother's bed.

"Dieter. Air raid. Come on, get up. They'll drop bombs again. We have to go to the shelter." I had located my brother's clothes and was holding one piece up towards the little shimmer of night sky I could see through the crack along the edge of the blackout blinds. It was not much but enough to verify the pants. I hugged my brother's warm body, again to orient myself, and also to ease the scare for both of us. My own and Dieter's.

"Why don't you turn on the light?" Dieter asked with sleep slowing down my words.

"We must not. If the bomber pilots cannot see any lights they do not know where we are. Then they cannot hit us. See?"

"But we have blinds."

130

"Yes, Dietz, but a little bit of light always shines through. Remember I showed you when we came home the other night? Come on now, put on your socks. I am taking your blankets. Let's go. Can you carry your shoes?"

"Can I sleep in the bed down there?"

"Sure, but you still want your shoes, maybe we have to run outside."

"Why outside?"

"Dieter please shut up, pick up your shoes and come!"

"Where is my other shoe?"

"Just feel for it. It must be right where the other one was."

"You have it? Let's go." I rolled up the pillow in the blankets and took the bundle under my arm. With my free hand I grabbed my brother's hand. "Careful, so you don't fall down the stairs." We came down the big wooden staircase slowly, I dragged my brother behind me, supporting him with the softness of the bedding. Dieter was still half-asleep. "Watch your step, just a few more." I followed a slight ray of light, which came up the staircase from the cellar. My mother was in the kitchen talking to Erika, our live-in household helper.

"Erika, it's an alarm. Get up and go down to the cellar, please, quickly. The sirens went off a long time ago!"

"The Flak is shooting already," I said, "do you hear it?"

There was a series of ugly, hollow sounds high up in the sky.

"Here they are—I told you they'd be quick. Everybody down, this instant. If your father would know we are still up here, he would be very disappointed, go, go fast, please!"

"But Mama, it's only the Flak," I said.

"Yes, I know, but what do you think they are shooting at? The clouds? Or the moon? The bombers are here!" my mother was herding us towards the stairs. Ina in her arms was quiet.

"I cannot hear any planes." I stopped at the top of the staircase to the cellar and cocked my head. "Normally I can hear them."

"Please, Peter, go—no arguments. Maybe they are higher or not so many—who knows?—I want you all down there, fast. You too, Erika."

"I am coming. Shall I bring some food?" Erika said from the kitchen.

"No, not in the middle of the night. The emergency stuff is down in the shelter anyway. Hurry up, it is getting dangerous up here."

There was more bellowing outside, although from a different direction.

Ina started to cry. "I don't like noise." Mother pulled her tighter going down the staircase behind Erika. She shut the upstairs door behind her, and now closed the fire door to the shelter.

"Here we are again. Let's hope this raid doesn't last as long as the one the day before yesterday."

"I want to sleep!" Dieter had climbed into the lower bunk bed pulling the blankets out of my hands. On one of his leaves my father had set up the old bunk beds down here so we would have a place to be safe and comfortable.

Erika headed for the upper bunk.

"What if the ceiling collapses—it will be all on you. Don't go up there."

"Down there the bricks will hit you harder, it does not make any difference." Erika settled in smugly. She liked to read. Up there was the only electric light in the room, and with a fifteen Watt bulb one had to be pretty close to see well enough to read. Erika was doing her obligatory household service with us. Every girl at the age of sixteen had to help out for one half year at a family with three or more children where the father was in the army. She was from northern Germany; her parents had moved to Austria and lived nearby. Boys at the same age had to sign up for six months in the *Reichsarbeitsdienst,* a youth work brigade, working on all kinds of maintenance and repair jobs, towards the end of the war, they were asked to man the anti-aircraft batteries around cities.

There was a big long rumble outside. And a burst of bellows. And another rumble. And many more bursts.

"Oh, oh, they have started the bombing now. But we cannot feel anything, so it must be pretty far away."

"The steel works again?"I asked.

"Probably, that's what they want to destroy."

"That's because they make tanks there and parts for U-Boats."

"Peter, please do not talk about that. You know it is a secret. Nobody is supposed to know what they are making there. The people who know must not tell. Otherwise the spies find out and then ..."

"... they bomb it ...' I finished. "So they already know, no?"

Now the anti-aircraft battery closest to them- a few miles away on a hill next to the remains of an old fortress—went into a spasm of firing. Even the smaller guns, the ones with the four barrels were going at it. They sounded like machine guns. TAK TAK TAK TAK, a burst, then quiet, then another burst.

"I bet they are firing at parachutes with the flares," I said loudly over the noise.

In between the explosions we could hear the humming of the planes.

I wished I could be outside watching. My uncle had taken me once. Quickly, avoiding the *Luftschutz* patrol, we had gone into the garden. It was a spectacle, all right. The Flak grenades exploded high up with a burst of light, then followed by the noise, the bellowing, hollow and sharp. But most exciting were the 'Christmas trees,' flares dropped by the bombers to light up the target areas. It was like lightening, but it lasted for a long time. I had felt exposed, like everybody was able to see me. Just like in daylight. The small anti-aircraft guns fired tracer bullets at the parachutes floating the flares down slowly.

Out of nowhere, without warning, there was an explosion, everything in the shelter jumped up and sideways, dust came off the walls and the ceiling. The light went out.

"Mama!" Ina and Dieter screamed. I reached out for my mother's arm. We all came together in a huddle with our heads stuck under the upper bunk. Ina clung desperately to my mother and cried.

We could hear the dust falling inside. Then a hiss started afar, came closer, and closer and louder, followed by an instant of quiet. Then another huge explosion. The whole room rocked again. The walls were cracking, the potatoes and the jars in the wooden bins seemed to be talking. Erika joined the huddle voluntarily or by force, it did not matter. Nothing broke. Nothing came flying. We all were absolutely quiet. The hell outside continued. Some hits close, some far: Flak, planes, bombs, planes, bombs, Flak.

"When you hear the hiss, the bomb will not hit you, remember that?" Mother was the first one to speak. "That was close."

"We did not hear a hiss before the first one ... how close, do you think?" I was thinking and shaking.

"Maybe where the Flak is, I have no idea. It sounded like the Mayer's house or thereabouts, but then our walls would be cracked open.

"We don't know whether they are or not, there is no light. Let's light a candle."

"No light, the pilots will see us." Dieter's voice was muffled by the featherbed he had pulled around himself.

"Down here it is all right, Dieter. The steel window is totally airtight. It will not let any light through." Mother started to move her hands from the pyramid of heads and arms and hands but the two little ones held on tight.

"Don't go away, Mama, please," Dieter said in a teary voice, which was the signal for Ina to burst out into one of her better cries.

"Oh hush, my dear, it's all over, we are fine." The noises were more distant now than they had been. But after that close hit, all the others sounded more distant all of a sudden.

"Do you think somebody got hurt—or ...?" I was not sure whether I really wanted to complete this thought.

"Where are the matches?" Erika asked.

"On the shelf at the end of the bed. Same place where the candles are." My mother had stocked the room carefully with all kinds of emergency items following the list that had been handed out by the *Luftschutzwart* a long time ago.

"I can feel the candles but no matches." We could hear Erika move and grope in the dark.

"They are either to the right or to the left ..."

"Yes, I found them, hold on ..."

There was the noise of the wooden matches rattling in the box, then the scratching of a match against the box and then there was light! Erika reached for one of the candles and lit it.

"We do have a crack in the wall!" I shouted. I had gone over to the far wall and was tracing the crack with my fingers.

"I can put my finger in it, it's big," he said, "We were lucky that bomb didn't hit any closer!"

"Look at you, you look all sugared," mother actually laughed a little. "You look as if somebody had put confectioner's sugar all over you!"

We all looked at each other and we started brushing the mortar dust off our clothes and hair. Erika was the whitest since she had been so close to the ceiling.

"Please stop!" mother said, it is getting too dusty in here. We'll clean up later, when we are back upstairs.

It took another hour before the sirens signaled the end of the raid. We all headed back to our beds. Dieter and Ina insisted that they crawl in bed with Mother.

When I woke up the next morning, I went from window to window to check the neighboring houses. At the bottom of our garden, another garden started uphill towards a house. Next to it was a huge crater, earth and plants were splattered onto the broken wall of the house and against another house next door. People were standing there and pointing. I recognized the family whose house was damaged. They were all there.

HITLER YOUTH IS PLAYING WAR

I plopped down on some moss and caught my breath. I was shaking all over. I felt safe now in the small space between some cool rocks.

The first battle in this giant maneuver of the combined Hitler Youth groups of the whole area had ended in chaos. My group of thirty had run into another group that already had been through some action. What was supposed to be a simple taking of armbands had escalated into name calling, pushing, wrestling, and finally into an outright fight with sticks and stones, fists and brutal kicks. The two leaders were powerless in their efforts to stop the violence. I managed to keep on the fringes of the fighting and finally headed for the woods in terror. I was running for cover as fast as I could, checking only once or twice to see if anybody was following me. Luckily, nobody had noticed my flight.

When the battle noise died down, I started moving downhill. I stopped several times to listen, but all I could hear were the voices of the birds in the trees high above me. For a moment, I settled into the excitement of being the explorer in an unknown forest, into the comfort of being one with the trees and being serenaded by the birds.

I jumped when I heard a loud noise. Something moved through the underbrush in front of me. I froze and waited for the deer to emerge. But it was a boy. Just like me, looking shaken and fearful.

"Did you run, too?" I asked.

"Yes, I got hit twice with a stick, after that I just ran. They were supposed only to take our armbands. What are you, red or blue?" the kid asked.

"Blue, and you?"

"I am red," he said, pulling his armband out of his pocket. "But I am not going to wear it any more. I hate fights. Where do you think our groups are?"

"I have not the slightest idea, I just came down from the rocks up there after everything quieted down," I said.

"Do you think we can go home?" the boy asked.

"Do you know the way? I have never been out here. You know that there are several 'armies' and even smaller groups in this area. If we run into one of them they'll make us go with them, if they don't beat us up," I said.

"We met a whole group of wounded boys before we got into our skirmish. They had bandaged heads, arms in slings, I got really scared. I thought this was a game, they told us we should trap enemy groups and take their arm bands," the boy said.

"I know, there was this big plan. We discussed it last night at our regular meeting. It never happened today, not with my group and not with yours. Maybe the others out there fought the way they were supposed to."

"What's your name?" the boy asked.

"Peter. And what's yours?"

"Herbert. Where do you live?"

"On the Keferfeld, by Untergaumberg, you know where?"

"That is a station of the Eferdinger Train, isn't it? I am from Urfahr."

"How long did it take you to come out here this morning?"

"We marched almost three hours, how about you?" Herbert asked.

"Not quite two hours, we started at seven."

"Let's go down to the path where our groups met and follow it home," Herbert said.

"Yes. I think where we came from would be closer to the main road. I don't think we hiked more than forty five minutes from the staging area," I said.

"Let's try that. What time is it, you think?"

"I don't know. I cannot see the sun. It should be close to noon. We got here around nine, it took us almost an hour to get all sorted out and banded and instructed ... and we went into the woods not much longer than half an hour ..."

"That's what I figured, too." Herbert said. "I am hungry, it must be lunch time. Did you bring any food?"

"No. They told us we would have a kitchen set up. They did not want us to carry packs. I have some water left in the canteen, do you want some?" I asked.

"Yes, I'll have a sip, thank you," Herbert said and reached for my canteen. "I shared mine with my friend, and he is carrying it."

"We'll find some water, I'm sure. It is pretty hot, we'll need more later on." I said.

We reached the battleground where my group had met the enemy.

"Look at this handkerchief. Somebody was really bleeding a lot. I am sure glad we escaped," Herbert said.

"Which direction shall we go? Where did you start from?" I asked.

"Hey, are you survivors or scouts?"

The voice startled us. We both looked where it had come from, ready to run. We saw two boys coming down the hill opposite the one we had sought refuge on.

"Survivors—deserters—we ran from the first battle, it was bloody." I said. "How about you?"

"Same thing, we got beaten up by a group way over there," he pointed back over the hill we had come down. "Where was your battle?"

"Right here. Herbert was a Blue. I was a Red. We both escaped when the going got rough. I guess they didn't miss us."

"I am Otto and this is Wolfgang. I am a *Jungenschaftsführer* from the first district," Otto said. He pointed at his red and white cord hanging from the epaulet on his shirt to the button on the breast pocket.

"Are you going to turn us in?" Herbert asked.

"No way! Let's get out of here as fast as we can," Otto said.

"Can you hear something?" I asked and pointed straight ahead into the woods.

We stopped and listened. Far off there were voices.

"Does not sound like a whole lot of them," Wolfgang said.

"Over there is good cover. Let's hide in there," Otto said. "They must not see us."

We moved quietly towards the thick undergrowth and found a small clearing that was protected from all sides. Otto nodded and sat down. The others followed suit. Once we were settled, we kept listening for the other group. The voices came closer for a while, we could hear dry twigs snapping under someone's foot a few times but we never could detect any movement in the shadows of the thick green forest.

After it had been silent for a long time, Otto stood up.

"I think it is safe to move on again," he said.

We followed his lead. He had the rank and looked older than the rest of us.

"How are we going to get home without running into someone?" I asked.

"Does anyone have a clue where we are?" Otto said.

The other three shook their heads.

"We don't have a map, we don't have a compass, and there is no water flowing anywhere which we could follow," Wolfgang said. His voice sounded weak and discouraged.

"I'd like to find some water to drink, I am really thirsty!" Herbert said.

"If we keep going in one direction we must come across a path, or a landmark of some sort, eventually," I said. "That's what my father taught me."

"Well, we have been trying that for the last half hour, but with the up and down on these hills and the trees so dense in places it is easy to lose direction. If we could see the sun, we could orient ourselves to that but it has been cloudy and through the trees you couldn't see it anyway." Otto shrugged his shoulders. "Maybe we have to sleep out here tonight."

"Without food and water it would not be fun. I'd rather go home," Herbert said.

"Shut up, Herbert! We are lucky that we haven't been beaten up like these other kids we saw. I'd rather be hungry than beaten bloody by some idiot bully."

"You all agree that we avoid all contact and not join any group until the war games are over?" Otto asked.

"If there is a way to tell that they are over. Probably by the end of the day it will be safe to go with another group and march home with them. They'll be all over the main roads," I said.

"Right. It would be hard to find a way into town that does not have a column on it. That's a good idea, Peter!" Otto said."Let's go!"

After two and a half hours we found ourselves back at the same battleground again.

"I don't believe this. I could have sworn we went straight east, all the time," I said.

"Well, I guess we did not," Otto said.

"Is there any water left?" Herbert asked.

"Sorry, no more, we drank it all," I said, knocking at my canteen making a hollow sound.

"How come, we did not come across any streams?" Herbert asked. "When I hike with my parents, we always find streams."

"Probably you do not hike here, and not in circles," Otto said. He seemed less sure of himself now. He was disappointed we had not made any progress.

"I am really thirsty and hungry," Wolfgang said.

"I wish you would concentrate on getting us out of here, instead of complaining." Otto stumbled over a big branch on the ground and almost fell. "I could handle a big slice of farmers' bread just with butter, or maybe some smoked ham?"

"Stop it, please ...," I said. "I am ready, too ... maybe we'll find a farmhouse and they'll feed us ..."

"Yeah, and five hundred others before us; I wish you were right, but I'd settle for some water," Herbert said.

"Water! Water! Water!" Wolfgang was ahead of them and had just disappeared around a bend in the path. We had been heading downhill for a while now.

"Let's see what it looks like," Otto said and started running. Herbert and I followed him. My legs felt wobbly. I had been on them for about nine hours now. I was exhausted.

When we rounded the bend, we saw the water. A small puddle had accumulated at the bottom of the hill in the ruts left by the wagon wheels that had cut into the trail.

"I am not going to drink this!" Herbert said. "It has green slime in it and probably polliwogs."

"Do you think it's safe to drink?" I asked, looking at Otto.

"Doesn't look it, but I'll drink it anyway," Otto said. He crouched down on all fours, avoiding the mud around the puddle as much as he could. With one hand he pushed away the greenish bubbles and the algae that produced them. The water underneath was clear. He scooped up a handful and tasted it.

"It's warm but it doesn't taste too bad."

I walked around looking for a better spot to access the water. I chased up a flock of little blue butterflies. They fluttered around my bare legs, and I could feel the faintest tickle when one of them touched me. I found a clear spot where the water was a little deeper. I filled my canteen, using a stick to keep the green stuff from entering the small neck.

I took a sip. "We'll turn into frogs, for sure, but it is not as bad as I had imagined," I said.

Both Wolfgang and Herbert were down on their knees and drinking directly out of the puddle.

"I never thought I would touch water like this. I wouldn't even swim in it if it were a lake," Wolfgang said, "but I am all dry from this heat, I don't care. We'll find out tomorrow if we have typhoid fever. I better not tell my mother what I did."

"Typhoid fever doesn't show right away, my brother had something like it before the war, boy, he spent more time on the potty than elsewhere for over a week," Herbert said. "We better not get that sort of thing."

"Shall we continue this way?" Otto asked.

"We are getting lower, so maybe we will hit a valley that takes us out of this forest," I said.

"It looks like they have done some logging here, so this trail should lead out," Otto said.

"The question is just where it will come out, we could end up in the Welser Heide," Herbert said.

"Oh, come on, the Welser Heide is way out West, and it does not have any forests ..."

"But we have walked almost all day, if it is all in the wrong direction, we could be there," Herbert insisted, but he was smiling.

"Well, luckily, we went in circles for half the afternoon, so we really should not be too far ..." I said.

"You've been saying that for three hours, it only took us one hour in the morning to come in here from the main road, so we were really off," Wolfgang said.

"Let's go. We need to get out of here before it gets dark. It must be going on five or six—next time I bring a watch and a compass—but I didn't want to lose the watch or have it broken, I just got it for my birthday," Otto said.

"They would have whacked it good, your watch, good thing you did not bring it," Wolfgang said. "I can't believe this all happened. Wait till my parents hear about this."

"Why, what are they going to do?" I asked.

"They will tell their *Ortsgruppenleiter* and they will come to the meeting and talk to the Scharführer. They'll raise holy hell."

141

"Our Scharführer does not listen to parents. They have to go higher. When I don't go to the meeting, he sends two boys to get me. He threatened my mother with an official complaint at the Party Headquarters, if I did not show up," I said.

Otto came up in between them. "It's not that bad, is it?"

"Yes it is, and you know it. Is it different in your district?" I asked.

"Not really, we allow one unexcused absence a month, and more if you have a good story. But if you miss all the time, we come after you, sure."

After a while, the forest started to get thinner and all of a sudden we found ourselves at the edge of a large meadow.

"I see a church tower," Otto said.

"Good, that's where my group came in—we are right, we are out, hurrah!" I shouted.

"Thank God, we are on our way! What are we to do if we run into any groups still playing war?"

"I think we should call them stupid and run!"

"No more running, it could be into the wrong direction."

"Thanks Peter, for getting us out, even if it took a long time! You should get a badge for 'sense of direction.' We will put you in for it!"

They all laughed and picked up the pace.

"Once we are at the church we can split in different directions, I guess everybody knows their way. Maybe you from the other side of town could catch a train somewhere, save yourselves some walking."

The people in the village looked at the boys and shook their heads. "Were you with all the others that bashed each other?" they asked.

"Yes, we were but we were the lucky ones, we quit early!"

"Never seen anything like it, I say, hope nobody set fire to them woods in there. Boys coming out every which way..." the old man walked off shaking his head.

RECORDING THE WAR

"I need two volunteers to pass out the diaries, please," the teacher said, as he did every day at 9 o'clock in the morning.

Hilde went up to the desk from the girls' side of the room. On the left side, where the boys sat, nobody had moved yet.

"Well," the teacher said, "I am sure somebody can do this task for me, how about you, Peter?"

"I can. Yes, Herr Schleier." I got up. I slipped out between the bench and my desk and went up to stand next to Hilde.

The teacher had given Hilde the girls' diaries already, now he handed the remaining stack to me. I looked at the notebook on top and saw Egon's name on it. I went over to his desk and gave it to him. The notebooks were bound in dark gray covers made out of flimsy paper that felt like blotting paper. The pre-printed label said "War Diary" on the first line, and it had space to insert a "from" and a "to" date as well as the student's name. I distributed all the notebooks and sat down with my own copy.

"Let's start with the Eastern front," the teacher said. "Who can tell me what happened there?"

There was silence in the room.

"Nobody listened to the *Wehrmacht* Reports?" The teacher looked around at the students.

"Yes, I did, with my parents, but I forgot what happened on the Eastern front. They bombed London again," Egon said after holding his right hand up to be heard.

"Very good, Egon, thank you, we will get to the air raids later. Everybody open his or her diary. What is the date today?"

"Wednesday, October 14, 1942," a boy said from the back.

"Good," the teacher said, and wrote the date on the blackboard. "Start a new page, put down the date, and let's go, write ...

"Eastern Front, German tanks are now within 100 kilometers of Moscow. In the Southeast the Sixth Army is closing in on Stalingrad, meeting with very little resistance."

The room was quiet except for the sounds of scratching of pens and the clinking of penholders against glass inkwells. I disliked the coarse paper in these diaries. My pen kept getting caught in the fibers, punching holes in the paper and leaving ink spots. It did not look very neat. The dictation went on.

"The German *Luftwaffe* continued bombing strategic targets in and around London. Another attack concentrated on the industrial center of Coventry. Several important targets were completely destroyed. All planes taking part in the raid returned safely without losses."

"Any questions?" the teacher asked, looking around in the classroom.

"What about Africa?"

"Well, I have no news, I will check and we can make an entry tomorrow. Good question, thank you Grete."

"That will be it for today. When you are finished, close your diary and pass it to the left. Hilde and Peter will collect them. Make sure that your entries are complete. As you know, I will be checking them all. Anybody not finished?" The teacher looked around the large classroom.

"Anna, you are still writing, do you need more time?"

"No, I'm finished. Here ..." she closed the notebook and handed it to Hilde who had just come to her row.

"Our soldiers are doing very well out there. We have to support them as much as we can. Are you writing to your fathers or other relatives out on the front?"

I raised my hand.

"Yes, Peter?"

"I finished a letter to my father yesterday. I told him we wrote about Voronezh in our diary. He went through there."

"Good," the teacher said. "Anybody else? Yes, Anna?"

"I keep writing to my father, but he does not write back. We have not gotten a letter from him in four weeks. My mother is worried. Something might have happened to him ..." Her eyes filled with tears.

"I am sorry to hear that, but you must keep writing. He will get your letters. It is very difficult to distribute all the mail with all the disruption of railroads and roads by bombs and mines. You have to be patient. I myself just received a letter from my brother who is in the Africa Corps. It took seven weeks to get here!" the teacher said.

I felt sorry for Anna. My mother always panicked when we did not hear from my father for two weeks or so. It happened all the time. The other day we received four letters in one day, after not hearing anything for weeks.

I liked the idea of having girls in the class. Before we had moved, in first and second grade at the other school in town, it was only boys. Out here in the country, we had boys and girls in the same class. My favorite girl was sitting in the second row, all the way to the right. She had black hair and her skin looked very tan. My eyes were resting on her now while listening to the teacher talk to other students about their letters.

Looking at Maria made me feel warm and excited. I imagined taking her hand and walking with her out into one of the meadows with the high, high grass. I wanted her to look at me and smile at me. We were sharing some secret, which was so secret that I did not dare even to think about it. I felt the warmth and the smoothness of her hand, I imagined being closer to her in some way, to make that feeling of her hand extend over all of me. I had never even talked to her. When there was laughter in the class, I always looked her way. Sometimes she too turned and our eyes would meet for an instant. This instant would be like a flash going through my body.

It was very different with Hertha. I talked to Hertha all the time. I walked to school with her almost every day. She lived across the street from us with her mother. She was a little older than I was and she was more serious than the other girls in the class. She got all A's and she never behaved badly. She had curly dark blonde hair, tamed into two thick braids. Although they were braided very tightly, they still looked curly. Looking at her against the light, the little blond curls sticking out everywhere caught the light and gave Hertha a luminous outline.

Hertha had never made fun of me. Not about my tallness, not about my thinness, not about anything I had said to her. I trusted Hertha. She was my best friend. The other boys had teased me about her because we always came to school together. They did not see any beauty in her. She was boring to them: A good student on good behavior. I ignored them.

I needed someone to see the flowers the way I saw them, as the most beautiful creations of nature, along with the butterflies, the bark of the trees and the colorful rocks. We had spent hours together, mostly in her mother's garden, exploring every corner, every living thing, looking and touching it. Hertha's mother was rarely visible, except when she brought us lemonade and snacks or when she called Hertha in for meals. She was so different from all of my other friends' mothers—she was quiet, friendly, private, and understanding. All of these qualities had rubbed off on Hertha. Her father had been off in the war already when we moved into the neighborhood. I had never seen him other than from afar once when he was home on a short leave. Hertha never talked about him. She showed great understanding for my missing my father though, which made me believe that she must be missing her dad very much, too. I never asked her about him, I was too shy, too afraid I might hurt her by bringing him up.

Just before the class was going to be dismissed, Herr Schleier brought up a new topic. The schools were required to participate in the next drive of the *Winterhilfswerk*. The *WHW* was a fundraising organization, which sold sets of Christmas ornaments or other collectables and used the proceeds to buy necessities for the soldiers out on the various fronts. Most of the money went for warm clothing for the soldiers fighting in Russia.

"We want you to pair up so you will not be alone out there when it gets dark—you will be collecting when people come home from work, in the streets, by the bus stops, or you can go from house to house. You will receive a box with ornaments—this year they are very beautiful again, made from cut glass. You will have no problem selling them. If you run out, you can come to me for more. The money goes into a sealed collection can; you all know the red cans the WHW has been using for years. There will be prizes for those of you who bring back the most money.

146

I will get a list of these prizes next week. I just wanted you to start thinking about with whom you want to go with, and to let your parents know that you will be doing it. Are there any questions?"

"How late do we have to stay out?" one of the girls asked.

"Well, there are no rules about that. The longer you stay out, the more people you will be able to ask and the more ornaments you will sell. It is up to your parents when they want you back home. Anybody else?"

"Can I go alone?" Alfred asked.

"You have to go alone, I won't go with you ..." many voices came from the boys' side at once.

"Quiet please!" the teacher said. "Somebody will have to go with you. We do not want you to be alone out in the street. You might have a lot of money in the can. You know the foreign workers here have been known to steal. They cannot be trusted. It is better when there are two of you, it is safer."

Alfred looked around for a sympathetic face. Nobody volunteered.

"I go with Hertha; we live next door to each other!" I said, looking over at Hertha for her approval.

There was a storm of laughter cresting over the classroom. "What is the matter, Slonek, you like Hertha?" Are you going with her?" The other pupils were screaming and laughing.

I blushed a deep crimson. I looked down at my desk. Why couldn't I go with her? We would start at the same place, and we would end at the same place, at home. None of the boys lived on my street. Only one, all the way up by the intersection, but my father would not allow me to play with Roland. He used bad language and his whole family was somewhat rough. I liked Roland, he was in trouble often, but I was not going along with him on that.

The teacher calmed the class down.

"I am afraid, that is not possible. The instructions say pairs of boys and pairs of girls. Boys cannot go with girls," he said.

There were more comments from my classmates. Some open, some hissed. I was distraught. I could not see anything wrong in going with a girl to collect for whatever. We could have fun talking to the people in the street. I did not want to look at Hertha now. I probably had embarrassed her, too. *Will she ever talk to me again?* I worried.

When the bell rang, I was the first one out the door. I did not want to see anybody or talk to anybody. I started running to get away from the others following me. They were shouting all kinds of words after me "Girl boy," "Sissy," "Want to wear a skirt?" "Want to make Boom-boom?"

Why? Why can I not have a girl for a friend? I kept saying over and over in my head. I was going to ask my mother. I knew my father liked Hertha. My father who had objected to so many of my possible friends, he must think she was all right.

Most of the boys in my class were either boring or trouble. I did not want to go with any of them. I would have liked to go with August, but he was in a different school. If these WHW people want us to help, why don't they let us help the way we want?

Hertha waved for me to come over. I had not talked to her since this morning in school. I was apprehensive about facing her.

"Mama, can I go over to Hertha's for a while?"

"Did you finish your homework?"

"Yes, I only had a little bit."

"Where is Dieter? Have you seen him around?"

"Yes, he is playing with the twins, over in their garden."

"Good. I'll watch him there. Come back for dinner, at about six."

I ran across the street and let myself into Hertha's yard through the garden gate.

"I am sorry for what happened this morning," Hertha said, before I could even say my greeting. "They were so rude to you."

"Did they say anything to you?" I asked. "I should have asked you first, but I thought ..."

"They called me some stupid names, too, but that does not bother me. You were fine to ask him," Hertha said. "I enjoy walking to school with you. I would like to go collecting with you."

I felt relieved. I felt a big weight falling off my chest. "Thank you!" I said.

"I want to show you the new chicks next door, come!" Hertha said and ran towards the back of the garden.

We looked over the fence where her neighbors kept their chickens. There were a dozen yellow fluffy balls running around, making the tiniest noises from their orange beaks.

"They look so soft," she said, "I wish I could pick one up. We never had any pets, I want something live!"

"We never had any either. My mother said she might let us have a rabbit next spring, if I take care of it. I think my father does not like pets. I don't know why, because he grew up with a donkey even, and his father had hunting dogs."

"Watch this one, Peter; it wants to go through the fence."

"Maybe it believes there is more food on our side."

"It is flapping its wings like crazy. It surely looks like it wants to go somewhere."

"You really wouldn't mind going collecting with me, even if they make fun of us?"

Hertha turned towards me, "Why, don't you believe what I said? Come, let's play on the swing." She took my hand and led me over towards the lawn where the swing was.

CHRISTMAS SURPRISE

"Mama, what's the matter?" I asked. I always watched when my mother read my father's letters. That way I had some idea what my father had written. Just now, my mother's face had changed, gone pale and then red.

"There's been a change, changes on the front. All leaves are cancelled. Papa is not coming home for Christmas."

My mother took a deep breath and then tears started running down her cheeks. The letter hung by a corner between thumb and index finger in her dropped hand.

"He already had his pass. It was a special pass, because Uncle Otto was killed in Kiev. Papa is the only son left for Omi and Opapa."

"They cannot do that!" she added.

I was angry. I went closer to my mother and put my arm around her shoulders.

"They'll change it again. They have to," I said. "What are you going to tell them?" I pointed towards the guest room.

"Omi and Opapa? I can't lie to them. They are so depressed already. I don't know how to break the news to them. Where are they?" my mother asked.

"Opapa walked to town to get some more cider. I think Omi is upstairs." I went to the door and listened. "I can't hear anything, she'll come down soon."

"What is going on in Russia that they cancel leaves, do you know, Peter? What did you write in your war diary in school? Anything special?"

"No, it is always boring. Always the same. The Germans march forward and win. There is some heavy fighting around Stalingrad. It is much colder there than here. Papa is sick, why don't they let him come home?"

"I do not understand it, either. What am I going to do about Dieter? His only wish for Christmas was to have his Papa under the Christmas tree. He'll never stop crying now." My mother let out a deep sigh. She had wiped her tears with a handkerchief. She looked sad and small sitting on the big sofa bed in the living room. The letter was now in front of her on the table.

I imagined my brother screaming again. He howled regularly, almost every night before going to bed, always the same, "I want my Papa ..." The more tired he was the louder his crying. I had a hard time with it. My brother's pain penetrated me. I felt though, that I was not allowed to cry. I was the oldest, the *man* in the house.

"Will you help me with the cookies? We can finish a batch before I have to start dinner." My drifting thoughts were disrupted.

"Which ones are we making?"

"The Lebkuchen. Would you like to be in charge of the dough?"

150

I liked all chores in the kitchen, except washing the dishes. I did not like my hands in the water, but I thought drying the dishes was acceptable. Weighing and mixing were my favorite tasks. I loved the old set of small weights for the kitchen scale. They were polished brass, a whole set in a smooth little hardwood box with a cutout for each weight. Their round bodies sat flush in the wood. The mushroom-shaped handles stuck up. The lightest was five grams, the heaviest twenty dekagrams. Ten grams make one dekagram. Most of my mother's recipes specified ingredients in dekagrams. Everybody in Austria called them 'Deka's.' Only the Germans used 'grams.' I loved to handle these weights and combine them in the correct way to come up with the needed total quantity to weigh.

"Do we have to use the water glass again instead of the cookie cutter?" I asked.

"Yes, we do not have the right size cookie cutter to make a big enough Lebkuchen that will hold the glaze." I was relieved that my mother had returned to normal. The matter of telling Dieter that Papa was not coming home for Christmas had been pushed way out to somewhere where I could not sense it any more.

"How did Uncle Otto die, Mama?" I asked in the middle of creating patterns in the sugar glaze on the round Lebkuchen with the blanched almonds.

"Please don't talk about this in front of Omi and Opapa, Peter. They are still in shock about his being killed."

"I will not say anything, of course not. But can you tell me?" I insisted.

My mother wiped her hands on her apron. "Another soldier in Uncle Otto's unit sent a note telling them. It was early in the morning when the rockets hit. Everybody was still sleeping. It was an attack with *Stalin-Orgeln*. His friend wrote that Uncle Otto died instantly. They buried him right next to the house that was hit. They used some loose bricks from a damaged wall to frame his grave. He also sent a picture of the grave. Opapa has the picture.

I had seen pictures of the *Katyusha* rocket launchers, nicknamed "Stalin Organs" in the newsreel. They looked very primitive, like a bunch of large organ pipes bundled

151

together on top of a vehicle. When they were fired, they looked frightening: One rocket after another came bursting out of the pipes, with a trail of smoke behind it. The explosion upon hitting the target was so strong, they said, that even people way off the site of the impact died of burst lungs.

"What would it feel like to have my lungs burst? Would I even know?" I thought.

"What did Omi and Opapa say, when they found out?"

"You are full of big questions today, aren't you?" my mother answered. "Omi cried and Opapa just turned and looked out the window. We have to be very nice to them. It is very hard on them. I am so glad I have you, you at least understand. You do understand, don't you?'

"Understand what, Mama? Were Papa and Uncle Otto close? Papa must be very sad, too. Did he write something to you?"

"Not so far. Opapa sent him a telegram. He should have received it by now, but you never know. I am sure it is a big blow to him, they were close, and Papa had been looking forward to Christmas with his brother and his parents here. Remember, Uncle Otto had been approved for a leave, too. Now it will be just us." My mother started stirring the pot of potato soup on the stove and became very quiet.

"I'll go and sit with Omi and play with Dieter and Ina until dinner time."

"Yes, that is a good idea. Thank you for doing the cookies. They came out beautifully. See, you did not burn a single batch today. You did well. You were concentrating. Thank you. I'll clean up what's left. All the extra sugar cookie rings we made the other day are in this tin. We'll put strings on them after dinner, or tomorrow."

"How are we going to do Christmas Eve, Mama?"

"Well, I thought we put the Christmas tree into the living room, there is more space for the six of us. We will do that a day ahead and lock both doors. We will tell Dieter and Ina that the *Christkind* needs some quiet to prepare the tree and the presents—Dieter might have some doubts but he loves to believe in the *Christkind* bringing all the presents, Ina is too little to understand.

That gives us enough time to decorate the tree. This year you can help."

"Oh, yes, please!"

"Only five more days," I held up one hand, smiling and spreading my fingers, "I am so sad about Papa not being able to come ... stupid Army, stupid war ..." my smile disappeared and I fought back the tears.

My mother did not answer. She turned away and started cleaning off the big *Teigbrett*—the wooden board we used for kneading cookie dough and cutting the cookies on.

I loved Christmas. I loved it even more so now, since I had become an accomplice with the adults in making it into the big surprise for my siblings. I still kept away from the presents hidden in various places but I took part in smuggling the Christmas tree upstairs from the basement, where it was stored away from the children's eyes. A few days before Christmas my mother had left a very small branch—a fork-shaped end thick with needles, decorated with one or two icicles–, in a conspicuous place in the hallway at night. In the morning, the children found it and got all excited: *"The Christchild must have been here, look Mama, it lost a part of the Christmas tree, can we look in the Christmas room?"* Of course, the answer was "no" because the Christmas room could only be entered on Christmas Eve, when the Christchild was finished with decorating the tree and had laid out all the presents and rang the little silver bell. The parents could go in there before and "help" the Christchild with all these chores. They never told what was going on in there.

"We need to wrap the candy that Omi brought from Vienna so we can hang it on the tree. Would you do this with Omi while I take care of Dietz and Ina?"

"Yes, that would be fun. Do we have enough tissue paper cut?"

"I do not remember but the tissue paper is in the box with the other wrapping things. There is a sample of how big the papers have to be and then how far you cut in for the fringes. Be sure to use different colors so they will not all be white. Omi likes them all white; I think different colors look nicer on the tree."

My mother went upstairs and sent my grandmother down.

"Mama said we have a chore to do for the Christchild?"

"Yes, Omi. Mama wants us to wrap the candy you brought in tissue paper."

"Oh yes, where is the candy and the paper? Do we have two pairs of good scissors?"

"I have Papa's paper scissors and the ones from the kitchen are good, too. Mama and I used them when we did the first batch of papers."

"Good. We will have to do this in the Christmas room, so Dietz and Ina won't catch us!" Omi said and winked at him.

They sat down by the small table and found the paper sample.

"I'll cut the squares, you can do the fringes." Omi reached for the pile of white tissue paper.

"Mama wants us to cut some colored papers, too."

"We'll do those next. Which colors do you like best?"

"The light blue and the pink, they look nice in the candle light." I liked many different colors on the tree.

Omi handed me the first stack of paper squares. I took three off the top, lined them up as well as I could and started to cut into the short end. The cuts had to be close together which was not easy to do with the flimsy papers but I managed.

"I like how they look when we twist them at the ends, the tassels look almost as nice as with the bought papers," I held up my handiwork.

"It was so much faster with the ready made papers, the cutting takes such a long time."

"Well, we have five more days before we have to be ready."

"And in four days Papa will arrive. I hope he will get a good train connection. It will take him almost two days to make the trip." Omi's face did not look as happy as the anticipation of seeing Papa would warrant. Maybe she was thinking of her other son who would not join us for Christmas this year—or any other year- again.

I looked down at the papers and cut another batch. *What will Omi say when she hears that Papa's leave was cancelled?* I had promised not to say anything. Now I was glad I did not have to.

"That looks enough, I think," Omi said after we had been cutting for a while. "Let's start wrapping some of the candy."

"Can I eat one, please?" I begged and looked at my Omi.

"Well, I don't think one will be missed; go ahead but do not tell ..."

"Thank you, Omi! Thank you for bringing them. Where did you get them?"

"Musch-Omi gave me some extra coupons and I asked my grocer down the street—remember the little store around the corner from my building?—I told him about visiting you,—he pulled the candy out from behind the counter—and here we are! He is a nice man. He remembered you from your last visit."

I picked a white piece and bit off half. I let the fondant melt slowly in my mouth before I put the other half in.

"Oh, this tastes so good! Thank you, Omi!"

"Well, you will have lots of them on the tree. Do you remember last year? You were allowed to pick one every day—and when we took down the tree there were still a few left. How many cookies did you make? Were they the ones we are hanging on the tree, too?"

"Yes, we made the decorated *Lebkuchen*, two batches—and we made a bowl full of sugar cookies—the rings with the hole in the middle -before you came."

"You must have been very busy then. We'll have to put strings on them after we are done with the wrapping."

"Can we use the red wool again like last year? I liked the way the red looked with the green needles and the brown cookies."

"If there is any red wool left, Mama has been knitting a lot this winter and maybe she used it all. But we will not need very much, maybe we can use another color."

"I will ask her when she comes down." The more we engaged in these chores, the more I was taken in by the Christmas spirit. I loved the smells, the secrecy, the little jobs leading up to a tree full of colorful ornaments and edible decorations. Behind my Omi I saw the big brown cardboard box, which had not been opened yet.

"Omi, do you know what Papa ordered from *Olbernhau* this year?"

"No, I think he did it on his last leave. I am surprised that they still make and send these wonderful handicrafts."

"Can we look in the box?" I said in my sweetest voice.

"I don't think so, Peter. Mama will do that. There might be presents for you, Dieter and Ina in it. And you do not want to spoil the surprise, do you?"

"Where is *Olbernhau* anyway? Is it very far?"

"I only know it is in a region in Germany, called the *Erzgebirge*—I thought there was mining, because 'Erz' means *ore* as in iron ore, so there must be some mines. Maybe the miners carve these little toys when they are not mining?"

"I like the deer family we have in the glass cabinet the best. They are so tiny and look so much like real deer. The wood they are carved from is so smooth, like the kayaker that Papa carved when he was a boy." I had always admired my father's handiwork. A tiny kayak with a man sitting in it, carved from one piece, and a glued-on paddle. I always thought it was an Eskimo but my father had actually modeled it after a photograph of himself in the boat. I wanted my father to teach me how to paddle and how to carve.

"Do you think we have enough candy here for the tree?" Omi asked, "Mama does not like it when the tree is too overloaded." She ran her fingers through the pile of candies we had wrapped so far, making the tissue paper rustle.

"I think, we have enough!" I said quickly as I wanted to move on to another task. "Maybe there will be some new ornaments in the box—I like the little angels, the rocking horses, the Santa Clauses—they all have such bright shiny colors, they really make the tree look happy!"

"I have never heard anybody say that 'a tree looks happy' but you are right—with all the colors and shapes on it, it does look happy!"

"Will you help me tie strings on these candies so we can hang them?"

"I will cut them and you can tie them," I replied quickly because I had a hard time getting the thin strings to make a knot at the place where the tissue paper was twisted to hold in the candy. I wrapped the string around my hand many times until I thought I had enough and then cut one side. I handed Omi the bunch of even-length strings.

"Very clever how you did that!" Omi said. "Did somebody show you or did you come up with it yourself?"

"I read it in Papa's old 'Crafts for Young Men' book. I like that book. I did many projects from it already."

Omi started to tie little loops of string to the pieces of candy. She laid the finished ones side by side on a big tray, so they too could be picked up easily when it was time to hang them.

On the night before Christmas Eve, after Dieter and Ina had been put to bed, my mother asked me to help her bring the Christmas tree up from the basement where it had stood in a pail of water.

"Peter, can you put the stand on for us? Opapa can help you."

"Do you think it will fit into the old one we have?"

"I already measured the trunk and the stand—it's a good fit, we are lucky, we do not have to trim anything off," Opapa came into the room holding a little ruler. "Peter, let's go down and get it!"

All four of them agreed on which side of the tree should face forward in the room.

"Is it straight?" my mother asked and walked slowly around the tree.

The doorbell rang.

I looked at my mother and the grandparents looked at her and shook their heads. It was too late for visitors. The neighbors always just knocked, they never rang the bell.

My mother turned towards the door.

"Be careful, Lisl. Ask who it is before you open!"

"Yes, I will do that."

It was a mailman delivering a telegram.

"ARRIVING CHRISTMAS EVE EIGHTEEN FORTY STOP KISSES PAPSI STOP" my mother read out loud after ripping the telegram open.

She burst into tears, I cried, and Omi cried. Opapa sat very quietly in the corner looking at us.

"But the first one said his leave was cancelled," Opapa contributed matter-of-factly.

"Yes, but that was a week ago. I knew it would change!" my mother said.

"When was the telegram sent?" Opapa did not trust this development.

"Let's look. Peter, can you see if it has a postmark on it?"

"It was stamped at the Linz Main Post Office at four this afternoon. Yes, here it is, it came from a German Army Post Office, with yesterday's date." I had deciphered the codes and the uneven printing on the narrow telegraph strips of paper glued on the telegram form.

"That's good!" Opapa said and planted his walking stick firmly on the carpet in front of him. "I will go to the station in the morning and find out which train he is on and see if there are any delays." He was the expert in the family on reading train and other schedules.

"Why don't you go later, then you do not have to go twice, it is a long way, you know!" my mother said. "I am sure the train will not be early and if it is late you can sit there and wait."

"Schedules are such a mess with all the bombing raids and partisans blowing up rails, especially in Russia. I would rather see in the morning where he is coming from and what the current situation is. I do not mind going twice. There is not much snow on the ground and it is not so terribly cold. I have my good walking shoes and warm clothes."

"Thank you, Papa!" my mother said. "Dieter and Ina will be delighted to hear the good news. I still cannot believe it's true. He is coming for Christmas even!"

"We could put him under the Christmas tree as a present," I said.

"That is a wonderful idea, Peter. Just what Dieter had wanted all along!" my mother agreed. "But we do not know yet when he will be arriving."

All three of us began hanging cookies and candies on the tree.

"May I start with the ornaments, Mama?"

"Yes, as long as you distribute them evenly around the tree!"

We kept at it until late. Opapa had nodded off in the easy chair.

"Let's go to bed and finish tomorrow!" my mother finally called a halt to our enthusiasm. Opapa was astonished when he saw the transformation that had taken place with the tree while he had been napping.

"It looks very beautiful already. I wish I could smell the greens and the cookies!" He had lost his sense of smell and taste after an accident when he was hit by a motorcycle last year. Luckily, his other injuries had healed up nicely and there was no other permanent damage.

Before turning in we went over the sequence of events for tomorrow, Christmas Eve. Opapa insisted on going to the station early to check up on schedules. Omi and I would finish the tree in the morning and my mother would keep my brother and sister busy. After lunch we would trade duties. My mother would then go and unpack the big box of Christmas things my father had ordered and lay out the other presents for the grandparents and us.

Depending on my father's arrival time, we would schedule the Christmas Eve celebration.

My grandfather came back from his reconnaissance trip to the railroad station very hopeful.

"As far as I could determine by talking to different railroad officials, the train Emil must be on is moving along as scheduled. It is scheduled to arrive in Linz at 5:30 in the evening. I will call the station once before and then, if nothing has changed, I plan to be there at five, just to be sure."

"What would we do without you, Opapa?" my mother said with a sigh of relief. "I will start preparing dinner. First, I will make the mayonnaise for the potato salad. The potatoes and the red beets are already cooked, I just need to slice them and make the dressing for the beets. The carp we do last, it needs to come to the table fresh from the oven. It can cook while we look at the presents."

"If Opapa and Papa can catch a bus right away, they will be here by seven. Do you think Dieter and Ina will be able to hold out that long for the *Christkind*?" I had visions of them being impatient and cranky.

"Well, we will have to do our best to keep them entertained until then!" my mother said, looking at Omi and me.

"They are so jittery with anticipation already, it will be hard. We have to think of something special, otherwise they will lose it." I had taken care of them often enough, I knew how hard this would be. The big surprise though, was worth it. We will manage. I was determined to make this the best Christmas ever for them. If only my father was on that train and it would arrive when Opapa had said it would.

"Mama, how much longer before the Christkind comes? It is getting dark outside already. Nobody can see it flying around anymore. It will come soon, I think!" Dieter was starting the questioning.

"Christkind?" Ina's face and eyes lit up. She smiled.

"We do not really know when, Dietz. There are so many children around Linz; it is a really busy time for the Christkind! We will have to wait our turn. Some years it comes early and some years it comes late. It depends on where it starts from and how many presents it has to carry."

"I want it to be here early and with many presents!" Dieter retorted.

"Peter will play with you with all your cars. You can make a garage under the bed. You had fun with that the other day! Or Omi could read you a book: Struwelpeter or Hansel and Gretel ..."

"Not Struwelpeter, he is ugly with his long hair and long fingernails. I don't like to look at him!"

"Come, Dietz, we will go upstairs and get the cars."

"Can I play with your blue truck?"

"If you say 'Please' and promise to be careful with it, you can have it for a while!"

I started upstairs and Dieter followed me right away. Ina felt left out and cried. She went after my mother but Omi intercepted her and picked her up.

"We'll play with the doll. Where is your doll? Is it in the baby buggy? Let's go look."

My mother went into the Christmas room and started to arrange the presents. When she came back out after a long while, we were still waiting for Opapa and Papa to appear. No word, just darkness outside.

Dieter kept asking when the Christ child would come. We were running out of stories and excuses for the delay. My mother got busy with the preparations for Christmas Eve dinner. Although we were not practicing Catholics, we still observed some of the church's traditions. Christmas Eve was a fast day, meaning no meat. The custom was to have a fish dish. For our family this meant Carp, either baked or jellied, which created great anxiety in my grandmother who was deadly afraid that one of us would swallow a fishbone and choke to death. In the years when she was not with us at Christmas Eve, she would call from Vienna at great expense several times during our mealtime to make sure everybody was still all right. Her calls became a family joke, which was used at all kinds of perceived crisis times.

The good carps came from monastery ponds, where the monks would raise them, mainly for their own consumption on Fridays throughout the year, which were fast days without meat. Extra supplies were sold at Christmas and other Holy Days, calling for a meatless diet. I loved the big fish lying on our counter, one big eye staring at us, his slippery scales glistening with different colors. Ever since another fresh fish had started flopping violently when my mother had started to clean it, which had scared her no end, I was in charge of testing if the fish was really dead. Of course my tickle test was useless because the flopping was not a sign of life but a muscle spasm that could occur at any time during the cleaning process. This year we were in luck, the fish did not move. It probably had been dead for a long time before it arrived at our household, another casualty of the war. My mother had assembled all the herbs and spices that would flavor the liquid, which would surround the fish while being baked.

When my grandfather finally came through the door, all eyes were on him. He nodded and winked at us while asking my brother and sister: "Has the *Christkind* been here yet? Did I miss it?"

"No, we have been waiting all this time, it has been dark outside for a long time and the *Christkind* still is not here. We do not know what is keeping it!" my brother was quick to answer.

We assumed my father was hiding outside. Now we needed to get the children out of the way so he could come in without being seen. There was a moment of great confusion and excitement. We all wanted to greet my father, but there was no way of doing that without spoiling the surprise for the children.

"I have a feeling that the Christkind is very close. I think when Opapa came through the door I could hear a little bell and I smelled the branches of a Christmas tree. Shall we go upstairs and look out the window? Maybe we can see something!" My mother had come up with a good solution.

Dieter and Ina ran up the stairs, my mother with them. She turned off the lights in the bedroom and lifted the air raid blinds. The kids were glued to the window in an instant.

My grandfather opened the door to the outside, let my father in and went out to fetch his bags. Omi and I hugged my father quickly and very quietly, exchanging conspiring looks. It was very hard for me not to let out a loud scream of joy when I first saw him. My grandmother led him into the Christmas room and closed the door behind them. They both were to light the candles on the tree. I still was not allowed in there because the presents were all spread out already.

Omi came out of the room sobbing with joy. "We are ready!" she whispered to me.

Within a moment, a little bell began to ring from the Christmas room. It rang once, twice, and one more time. I heard running and then the door upstairs flew open.

"The Christkind is here! Did you hear the bell?" Dieter called from above starting down the stairs. Ina stepped down after him as fast as she could make it, repeating "Christkind is here, Christkind is here!" My mother held on to her hand so she would not fall.

"Well, shall we go in? I think it is time!" My mother let Dieter open the door.

"Papa!" he shouted and ran towards my father sitting in a chair next to the Christmas tree. Ina's eyes went wide and she hesitated before she started to move. "Papa" she said and cried when she reached him. They both were on his lap holding him tight. The four of us stood in awe of the scene. The man in uniform with the children, under the Christmas tree, candles ablaze. We all started to cry. It truly was a Christmas miracle. There he was, our father, mother's husband, and the one son my grandparents had left.

We did not pay any attention to the Christmas tree and the presents. My mother went to my father, he stood up, also in tears now, setting down the two little ones, and they embraced.

"My Lisi!"

"My Emil!" was all they could say to each other.

I wanted a second hug but there was no chance right now. My grandparents were standing back, taking in the scene with tears flowing freely.

"Watch the candles! Please watch the candles!" my grandmother said to nobody in particular. She was afraid the tree would catch on fire. My mother always placed the candles very carefully near the tips of the branches so they were never near another branch.

"Otto, oh my Otto, oh, where are you, my Ottolein?" Omi sobbed suddenly very loud. Uncle Otto was supposed to be here on leave with us. But he was dead, another victim of the war. He had gone on his last leave.

There was a short silence in the room. My father was struggling with tears again. My mother put her arms around my grandparents.

"Shall we sing 'Silent Night, Holy Night'?" my mother finally asked.

"No, no, later!"the children shouted.

"Well, we want to do it while the candles are still burning,"

"No Mami, no. We can do it later! I don't like when you sing." Dieter was adamant.

"All right, then we will blow out the candles now and you can look at your presents."

"I want my Daddy!" Ina stretched out her arms and Dieter did the same. They both sat on Papa's lap again. My grandparents started to blow out the candles on the tree. I helped them with the ones higher up but at the same time, I was glancing around for my presents. We each had our own little space where they were laid out. I spotted what looked like my area on the big easy chair in the corner. But first, I wanted to be with my father. He looked tired. His uniform was all crumpled up from having traveled on the train for a long time.

"How long did it take you to come home?"

"I left my unit three days ago. I had to change trains four times. Luckily, there were no air raids but one of the main tracks had been destroyed, so the train had to make a long detour."

"Where did you sleep, Papa?" Dieter wanted to know.

"The trains were very crowded. I could not stretch out on a bench as I had hoped—so I slept some, sitting up. I used my coat for a pillow. I am very tired now."

"The fish is in the oven, the salads are made. We can probably eat in fifteen minutes." Mama had ducked out earlier and had started the fish.

We had set the table while waiting for Papa to arrive. It looked very festive. There was a big advent wreath hanging from the chandelier over the table, with four fat red candles. Between our plates there were little pine boughs with one or two pieces of tinsel on them. The centerpiece was a bigger branch with two white candles in clip-on holders, just like the ones on the Christmas tree. My mother asked me to light all the candles, even the ones on the advent wreath.

My parents had received a special set of fine china meant for serving fish as a wedding present. We called it the 'fish china' and never used it. It stayed hidden behind all the other good china in the credenza. Today my mother had brought out the salad plates and she was serving the carp on the huge serving platter that was deep enough to hold the liquid the fish had been cooked in. My father looked at the plates and smiled.

"That set is still intact, isn't it; maybe we should use it more often so some of it will break." He never had liked the design, which showed different romanticized fishes swimming through very murky, greenish waters.

"Let's turn off the lights, there are enough candles burning. It will look more like Christmas," Mama said. The tree was showing through the wide-open double door in the next room.

"No, please, we need the light, otherwise we cannot see the bones. Somebody might swallow a bone!"

"I'll make sure I serve pieces away from the bones, this fish is large enough to have big pieces of meat without bones. Mutti, please relax, we will be fine."

Papa was firm and started serving. Nevertheless, as was her habit, Omi was intently watching every one of us, every time we took a bite of fish, to see if we would be able to swallow it without swallowing a dangerous bone.

I sat next to my father and kept looking at him. I still could not believe he was here with us on this special night. Halfway through dinner, my grandfather cleared his throat noisily, stood up, and raised his wineglass. "Welcome home my dear Emil! Let us toast to you and all of us, and to your dear brother, our dear son Otto." He lifted the glass higher and looked at the ceiling "who is watching from above. Merry Christmas to all of us! Prost!" Omi, my mother and my father all wiped tears off their cheeks with their napkins. Dieter and Ina looked around not knowing what was going on, I looked from Opapa to Papa and then at my plate. It was a good Christmas but also a very sad one.

"Can we go look at the presents?" Dieter finally broke the silence.

"Yes of course, you can. I will bring some cookies to the other room. We can eat them there," my mother said, "Peter, could you help me clear the table, please?"

My grandmother and I quickly moved all the dishes, silverware and leftovers to the kitchen. Omi made sure that the fish skeleton disappeared into the garbage as fast as she could slide it in, so there was no chance for any bones to wander into our throats with some other food. We joined the others in the Christmas room. They had lit the candles again. Dieter and Ina were busy examining their presents. My father, thoroughly exhausted by now, sat closely by my mother and held her hand. My grandfather sat in the corner, one hand on his walking stick, the other holding his pipe, which spread the aroma of cheap war-quality tobacco.

When Omi and I had settled in, my mother suggested again that we sing 'Silent Night, Holy Night' as was our custom every Christmas Eve. She started to sing and we all fell in. The kids looked up from their toys but did not pause very long. The familiar melody and the words set the seal on Christmas. It made it official. Nobody ever sang that song before Christmas Eve. It was reserved for that night and it made it special. The flames of the candles flickered, maybe from our breathing with the old melody.

"Can we eat a candy from the Christmas tree?" My brother remembered from last year that we were allowed one candy each off the tree every night.

"Why don't you have a cookie first, we should leave the tree alone, at least for the first night."

"No, Mami, I want one of the wrapped candies, they are so good, please?"

"Fine, tonight is a very special night, so you can have one, but ask Papa if he wants one too. Then you can bring it to him. But first we will blow out the candles. Can you do the ones at the bottom for me, please?"

We all showed each other our presents. The excitement usually coming with the surprise and joy over the presents, tonight centered on Papa's presence. We were overly glad that he was here, the biggest and most surprising present of all.

Dieter and Ina were totally in awe of the magic powers of Christmas with their Papa appearing under the Christmas tree out of nowhere when he was supposed to be in a war, somewhere far away.

My mother and I, and the grandparents, knew that he would have to leave again in a few days to join that insane chaos that festered over the whole world.

OUR FIRST PET: A RABBIT

Most people living in our area had animals as part of their household. They had been resettled here from the site of the new steel mill, where they had lived a more rustic life, growing their own vegetables and fruit and keeping small farm animals to supplement their diet. They were allowed to continue this in their new environment on a smaller scale since the individual lots were not as big as what they were used to.

For a long time my father had resisted all begging from us children to let us have a pet. But we kept trying, although we had a hard time deciding what it should be. A dog was out because of my fears, my parents definitely did not like cats, I really wanted to have chickens but there were objections to the noise they make, so the choice narrowed itself down to rabbits since we were not ready for a goat.

Neighbors were constantly offering baby rabbits for sale or barter. When the family next door had a new litter we were allowed to choose a female since we had agreed that we wanted our own baby rabbits in the future. A big wooden crate was converted into a home for our new friend by adding a metal-mesh covered door. As the main agitator for this animal I was ultimately responsible for the feeding and care, no matter what my siblings had offered to help. We fed her kitchen vegetable scraps and let her graze on our clover beset lawn, surrounded by a portable fence.

It all went well until one winter morning I discovered that she had eaten a hole through the wood and escaped. My brother and I followed her tracks in the snow, they led us through two neighbors' gardens until we lost it completely. There was great mourning and guessing what had made the rabbit so unhappy that it had decided to leave us behind. Accusations flew my way for not feeding her enough, for not cleaning the den often enough but I

167

could convince my family that I really had taken good care of her.

Several days later, one night we were awakened by a piercing scream neither of us had ever experienced. We could not turn on any lights because of the air raid regulations. We tried to look out the window but it was too dark to see anything. Not knowing where the desperate cry had come from we did not know where to look in particular. Only the morning light revealed the sad truth: Our dear rabbit was laying in the snow, dead, obviously headed in the direction of its pen, surrounded by a pool of very red blood. When I went down to investigate I found that some animal had bitten through the rabbits neck and thus ended its life. It had not tried to eat any part of the rabbit. Our looking out the window must have scared it away. The tracks around the scene of the struggle were too messy to be identified, so we never found out for sure who had committed this murder.

My sister started to cry, then my brother joined her and I had a hard time hiding the tears running down my cheek. We had grown fond of this critter and to lose her this way was very sad.

"What are we going to do?"

"We will have to eat her," my mother said very matter-of-factly, I will take her over to the Mayer's and have their grandpa skin and clean it for us. I noticed she had not used the personal "her" which was how we usually referred to our pet.

"NO..."—my brother howled, my sister just kept crying harder and I bit my lip. It had been quite a while since we had had a good chunk of meat. And yet my eyes filled with tears again at the thought of putting the skinned rabbit in the oven.

My mother bravely did her duty, against her will and inclination, picked up the dead rabbit and carried it over to the neighbors. We watched her disappear through their door. She returned by herself.

"He will do it for us," she said.

Later in the day I kept peeking through the upstairs window to see if grandpa next door was headed for the shed where I had seen him behead chickens and skin a few rabbits. Nothing happened. After a while of puzzling over this, I finally realized that the carcass was frozen stiff from the night and probably needed to thaw out before grandpa could go about his gruesome task. I missed the actual operation and I was glad I did. I don't think I could have watched my dear bunny being dismantled very dispassionately.

In order to make things easier on us, my mother had decided to make rabbit stew rather than present us with the roasted animal all in one piece, which would have tasted better but would have caused enormous emotional harm to the three of us. Regardless of all the carrots, parsnips and potatoes, the herbs and the sauce, and the fact that the meat did not taste very much different from our usual chicken fare, we all cried during the meal. But eventually we finished the stew and our bodies were grateful for the additional nourishment.

In the spring we acquired another rabbit and she lasted much longer with us. She produced a litter of little bunnies who provided much pleasure for us.

PROPAGANDA MARCH

After my tenth birthday I had to report to the local DJ group. The *Deutsche Jungvolk* met once a week in the evening for a *Heimabend*, an "Evening at home." We were taught songs, we were quizzed on the different emblems of Army, Air Force, Navy, SA, SS, the *Reichsarbeitsdienst*—the "voluntary" Work Service, which I had a good chance of getting drafted into at age fourteen, and on all the insignia of rank within each of these services. We heard about heroic deeds in the Armed Services and saw pictures of the heroes; we were shown newsreel clips and propaganda films, mostly about victorious campaigns on the ground and in the air, of U-Boat attacks on enemy ships and convoys. The only movies I really enjoyed were the ones about air combat. It looked like every pilot had an even chance. It was man to man. The pilot with the better skills and the better plane mostly won. My endings never involved death of the enemy; the losing pilot always parachuted to safety. I wanted to be a pilot very badly.

169

My father was not in favor of me attending these 'evenings at home' as they were called, with the youth groups. He was aware of the brainwashing I would be subjected to. My parents invented sicknesses and trips, wrote notes and letters. Often on such occasions the leader in charge of the meeting would dispatch two of his trusty underlings to check up on me. If I was not in bed, shivering with fever, or protected by doctor's papers verifying contagiousness, they would take me with them under threat of an official report to the Party *Ortsgruppenleiter*, the local capo, who was a man not to be messed with. He could make trouble for my father at work, he could launch an investigation into subversive activities such as listening to enemy broadcasts, supporting known enemies of the state, and other charges easily proven with the help of people with no conscience, who did anything for little favors. So I went, as often as I had to, carefully instructed by my father not to believe everything I was being told, but to think on my own before I made up my mind. I could always ask him for advice when things were not clear.

I was supposed to follow the same rules at school, but only for certain subjects–, very confusing instructions at age ten. Of course, I could not apply this to whatever my parents were telling me, because they spoke the absolute truth and did not want me to second-guess them. As far as I was concerned, there was nobody else around me I could have double-checked with. I developed an extra inner skin shielding me from this outside information. I heard it and I absorbed it but only as far as that skin, it did not penetrate into my soul. There, in my soul, I slowly built another world. I read book after book, populated with other kinds of heroes: Noble Indians and trappers in North America; men who forged through eternal ice to find the North Pole; men who rode alone on horseback through the forbidding mountain ranges of Asia; men who sailed off into uncharted waters; men who crossed the big Oceans in small boats; men who explored the jungles of Africa and South America in search of new peoples, plants and animals; men who were concerned with illnesses threatening whole populations in far away places, and helped to find cures.

In these—my worlds—nobody was marching six, eight, ten abreast, singing, shouting, with hoarse throats, about conquests and victories, waving flags, saluting flags, blessing flags, bloodying flags, listening to never ending speeches promising everything the heart could desire, for *after the war was won.* Nobody had "Death, Blood, and Honor" engraved on their daggers and belt buckles, or tattooed on their arms. They fought nature and evil, easily recognizable evil like murderers and crooks, who had stolen from the poor or had done physical harm to people or animals. They did not go by ancestry or by yellow stars sewn on somebody's clothes.

Shortly after I had been drafted into the DJ—the *Deutsche Jungvolk*, I was caught up in mass hysteria again. There were rallies on all occasions: the anniversaries of great events of the Party, victory parades when Germany had swallowed up another of its neighboring countries or won a major victory on one of the many fronts.

It was another one of those propaganda marches. We had assembled at eight in the morning at "my unit's" meeting place; twenty-five of us had marched into town to meet with other units. At the designated assembly area, all units joined and marched in formation to the town's largest auditorium. We filed in and sat through a two-hour production put on by other Youth groups: There were gymnasts, choirs, and patriotic folk dancers.

There were even some attempts at humor, which were quickly outweighed by a very serious speech by a Hitler Youth leader, who told us how we had to sacrifice everything right now for the final victory, which would bring us everlasting happiness and bliss under the guidance of our Führer. Then several units carrying flags marched through the auditorium and onto the stage, greeted the speaker by lowering the flags and waving them in patterns around the stage. When they were finished and positioned along the front of the hall there was another lowering of the flags and a few moments of silence honoring the heroes who had already given their lives for the great cause. There was special mention of a large number of Hitler Youth members and what part of Greater Germany they had come from before they nobly laid down their lives for the Führer.

In my youthful ignorance or innocence, it was impossible for me to imagine how I would lay down my life for the Führer, or for any of the other causes I had just heard about. All I had to relate to were pictures I had seen in the newsreels: German soldiers, riding on fast moving tanks, smiling through their oil-smeared faces, waving at the camera, civilians lining the streets, waving at the soldiers, little girls delivering bouquets of flowers to commanders who then kissed them. But there were also battle scenes, heavy howitzers being loaded with huge shells, firing over the heads of advancing German infantry, Stukas whining their way towards the earth and their doomed targets, delivering their deadly loads causing huge explosions, smoke and debris flying through the air.

I also remember seeing columns of soldiers taken prisoner, Polish soldiers, French soldiers, Russian soldiers—with glum faces, marching slowly, tired and hungry, not knowing whether their survival was a good turn of fortune or a bad one. The backdrop to all these scenes was nothing but death and destruction. Buildings in ruins, still smoking, upturned vehicles, disabled tanks, horse wagons, wheels up, hitching poles sticking out like big antennas, sometimes the dead horses right next to them with bloated bellies. Occasionally I could spot a dead soldier sprawled out in a ditch nearby. I became an expert in watching the backdrops, because they told me the real story. Somebody had driven the truck with the missing cabin, somebody had manned the tank with smoke coming out of the hatch, and the horse that now looked three times as big as normal had been loved and fed by a person. I was not going to lay down my life for that, next to that. All I saw were things that make people sad and unhappy.

I had no elaborate concept of what it means to win a war or to lose a war, but if Germany would not win and not get the colonies back and I could not go to *German Southwest Africa*, to become a sheep farmer, I would be fine. I would live with my father and my mother, my brother and my sister. We would not have to worry about owning a flag and hanging it out on special days decreed by the government. I would not have to march on Saturdays and Sundays singing about fighting with the Boors in Transvaal against the evil British Forces, or about my best friend marching next to me, being felled by a bullet, and how he is now marching on in spirit, next to me, giving me strength. No—- what was I doing here?

The flags had cleared the stage, making room for a large group of girls, dressed in simple, colorful *Dirndls*, the Austrian Alpine national costume. They formed circles of eight and, holding each others hands, danced around, singing again and again—"the day begins with a happy heart, the day ends with a happy heart ... " their bodies twirling, their dresses flowing, their braids swinging—and their bright voices ringing .... A girl in the far right circle looked especially beautiful. From way up here on the balcony where I sat she was tiny, just a whirling little puppet on the stage, but I fell in love with her, her face, her movements, her colors. There was excitement in my whole body and I knew I would meet her some day.

Finally, it was all over. We all rose and sang *"Deutschland, Deutschland über Alles ..."* right arms high in place for *'der Deutsche Gruss'* the Heil Hitler salute. On the way out, we were handed a roll filled with sausage and cheese. It was way past lunchtime, and another group filed into the theater to see the same wonderful show. As they passed us, they asked how bad it would be. They were given a number of unflattering descriptions, some in crude dialect, until one of the lower ranking leaders threatened the offenders with an enormous number of pushups right here in the street or official write-ups in their reports. I thought of my girl and chewed on my roll.

We were marched to a soccer field quite a distance from the theater. There we were divided into small groups and engaged in harmless competitive games, running, tug-of-war, horse carriage races, building body pyramids—and singing. We had to pass the time until the other group was finished with the show. Then there would be a combined march through town along the main street. Several large groups of Hitler Youth would be marching with us. In the distance, we could hear the drum rolls and trumpet fanfares that were an integral part of these demonstrations of solidarity with the Führer and the Third Reich.

Very few people lined the streets when we finally started the march. The drums drummed left, two, three, four—left, two, three, four,—again and again. The trumpets joined, our steps made the pavement vibrate. Each row had to watch to be lined up with the leftmost marcher. Every man was lined up perfectly behind the one in front of him. *Im Gleichschritt*. Singing. The same songs again. "Louder" yelled the group leader, marching alongside the column. We arrived at the main town square. We marched to form a huge block, facing yet another rostrum. More flags. Another pep talk. Cheering. *Sieg Heil*-ing. Finally the commands came to start marching again, in the other direction. "*Achtung! Ganze Abteilung, rechts um! Im Gleichschritt, Marsch!*"

"*Ein Lied*" The designated song-keeper had to come up with a title quickly. "With a happy heart the day begins, with a happy heart the day ends," I was singing to myself. My little angel floated in front of me, *im Gleichschritt*, of course.

The other dry mouths intoned the "*Horst Wessel Lied*," about some heroic young Hitler youth who had been shot in a political shuffle. I particularly disliked this one, because I never could understand why people would kill other people just because they did not believe the same thing. There was so much to believe in and so much not to believe in, who could keep it all apart? Who was the judge of what was right? My father? My group leader? My teacher? My friend's father? Who??? Tell me WHO? The Führer? Of course, the Führer but the only concept I had of him was that he spoke very loudly. He shouted. So the one who talks the loudest is the one who is right? No, I knew that one from school. Loud had nothing to do with the truth. There was no answer. Maybe God. God who? My Grosse Opapa went to Holy Mass every morning. Praying to God, receiving God in the Holy Communion, talking with God. Did my grandfather know the truth? Is that why he ate the spinach first, and then the meat, and then the potatoes? Is that why he did not talk nicely to my grandmother? Because he knew the truth? There is no truth. There are the people in my books who do good deeds. They make other people happy. That might be true—but is it the Truth?

More and more people kept stumbling, getting out of step—I had seen a few even dropping to the ground, being picked up by the special helpers with the Red Cross armbands and being put on stretchers. I was nauseated and thirsty, my legs hurt, my right foot felt like it had a blister on the heel. At the Blumau, a widening of the street, not quite a square at the opposite end of the main street we were marching on, one column after another was ordered to halt. The big loudspeakers announced individual meeting places for the local groups. We were to gather there and check in with our group leader. He was to arrange for our marching home.

"Marching" home? They must be kidding. Dissenting voices rose all over. The group leaders called for quiet. "If you do not check in at this time with your group leader, you will be reported to the central council for not having participated in this important event. That will have serious repercussions. *Mannschaft Stillgestanden! Heil Hitler!*" The mass of voices answered "*Heil Hitler!*"

"*Alles Wegtreten!*" The final command for the day was to leave the formation and join the local groups. There was an uproar of voices and pushing in all directions at once. I fought my way to the central bus stop where my group was to assemble. Two of my cohorts were already there, slumped on the bench in the bus stop. "Boy, am I tired. I cannot walk another step!"

"But we have to walk home!" the other one said. "He better not make us march! That was enough for the day. Next time I'll be sick!"

"Quiet, here comes Rudy."

"Did you have fun? That was quite an event, I have never seen so many Hitler Youths in one place. Good for Linz. We'll be in the newsreels." Rudy looked around for confirmation. Twenty somber, tired faces looked back at him.

175

"We are tired, very tired. You know, all we had to eat all day was that measly sausage?"

"Yes, and nothing to drink other than what some of us had in our canteens!"

"I told you, be prepared. Eat a good breakfast, and you'll be home for dinner," Rudy said defensively.

"At my house, dinner is done by now!" somebody said.

"All that singing makes you really thirsty!"

"And they would not let us out of formation at the fountain. We could have drunk some water there!"

"Is anybody missing?" Rudy asked.

In the meantime, more of our group had struggled in. We looked around and counted.

"Alfred is not here," somebody said.

"I just saw him over there, a moment ago, let's wait."

"Yes, but not much longer, it will be dark by the time we get home."

"Hey, Alfred! Over here, we are leaving. Want to be reported to the central council?"

"No jokes about that! We do not want people to show up in the morning and then disappear. Imagine the soldiers would do that at the front? We'd never win the war."

"We'll never win it anyway," somebody murmured close to me without being heard by Rudy.

There was no mention about marching. We set off walking in "loose formation," together but not lined up, and not in step. We were about forty-five minutes' walk from our part of town. We were dragging our feet. Nobody talked.

"Can I split here?" Alfred asked when we reached the road that lead to his house.

"Yes," Rudy said, "Good bye, *Heil Hitler*!"

"*Heil Hitler*" we all said, "see you on Thursday!"

"Thursday" we heard from a distance. Thursday was the Group's meeting night.

By now it was pitch dark. One after another of the boys said their "Goodbye's and *Heil Hitler's*" and went off into the dark. There were three of us left. I had never come home alone in the dark before. I was sweating with fear. I had thought of several ways of saying that I would like someone to come with me, all the way home. I lived in a dead end street, so nobody would walk with me unless he wanted to see me home.

"I guess, here we are. Everybody is on their own from here. Everybody fine with that?"

"Paul could you walk down to the corner with me rather than going the other way around? It is the same distance." I asked in a low voice.

"What's the matter, Peter, are you afraid?" Rudy asked. "I'll take you home if you want me to."

"No, it's fine," I lied, "I just thought it would be nicer for Paul and me to walk together."

"I don't mind to go that way, Peter, I'll walk past the milk store with you."

"Thank you, Paul!"

"So you are fine, you two?" Rudy asked again, anxious to get going for himself.

We said our greetings and left in different directions. Only Paul and I walked together. Paul was not a real friend of mine. I had met him in the group but never saw him outside of it. My secret plan was to talk him into going all the way home with me, a detour of five minutes, and then have my mother take him home. I knew she was up and worrying about me. First, I had to admit to Paul that I was scared. Scared to death, actually.

This last piece of road, from the milk store to our house was the most awful piece of road I have ever known. There were those two dogs on the way. The German Shepherd normally calmed down as soon as one had passed. The Bulldog was always ferocious, beginning with the first whiff he would get of me until I was almost home, he would bark, foam at the mouth, jump up on the fence, race back and forth along the fence, I was convinced that if he ever made it over the fence I would be a bloody mess. I swear, I had never teased him. I was much too afraid of dogs to think of teasing one, I was just afraid. Afraid of the day he would find that gate open, afraid of the day he might get enough ferociousness to jump the fence. I had to go through this ordeal twice every school day. Mostly I timed myself so that I could walk with one of the other kids on the street, then it was not so bad. As long as I was not alone, I felt protected, my odds of being torn to pieces were at least less than one hundred percent. Sometimes, when there was nobody else in sight, I would beg my mother or father to guide me past that ugly beast. If they had time, they would do it. Only very, very rarely was the beast with its owner, or somewhere in the house and not in the garden. But I never knew if he would not come racing to the fence at the last minute, and be even more ferocious because he had missed the greater part of the window for barking at me.

I had never been by there alone in the dark. I was sure the dog would feel much more threatened or defensive when somebody walked by during the night. There was no way around, other than crossing fields and passing more unknown and treacherous places in the dark.

It was really dark now. I could hardly see my hand in front of my face. Nobody was allowed to have any lights outside and all the windows had to be covered to let no light shine through because of air raids. Violations counted as treason, since you were obviously giving light signals to enemy aircraft. There were a few stars but no moon.

We came closer to the point of separation. I finally took heart: "Paul, there is a dog down my street and I am really afraid of it, would you mind walking with me, all the way to my house and then my mother would walk home with you?" I looked at him as well as I could in this darkness and waited for an answer.

"Peter, that dog is inside, asleep, you don't have to be afraid. I really want to get home. It's so late and my parents will be worried already."

"Oh, please Paul, it is just five minutes more ...," I pleaded.

We had arrived at the milk store.

"Really, don't be silly. Did the dog ever bite you? No— it's behind a fence. It is sleeping, believe me. All dogs I know go inside at night. Did you ever see it at night?"

"No, I never have been by here at night."

"See, it's alright. Good night. Be brave. Sing one of our songs. Everything will be fine, believe me. See you on Thursday!"

Off he went. Whistling to himself, "A comrade I had, a better one cannot be found ..."

"A comrade I had ..." I thought, but now I was alone in the dark. Panic rose from deep down within my body. That's where that dog fear lived ever since that big wooly thing had jumped up at me when I was a two-year old little boy, had knocked me over and then had stood over me panting, teeth showing, tongue hanging down ... a beast so much bigger and stronger than me ... until someone had come and rescued me. That push and that dog's face had followed me into many nightmares, over and over, and in every dog I saw that beast, jumping...

I was trembling all over. I took a deep breath and started down the street. I was very careful not to make any noise walking. Although my feet were aching, I lifted my feet up high with every step so I would not kick any pebbles. So far so good. The house with the dog was on the left. I moved as close to the right side of the road as I could. I stopped and listened. Not a sound anywhere. Cautiously I moved on. Two more houses, then—there was a noise. My heart stopped. Something was moving through the bushes inside the garden. I screamed at the top of my lungs and started to run as fast as I could, all the way to where my mother stood, in the light of the open door, arms outstretched "Where have you been .... are you alright?"

I could not talk. I cried and sobbed for a long time. Finally my heart came to rest, my mother sat me down in the kitchen and wanted to know all about my day, while she was heating up some vegetable soup she had saved for me from dinner. I told her all except about the girl I had fallen in love with.

DID YOU KILL?

I did not like the hectic atmosphere when my father was home on leave. It had been that same way last time. This time he only had a week before going back to Russia. There were long lists of things to do, to buy and to pack to take with him.

"Are you taking me to the movies today, Papa?" I asked.

"Yes, we do some errands in town. I've got to get film and some more pocket knives—I need more pocket knives to trade for eggs, the Russians love these knives—..."

"Papa, they do not have any film, Mama tried before you even came. No more, they are out."

"I'll get some, trust me. You will see. There is always more, they just keep it hidden and you have to talk them out of it." My father winked at me, "I will give you a lesson," he said. "We will have to catch the two o'clock bus. That will give us enough time for shopping before the four o'clock show, and we will be home in time for dinner, so Mama will not be upset. Good?"

"Are you sure we will get tickets, they have been sold out most of the time, Norbert told me." I said.

"Soldiers on leave have special privileges. We can go to the front of the line, and they hold extra tickets for soldiers. There have to be some advantages to being in this hell. If I have to go to the front out there, I can go to the front at home, too. *The Home Front*, they call it," my father said. "You get ready, so we do not miss the bus. You know I do not run to the bus stop. I like to walk and be there a few minutes before the bus arrives."

I felt a little uneasiness creeping up my spine. I knew my father was talking about my mother, who always left late and had to run to catch the bus. She did not look very dignified when she was running, all dressed up, wearing her city shoes with the big block heels. I felt sorry for her. Whenever my father said something about one of her weaknesses, either in front of her or just to me alone, I cringed. I wanted total harmony. I did not want to hear sharp edges or harsh words, I did not want to see hurt in her face or tears. Maybe this could be fine for children, but it was not fine for adults.

"Papa, may I look at the pictures you developed and printed yesterday?"

My father had been to the lab while I was in school. There was a big stack of proofs on the table in the living room.

"Sure, I will be ready in a few minutes. They are small but you will get an idea on how flat that country is—really depressing at times, especially in the winter with no colors, just gray, gray, and gray as far as you can see."

I sat down and looked at the first sheet. These proofs were a lot smaller than the ones my father normally made. He had exchanged his beloved Rolleicord for the smaller Leica, the thirty-five millimeter camera that had belonged to his brother Otto, because it was smaller and the films were easier to get. He also wanted to save the Rollei in case something would happen to it out there in Russia. All of Uncle Otto's belongings had arrived at our house a few months after we had received the notice that he had been killed in action.

Wanting to be prepared for the worst, the uncle had packed up everything during his last home leave before he left again for the front. My grandfather had arranged for the shipment.

I kept looking through the proofs.

"Is this the house with the crooked windows that you painted?" I asked my father.

"If it looks like it, then that's it. I took the picture so I could prove to you that the windows really were crooked, not only in my painting."

"I cannot see that here, it is too small. Are you going to make enlargements?"

"Yes, if I have time, I want to. Surely not all of them but a few I would like you to see a little larger. They would be nice for showing to other people too. Russia is a very different country. It is hard to imagine without having been there, or at least seeing some pictures."

"Are the people different where you are now than the ones where you were before?" I asked.

"Not much. The Ukraine is all farmland. At least it used to be. The people used to have good crops. Now they are as poor as the rest of the Russians. Everything is destroyed around them. All their animals are dead or they are starving to death. It is very sad to see all the destruction and the poverty, there seems to be no hope for any recovery."

I noticed the change in my father's voice. It was slow and thoughtful, dragging as if it wanted to keep pace with the images that certainly must pop up in his brain just as in a newsreel.

"Here is a picture of the horse with the weird arched hitch, the one you drew for me in the letter." I loved my father's drawings. They established a special connection between us. Many times my father would draw things in his letters rather than explain them with too many words.

There was no time to draw together on these home leaves. Too much of an agenda was cramped into a few hectic days: shopping for rationed items only my father could get, visits with a few old friends, fixing the leaky faucet, and a review of garden planning. Then there were endless discussions about how my mother should budget the scarce military pay, what to pay now and what to pay later, or about how our situation would get better once my father came home again. The least time was spent on a few frivolous activities like going to the movies or to a gallery. Some of these excursions happened just with my mother and others included us children.

I felt lucky today. It was my turn with my father all by myself: The privilege of the oldest. The movie we were going to see was only for fourteen-year-olds and up. I could pass at not quite thirteen because I was tall and my father was with me to fend off any questions for a school I.D. or any other proof of age.

"There is one picture of you in a trench, with a rifle. It looks like the trench is dug in the snow." I held the sheet up to the light to see better.

"That was taken outside of our quarters. We are far behind the front but there are so many partisans, we always have a guard on duty and we are supposed to be ready to defend the house. Normally the partisans do not attack houses, they like bigger targets."

"Like what?"

"They like to blow up trains or truck convoys. They put out mines at night. You know, on every train the army puts a few extra freight cars in front of the engine, the first one filled with sand or rocks—so when the train hits a mine on the tracks the locomotive isn't damaged." My father looked at his watch.

"We need to leave, Peter. I am ready. I'll talk to you about it on the way to the bus, yes?" my father said.

"But if it blows up the car with the sand, there is a hole in the tracks and the locomotive will run into that and into the damaged car?" I kept with the story.

"Not all the time. The engineers are very careful, they are moving the trains slowly. Many times the explosion will stop the train, until they can repair the tracks. The soldiers of the pioneer corps can do that very quickly. It gets bad when the partisans attack the stalled train and try to take guns, ammunition, food, supplies and clothing. That always ends up in a fierce firefight."

"What happens to the soldiers on the train? Or the engineers?"

"If they are lucky, they get locked into one of the freight cars, if they are not so lucky they get shot."

"Have you shot at people?" I asked.

There was no answer.

We put on our coats and gloves and hats.

"Have fun and don't come home too late," my mother said from the kitchen door. "I'll have dinner ready at seven. You should be able to be here by then, easily."

"Yes, we will be back by seven, even if we miss the first bus, we can still catch the 6:15, so we will be home a little after seven at the latest," my father said before kissing her goodbye.

"Let's go, Peter. The town is waiting for us!" He extended his hand to me. I grabbed it and followed him out the door.

My father walked determined and fast. With my long legs I had no problem keeping up with him.

"Papa, I mean how can you shoot when you know there is a person on the other end? You could kill them. Have you killed a Russian soldier?" I asked.

"You must know every little stone on this road, you walk here at least twice a day, don't you?"

"Maybe once a week I go the other way around, behind our houses and along the street over there," I pointed across to another row of houses, "but this one here I know. I have time to look since Hertha moved away I am always walking alone."

"Where did Hertha move to?" my father asked.

"I don't know. It went so fast, all of a sudden she was gone."

"Do you miss her?"

There was a pause before I answered.

"Yes, I do. I liked her the best of all the kids in the neighborhood. I like Pepi Steyrer, who lives two houses down from us, but he is so much older. He has friends his own age."

"Didn't you build that hot air balloon with him?"

"Oh, yes, that was a fun project. Except the balloon burned before it flew anywhere. I wrote you about that."

"Yes, I laughed when I read your letter, I am sure it was not funny at the time. You had put so much time into it. The accident must have been a big disappointment for all of you. How did it catch fire? I don't remember what you wrote."

"The balloon was made of strips of tissue paper. The only paper we could get was too thin, I think, it did not hold up very well. Instead of a gondola at the bottom, there was a small white gas burner, a little cup with a wick in it. The heat from the flame was supposed to rise into the balloon above and since the hot air is lighter than the air around it, the balloon would take off."

"How was the burner fixed to the balloon?" my father asked.

"With a very thin wire. We built a structure to hold the paper in place with the wire. It held up well, actually."

"So what happened?"

"We had it all set up for take off, for its maiden flight, and after we lit the burner there was a little gust of wind which tilted the balloon. The flame got bigger and too close to the paper—the whole balloon was gone in a flash. We could not get to it fast enough. Pepi almost burned himself trying to extinguish the fire."

Did you build another one?"

"No, Pepi had a big project for school and it was such a pain to paste these strips of tissue paper together, we let it go. We talked about a glider. You know Pepi is now building gliders, he is in the Flight Training group of the Hitler Youth."

"You see a lot of August now, don't you?" my father said.

"Yes, he is my best friend. He comes over every day. Mama likes him, too. He is polite and he does not use bad language."

"Not like this little twit that lives at the end of the street. You don't play with him anymore, do you?"

"Not since you told me not to. He isn't that bad, Papa. His whole family talks that way, he cannot help it."

"That is exactly what I mean, they are all Proletarians. I don't want you to have anything to do with them."

I did not like these pronouncements. I did not think Karl was that bad. He had a loose mouth and he picked fights but not with me. He was hard to avoid. He lived on the same street, went to the same school, and he was the same age as I.

I did not feel comfortable with this subject. We were walking by Karl's house just at this moment.

"You promised to tell me about the war, about shooting at people."

"What do you want to know?" My Father seemed off somewhere else.

"How can you shoot at another person? If you hit him right, he is dead. We play war and pretend to shoot at people, but they never die. It is all in fun. What do you think when you aim at another person?"

"Well, I am not really at the front. I have never been in any combat. Thank God. I am too old for that. But there are a lot of partisans where we are stationed now. We have to be careful." My father's voice trailed off.

"Have you killed a Russian soldier?" I asked.

"No, I don't think so. But I have shot at them."

"You wanted to kill them?"

"I wanted them to stop shooting at me and my friends."

"So you wanted to kill them?"

"I guess. It is either them or me. I want to live for you, your mother, your brother and your sister! I want to be with you as soon as this madness is over."

"But still, how can you shoot to kill another person?" I wanted to know. I could not reconcile the gentleness I knew in my father with the act of killing.

I felt my father's grip on my hand getting a little tighter.

"After I finished basic training—remember, I stopped at home for two days?—We took a train into Poland and from there we marched for weeks, sometimes close to thirty kilometers a day, into Russia. What I saw along the way was ugly. At first it was only destroyed houses and burnt-out tanks, trucks and cars, sometimes a cemetery with lots of fresh graves, long rows of them, extending outside of the cemetery. People's belongings were strewn all over in places, furniture, horse carts, things that had been put together with a lot of effort and love, no longer functioning, they were kaput, most of them forever.

"One day, after an air raid we marched past the remains of what had been a supply train, just a few hours ago. That is where I saw the first dead German soldiers. Well, we could tell from the uniforms that they had been German soldiers. There was not much left of them. And not much of the horses and the goods on the train, not even much of the train. There was blood everywhere. Luckily we did not have to help with the cleanup. We had to make time to get to our destination."

"Later on we saw more dead horses along the way. They had been dead for days. Their bodies were bloated to two or three times their real size. There were flies all over them. There was a terrible stench around them. We were tired and hungry."

"Why didn't anybody bury them?" I asked.

"There were very few people left. All but a few very old men were gone with the army, or as prisoners, or dead. Nobody was left to do the burying. Also, there was no equipment. Nothing left.

"One day we were hit by sniper fire. Partisans. Two hundred kilometers behind the front line. Out of the blue. Looked like a peaceful village. Not even a lot of destruction. They were hidden somewhere in an attic, or in the church tower. They killed two of my marching buddies, just a few rows away from me."

"Were you hurt, Papa? Were you scared? You did not write about that, did you?" I said. "You could have been killed, too!"

"No, I was fine, except for the blisters all over my feet. But I was angry because there was nothing I could do. Nothing we could do, a whole regiment of soldiers. There was no enemy in sight. Our commander wanted to shoot up and burn down the whole village as a punishment. There was no heavy artillery around that could have done the job. The local commando probably rounded up some of the villagers and shot them or sent them to a prison camp. We just moved on."

We had arrived at the bus stop. A few other people were waiting. My father looked around. There was nobody we knew. We went a little bit off to one side and stood there.

I looked at my father. I had let go of his hand when we came to the stop. My father looked very serious. His forehead was all furrowed and his skin seemed paler to me. His black beard stubbles looked almost as if he had not shaved today. But he had. Except for his little mustache, which had always been part of his face.

"After these things happen a few times, and you lose more of your group, after seeing so much death and destruction all around, one gets numb. If you would not be numb, you would be crying all the time, from the pain and the overall ugliness. Soldiers don't cry. They are supposed to fight back. So when there is an attack and you can see where the fire is coming from, you run for cover and you shoot back, to protect yourself and your friends.

"First time I aimed at a partisan, I could not shoot at him. I shot in the air. If my sergeant would have noticed, I could have been court-martialed or shot on the spot for treason or whatever. When the partisans started throwing hand grenades, I started shooting for real. I did not want to be blown to bits."

"I don't want to hear this, I get so scared, I don't want you to go back there, Papa," I said. I grabbed my father's arm.

"You don't have to worry, Petz, it does not happen that often, I am so far away from the actual fighting—you asked me and I did not want to lie." My father put his free arm around me and pressed me against his side.

"Here comes the bus!" my father said. "Let's go."

The brakes squeaked when the bus stopped. It was one of the very old ones, which had been converted to run on wood gas. It had a big cylindrical burner mounted on the back, looking like a misplaced smoke stack on an ocean liner. It smoked all right. The driver had to climb up on the roof every so often and keep filling the burner with wood chips, stir them with a metal rod until they fell onto the fire in the bottom.

My father paid the fare, I showed my student card to prove I qualified for the student fare. We went towards the rear and took a seat.

"I ride with this driver at least once every day of the week. He still does not know my face. He always asks for the card." I said.

"Well, he has to do his duty. That makes him feel important. Just show it to him before he even asks, then you stay out of trouble."

"I do, anyway. I don't like to get yelled at."

"What do you know about the movie?"

"Norbert in my class saw it last week. He thought it was really good and exciting. Story happens in the *Luftwaffe*. Lots of good dog fights."

"I really did not need to see a war movie; I thought it was about a family"

"It is about the family. But the son is in the *Luftwaffe* and he is a fighter pilot." I said. "Do you want to see another movie?"

"No, there is nothing worth seeing. This one has the best reviews. The war is on. It is part of everything. Unfortunately, we cannot escape that. I hope it will be over soon."

"Do you think it will be over soon?" I asked.

"I hope so. If we take Moscow, the Russians will capitulate. Then all the German troops can go to the Western front. They'll take England and that's it. The rebuilding afterwards will take forever. Everything is destroyed. Wherever I have been so far, nothing but ruins."

"The Germans are good, aren't they?" I said.

"The Russians have terrible equipment. Very primitive, but some of it works better than ours in the mud and in the snow. They have unlimited reserves of people, millions of them. Let's talk about something else, please. How are you and August getting along. Are you still planning that expedition? Mama wrote you are sitting on the posts for the clothes line and discuss your plans."

"Yes, then Dieter and Ina and their friends cannot disturb us. We are all done with the planning. We know we will need sixteen camels to carry supplies and four for riding. It is two weeks through the desert, with only one oasis along the way. There we can get more water."

"You sound excited and very sure of your plans."

"We wrote everything down and figured out how much of everything we would need for the trip."

"And at the end there will be the treasure. How do you know where it is?"

"Well, in the story I read, they have an exact map. But they never made it all the way. They had to turn around. That oasis used to be very busy because it was along one of the major trade routes. Later the traders found a shorter and less dangerous route for their caravans. From then on this oasis we want to go to was only used by local Bedouins and robbers. Some outlaw band hid their booty there and then they all got killed. So the treasure is still there."

"How do you know the story is true?"

"It is an old magazine and the story was written by a father and his daughter. Why should they lie?" I had thought about that a lot. What if this whole tale was made up? No, they had been there and they had the map and they had verified the sources.

"Even if you don't find the treasure, it will be a very interesting trip," my father said.

"August and I will save all our money when we start working. It will take us at least two years to save enough."

"What if someone finds the treasure before you go there?"

"This magazine is so old, I am sure there are no more copies around. Oma had saved them for a long time. I had them disinfected after the scarlet fever so I could keep them. Remember, they burned all the other magazines and papers."

The bus squeaked to a stop at the end of the line in town.

"Here we are. Shall we transfer or walk the rest of the way?"

"Let's walk. It is faster anyway. I don't want to wait for the dumb streetcar."

"You can come with me to the photo shop. That is on the way. Then I'll drop you off at the theater, you can get in line and get the tickets while I do my other errands quickly."

I was very uncomfortable with the thought of having to buy the movie tickets by myself. What if they are sold out? What if they don't believe me that I am over fourteen? What if they push me out of the line? What if Papa arrives only after the show starts?

I did not say any of these things to my father. I just held on tighter as we marched down the quiet part of main street towards the center of town.

"Frau Helga, I cannot believe you are still holding the fort!" my father said to the pretty, youngish woman behind the counter. He had changed personality as we walked through the doorway of the photo shop. The stern, serious father had stayed outside, the charming photographer-doing-his-duty-in-the-army had entered.

190

"Where else could I be," she said with a big smile that looked very personal to me, "but defending the *home front*. Tell me, did they send you home for good?"

"No such luck, they need us old ones to occupy the territory behind the front, keeping the partisans in check." He leaned slightly over the counter and said in a much lower voice "It is all so stupid, I tell you, we can only hope it will be over soon."

I had been in this store many times before. My father bought all his film, photographic papers, developers, fixing salts and whatever else he needed for his hobby at this place. Through the photo club he got a discount. He knew the owner and most of the regular staff and they knew him. Another woman behind the counter waved at him from across the store. He acknowledged her with a smile and a nod. Then he leaned over the counter again.

"And how do you imagine, *sehr verehrte Frau Helga*, that I will be able to record this great victory of the *Grossdeutsche Reich* over the Bolsheviks and all their slant-eyed allies—WITHOUT FILM? My son here tells me that his mother tried in vain to talk you out of at least one lousy roll of Agfa's best."

"My dear Herr Slonek," Frau Helga said, picking up my father's mocking tone, "as far as I am informed you are not an accredited *Kriegsberichterstatter*, and therefore not entitled to any film over your regular allotment of two rolls per year, which—as I remember—you picked up as soon as you had your ration card in hand at the beginning of the year." She took a deep breath and said, "And how many rolls did the Führer ask you to take back to wherever you came home from?" I could hardly hear the words, they were spoken so low.

My father clicked his heels in a mock 'attention' and said "He said at least six thirty-sixes, because exciting things are going to happen in Russia very soon ... not to mention the scenery which is the most depressing I have ever seen in my life."

"Is that so. I am sorry about that." Frau Helga said. "We still have our scenery but from all I hear, the bombs will start working on that pretty soon, don't you think so?"

"Unfortunately, yes. They are making a mess out of Germany already. I want my family to move to the country immediately, I want them away from this town, away from the steel works."

My father had grown very serious in a matter of seconds. I knew about his concern about us being exposed to the bombing.

"Under the circumstances, I can give you four rolls, no more, because I have no more. Please don't tell anybody where you got these. Because if an official *Kriegsberichterstatter* walks in here tomorrow and needs film, I am in big trouble, we have orders to keep an emergency supply."

My father winked at her. "I am sure you could drag up a roll or two for the emergency supply, couldn't you?"

"No, I swear, that is the bottom of the barrel." She sounded very honest to me.

"I am ever so grateful for what you are offering, Frau Helga. It is more than I could have hoped for. And when I come back, I'll hire you to manage my studio, advertising agency, *Peace-Reporting* agency, just to show you how grateful I am."

"I'll be waiting, Herr Slonek, but now let me pack up the goodies. Anything else today? Not that we have a terrific selection but we do have a few things left. Let me see, I have some post card stock, you always use that, don't you? And some fresh developer, if you are planning to do some work before you leave."

"I'll take a box of the postcard paper, please. No developer, thank you, I am leaving and I don't know when I'll be back," my father said.

I was wondering what kind of postcards my father would produce next. He always took a few of his best family or scenery shots and made them into postcards, which he then sent to my grandparents and other relatives in Vienna. My Omi was especially fond of them. She already had a whole collection.

My father looked at his wristwatch.

"We better go, Peter, or that movie will start without us. How much do I owe you?" he asked Frau Helga.

After he paid, she wished him a safe tour and a speedy homecoming. She smiled and shook my father's hand. He thanked her profusely for the special favor, waved at her and we left the store.

"Well, that was not so difficult, was it?" he said to me as soon as we were outside.

"No," I said. I did not know what else to say. Maybe we just came at the right moment when she had some film left. Maybe she likes my father better than my mother. He is the one who always shops there. But still when my mother asked for film she said it was for him, in Russia.

"Frau Helga has been helping me out all along. She is very nice. I have been shopping there ever since we moved to Linz. That has been a while. It is always good to go to the same store, once you like the people there. They get to know you and then they help you.

"Here is the theater. Take this money. Get two tickets somewhere in the middle, I don't mind where we sit, as long as it is not all the way up front. Yes? I'll run over to the craft store where they have the pocketknives. I'll be back quickly. Just hold on, you are a big boy now."

"Papa, please don't be late. They won't let us in after it starts," I said.

"I'll be back in time, I promise. All we would miss is the dumb newsreel. I don't need to see the war pictures. You are better off without seeing them, too. We'll be fine. Don't worry. Bye!" my father said, and walked away quickly.

I crossed the street and walked up the stairs to the Coliseum theater entrance. It was the most modern theater in town. It's front wall was all glass and the inside hall was huge. I felt the butterflies in my stomach flapping their wings stronger and stronger. There was a long line in front of the ticket window.

Thank God, I thought, Maybe Papa will be back before I get to the window.

The line moved slowly but still too fast for me. Although it was more than half an hour before show time there were quite a number of people waiting already. I glanced ahead at the price chart above the ticket window. None of the categories showed the 'sold out' sign yet. So there was no real danger of being shut out if I did not manage to get the tickets.

I rehearsed the words with which I would order the tickets: "Please, two Parterre seats, by the middle aisle if you have them?" or "Two tickets, please, by the middle aisle, at the Parterre level." I could not decide which phrase was more effective. Which one would protect me better from a question about my age? Maybe I should get a look at the lady in the window first.

There were only four people left in front of me. I could see the woman. Her hair was curled up into a big bun and dyed an intimidating shade of red. I had never met a person with their hair dyed red whom I liked. I tried to remember my line. I drew a blank. I panicked and stepped out of the line.

I'll go to the back and start all over again. There are plenty of tickets, I said to myself.

When I turned back I froze: The line had grown behind me into a double snake, winding its way through the modern chrome railings all the way to the entry doors. I began to shake. I was not going to make it to the window before my father would come back.

I had just added another level to my panic: Not only did I have to get the tickets but now I also had to explain to my father why I was so far back in the line—or would I get to the window, or would my father arrive ... I was utterly confused in my fear.

Between rehearsing my lines and watching for the "sold out" sign to light up for one of the sections, I had forgotten to watch for my father.

"You still don't have tickets?" Was the window closed? Or were there so many people in line? The place is certainly mobbed now. Come!" My father took my hand and pulled me out of the line.

"But I was holding a place for us ..." I was holding back tears.

"No, we'll pull rank here," my father said and walked up to the front to the window that said "Military On Leave." It was closed, with nobody standing in front of it and with nobody visible inside.

My father knocked on the window. A woman appeared inside and opened the window. Her expression was not particularly friendly. I braced for a battle of words.

"Good Day," my father said, "I am on leave from the Russian front. Can we have two tickets, parterre, somewhere in the middle, please?"

"Let me see what we have left. One moment, please."

"You still have the money?" my father said, stretching out his open palm. "How come you were not able to get the tickets?"

The woman in the window came to my rescue.

"I have two in the sixteenth row, three seats in from the center aisle. Do you want them? Or do you want to be further up front?" the woman asked. She held the pad with the bright green tickets in front of her, ready to tear the perforation.

"No, thank you, those are perfect. How much are they?" my father asked.

"Two Marks total, that is the military price," she said and I heard the tearing of the flimsy paper and watched her hand them to my father. He counted out the money, thanked the woman again and turned to me.

"Well, we made it. But before we go in, tell me what happened."

I looked at my father and my eyes filled with tears. During the whole transaction, my mind had been racing through all the possible stories I could tell my father, which would make me look better than I felt.

"I was afraid they would not give me the tickets," I said in a very low voice, "I went to the back of the line again." I stepped back as if I could protect myself from my father's answer with added distance.

"They would not even have asked your age, you are so tall, and look so much older, don't you see that? The lady would have had to look UP from the window, just like for an adult. I should have let you ask, waiting behind you. Would you have done it with me?"

"Yes," I said. I felt a huge load drop off my chest and out of my tummy. "Yes, I would have asked for the tickets with you backing me up."

"Good." My father reached into his coat pocket, pulled out a small sack and opened it. "Look what I have!"

"Thank you. Where did you get those?" I asked, surprised at the colorful hard candy in the bag.

"At the craft store—no, I dropped by Jindrak's, they had some left behind the counter." My father smiled and offered me the open bag.

"Can I have two?" I asked. They were my favorite fruit filled bonbons.

"Sure," my father said, "let's go find our seats."

EASTER PRESENTS—4/4/44

The *Feldpost* parcel my father had sent from an unidentified German army post office somewhere in the vast occupied hinterlands of the Soviet Union arrived just before Easter. Like all of his packages before, it was wrapped in strong brown paper and tied with good hemp string. Both the paper and the string had made the journey between Russia and Linz several times already. These materials were hard to come by and had to be treated respectfully to make them last.

There was a ritual for unpacking my father's parcels: We would wait until the four of us could gather— my mother and the three of us because we would never start opening anything without all of us present. These rare packages had become the only tangible links we had with my father. My mother patiently untied the string, knot by knot, without cutting. She rolled it up neatly and put it away before starting to unwrap the paper. There were several layers of it, before we could see the somewhat battered box made of ugly, brownish-gray soft cardboard with stapled corners. Once that was open, we could see several small packages wrapped and nestled in old newspapers.

Our hands were getting impatient. All we had done so far was watch my mother, it should be our turn now. The biggest little package had my sister's name on it. She was four at the time, the youngest, and not quite aware of why all this was going on to begin with.

"Where is Papa?"

"He is far away with the soldiers, but he will come back soon," my mother said, pulling her closer, handing her the package.

The present was red, had a wooden handle and looked like a table tennis paddle, with a hole in the center. Completely unpacked we saw that there were four bright red chickens perched around the hole, and strings going from their necks to a little pebble dangling in the hole. My mother held my sister's hand around the handle and started to swing the pebble slowly, in a circular motion. The chickens started to peck loudly at their imaginary food, little kernels painted in loving detail on the board. The chickens themselves were quite ornamental, too: little patterns on their heads and wings, and the heads and tails finely tapered and detailed with a sharp knife, it seemed. We all touched the little chickens because they looked very touchable. Maybe we were also reaching out to touch our father, who had made this magic toy from wood and paint found somewhere out there in the desolate steppes of Russia, with makeshift tools, probably patterned after a toy he had seen in the hands of a Russian child. Later I found out that he had made quite a few of these pecking hens and given them to the local children.

Now it was time for us boys. My brother was already reaching into the box to retrieve the package my mother pointed out to him. The sequence from youngest to oldest was part of the ritual, as was unwrapping everything piece by piece with everybody watching, so the joy would last longer, and all could participate in the other's excitement as well.

What my brother had in his hands looked like a nice piece of wood, with the grain running parallel with an obvious top and bottom. From the lines visible on the wood, we assumed it must be possible to open the "board." My mother who had already read the enclosed letter from my father said, "there is a trick to opening this box, you must find out by yourselves" while she handed me a package exactly the same size as my brother's. My box was identical with my brother's except for the outside decorations. My father had painted on the finished wood with his poster paints, which he had taken as a part of his boredom-emergency kit. Both my brother and I had our initials in big stylized letters on one side, surrounded by a border, just like the logo of a big company, very elegant looking, and underneath, finely hand-lettered *"Russia Easter 1944."* That layout influenced my graphic aesthetic sense forever.

On the other side of my board box there was the outline of a mountain topped by a white cloud in the background, a lake with a tiny sailboat in front of the mountain, and in the foreground there was a small car pulling a small camper. I remembered immediately what this scene stood for: Our promised camping trips! On his last leave my father had promised us that once he was back, and our car was back from the army, we would go on frequent camping trips.. We were hoping that the car was in good enough shape to pull a small tent-trailer, which at the time was the most modern mobile camping gear available. We would drive to the mountains to hike, and go back to the beautiful, clear mountain lakes with a new sailboat. My father would teach me how to sail, which I knew he did well. I had seen all these photographs of him, standing on the side of the boat, hanging on to the rigging, and -with a sporty cap and scarf -, on a sleek one-man ice sailboat.

My brother's box had the same symbols but in a more childlike version, which he understood as well as I did. Now we had to figure out how to open this treasure box, so we could hide our smallest and most valuable items in it. One end of the lid was held down by a screw, and part of the lid would swing out revealing a second board and, if opened wide enough, a little slot towards the screw. After much experimenting with moving the board in different directions, we finally figured it out. The second board slid along the screw slot and then turned sideways to give access to the hollow core of the board. All the pieces fit together perfectly, so the mechanism was not obvious and for months we had many a friend puzzled over our father's secret lock fashioned from an old bed board, as he told us later. To this day, I love to feel the smoothness of the wood, the slight roughness of the ends rounded with a wood rasp and to play with the cover pieces that still slide in and out without making a sound.

A LONG WALK HOME

At ten thirty in the morning, the sirens went off. They signaled relief for me and my classmates because they interrupted the school day as they had all throughout this school year. Without being asked, we lined up in pairs by the door. It was somewhat demeaning for thirteen year-olds to follow these rules but we had been told discipline was essential in the face of danger. The teacher waited for us to quiet down before he let us start downstairs and out towards the shelter.

We crossed the yard with the teacher leading us, just like all the other classes spilling out of the building from various doors, looking like ants leaving their anthill in an orderly fashion and crawling underground again not too far from where they had emerged.

The shelters were long concrete tubes with steel-reinforced roofs and airtight steel doors buried under the playing field. When my class entered, another group was already sitting down in the back. There were enough seats left on the wooden benches lining the walls. I managed to sit next to my friend Georg. A few of our buddies were right across from us.

Recently, it had been the same routine almost every morning: The American bombers came in from Southern Italy, flew over the Alps, and on the way to the cities and industrial centers in Czechoslovakia, Hungary and Eastern Austria. They came close enough to Linz to put us here on alert. The large steel mill at the edge of town had been targeted several times but the damage had been mostly in the surrounding fields and residential areas.

"Quiet please!" It was Mr. Krenn, plugging in the little radio so we could listen to the official civil air defense broadcast tracking the movements of the enemy bomber squadrons.

"I'd rather have Mr. Schmidt here this morning," I said to Georg in a low voice. "He makes jokes about the planes and the bombs. But remember when he told us how scared he was?"

"Yeah, I like him better, too," Georg said.

Herr Krenn was without emotions.

"This is the German Civil Air Defense Warning Service with an update at 10:50. For Sector Southeast: Bomber formation consisting of four squadrons moving Northeast over the Salzkammergut, two squadrons on course towards the areas Linz and Vienna. Level 4 alert for these areas immediately. Estimated arrival of aircraft within 15 minutes Sector Southwest: Four squadrons heading for the areas Bavaria, Hessen..."

Herr Krenn turned the volume down.

"Sounds like a lot of planes coming in this morning," Georg said. Herr Krenn closed the second set of heavy steel doors at the entry to the shelter.

"Where were we when this stupid siren went off?" Herr Krenn asked.

"Oh no studying, Herr Krenn, they will be here any minute anyway," said Karl who was the most clever in the class when it came to distracting teachers from their subjects. Karl was the one who took over when one of the teachers was late. He could do all kinds of neat tricks to entertain the class.

"Let's review the Alps, it ties in with the approach route of the bombers. Peter, which mountain range would the planes fly over first, heading straight North from Torino?"

"I Dolomiti" I said in a tiny Italian voice.

Everybody who had heard the answer laughed loudly. Herr Krenn was not amused although the answer was correct.

"Achtung, Achtung, this is an important update ... Sector Southeast." The teacher leaned over and adjusted the volume on the radio again. "The two squadrons approaching Linz have changed formation. We have reason to believe they will be attacking Linz. Level six Alert for Linz and surrounding areas. Everybody must enter a shelter immediately. Shelters to be locked. District Civil Air Defense stand by for further instructions. We repeat, everybody in the area Linz except authorized Civil Air

Defense and Anti-Aircraft personnel must be in a shelter...
End of update for Sector Southeast ..."

I always felt goose bumps crawling all over my body
when listening to these announcements. This one sounded
very serious—the planes must be pretty close ...

As soon as the radio had gone quiet again, we could
hear the angry bellowing of antiaircraft guns. All of Linz
was surrounded by a ring of anti-aircraft batteries. It
sounded as if all of them were letting go, all at the same
time now. Then there was a heavier thump. And another. I
looked at George next to me: "I think we're getting some
today."

"Oh, think of all the shell fragments we'll find on the
way home—with all this Flak shooting off—there'll be nice
pieces, no?" Kurt said looking at me.

That was not what I had been thinking. The area
where I lived was close to a railroad junction where the
major East West track joined a line coming up from the
South. My father had said a long time ago that that would
be a bad spot to be close to in case of heavy bombing. I
thought of that remark every time there was a raid with
bombs falling and I was not at home. So far, nothing had
happened. A few stray bombs here and there but
obviously the junction had not been targeted the way they
had targeted the steel mill a few raids ago.

The noises outside were getting louder and angrier.
Now we could hear the engines of the planes blending in
with the anti-aircraft fire and the exploding bombs. The
engine noise was an ugly hum that penetrated the yards of
earth and concrete on top of the shelter as if there was
nothing between them and the planes. It sounded as if the
sky was covered with airplanes.

I had seen them fly high above, little silver birds way
up in the blue sky, in formation, just like for a parade. But
that was on days when those planes had had orders to go
somewhere else but Linz. Today apparently it was our
turn.

A whole string of bombs hit closer and shook the
bunker violently. Concrete dust came down from the
vaulted ceiling and settled on our hair and laps. Another
big thump and explosion and the whole shelter jumped as

if it were a ship at sea, dust flew all over, the benches rattled, and the lights went out.

The teachers flicked on their flashlights. We were between fear and delight. This was exciting stuff. Hits close by. The noises moved away gradually. Without the radio, we did not know what was going on. Only the sirens would tell us when it was safe to go back out.

Then there was more flak, more engine hum, and then, out of nowhere there was the angry hiss of a falling bomb.

When you hear a bomb it will hit somewhere else, I remembered. But what about the next, and the next? In the newsreels I had seen them dropping out of the planes, a whole string of bombs at a time.

The impact was loud, the explosion louder and the ensuing earthquake threw most of us off the benches onto the ground.

"Stay down, heads down, grab your gas masks." Oh, yes, the gas masks, I remembered the drill, the awful rubbery smell of the mask and the funny noise the filter made when exhaling. We had had some fun with that. The thought of putting this gadget on in the dark—for what?

"Do you think they are using poisonous gas this time?" Georg asked between his hands.

"You never know, so just keep them handy," the teacher said.

I felt for the big metal canister under the bench behind me, grabbed the ribbed metal and pulled it close to my body.

Both teachers had turned off their flashlights to preserve the batteries. No light came into the shelter from the outside. This meant that there were no cracks in the cement. The hits had sounded closer than they actually were.

Outside it was silent again. A few flak shell explosions could be heard in the distance. The planes had come back for a second wave. Will they come back for a third, or are they low on fuel, or out of bombs? I was familiar with the patterns from reading the newspapers and watching the newsreels.

"Is everybody alright?" our teacher asked. "You can get up and sit on the benches again. It sounds like they are gone."

There was a noise at the steel door. We heard the sound of rubber seals on the outer door being pulled apart, then the inner door opened letting the bright daylight in. I looked into the blinding light and saw the school civil air defense chief with his armband and helmet waving to Herr Krenn.

"Alles in Ordnung bei Euch?"

"Yes..." as a long drawn-out scream relieved the tension of the past half hour from all of them.

"The radio is out, of course, but from all we can see they seem to have gone. The closest hit is four blocks away, on Weginger Strasse. We went up on the roof to check the situation. I think most of the damage was done at the steel mill and there is some heavy smoke from fires on the other side of the Danube. As soon as the siren comes on, let them go home." He waved a modified and abbreviated "*Heil Hitler*" and left.

"Put the gas masks back under the benches. Let's sit up straight again. This was not a fun raid. Does anyone live near the steel mill?"

Nobody answered.

"Will the streetcars run?"

"No, with the electricity out and that many bombs it'll be a while, I guess."

It was shortly after noon that the siren signaled the end of all danger. The long drawn-out pitch was greeted with a burst of cheers inside the shelter. We all gathered our satchels and got up. We started to march out in pairs, the same way we had come in.

"Please be careful on the way home. Stay away from any rubble and fires; there could be unexploded flak shells and bombs, and there are time bombs. Remember Munich last week! School starts tomorrow at eight. Good luck."

We all ran for the main gate leading out of the yard.

I headed for the bus terminal at Blumenau near the railway station. Georg and I took separate busses from there. Without using the streetcar, it would take us about 20 minutes to walk there.

The air smelled of sulfur and dust. Black smoke billowed over the center of town. There were hardly any people in the streets. Georg stopped an older man, the first person we met.

"What happened? Where did they hit? What is burning back there?"

"I don't know. Sure rumbled a lot. Must be bad wherever it is bad. Where do you boys live?"

"I live on the Keferfeld, out by Untergaumberg," I said.

"I live on Wiesenstrasse, towards Kleinkirchen," Georg said.

We hung on the man's lips as if he were the oracle that could tell us how our neighborhoods had fared in the raid.

"Sounds pretty safe to me," the man said, "sounded like most of the bombs came down around the steel works. What's burning back there, I do not know. It is opposite of where you are going anyway, so you are pretty safe. Hurry home boys, your mothers will be worried, too."

We sped up along the familiar route towards the bus terminal. Everything looked the way it always looked. There were no signs of damage along the way.

A small crowd was gathered outside the waiting room in the terminal. Rumors were flying about like the concrete dust in the school shelter.

"Half of Urfahr is wiped out—just flat," one man said.

"They missed the steel works, but they hit everything around it," said another.

"What about Wiesenstrasse?" Georg asked him.

"Don't know about that," the man answered.

It turned out that nobody had actually seen any damage yet. They were all concocting pictures from the noise they had just lived through and were repeating what others had said.

"There will be no busses," said the old man in a bus drivers' uniform. He did not know any details about why or for how long.

"Did they hit the depot?"

"Is the road out?"

"I don't know. All they told me was that there would be no busses, now. They drove off. You had better walk, if you want to find out about home. I'm going home myself."

The driver without a bus stepped into the waiting room to post a note over the schedules.

"I'm going," I said, "Are you going to wait?"

"No, I'll be home sooner than you. See you tomorrow. Want to meet here at seven thirty?"

"No, I think I'll take my bike. Who knows when the busses will start running again?"

"Good. At school then. Good luck, Peter!"

"Good luck, Georg!"

We walked off in opposite directions. I headed for the railroad station. That was a slight detour but I wanted to see if anything had happened there.

As I approached the large, stretched out yellow building I noticed people running in and out, more so than normal, but the front looked intact. A few mail trucks were parked outside, nothing else.

I turned right up the hill towards the main road home. When I was all the way up, I looked back. Now I could see behind the Main Station building and across the main switching yard just outside the passenger station. I shuddered. What I saw looked like my model train after my little brother had walked across it: passenger and boxcars laid out on their sides in neat semi-circles around craters that were decorated with upended steel rails all around. I had never seen such destruction. There were rows of craters across the yard where the bombs had hit. Looking down on it from a distance it almost looked orderly.

There was nobody to talk to on the street. All the ugliness went inside of me. Confronted with the incredible destruction below me, my body re-lived the last hit. The whine, the hiss of the bomb, the explosion, and the vibration throwing us all to the floor. How would it feel if it came through the roof? Would you see it or would it go too fast? Would there be a moment before the big flash?

I thought of my house. My mother, my brother and my sister, they were all there. Were they still there? I panicked. Pictures tumbled through my head, an uprooted garden, a big hole in the red tile roof, the front door blown open, all the windows shattered with the glass all over. I turned and ran further up the hill. My throat hurt. It was from the chemical smoke they released before air raids to obscure the railroad tracks and the area of the steel mill. Had not done much good, this time.

I stopped at the top of the hill and looked around. I was surrounded by buildings so I could not see very much. Nothing was destroyed here. I moved on, directly towards home. It would take me close to an hour to get there. I knew the route well from my grade school days when we had moved to the new house. For the last two months of second grade, I had walked this way twice every day to and from my old school.

As I moved out from in between the buildings, up another little hill, I saw more damage: A small apartment building was missing half of the top two stories. The remaining floors and ceilings were hanging down sadly, steel rods severed from their anchor positions swung slowly with the weight of chunks of concrete still attached to them.

I felt like I was intruding on these people, their privacy ripped open for all to see: their dark green walls in the bedroom, the bed on top of a pile of rubble down below, clothes and pieces of furniture strewn all about, a few feathers from a comforter or a pillow hanging in midair along with the dust that kept trickling down from the broken walls.

Last I saw the people, stumbling around on the remains of their dwelling, one woman crying, two children sitting off to the side, in shock, holding on tightly to their teddy bears.

I stopped. My mouth was dry, my eyes were burning, I was shaking—I was angry. Angry at the planes, angry at the bombs, angry at the people responsible for all this chaos. When I realized that I was no longer moving, I promised myself to continue on my way home, never mind what I would encounter along the way. I had to find out whether my house was intact. I did not want to think the other thing. The house. I wanted the house to be in one piece and everybody in it, too.

206

Up to the right was my friend Hans' house. The big gray block, partly overgrown with wild grapes, with the huge balcony, where Hans and I had played with model cars and railroads. The house looked fine. The garden on the slope below was not fine. But that was where my friend's parents and the other occupants of the house had built their shelter, into the hillside, carved out of smooth yellow clay, because the basement of the house was half above ground and not safe.

Right next to the shelter there was a big crater in the hillside. The garden, wherever it was not covered with loam, was blown bare from the explosion of the bomb that had hit there. I kept my promise to keep walking and I actually walked faster than before. I was almost trotting now. Looking back, I saw that the doors to the shelter were open, not broken and that the cave had not collapsed. So the shelter must have done what it was supposed to do. It had sheltered. I did not want it any other way.

I was now on the stretch along the main railroad tracks leading out of town. Nothing had hit here. The little gardens on the other side of the road tended on weekends by retired railroad workers looked as peaceful as ever. The boughs of fruit trees were full of apples, pears and late plums; the gooseberries had rosy cheeks under their prickly hair, and there was cabbage and red beets, cauliflower and the beginnings of Brussels sprouts on the stems in the little orderly beds around the sheds full of tools and garden chairs.

This always had been a good stretch to walk. Even now, I remembered the excitement of the passenger trains passing with people waving at me and the long freight trains with platform cars full of trucks and tanks on the one side, and the peaceful gardens on the other, with blossoming trees in the spring, flowers throughout the seasons and the smell of soil and growing. I never got bored here. At the end of the stretch I had to cross the railroad tracks, which sometimes was a bore because they kept the bars down forever, before and after each train.

On the other side of the tracks there was the other hill, short and steep, right next to the huge old farmhouse, the one that had given the whole area its name.

I started wondering about what it was like up there, beyond the hill. All my discoveries today had been sudden and around corners. I hurried up the hill, all sweaty now, although it was a cool day, and I kept switching between running and walking, as fast as I could. Two more corners then I would be at the cul-de-sac where we lived. I finally met one person in the street.

"Any bombs come down around here?" I asked the woman who looked at me from her garden.

"Further out by the Leondingerstrasse they say, on the West side."

"Thank you!" I said.

That did not sound close to my house. But I had heard enough false information already. I would not believe anything and anybody but my eyes.

Everything looked peaceful up here on the plateau, the houses, the gardens, the roads. Finally, I turned into my strect. It was straight from beginning to end. But it was not quite level, it had that small rise somewhere half way down its length. All I could see now was the big building next to our house ahead of me, or at least the top of it. It looked normal. So did all the houses on the street.

I ran to the top of that little rise and stopped. I could see my sister on a tricycle pedaling as fast as she could to escape my brother running after her. When I heard their laughter, I started to walk again. I looked very tenderly at the fence around our garden, at the walls of our house, at the flowers growing in the beds along the house, and the big lawn sloping down towards the area where we grew our vegetables and fruits. My mother was coming up the path with a bunch of carrots. When she saw me, she looked at me for a long time before she said, "Thank God, you are here!"

Papa's "Official Portrait"

Wedding August 16, 1931

On the Banks of the Danube

I arrive September 1932

Nasi Bussi - Eskimo Kisses

Hammock Time

Loving my Papa

First House in Linz

Playmate Hertha

Flowering Meadows

Sunday Breakfast

Uncle Otto and Cousin Meta

Uncle Niki Visiting

My Fourth Birthday

Sunday Afternoon

Any Creepy Crawlers?

Being Grownup

First Taste of the Alps

Time for a Rest

213

Papa's Linoleum Cut

Announcing Dieter's Arrival

Proud of Little Brother

Official Peter/Dieter
Portrait

Winter Sports

Visit to New House

Home from Work

Dressed up Brother

215

Summer Vacation

Evening Dip

Playing all Day

My Precious Barges

Our Pride and Joy

Fishing in Boat House

Coffee at Aunt Martha's

Dreaming of Sailing with Papa

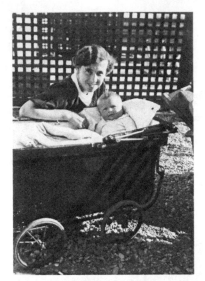

1940: Sister Arrives

First Outing with Sis

Christmas 1940

First Steps

Papa's Merry-Go Round

Little Opa Visit

Backyard Water Games

My Horses Pulling Wagon

Lederhosen Talk

Leave from Army

Mama Visit to Boot Camp

The Five of Us

Scooter Vintage 1941

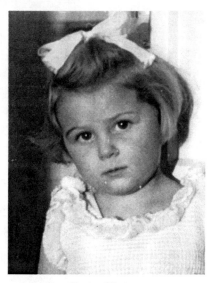

Cute Sister

Portrait for Papa

Vacation with Cousins

Smiles from Hospital   Papa's Parents: Omi and Opa

Sketches from Russia

Christmas Eve Telegram

Uncle Otto's Grave in Kiev

Papa's Grave in
Belgium

A Letter to Papa

3. THE CHAOS

SEPARATION

"Entschuldigen Sie bitte, wo geht's hier zum Schloss?"

"It's easy, Mum, you cannot miss the Castle. Go down to the main road there and then keep on going up towards the lake, about half an hour, there you'll see it on the right, sort of up on the hill, hidden in the trees. It has a big iron gate, no other one along the way, that is where you go in.

"Young man there joining that school in the Castle, maybe?" He said to my mother pointing at me.

"Yes. We live in Linz and my husband, he is in Russia, wants us to be away from there, somewhere safe. You wouldn't know any quarters for us, five of us, by chance?"

"No, sorry, everybody I know is doubled up and tripled up already. They just keep stuffing refugees and the bombed out people in here. We are bursting. Surprised we can still feed them all. So many people in one place. This was a quiet town, I tell you, even with all the tourists in the summer, no more. Just too many people."

"I have been finding this all over, I have looked for quarters in so many places in Upper Austria," my mother said.

"Don't blame you for wanting to get out of Linz, hear it is pretty bad there. We see the planes flying over here, nobody seems to bother them anymore, mornings and afternoons they come and go, never drop anything here. Nothing to hit."

"We saw the station at Attnang-Puchheim on the way up. That place was really devastated. It is because of the railroad, they say. You must have heard the bombs when it happened?"

"We sure could hear the rumbling last week. Sounded like everything was flattened out."

"Yes, it was. I wonder how they can keep the tracks fixed with all that destruction going on, the station is still standing. So far they just hit the tracks and the trains. Well, we had better move on. Thanks for the directions. Good day!" My mother shook the man's hand, I waved, and we turned up the hill.

We found the gate easily, just where the old man had said it would be. It was good to know we were allowed to enter, since it was such a forbidding structure. A fifteen feet high wrought iron gate between solid granite posts and granite block wall. The gravel road led straight up the hill through a dense stand of old oaks and some blue spruces. The road forked around a big fountain right in front of the main entry to the castle. That gate was equally imposing, made of solid wood, with elegantly twisted wrought iron hinges and massive door handles. There was a smaller, regular size door cut into it. It was unlocked.

"Where do we go now? I am lost," I said, looking through the long arched hallway into a big courtyard. My voice echoed from different directions. Smaller hallways lead off right and left, and there was a wide stone staircase right where we stood.

"This looks official to me, let's try it first," my mother said, "Or do you see any signs?"

"No. Let's go and find out!"

I was curious to see more of this huge place where I would live and attend classes until my mother would find someplace where we all could stay together and wait things out.

"When can Ina come home from the hospital? She is well again, isn't she?"

"She is over the scarlet fever but they want to watch for any damage, still. Remember that was a big deal when you had it. Last time I saw her, she was very weak and thin. I'll bring her home as soon as I have found a place for us."

"But that could take a while longer, Mama, you have been looking for a place so long already, she will be scared alone … Why didn't Uncle Leopold with the tree farm take us in? He is Papa's cousin. They are friends, they went hunting together. They have a big place. They have the cage with the little monkeys, I remember. I would love to stay there."

"I don't know why he did not want us. He said they were full, workers and their families, no extra space ..." her voice was trailing off and I thought I could see the sadness, the disappointment in her face again. When she had come home from the day trip, she had had tears in her eyes. It had been the third relative to turn her down.

"Maybe they think they'd get stuck with us forever," she said.

Two flights of broad, well-worn stone stairs had taken us up to the second floor and there we finally encountered a person, a boy who looked at us curiously.

"Heil Hitler, young man. Can you tell us where the Director's office is, please?" my mother asked.

"Yeah, I'll take you there. It's such a big castle, you can get lost in it! Who are you coming to pick up?"

"Well, actually, I am dropping off my son Peter to join you."

"It's fun here, school is easy" he said to me. "What district are you from? We are all from the fourteenth."

"I am from Linz. Realgymnasium."

"We even have locals in class. But they don't live here. Even girls. They're weird. Here we are! See you later!"

He ran off and left us standing in front of another huge door with a small sign that said "DIREKTOR."

They knocked. There was no answer. But we could hear a chair scrape the floor and through the matte glass we saw a figure approaching.

A tall, thin man with gray hair and a tiny mustache opened the door slowly as if it were very heavy. He looked through the opening. "Yes?"

"My name is Mrs. Slonek, this is my son Peter, I talked to you on the telephone last week. We are from Linz, moving into the area, and you said you could take my son until I had found quarters for all of us. We have a relative who owns a house up towards Attersee, we might stay there for a while, and Peter could come to classes from there."

"Yes, I remember. I am *Oberstudienrat* Staudinger, Heil Hitler."

He shook hands with both my mother and me, bowing formally each time, which did not match the official "Heil Hitler."

"Please come in. Have a seat." He pointed to two regal chairs in front of an even more regal desk with curved edges, a cardinal-red velvet inlay for a writing surface, and delicately sculptured legs, which rested in the colorful plush of an oriental carpet.

I immediately disliked this man. His voice and his behavior were that of an old man. But his looks were that of a mean teacher. He reminded me of Oberlehrer Veith, my first grade teacher, same height, same gray hair, same tense expression, same lean look, but he was dressed in brown tweed rather than the black cloth suit that had made Herr Veith look stern like a priest.

"I did tell you, Mrs. Slonek, that what we have here is a closed relocation project for one complete school, the *Third Bundesrealschule* from the fourteenth district in Vienna. We feel very fortunate that we have been given use of a wing of this castle to continue teaching away from the constant disruption of air raids and the threat of bombs. Our school building in Vienna was leveled by a direct hit over six months ago. Luckily it happened at night when nobody was present. There was no chance to rebuild. It will have to wait until after the war. But that is beside the point.

"I also told you that we can make an exception in your case and take your son in on a temporary basis. We also have local students attending classes since their parents do not want them to take the risks of commuting by train to the Realgymnasium in Attnang. The way the raids have been going, I do not blame them.

"When are you moving in, Peter? You will like it here. The boys really have taken to the castle. We have a regular operating *Jungenschaft* so you can work towards your special certifications. And after here, you will never have a classroom like this again, I am sure—magnificent architecture, early *Biedermeier*, tall windows with crystal panes. When are you coming?"

"I brought all my things, they are at the station. I'll take my mother back to the train and then bring my suitcases."

"They have a man here at the castle, Jakob, he takes a buggy to town at least once a day. We will tell him to fetch your luggage, then you don't have to carry it. It is a long walk. Why don't you let me have your claim check?"

"Mama, you put it in your purse."

My mother searched briefly through her purse and brought out a small green ticket.

"Yes, that's it." I handed the ticket to the Direktor.

"Thank you, Herr Direktor Staudinger, that will be easier than carrying them. But I still want to walk my mother over to the station. We have not had much time together lately."

"That will be fine, Peter. Dinner is a six. You can make it back by then. Mrs. Slonek, we need to complete some paperwork before you go, please. Just formalities, but necessary. As I mentioned, there are no fees, the State pays for it all. It comes out of some emergency fund. I assume your emergency is as much of an emergency as ours. We must keep these boys in school so they can carry on the good work after the war. They have a great future ahead of them."

"That was easier than I thought," I said after we closed the door to the Direktor's office. "Let's go so you can catch the early train back."

"We can say our goodbyes here. There is no need for you to walk me down to the station ..."

"No way will I let you go alone," I interrupted. "Who knows when I will see you again." I hooked my arm under my mother's, we found our way out the door and headed past the fountain back out onto the street and towards the train station.

"I hope they feed you enough. Write me right away, please. Also write to Papa. He is waiting for mail all the time. He feels so separated from us. He will want to know all about this school."

"Do you know Mama, that as soon as you leave on this train today everybody in our family will be in a different place. Ina in the hospital, Dieter in this strange camp you put him in, you in Linz, Papa—we only know where he was when he mailed the last letter. I am here, the last of the displaced persons."

My mother squeezed my arm and looked at me. She then let out a deep sigh. "Petz, I do what I can. I did not plan this. I looked forward to a great life in the new house. Look what kind of a mess this has become. What will happen next? I do not know."

I felt sorry for her but I had no idea of how to convey that to her. Everything I thought of to say was either clumsy or would lead to an argument. "We need to find a place where we can be together. Did you see all the refugees on that train we passed? They are all looking for a place to stay ... and that was just one train of many. People and trains are moving in all directions. The armies are moving in all directions. By now, the German army is mostly retreating. We will lose this war and then what?"

'Peter, don't say such things. The Gestapo will lock you up. There is hope. There is the *Wunderwaffe*, you will see," my mother said in a weak voice.

"You don't really believe that, do you?' I had let go of her arm and stepped in front of her. "Mama, please collect Ina and Dieter and come out here. We will camp outside of Aunt Martha's house until she lets us in. She is your father's first cousin and very Catholic. How can she refuse us?" Exasperated I started downhill again.

We walked quietly side by side all the way to the station.

"Please write to me and let me know how you are doing. If there is not enough food, maybe we can get you some extra ration coupons from Musch-Omi."

"If you get extra, keep it for yourself and the children. The children need it the most. They are growing ..."

"Peter, you are growing the fastest, you are getting so tall, your body must stay strong," she pleaded.

We turned a corner down in the village and the station appeared before us. This was where we had to part.

She is going back to an empty house except for Tante Gmeiner, who is no help at all. There will be more raids, more bombs, who knows what is going to happen to Dieter and Ina. When will I see them again? Will I see them again?

229

On the train, on the way out here ... there will be more bombs ... these people in the castle, they are all strangers, I do not know anybody here but Aunt Martha and she does not want anything to do with us ... where is Papa? Still in Darmstadt?

"Mama, I will be fine. Please do not worry about me. Take care of the little ones and yourself. Come back safely—- and soon, please!"

My mother looked at me with that forlorn look I did not care for at all, close to tears and apparently at a total loss what to say next.

"You have an hour until the train leaves. I would like to stay but I cannot miss the first dinner ..."

"Oh, please go, Peter, I can read a paper or walk around town for a little while. I can use a rest. It has been a pretty full day."

"Gute Fahrt"-safe travels- I said to her and kissed her on both cheeks. I looked into her eyes and held her hands. I felt tears welling up.

"Good Bye!" we both said at the same time. We had to laugh. I squeezed my mother's hand and kissed her cheeks one more time. Then I turned and walked away. Before passing the corner, I looked back and waved. She waved back and sent me a kiss. I picked up my pace and headed for the Castle.

I entered the big hallway and found the boys assembling for dinner. It looked like a rather formal procedure.

"You the new guy?" the Group Leader asked me.

"Yes, I am. My name is Peter Slonek."

"Greyhound told us you were coming. Get in the lineup here. Guess you are up front, you are the tallest. You are in the second year?"

"Yes," I said, as I took the first spot in the lineup, looking around self-consciously. I never had liked my tallness because it always put me at the front of the line and made me go first. People wanted me in the back row so others could see and people behind me in the movies complained. In the streetcar or on the bus I hit my head. All the relatives who had not seen me in a while always had to say *'Oh, where are you growing to? You are so tall!*

How tall are you? How is the air up there? I was sick of it. Now, here again, the same deal. I was number one in the lineup—nobody in front to look at to see what to do next, in case I missed a command.

The group leader started to shout his commands.

"Attention!"

"Face right!"

"Abteilung Marsch!"

The thirty-five boys marched through the ground floor hallways, stone floors and archways reverberating with our marching steps, dragging of soles and heels echoing off the walls and the ceiling. Apparently, there was no talking allowed until we all had sat down for dinner.

I was inundated with questions, immediately.

"What does Vienna look like? What is still standing?"

"Is Linz as bad or worse?"

"Is your school gone, too?"

"Did you see any planes downed? Any prisoners?"

"We saw an American pilot come down with a parachute over the lake. The *Wasserschutzpolizei* went out to get him."

"Are you good with the Beebe gun?"

"Do you have a girl friend? You can pick one at the girls' school. We go there on Saturdays for a dance."

"I can't dance. I've never danced in my life!"

"Oh, they call it out, it's just walking, and bowing and linking arms. But you can talk to the girls! If you want to send a letter afterwards, Ollie will take it there. He has connections." The boy next to me pointed at Ollie at the other table.

The food was bland but good. There were seconds and there was a piece of cake for dessert.

After dinner, I found my suitcases standing in the hallway. I picked them up and followed the others to our sleeping quarters. One group split off and led me to a room with twelve wood-frame bunk beds. There was a row of wooden lockers against one of the walls, one for each bed.

They pointed to the one unoccupied bed. It was a lower bunk. I sat on it. The mattress answered with a dry rustle, a strange smell and a lumpy feeling. I looked at my new roommates.

"Straw! You can feel it, can't you?" One of them said with a smile.

I had heard of straw mattresses but had never touched one. There also was a funny looking pillow and two army blankets. "*Well*" I thought, "*it's not going to be for long ...*"

"Keep your stuff in the locker neat. One of the group leaders does an inspection almost every morning. If he doesn't like the way you fold things, he will dump them all on the floor."

"Do you know how to make your bed?"

"Yeah ..."

"No, it has to be a certain way. The edges parallel, tucked in at the foot end. Look at Frank's bed over there. He is the best bed builder around."

I was overwhelmed. I was used to order at home and used to doing my chores. I had never heard of inspections and of things being thrown on the floor.

"The group leaders all have the rank of *Jungenschaftsführer, they* rotate weekly. This week it's Hermann, the one who marched us to dinner. Frank is the one living in this room. He is visiting his parents in Vienna. He is the meanest. Better get on his good side, right from the start or you've had it.

"We don't see the teachers other than in class, in study hall and at meals. They are not around in their spare time."

Hermann came by at nine and turned off the lights.

I lay on my crackling straw which I could feel through two folded up blankets. *Please mother, find a place soon*, I thought. *But who knows what will be waiting for me in a new place.*

Being with all these boys all of a sudden felt strange, living here with them in a castle. The bunkroom was not as splendid as the office of the Herr Oberstudienrat, it must have been some servant's room or a storage place. Plain walls, four feet thick all around, as you could tell from the window and doorframes. It housed twelve boys right now. This was different than all-day war games or track meets, or all-day propaganda marches. I had never stayed anywhere alone over night, away from home, other than a week in the hospital after I had my tonsils removed. Nobody would watch out for me here except I myself. What about inspections, drills, and certifications? I had thought I was coming to a school where you stay after class to eat and to sleep.

I felt trapped. I remembered the letter from my father after we had received a formal invitation for me to join the *NAPOLA* at twelve, an elite political academy, where promising young men were made into young model Nazi adults, trained to be future leaders. *"We will not let them take you, I promise,"* my father had written.

"Your son Peter has been brought to our attention. His scholastic accomplishments have been consistently above average, there are no problems with discipline, he has scored well in sporting competitions sponsored by the school and the Deutsche Jungvolk. We offer you an outstanding opportunity to have your son develop all his talents to his limits, which will serve the *Führer* and the *Vaterland* the best. He is eligible as of now to enter the NAPOLA this fall. Please come and visit one of the NAPOLA'S listed below and convince yourselves and your son of the excellent opportunities these educational institutions offer for the selected few who will be needed to govern the Third Reich ..."

I was wet with sweat just remembering the letter. I had heard about these schools. The boys were pushed to the limits on all counts: Academically and physically. My one big fear was about water sports. I could not swim. I knew they would throw me into the deep end of the pool as soon as they found out. My parents were concerned about other angles. Never mind the swimming. Mind the mind. My father did not believe in the party line. He believed that his son was a sensitive, creative human being who would be destroyed by this environment, disassociated from his parents' heritage and finally swallowed up in the party machine. My parents refused the offer and I was saved from drowning in the NAPOLA swimming pool.

I heard some boys moving about the room. They were whispering and giggling. I was not included and I did not feel left out. I made a mental note to ask them in the morning about what they had been up to.

What was I doing here? Was I any safer than all the others? Mama is in Linz, Dieter will hopefully be back home soon, Ina is in a children's hospital somewhere two hours by train from Linz, Papa is in Darmstadt, maybe already on the way to the front. Linz is being bombed, every city, every railroad station, many living areas are being bombed daily, everything built up is destroyed. People die, Mama could be killed at any moment, Dieter, Papa—how will I know, how will I find out? Who even knows where I am? This is not my school. These people do not know where I come from. Omi and little Opapa, Musch-Omi and Opapa, uncles and aunts, they are all in Vienna. People say Vienna is going to be overrun by the Russians soon, if anything will be left of it after the bombs.

I want to go to Africa when the war is over. Will it ever be over? If the Germans don't win, they won't get the colonies back, then I cannot go to Africa. The Germans cannot win. They are being beaten. But they have new rockets, rocket planes, I've heard them high up in the air— they are testing them, they say they will be ready soon. Then we will beat the hell out of them all, Russians, Americans, English, Canadians, Australians—the whole world is fighting against us. Why? How can one win against all? Those soldiers have been out there for four, five, six years—in Poland, in Africa, in France, in Russia. Papa will be 42 this year. He was forty when he marched through Poland towards Russia, his feet covered with blisters and infections. After almost a year in Kiev he came down with Malaria fever. Finally they sent him back to Germany, to recuperate, now he's going out again, East, West, South? To do what? He writes 'don't worry, we are too old and incapacitated to fight, they'll put us behind the front.' Where 'behind the front?' With all the bombing, 'behind the front' is just as dangerous. The whole of Europe is a front and dangerous. There is no safe place any more.

I liked my new "classroom." It was huge, with a high stucco ceiling, chandeliers, high, arched French windows through which the light streamed in unhindered, warm fruitwood paneling and old-fashioned wallpaper with large flower prints. The furniture looked as it had been collected from all over the castle household: chairs, desks and tables, arranged loosely around the oversized room on the shiny inlaid parquet floor. I found an extra chair and moved it to a table close by one of the big windows. I loved the light. My father always kept after me to be in good light when reading, writing or drawing.

I borrowed my neighbor's Math book.

"What page are you on, Ernst?"

"Oh, I marked the last problem with red pencil, I think it's number 83 or so."

I leafed through the book. It was the same book we had been using in Linz. I found the marked problem.

"Thanks" I said, "That's great, you are about twenty pages behind where we were. I've done all these."

"Wow, who's that?" I nudged Ernst, pointing to the door.

"The tall one is the Mayor's daughter, Anneliese. The little one is Helga. They've been with us from the beginning. They are smart. They used to go to the Gymnasium in Vöcklabruck. But they don't talk much. They are shy. Ollie teases them a lot."

"Anneliese is beautiful" I said without taking my eyes off her. She moved naturally and smoothly, her Dirndl dress flowed elegantly around her tall girlish body.

The two girls took their regular seats that happened to be at an angle to where I was sitting. Looking straight ahead, I was looking at them but they were looking towards the podium where the teacher was getting ready to start the class.

DANCING WITH THE GIRLS

"Peter, you are coming with us tonight to see the girls, aren't you?"

"Oh, it is tonight? Well, I want to, but I don't know what to do. I have never been to a dance before."

"Well, don't worry, it is not exactly a dance. We just walk around in a circle, and the girls walk in the opposite direction. Then if you like one of the girls, you bow to her and then she will join you, link arms and walk with you. All you have to do is hold out your arm, like this," he showed me the position, "and she'll hook under. Then you have a chance to talk to her. It is fun, I tell you. It is very exciting, too, because they don't have to go with you."

"How embarrassing," I said. "What if she refuses me, I wouldn't dare ask another."

"Ah sure, you would. That is the whole game. See whom you can get, who likes YOU. Later in the evening they switch and then the girls can ask the boys. If she asks you back you are really in!"

"What if nobody asks me?"

"You just keep walking until the music stops, then you can sit down. Everybody gets picked sooner or later, it's just a fun evening."

I put on my favorite white shirt with short sleeves and over it the vest my mother knitted for me last Christmas. The Area Group leader for the *Hitler Jugend* came by with a bunch of other boys from another school and picked us up. We marched in formation but not in step, after all, this was a recreational outing.

The girl's school had been relocated in a summer resort, near the lake, in several buildings surrounded by a spacious park with old trees. We entered what looked like an enlarged veranda with wide double French doors and paneled windows all around. The ceiling felt oppressively low to me after the huge halls at the Castle.

There were about thirty-five girls seated along the walls of this room, all looking at us as we entered. The chaperone of the girls rose and came to greet the Group Leader. They talked for a while, laughed and then walked over to an older woman who sat in one of the glass-walled alcoves surrounded by potted plants. She was holding an accordion in her lap. She started to play a frilly polka immediately. The girls' leader motioned the girls to form a circle in the center of the room and told them to wait for the proper music. We had to move into the chairs against the wall. The accordion player switched to a folksier polka and the girls started to dance. Most of them moved very gracefully, making their turns, arching their backs, doing their little steps and big hops. They seemed lost in the music and their movements. All of us did not watch the dancing, we watched the girls. The girls looked rather refined in their dirndl dresses, white blouses and white knee socks.

Ollie, the contact man, sat next to me.

"Do you see one you like, yet?"

"Several, actually, but I need to do more looking!"

"Look fast because the dance will begin in a minute and then you will have to choose. Good luck. Have fun!" Ollie went off to a group of older boys from the other school across the room.

I felt very alone all of a sudden. What would it mean to nod to one of the girls and thus make her aware of my preference, my liking her appearance, my being drawn to her? Would she accept my invitation in front of all the others and come and walk at my arm until the music stopped? What would I say to her? I would have to ask her for her name.

"I am Peter. I am new at the Castle. I just came there from Linz."

"I am Elspeth. Aren't all the others in your school from Vienna?"

Her voice was firm and melodious. She was very slender. Her blonde hair seemed very thin, with curly strands framing her face. She walked matching my steps easily. I could hardly feel the weight of her hand on my arm, but I could feel the electricity, the warmth of her closeness and of her words.

"Yes, they made an exception for me. My father wanted us out of Linz because of the bombing. We will move in with my aunt here along the lake. She has a house but there are other people in it now. So my mother enrolled me in this school."

All the while I spoke she looked at me with little blue eyes, listening to my words. I was wondering if she noticed my nervousness, my sweaty palms and my slightly unsteady step.

The accordion player started giving instructions for a simple dance: Singles sit down, please, pairs switch sides, the boys are now on the inside, the girls on the outside, girls reverse your direction, find your partner, swing him around, one, two, three times, continue ...

There were little mishaps here and there, toes stepped on, partners missed, I felt lucky, I had not missed a step.

"Have you ever done this before, Peter?" Elspeth asked.

"No, never—I really have to pay attention. I am so afraid I will make a mistake," I said smiling a nervous smile.

"We dance almost every night. She is our music teacher," Elspeth said, pointing at the accordion player. "She knows all the songs; we have lots of fun with her. Are you homesick yet?"

I thought for a second.

Yes, I was homesick for my family, for all of my family: my father, my mother. I wanted to be back in our garden, with my brother and my little sister, my friends and their friends, playing games, teaching them gymnastics tricks and doing puppet shows for them. What I really wanted was my father back. Papa had promised to teach me about the garden, the house, photography, drawing and painting, the woods, animal tracks, how to make a bow and arrows, how to make a sling shot. I wanted to learn it all.

"No, not really. I am just getting used to the castle and my classmates, it is all so new. And my mother will be here in a few weeks."

'*If she is not hit by a bomb before then,*' the sentence went on in my head.

The music stopped. I took her hand and bowed to her, the way I had seen in the movies. "Thank you for dancing with me!"

"Thank you, it was fun," she said with a slight curtsy and ran back to the corner where all the other girls congregated.

I looked around for Ollie. A whole group of boys talking wildly surrounded him, but when he saw me standing alone by the wall, he came over to join me.

"How did you like it?" Ollie asked.

"I was nervous but it went all right," I said and nodded. "You said it would be just walking around, no dancing." I turned my head to see if I could spot Elspeth.

"Well, this is their music teacher, she must have taught them, it wasn't this way before, believe me, I was surprised. It was freaky."

"Same circle as before, boys on the outside, girls on the inside, facing one another," the music teacher said loudly over the chatting noise of the two groups.

Ollie rushed to the floor, dragging me behind him.

"Let's do it again, yes?" he asked.

"Sure, why not."

I did not recognize the girl facing me. I had not noticed her before. She smiled at me, I smiled back. We were waiting for the music to start.

'I hope I don't have to walk with her. I don't care for her,' I thought.

"Girls turn right, boys turn right, start walking ..." The accordion struck up a fast march.

I saw Elspeth coming around but it was not time for selecting a partner yet. Shortly after she had passed me, the signal came to pick a partner. I bumped into the boy in front of me because I wanted to go faster.

What if she goes with somebody else?

She did not. I also got to walk with her in the third round.

"Line up outside—we are going home," the group leader called out.

Ollie came up besides me in the dark. "You know what you did?"

"I picked a girl friend," I answered.

"You picked mean Frank's girlfriend. You had better watch out when he comes back from Vienna. Let's talk tomorrow after school."

Ollie was gone before I could answer.

DESTROYING EVIDENCE

"There is fighting in Vienna, did you hear?"
"Who said that?"

"My father sent a note through my uncle. He drove out ...h an Army convoy."

"Do you think they will be able to hold it?"

"Vienna? They have SS troops and a lot of Panzers there. They will keep the Russians out and beat them back."

"What if they don't?"

"They have to—otherwise it is over for us altogether."

"What about your parents, are they going to get out? Will they come and pick you up? What if they do not make it here?"

"Will the Russians then come all the way here?"

"The Americans are moving in from the West. They crossed the Rhine already ..."

"No, they were beaten back; they are still on the other side."

"What about the *Wunderwaffe?*"

"Oh come on, what is it going to be?"

"My uncle knows someone who works in this underground factory, under the mountains, they make and store airplanes there. Rocket-propelled airplanes! No more propellers! Faster than anything in the air. You know the V1 and the V2 rockets? It is just one more step. They developed them into a plane with a pilot and guns. They can shoot anything out of the sky they want, without being shot down themselves, they are so fast."

"Why are they not out?"

"They have been out. They have demolished some of the bomber squadrons that have come over from England. The Luftwaffe keeps it a secret, nobody knows why. But I heard them say it's a matter of weeks ..."

"Well, if it is a matter of weeks, the Russians will be here shaking hands with the Americans or the English or the French and those planes can fly as fast as they want. Where are they going to land?"

"Hey, stop it. No matter what, I think somebody will be coming through here. It will not be the victorious German army. It will be the Russians or the Americans. And if we are lucky we will get a swastika armband and be asked to take a big *Panzerfaust*-Bazooka-Stovepipe under our arms and go out on the roads and fields and wait for the tanks to show up."

"Oh, shut up. You should be arrested as an enemy of the people, a spy, demoralizing the *Hinterland*. And the age limit for fighting is fourteen—you are nowhere near fourteen and neither am I ..."

"Primitivo, give up. It is too late. What will you tell the Russian officer taking over this castle, when he finds the *Hitler Youth* Uniform in your locker? When he finds one in every locker in this place? And your belt buckle and your little bayonet with *Blood and Honor* engraved on them?"

"He will say, oh, yes, you are these good Nazi kids, we do want you to learn something, we have this nice school in Siberia and the next train will leave tomorrow morning and the fare and tuition are free for all you little Nazis ..."

"Shut up, Peter, you pessimist, you *Schwarzseher*, you..."

"Wait a minute, Thomas, he is right. We are not going to win this war any more. That means we are losing it. We will be the losers. You know what happens to the losers. Remember last month in History, he told us about World War I how they treated the captured soldiers..."

"That is against the rules of the Geneva Convention..."

"That only protects the wounded soldiers not prisoners of war. Peter is right, we should think about the uniforms, getting rid of them, maybe hiding them? What do you think?"

"Let's ask *Herrn Direktor Staudinger*, he should know."

"Are you crazy, he is a Nazi as big as any Nazi. He will have you arrested."

"What about Mr. Obermayer? He is reasonable."

"Yeah, he is reasonable. But you know what he is going to say? He'll say 'these are good clothes made of good material, especially your winter uniforms—good thick wool, pants and jacket—it will be a long time before you can buy something like that again, hang on to it. Cut the swastikas off, the buttons, and the epaulets but don't throw them out, please.'

"He's right. They are good clothes. Let's just burn the belts and buttons, and bury the knives ..."

"And you think the stupid enemy is so stupid that he will not recognize a *Hitler Youth Uniform* without buttons and belt? Come on people, be reasonable. They've got to go!"

"If they do not find a uniform on you, then they'll think you have been in the resistance movement... you think? They know we all had to join, everybody, no exceptions. Otherwise you were a goner, harassed ... so what is the big deal?"

"Wassily Ivanovitch might not have had time to read the newspapers and the history of the Hitler Youth movement in the Third Reich. All he knows is that when he finds someone with a few swastikas on his uniform, that that is an enemy. The same enemy that devastated his homeland, who killed millions of his kamerads, somebody loyal to the great *Führer*. And then he goes *Boom Boom* because that is how one wins wars."

"Well. I do not want anybody go 'boom' on me. I'll get rid of mine. Everything. I tell you, we find a spot—maybe up by the Autobahn construction site, by the tunnel we went climbing on last week end—and bury all the uniforms in one spot. Then, when the air is clear, we can dig them back up and have them reworked into something wearable. Just now they are a bad thing to have around. What do you think?"

"What if some clever little weasel goes up there after us, digs them up, and sells them on the black market?"

"Oh, come on Peter, it will be just us and nobody would do that, nobody outside of us will know about it."

"What if we have to wear uniforms for an exercise or a rapport?"

"When was the last time we did that?"

"You never know what some of these *heinis* come up with."

"So we save the brown shirts and the scarves and the knots—they let us get away with just that if they want uniforms. And these we can burn in a flash in the big fireplace upstairs if we are surprised ..."

"Yeah, I go for that."

Sunday morning early, right after breakfast, the six of us carried our bundles through the woods up to the

Autobahn construction site, long abandoned for some more urgent defense work. We had borrowed two shovels from the castle gardener, without his knowledge, of course, and in an open spot where the vegetation had not taken hold again, we dug a rather deep hole and threw our bundles in.

"Are you sure we are doing the right thing?" I asked when the first shovels of dirt fell on the good blue cloth at the bottom of the hole. I was cold, the fog was eating through my thin sweater and I remembered Otto's pointing out what the reasonable Mr. Obermeyer would have said: Warm clothes will be hard to come by ..."

"How would I tell my mother—this uniform was not even mine, it was on loan from my young uncle who had gone on to become a career soldier—officer—what would he think of this cowardly behavior? Well, uncle Hans was in Denmark or wherever, if not long dead, and my mother might never show up here any more ... but I might freeze just all by myself—which would be the worst case—worse than being dragged through an interrogation and being accused of having been active in the Hitler Youth Movement? They cannot take the whole Nation prisoner. They cannot try every one of us. They cannot kill every one that was "active." How could they prove who was active? Do they need proof?

However, there are lots of stories floating around. Reasonable people are committing suicide, just because they did not dare to face the end. Was this the end? The end of what? Are there ends? History does not end. We do end. Do we? Would I end like that Concentration Camp prisoner ended? All bent out of shape and stiff and pale? Maybe it is better to be dead than to live through all this? All this what? All you know is hearsay. Stories. Propaganda? Truth? How much propaganda and how much truth? Can there be truth where there is propaganda? There always is a truth. But who is the keeper of the truth? How do I find it? Is it German? Or AUSTRIAN—what is Austrian? Or American?

My father? Where is my father? Would he have let me bury my uniform? He probably would have thought that is stupid. Why? Because that is how he is. I don't know. I

243

*don't know him. He has been gone for two years. He writes
me letters but they do not contain advice on burying
uniforms. He just writes "It will be good for you to know
what to do in case something happens .. something happens
... something happens ... "death could part us any minute
now" my father had written in his last letter, that sounds
like from a play, play, play—are we all playing this?*

Thump, thump—shovel after shovel had gone on top
of the uniforms. Nobody could see the uniforms any more.
Nobody would know we were involved in the *Hitler Jugend*.
Well, it was only the *DJ—das Deutsche Jungvolk*. You had
to be fourteen to enter the *Hitler Jugend*.

"Let's all promise one another that this is our secret,
no one shall know what is buried here, nobody shall know
that anything is buried here. Promise not to tell anyone
and not to come back alone?"

"Promise!" came from all six with a sense of great
seriousness and a great deal of visible breathing into this
foggy morning.

"Grave diggers, let's go home to the castle before they
start looking for us!" Otto shouted. He put one shovel over
his shoulder and started downhill. I picked up the other
shovel and followed Otto and the others quietly.

REFUGE WITH AUNT MARTHA

Not being able to find quarters for us outside of Linz,
my mother grew more and more desperate. Finally, she
had approached Aunt Martha again, laying out our
situation and appealing to her kindness. My mother
promised that we would move on as soon as we would find
other quarters. Aunt Martha agreed and I received the
good news that we were allowed to move into her house
temporarily, into the big bedroom upstairs with the
balcony looking out over the lake. Everybody in the
surrounding small towns and villages with unoccupied
rooms had to take in people who had lost their homes to
the bombs or refugees who were arriving in long convoys
from areas where the German army had already retreated.
Aunt Martha had held out for a long time, due to good
connections in the community and because she had

registered her three children as living there, too, when in fact, they really lived in their large apartment in town. The Doctor Uncle had died in 1940, prematurely and quietly. Their oldest daughter lost her life in a tragic accident less than a year later. These unexpected losses had made Aunt Martha even more serious and god-fearing than she had been before.

After another heavy influx of refugees coinciding with stricter enforcement of the double-up rules, a family of four had been assigned to Aunt Martha's extra living space upstairs. They had not done things the way Aunt Martha liked them done. They were neither really clean nor had they ever lived in an elegant, spotless house like hers. Through her connections, she had them assigned to other quarters. In order not to get other unwanted tenants, she yielded to my mother's request and took us in, except for Frau Gmeiner, the woman from Berlin who had been living with us in Linz and had become part of the family. There was no extra room in Aunt Martha's house and she did not want the extra person in the one bedroom we would have. In her friendly ways, Aunt Martha was very firm.

She had principles. She went for a swim every morning before anybody else was up, in any weather, except on the coldest winter days. She also went to Holy Mass almost every day. She rode there on an old beat-up bicycle with a creaky chain. She came back with rosy cheeks and her toothy smile was even more beatific than usual.

Aunt Martha and her place were faint memories for me. Like a movie seen a long time ago with some scenes sticking out very vividly but the whole story forgotten. Years ago, on our first visit to her house by the lake, we had driven there in our new car. There had been ample warnings about behaving, being quiet, not touching anything. I had not been looking forward to the visit. It had sounded like going to a dull museum with live people in it.

The house by the lake was a sight to behold. A large modern structure copying the region's farmhouse style, the second story sided with dark stained wood, a pine balcony including a fancy railing all around the second story, wooden window shutters with cutout designs, and flower boxes with red geraniums at every window, wrought iron window grates and door fixtures.

Aunt Martha seemed friendly behind her honey-colored horn rimmed glasses with her big smile, showing large teeth, some of them capped in gold. Her voice was very guttural, I thought it was coming from somewhere else rather than from her own throat. Her husband, Uncle Franz, had been a well known physician, *Herr Primarius*, who always managed to be in another room when we were visiting and only showed up for hellos, goodbyes and for meals.

There were four children, who were aunts and uncle to me since Aunt Martha actually was a Great Aunt—my Grosse Opapa's first cousin. The 'children' were a lot younger than my parents but they behaved and looked like adults to me. They had benign smiles on their faces, never moved faster than in a church procession, and always did the right things.

The real memory for me was the boathouse. Every nice property along the lake had a boathouse. Aunt Martha's held more than just their three boats. It was built on stilts about 30 yards offshore where the water was deeper. It had a boardwalk leading to it with a railing on one side, and nothing on the other. There was a narrow dock on the outside facing the shore for taking on passengers, and there were two cabins to change in, one for men, one for women, a small sun deck facing the lake and steps with a handrail leading into the water. One of the two rowboats was hanging high up on pulleys. It was a sleek racing boat with a seat on rollers and it was off limits to everybody but Uncle Franz Jr. The other was for daily use. It was an expensive-looking craft, with glossy varnished wooden planks, brass screws and fittings, and a real rudder with strings fastened to the sides so the helmsman could steer facing forward. I liked to feel the smooth surfaces and watch the sunlight reflecting in the shiny layer of varnish on top of the rich teak color of the wood. I was not allowed to row this boat. It was too precious. There was the danger of running aground or ramming the boathouse when coming back. The third boat in there was a small sailboat hung flat against one of the walls.

Once we moved in, I liked to spend time in the boathouse by the boat slips. The water was turquoise and clear. I could see all the way to the sandy bottom and watch the little fish darting around the stilts. The fish were almost the same color as the water but they had black stripes across their backs that made them visible. My uncle called them *Schrazen*, the local name for them. I would have given anything for a fishing pole. There were several in the house I considered borrowing. My mother told me that was not up for discussion.

I had another favorite place on this property, the shoreline itself. The lawn came down to the water; there were shrubs and a few larger trees growing along the edge between water and lawn. Where the water started there were pebbles of all sizes and colors. The water was never quite still enough not to make that lapping sound all along the shore, moving from one side to the other, depending upon the angle the waves were coming in from the open water. I enjoyed sitting there, looking at the pebbles, listening to the small waves. Some days I would collect several of the most attractive stones, the reddish ones, or just the clear quartz ones, until my hand could no longer hold them all and then I would slip them into my pocket. There the stones would feel cool and heavy against my warm body, which would make me feel part of the earth.

One of my regular tasks was pumping water from the well under the house into the holding tank upstairs so there would be running water throughout the house all day. The pump was driven by a solid long handle located in the doorway to the cellar. It was made of polished wood and felt good to the touch. I had to push it back and forth along the wall for at least half an hour, if not longer. I could feel the water being pulled up in the pipe and then running into the tank, relieving the pressure on the handle. I was allowed to stop only when the tank was full. The water level in the tank was indicated by a metal weight moving along the wall to a certain mark, much like the weights on a grandfather clock. Some days it took a long time before that thing would even start moving. I had to rest several times on the way, which brought Aunt Martha's smile looking through the doorframe above: "We are not full yet, are we? You are a good boy, just keep at it!"

There are two distinct food memories in my mind from that stay that over-shadow all others: *Hallimasch* and *Asperln*. Both items were edible -of sorts- and therefore prominent in our diet of diminishing rations.

Hallimasch is an edible mushroom that grows along roadsides and almost everywhere else. It is abundant and easy to find. It does not hide under fallen leaves or moss. It comes out of the earth a dirty orange-yellow, with a tall stem and a big cap, frilled at the edges. It had always looked poisonous to me and we had never picked it before. Aunt Martha had declared them edible. After eating these revolting mushrooms for weeks on end without any discomfort other than its horrible slimy taste, even I had to accept its edibility. No matter what my mother and Aunt Martha did to these fungi, they tasted vile. With shrinking rations and frequent shortages in the stores it was essential to supplement our food supply with creative other edibles. I was always hungry and my siblings no less so. Our choices were limited. We had to eat something. Hallimasch were better than nothing, probably full of vitamins and other natural goodies.

Asperln were the dessert. This is a fruit unlike any other fruit. About the size of a large walnut, brown in color, with sandpaper-like skin and a crown of dried spiky flower petals. When ripe, the insides look like those of a rotten apple or pear and if that is not enough punishment, there are about eight stones somewhat larger than cherry stones sitting in a neat circle in the center of the fruit. The process of eating an Asperl involves pulling off the spiky leaves, as much of the skin as possible, munching through the pulp until all eight stones are spit out and then enjoying the pulp. If that was possible. Well, it was sweet and soft and you could eat ten or fifteen before your stomach said HALT. Just like the Hallimasch, they grew in abundance as the fruit of a large shrub in Aunt Martha's huge garden. They were harvested hard and green, ripened very slowly and, as one can imagine, were not much in demand. There were plenty to be had at any time.

After watching the fish in the boathouse for a long time, I decided to try my hand at fishing. Since I was not allowed to use the equipment in the house, I fashioned a fishhook from a pushpin, tied it to a length of strong thread and baited it with a worm I had dug up at the shore. The young fish immediately took to the new food. They converged in a fury onto the worm and tore it off the needle in little bits and bites. Without any barbs on the hook, that was an easy game for them. I never hooked one of these voracious feeders. My pail with water remained without fish for many days spent with great patience feeding those little *Schrazen*. One day, a bigger fish came darting out from behind one of the pilings and swallowed the whole worm and needle. I pulled excitedly on my string, unfortunately, halfway up to the surface the fish spat out the hook and swam away with a short piece of worm still hanging out of his mouth. I was very disappointed. When I related the story to the neighbor who was fishing off his pier every day, he explained to me how to 'set the hook' by yanking immediately after the strike.

I started another fishing day with new hope. I now had learned that I could lure bigger fish out from their hiding places and if I yanked the line right after the bite, I might be able to land one. I baited the needle time and again, mostly for fingerling food. Late one afternoon came the big strike, the yank and the landing in the bucket. I was jumping with joy as much as the fish was jumping with panic.

"I've got one, I've got one!" I yelled and danced around my bucket, which now held one Schrazen, about five inches long, desperately trying to find a way out of his round prison.

"What is the matter Peter, are you alright?" my mother called. She was out on the sun deck darning a big pile of my socks.

I carried the bucket out to her. "Look, I caught a fish with my needle hook!"

"Oh the poor thing, why don't you let it go!" she said.

"We cannot eat it? It's too small, is it?" I said with sadness in my voice.

"It will be nothing but bones, even the bigger ones people do not like to eat because they have so many bones," my mother said.

"Why don't you sit down with me here for a while? Give the fish and yourself a rest. You have been in there every day for hours."

"I enjoy it. It is fun. Aunt Martha doesn't mind, does she?" I asked.

"No, she gave you the bucket and told you on which side there are most of the *Schrazen* or whatever you call them. She's been awfully nice to us."

"Where are Dieter and Ina?" I asked. I did not want to get involved in a discussion about Aunt Martha's 'niceness.' I had formed my own opinions about her. Why hadn't she taken them in at the beginning when my mother had first asked her? Now we were the lesser of two evils, strangers versus family, but she was already scheming on how to get us out. This was not a refuge for us. My mother was still looking for quarters for all of us, including Frau Gmeiner, who was holding the fort in Linz.

"They are napping, Ina still is weak from her diphtheria, Dieter is out from running around here. He hasn't been outside that much for a long time. It is good for him. He has not been crying for Papa so much either."

The fish in the bucket had a nervous fit. It raced around and up and down, finally it jumped—but only to land back in the bucket. I stared at it. I felt sorry for the fish. That needle must have hurt his mouth. I felt the roof of my mouth with my tongue to see if I could find a wound there. After a short contemplation I emptied the bucket into the lake.

"I want to catch a real big one, so we can eat it," I said, "wouldn't that be nice?"

Before that big catch could happen my mother's perseverance with the local authorities to find us another place to stay—Aunt Martha had claimed officially that her family needed the space—paid off. We were given a name and an address a few miles from our current quarters, close to the little town of Attersee.

NEW QUARTERS AT THE LAKE

We got off the bus one stop short of the town of Attersee. The main road followed the shoreline as closely as it could. There were small parcels of land along the lake, too small to be built on, fenced towards the road. Some had small docks stretching like fingers into the water, others were just a place to pull an old boat ashore. The houses were built on the other side of the road, with a hillside rising sharply behind them. There were sloping meadows and many trees. The house we were looking for turned out to be a big farmhouse squatting broadly on an expanding hillside. The back of the house was buried partly into the hill and its front was grinning from ear to ear with a balcony full of geraniums looking out at the vast lake.

Herr Kastinger met us at the barn door.

"It must be you who's moving in with us, isn't it?"

"Yes," my mother said, "I am Frau Slonek. *Grüß Gott!*"

Herr Kastinger was a tall, well-fed man with a reddish complexion and an open, friendly smile. He kept swaying from side to side as he looked at the four of us, standing in front of him feeling like beggars. Our suitcases sat on the grass next to us.

"Let me show you this room. It's upstairs. It is our bedroom. My wife and I sleep there. Well, we did. I guess it's yours now for a while."

He led the way up an open staircase of well-worn wood, creaking under our steps. At the top, there was a small hallway, with a dark and a light end to it. The light end lead out in the back onto the hill and the dark end lead to three doors. Herr Kastinger opened the middle one.

"Here it is." He stepped inside and motioned us in.

"The lady in charge of the refugees said we'd have to double up for a while. No way for you and the kids to live where the bombs come down every day. No life. Bad war. I wish it was over. Don't make sense."

I noticed a slight limp on the man when he moved over to the windows. "You have a nice view of the lake here, keeps it cool in the summer, too."

There were two big windows overlooking the street below and the lake and the hills on the other side of it. It was very peaceful.

My mother looked around at the beds.

"Did we tell you, Herr Kastinger, that we have this lady from Berlin with us?"

"I was wondering where she was, they told me you were five, will be mighty crowded for you in here. Was plenty big for my wife and me."

"Do you think we could have another bed for her?" my mother asked, her voice trailing off slowly. There were two big double beds pushed together in the center of the room, and there was a couch in one corner.

"Well, I don't know. Getting mighty short of beds around here. We are sleeping on the couches downstairs in the family room, my wife and I and my daughter. The lady next to you—she's from Berlin too, coming to think of it—has one in there for herself and her little boy, no couch in there, and then the Yugoslavs down by the barn—well, I'll go have a look. But I'm not promising anything."

He swayed out the door and we heard him walk down the stairs slowly and mumbling to himself.

We looked at each other, out the window, and all around. The room had warmth. Somebody had lived in it comfortably and happily. There was even a tiny basin with holy water hanging next to the door.

"Please can you get our suitcases from downstairs," my mother said. I noticed her visible relief over finally having found a place for us. She seemed to enjoy the friendliness with which the man had received us.

"I am tired, Mama," said Ina, and sat down on the couch.

"Can we go swimming when it gets warmer?" Dieter needed activity. He felt frustrated living so near to the lake and not being able to go in it.

I dragged two more suitcases into the room. Mother had opened the bigger one of the closets, the one with the flowers painted on the outside. "Put them right in front of this, please Peter."

"Thank you."

"This room is bigger than the one we had at Aunt Martha's, isn't it? Where are we going to put Aunt Gmeiner?"

"If we get another couch, we can put it here between the big bed and the wall."

"Boo, but I am not sleeping on this side next to her, she's snoring all the time," Dieter was upset.

"I've told you many times, Aunt Gmeiner lost all her things when a bomb hit her house in Berlin. She has nothing left except what she carries in that little case of hers, so let's not make it more difficult for her, yes?"

"What if our house gets hit—how will we know? And people will steal my toys and my books when they are thrown all over," Dieter asked.

"Will they steal my toys, too? I don't want them to ..." a big howl came from the sofa corner. Ina had been very touchy ever since she had come back from her three weeks away from her Mami in the hospital.

Mother stopped putting clothes away and went over to her little girl, sat down next to her and put her on her lap.

"Now, where are you going to sleep, Ina-Maus?"

"With you Mami, in the big bed. And my doggie too, yes?"

There was a light knock on the door.

"Come in" my mother said.

It was Herr Kastinger, his ruddy face beaming: "I found a bed frame in the barn, need to dust it off and put it together. But no mattress. Guess we can put some straw in big sacks and a heavy blanket on top ... is that going' to be all right?"

"Sure, Herr Kastinger, I really appreciate your being so helpful and kind. I don't know where we would be without you. Thank you!"

"It's no fun for any of us. Can't last much longer. It's crazy, everybody is crazy. Who needed this war? Not me. Didn't get me at least, got kicked by a cow, broke my knee, hurts a lot when it rains or gets cold, and I can't move fast, but sure beats fighting this war. I'm too old, but they wouldn't care. They took old Alfred next door, just three weeks ago, he is 62. That's crazy. He'll blow up a lot of tanks. *Volkssturm*, what an insane idea. Children and

253

grandfathers, supposed to hold up the enemy. My ass -oh pardon me—I get carried away thinking of poor old Alfred."

"My husband was 40 when they called him up, not exactly soldiering age either. I wonder where he is now."

"Is your lady coming today?

"If she can get a ride, she will, but I'm not sure. It'll be all right, she can sleep on the sofa tonight, if she comes. Take your time with the bed. Peter can help you bring it up when you are ready. Just let us know. Thank you for taking such good care of us."

My mother's voice was softer now. She had found a home for her flock. It wasn't much but it was in an idyllic spot, it was safe from the bombs, and it felt solid. The man seemed to have a heart without boundaries. Strangers in his own bedroom, a family in the space next to the barn, a mother and child in the extra room. Four families in a house built for one.

"Let's have something to eat," my mother said, lifting the food bag up from the floor onto the table.

"Shall we leave the table right here at the end of the beds? That way we can all sit here and look out the window at the lake, yes?" my mother asked. She unpacked the half loaf of bread we had picked up yesterday as part of our rations.

"What are you putting on the bread?" Dieter asked.

"We have some nice fresh lard, which Aunt Martha gave us. It has little bits of bacon in it, crunchy ones." Mother was selling the only choice she had to offer.

"Can I have something on top?" Dieter asked.

"What would you like?"

"The green stuff we had the other day, tasted like onion almost," he said.

"Oh, you mean chives. I think there are some left. They would be in the bag over there, wrapped in wet paper."

Dieter went over to the other bag and retrieved a small bundle of chives, the tops sticking out from the soggy newsprint paper around them.

"The cutting board is ... let me think ... in the little suitcase. Let us set this up right, from the beginning. Where shall we have the kitchen corner?" She looked around in the room. Every space seemed to be taken already. There was a massive chest of drawers in the far corner. It had a marble top, which held a big porcelain washbasin and a porcelain water jug with a wide mouth and a big handle and two matching glasses for brushing teeth.

"We have to keep that for our bathroom corner, so we can all wash. How about one of the nightstands? We could move that one over here, it also has a nice marble top, just made for a kitchen table. Peter, can you chop the chives for Dieter, and for yourself, if you want some."

"I don't want green stuff on my bread," Ina said in a whiny voice.

"No, I know you don't like it. You just get the lard, yes?" Mother reassured her. She started to cut the bread.

"When I was a little girl after World War I the bread we had was so dry, my mother had a hard time to keep it from falling apart when she tried to slice it for us. Some ingredient must be in short supply, I think it is the shortening. This bread here looks just like the one back then."

My mother managed to keep three slices sort of together, arranging them on the small plates we had brought with us. The jar with lard was covered with one of Aunt Martha's washed and re-used butter wrappers, doubling for the parchment we used to use for our canning jars, and tied with a string. I untied the knot and mother spread a thin layer of the lard on each of the breads. She made sure that everybody got the same amount of bacon bits.

"What are you going to eat, Mama?" Dieter asked, looking at the three breads.

"Oh, I am not hungry right now, I think I'll wait for dinner," she said.

"Mama, you have to eat, too, I know you must be hungry, you only had a half slice of bread for breakfast," I said from the back of the room where I was scraping the finely cut chives onto a plate.

"We have to find the baker here and see when they issue the bread. I'll ask Frau Kastinger as soon as we are done. Maybe we all can go into town and see what it is like. I have not been to Attersee for a while."

"That will be fun. When will we go and get our bicycles from Aunt Martha's place?" I asked.

"We can do it tomorrow. Today it is too late. We'll have to ask Herr Kastinger where we can put them."

"I am sure they'll be fine in the back of the house," I said.

"Still, we want to make sure they are not in the way. There are a lot of people living in this house, you know." Mother was feeding Ina with pieces of the bread.

Dieter and I had spread the chives over our slices and were eating the bread keeping close to the plates so the crumbs would not fall on the floor.

"Do we have any milk left?" Dieter asked.

"No, sorry, remember, we drank it all before we left Aunt Martha's so we would not spill it, or have to carry it. Somebody told me we would have to pick up our rations at the milk shed, over in the little bay we came through on the bus. That would be rather far from here."

"I can go by bicycle once we get it," I said. "It is too far to walk from here."

"I'll put Ina down for a nap, when she wakes up we'll go to town. Herr Kastinger said you could go across the street and check out the dock. I think he has an old boat there, too. Take a look but be careful, the lake is still very cold, don't fall in!" She lead Ina by the hand to the bed and tucked her under the feather bed. She gave her a kiss. "Have a good rest! You need to be strong for our big walk later!"

LOOKING FOR GOODIES

The steep meadow up above the farmhouse had not been mowed in a while. That was the way I liked it best: tall grasses in all shapes and heights, big batches of marguerites and bachelor buttons, a few bright red poppies, lots of larkspur and dozens of other little flowers sparkling from below the greens.

My mother had asked me if I could forage higher up on the meadow for some *Saurampfer*. Aunt Martha had introduced us to this green leafy plant growing freely along roads, walkways and wherever greens flourished. It was tall and had graduated from neglected weed to a substitute for spinach as supplies of fresh vegetables got scarcer and scarcer. Its name contains the word *sauer,* which means sour. We all liked it fine as long as it did not come to the table too often.

I wanted company for this assignment. I had found a friend and mentor in Miro, who lived with his parents in the room next to the barn downstairs from us. They had fled from Yugoslavia when the German army was driven out by the partisans under Marshal Tito. Miro was a couple of years younger, a head shorter, and ages wiser than I who was learning rapidly from him. He spoke German better than his parents did but at times I still had trouble understanding what he was saying.

"Miro, I have to go for some *Saurampfer,* and maybe some mushrooms, my mother wants to have something different for us to eat. Want to come with me?" I asked but I knew that Miro would come anyway. Miro always went when he felt like it. He did not listen to his parents and they did not seem to care.

"Let's go—we'll get lots of eats first and then we go look for goodies." Miro was ready.

"What do you mean, goodies?" I asked.

"You'll see, we go higher this time, up past the top of Herr Kastinger cable car. That's where we find goodies," Miro said and smiled his Slavic smile—broad, full of secrets and mischief.

We started climbing up through the tall grass, mostly following previous paths under the cables of the funicular. We really wanted to ride that little cable car but Herr Kastinger refused to let us. He said the motor is broken. He used to use it for bringing hay down from the upper meadows and for going up himself to check on the cows on the pasture up there. The whole setup consisted of several wood beam supports holding up the cable and a big wooden crate suspended from two rollers by steel bars as the 'gondola.' A small electric motor at the barn-end of the contraption drove the pulley system for the car.

Miro went up the hill fast. He was tough. I had grown rapidly during the last few years and my organs had not kept up. I had trouble breathing.

"Wait for me, Miro, not so fast, I can't run uphill."

"I'm going slow, for you, alright I wait." Miro was impatient. He made a face. I threw up my arms. He laughed.

"Peter" he said "you must get more food, good food. Eggs, meat, meat from swine, bacon from swine, Herr Kastinger bread. He say he will kill sow soon. Then we will eat. You know, my father go work for other farmer, he bring smoked bacon, very good."

"Stop it Miro, please, I am getting hungrier when you talk. Let's find some *Saurampfer*."

"That is no good, taste like sour spinach."

"But it has iron in it, it makes you strong, my mother says. Here is some, but its old and the bugs ate at it. No good."

"I saw a big batch over by the trees up there," he pointed ahead of us, "I'll find it again. Come." Miro was climbing again.

"Here, here it is! Come, look! That's it, isn't it?" Miro had ripped a few plants out and held them up high.

I caught up. I was out of breath. "Yeah, that's them."

I took one of the plants and looked at it closely. It had nice big leaves, looking like big radish leaves, and a thick green stem curved back and forth between the offset leaves. It ended in a reddish "flower" made up of tiny red seeds. The birds loved those later in the season when they had dried out.

"You want pick them now or when we come back— then we don't carry them all the time. Only down to Mama." Miro always made fun of my errands for my mother.

"Break them off above the root, Miro, so they grow back again."

My father had told me to do that with all plants. Pulling out the roots means killing the plant. You don't want to do that. I felt badly when I pulled a whole plant out of the ground by accident, because the soil was moist, or the stem wouldn't give. I got rid of the root anyway, so there would be no evidence, not even for me to look at.

Quickly we had collected a whole pile of the edible plants.

"That enough for Mama?" Miro asked. There was a slight mockery in his voice.

"Miro, shut up. Yes, that looks like enough for one meal. Thanks."

"We will put them all here under the support for the funicular, then we will easy find it on the way down, yes?" Miro looked for me to agree.

"Yes, Miro, that is good. You will help me remember. It looks so different when we come downhill. Remember the day we collected all the mushrooms? We almost didn't find them again."

"Come, Peter, we go up in the woods. Maybe there are still mushrooms from the last rain."

"And what about the goodies?"

"Do you ever shoot gun?" Miro put his hands and arms up in a mock rifle aiming position.

"No. When we visited my uncle who has a nursery, he is a hunter. He took us to look at the deer, but there was no shooting. I wanted to try."

"Maybe today you can. Many bullets up there. Maybe also gun."

"Really? From the planes? Did a plane crash up there?" I was getting excited. I saw myself crawling around in a broken up enemy plane.

"No. Just bullets and guns. Soldiers throw them away," Miro said with authority.

"Why up there? We've never seen soldiers up here." I wanted a logical explanation.

"My father say they afraid. They hide. They no march with others on street. If SS men find them without gun, they shoot them. Deserter." Miro was excited now, too. That made his German worse, he kept forgetting his words.

"So, if we find a gun we can shoot it? What do we shoot at? Is it dangerous?"

"Mama says it is dangerous but if we careful like soldiers is not dangerous," Miro said, smiling.

259

"Did you shoot one before?"

"No, my father was with me when we found. He did not touch. He said I must not touch."

This was the first time Miro sounded not absolutely sure and positive to me. I seized the opportunity to go into the lead.

"Let's go and look. I want to try. We shot BB guns at the school. I hit a bird after everybody else had missed it. It was exciting."

We scrambled further up the hill and finally got to the edge of the patch of dense forest Miro had mentioned earlier.

"Let's look for mushrooms, too," I said, "My mother thinks there must be some left."

"I look for mushrooms, I always look for everything!" Miro said. He was laughing.

We moved along the edge of the forest, where the light was still getting through the trees. There was that certain musty smell in the air that could mean mushrooms but we did not see any.

"Let's follow this path. This looks like a path, doesn't it?" I really wanted to go in deeper and see if we could find a rifle.

"Soldier follow path, then they go hide," Miro said, nodding his head.

We came to a small clearing, which allowed us a view of the top end of the funicular. It was below us now, quite a bit.

"I've never been that high up, it is nice up here," I said.

"Nice woods—no people. My father see deer. Come in here." Miro left the clearing and disappeared into the trees.

It was dark in there. Although the trees were not very close together, there was not enough light for underbrush to grow.

"Ouch!" I yelled.

"What's the matter, you hurt?"

"I ran into a branch with my forehead. I did not think they were that low."

"Don't think, LOOK!" Miro said, mocking little binoculars with his fists in front of his eyes. "You are bleeding."

"Where?" I wiped my forehead with my hand. I looked at the hand and it was bloody. I pulled a handkerchief from my pocket and dabbed at my head where I thought the bleeding came from. It didn't hurt. There was just a little spot of blood on the handkerchief. "It's fine."

We came across some tracks. More than one person had made his way through here. It was not a path but we followed the tracks. After winding through the trees for a few minutes, we saw a few rays of sunshine shining through the canopy lighting up some ferns. There were some fallen trees and tree stumps.

"Here, look!" Miro held up a metallic blue barrel with some sort of wood at the end.

"They broke the butt off," I said as I came nearer. "Why do they do that?"

"My father say, army tell them to do, nobody can shoot any more." Miro turned the rifle around. Where the butt had been there was an ugly mess of splinters, all sticking out in different directions.

"If you hold this up against your shoulder and shoot, these splinters would go right into you. Even the BB gun we shot had some recoil. Imagine this one. Much more powder, much thicker barrel.

"Let me see!" I reached over and took the rifle from Miro. I felt the cold steel, the weight, and the remainder of the polished wood.

"Don't point at me, you don't know if it is loaded." Miro sounded serious.

"No, I would not do that. My father told me all the time. Not even with toy guns."

I brought the broken carbine up into aiming position, I looked through the sight and went "bang." I laughed. "It would be fun. But it is heavy! Do you think it is loaded?"

"No, no, don't shoot Peter!" Miro shouted and came closer.

"No, I mean open the bolt." I laid the rifle down on the ground, slid the bolt up and back. The smooth metal clicked into all the places the way it was supposed to. "The metal feels good. It is beautifully polished. This soldier must have taken good care of it."

The bolt was now all the way back. There was no shell in the magazine.

"Do you think we'll find some ammunition?" I said and looked around.

"We can look. When my father and I found there was many."

We both started combing through the area around our find. I had not gone far before I stumbled over a wide shiny leather belt. It had the leather cases for the rifle bullets on it. "Miro, come here, I found a belt!" I tried to lift it but it moved only a little bit. It was very heavy.

"It is heavy, Miro, the bullets are still in it."

I opened one of the cases. It was full of brass shells, detonators intact, and tipped with sleek projectiles. I pulled one of them out. I had seen soldiers loading their rifles in the newsreels, many, many times. I walked back to the rifle and fitted the bullet into the groove. Then I grabbed the shaft with my left hand and asked Miro to do the same: "Hold on to this, Miro."

I then copied the movement I had observed so many times. Bolt up to the middle, slide forward, and lock down to the right. The bolt clicked into place.

"We are loaded and ready. Want to shoot?" I asked.

"No, I don't want to get hurt. It is too heavy for me. It is too heavy for you, too. Don't be dumb." Miro said. He was serious. The steady smirk had disappeared from his face.

"If I hold it this way..." I lifted the rifle up and let it hang in my outstretched arms on my side "the recoil will just go by me. See? Like this."

"Put it against tree first, makes it more steady. But why shoot anyway?" Miro was uncomfortable with the idea.

"It's fun. And it is exciting. I love shooting." I said.

"What are you going to shoot at?" Miro asked.

"Nothing. Anything. Wherever it hits. We are safe here. Nobody around. It will hit a tree, or the ground."

"Do it. Put it down. Against the tree, is safer!" Miro pleaded.

"Yes, I'll hold it against the tree—see, here in this groove, and now, go behind me, way back—one, two, three ...." I counted and pulled the trigger.

The shot sounded like a minor explosion amidst all the trees, there seemed to be an echo from every tree along the way, the broken butt smashed into the bark of the big fir I had selected as my recoil-stopper.

I was shaking from the effort it had taken to hold on to the rifle.

"Boy that thing really jumped. Did you see where the bullet went?" I asked Miro who was still behind a tree in the back.

"No, went too fast, too loud. I close my eyes."

"I want to do it again. This time no tree for support." I was into the adventure. I took another shell out of the belt and loaded the carbine.

"This time I am aiming at the tree over there, the one with the big branch low down. See it?" I asked.

Miro pointed "That one?"

"Yes. Watch!"

I had the rifle in my hands, arms slightly bent both to my right, and the rifle pointing straight ahead at the tree. The butt end was sticking out behind me. I checked my line-up a couple of times, and then pulled the trigger again.

The explosion lacked the crackling impact of wood on wood but the rifle recoiled backwards and pulled me down. However, I had held on and had kept it pointed.

"Wow!" I shouted when I got up. I brushed off my hands and my pants.

"Let's go look if I hit the tree," I said and ran up ahead. Miro followed.

"You are stupid. You get hurt." Miro said once he caught up with me.

"I hit it, I hit it! See, here." I had my finger on the splintered bark where the sap started to ooze out of the tree's trunk.

"You want to try? It's easy!" I asked.

"No, I don't want to. We go home now." Miro said.

"I want to come back here. You think we can find the place again?" I was very excited.

"I think we can find it. If not, we find another." Miro said.

We followed the path back.

"Miro, are we going uphill?" I asked after a while.

"Yes, here we go uphill, but not all the time," Miro said as he looked around.

The dead brown twigs of the trees around us looked all the same. It was like looking into a big brown muddy lake. The path was mostly in our imagination: fewer twigs, more space between trees—winding along, always found anew at the next turn.

"We did not come this way before." I was not so sure whether we were heading into the right direction.

"Next time downhill, we go downhill." Miro was very matter of fact on this. Growing up in a refugee camp had reduced his sensitivity and made him numb to some fears.

"No—- a dead ..." I screamed but my voice went dry and silent. I stopped in mid-step and waved Miro up ahead.

"... soldier."

I looked in awe at the body curled up in the dry pine needles under the trees. I could not see the face, only one hand that was laying limp at the end of the arm, palm up.

"Maybe he is sleeping," I thought, "but the shots would have awakened him." I tried to get a closer look, but without moving. I was afraid to see the face. The uniform had the black ornamentation of the SS, with the white runes embroidered on them.

"There is blood by his head. He shot himself." Miro said. "My father found one before."

I noticed the big dark stain in the needles around the upper end of the body.

"Where is the gun?" I asked.

"You are going to look for it? Not me." Miro said, shaking his head vigorously.

"Not me either," I said. I felt nauseated—there was an odor in the air, not from pine needles and pitch, not from sun and decaying wood.

"I'll tell my father, he'll get the shoes and the coat. They are still good." Miro said.

264

I shuddered at the thought of going near the dead man and touching even just his clothes or shoes.

"It is getting late, we have to go home, pick up the Saurampfer on the way." I had turned and headed downhill, without a path and without waiting for Miro's reply.

The twigs scratched at my clothes and my bare arms and legs. I ignored the pain. I held my arms outstretched in front of me to protect my eyes and my face.

"We'll never hit the funicular if we go down here." Miro said.

"We'll turn left on the next path we come across." I said firmly.

"Maybe there is no path this way?" Miro countered.

"Well, the other one did not go anywhere but up." I was not paying attention. The dead man was on my mind. Why had he shot himself? Maybe somebody else had shot him? Should we tell the police? Would he be buried? Was somebody waiting for him at home? Where did he come from? My mother had said that the last SS Company through here had been all young boys from Hungary who had been made to look like SS to scare the enemy. This poor boy just scared himself.

Where is my father? Is he lying somewhere dead? Unburied or buried with many others? Or under a tank? Or sealed into a bunker after a direct hit. Was he captured? Starving? Was he being tortured? For being German? He's Austrian. He had told me once that in France, when the locals found out that he was from Austria they were much nicer to him afterwards. My father is gentle and loving. Nobody would do him any harm.

IS HE DEAD IS HE ALIVE WHERE IS HE I WANT HIM BACK I WANT HIM HERE WITH ME I WANT TO LIVE I WANT TO GO BACK TO MY HOUSE I WANT US ALL TO BE TOGETHER AGAIN NOT WANDERING THE STREETS LIKE ALL THESE REFUGEES NO HOME NO PLACE TO GO AWAY FROM THE WAR THERE IS WAR ALL OVER IN ALL DIRECTIONS THEY ARE COMING FROM ALL DIRECTIONS THEY WILL CRUSH US AND NOBODY WILL KNOW WHERE PAPA IS LOST GONE ALL OF US LOST

GONE DEAD NO HOME NOBODY HOME NOBODY
KNOWS WHERE ANYBODY IS ...

I was thrashing the twigs and branches in front of me
struggling downhill. After a while suddenly there was more
light and there were bigger trees and there was a path.

"Here we are." I stopped and turned around to Miro.

"You cry? You hurt?" Miro asked, looking at my face
and arms. "You bleeding again."

"Oh, just scratches from the trees," I said. I wiped the
tears off my cheeks with the back of my hand. I made an
attempt of laughing off the embarrassment. I'd only seen
Miro cry once after his father had beaten him with a belt.

"I want my father back."

"War will be over soon, then father will come home."

"They are still shooting. I am afraid they'll get him. If
he is not dead already. We haven't gotten any mail from
him in weeks."

"Too much confusion, roads all stuffed up with people,
how can mail come?" Miro was more practical.

"It always got through, so far." I said.

"You get mail, soon." Miro said and put his hand on
my shoulder.

The warmth of the little hand felt reassuring to me.

"You think the funicular is over there?" I pointed along
the path ahead of us.

"Maybe. We'll see." Miro said. "Let's go and see."

We fell into a downhill trot and with fewer dry
branches in our way we could move better. We saw more
and more sun coming through the trees and finally we
were out on a meadow in bright sunshine.

"I like the sun," I said and spread out my arms.

"I like it too!" Miro shouted and did three somersaults
in a row in the tall grass, tumbling downhill.

"You better not let Herr Kastinger catch you trampling
down his tall grass, you know he gets mad—it is harder to
mow and the cows don't like the smell of us ..."

"Cows don't smell. Cow shit smells!" Miro was off
again rolling down the hill sideways.

"Maybe the deer sleep here and break down the
grass," he shouted when he got up, "Let's find cable car.

Hey, here is more good *Saurampfer*. Want to pick some more?"

"Little bit, it looks nice and big. But the big leaves really taste sour."

"My father don't eat that stuff. He says is bad for him. My mother laugh and give it to me and my sister. My father like meat. From pig and from sheep. We had many pig and sheep on our farm at home. All dead now. Eaten by soldiers. First German then Serbian." Miro's face was serious.

"Why did you leave?" I asked.

"We speak German. Serbs kill all German speaking."

"But you don't speak German with your parents?"

"Ah, we speak Croatian, but my Great-Grandparents, and my Grandparents speak German. Great Great Grandparents come from Austria. Long time ago." Miro said. "Partisan know, they kill. They take land, house, animals. German soldiers only take animal for food. We walk many days. At night. Hide in day. Then we ride on truck go to camp. From camp come here."

"Where do you go from here? Back?" I asked.

"No back. Find new place here or Germany. My father say Germany bigger, more land. Maybe he can work on farm." Miro had told this story often. He was looking out over the grass as if looking for that new place his father has been talking about.

We had collected a bunch of the tall plants and headed off across the meadow.

"I think cable car is behind these trees there." Miro said.

"Maybe. Let's go look." I was not sure.

We ran through the grass with big steps holding onto our edible bouquets.

"There it is. I was right!" Miro was happy. He pointed at the supports visible through the stand of tall trees.

"We left the *Saurampfer* down there, at the second one. Let's pick it up." I went on ahead.

THE ENEMY IS HERE ...

"What's for lunch?" I looked over my mother's shoulder.

"What do you think?" my mother said and continued to sprinkle little sugar crystals over four thick slices of rye bread covered with an almost invisible layer of butter.

"Is the butter rancid or fresh?" I asked.

"I am afraid it is rancid, or what you call rancid. I've told you before, the farmers eat it that way all the time. The Kastingers are going to make a fresh batch this weekend, I am sure they will give us some again. Then you can have fresh," my mother said, putting a lot of emphasis on the 'fresh.'

"I am just kidding. But it does taste weird, sort of soapy...? Why didn't ours at home taste that way?"

"It's probably made a different way, not ladled off a bucket of freshly milked milk, and saved for a week and then churned in an old wooden butter churn. The cream goes to a real dairy, it is kept cold, it is sterilized in some way and when they make butter, they package it and store it in a properly cool place and it only goes rancid when it stays warm too long." While she was talking, my mother had put each slice of bread on a little plate and taken them over to the table at the foot end of the big beds. "Can you pour the milk, please?" she asked me.

I filled three cups with milk, a bigger one each for my brother and sister and a smaller one for myself. "Dieter, Ina, lunch," I called through the back door from where the voices of my brother and sister had been coming. I sat down at the narrow end of the table. They came running in.

"Wash your hands, please!" Mother said.

"Oh, can we do it with the hose outside?" Dieter asked.

"No, just rinse them off in here," she said, "it's quicker."

They both went to the big china washbowl sitting on the old-fashioned washstand in the niche against the wall. Ina had to step on a stool to reach into the water. They both piddled around for a while and then dried their hands on a towel before coming to the table. "Let me see," I said and looked at their hands, "pretty clean, well done!"

"Where is Tante Gmeiner?" Dieter asked.

"She went to town to get a letter mailed," my mother said and came to the table with another plate, which held an apple cut into four quarters. "See what I got? Herr Kastinger gave it to us from his cellar."

"I wish Tante Gmeiner would not stay with us. She is mean to me," Dieter continued without looking at the apple.

"Please, let's not say that. You know she has nowhere to go. Her house was destroyed by bombs. Almost all of Berlin is destroyed. She cannot go back there. We took her in, we are all the family she has and when things become settled she will find herself a place. When Papa comes home we will need the whole house." Mother let out a sigh.

Dieter's eyes got watery and he started to cry. "I want my Daddy. I want my Daddy." Mother picked him up, sat him on her lap and put her arms around him.

My insides cramped up. They always did when Dieter did the *'my Daddy'* thing. The pain in his crying stirred up all of my own pain of missing my father, of having to be serious and responsible, of being here and not home, of the uncertainty of what would happen next.

"Let's eat," my mother said, "You want me to cut your bread?" she asked Ina.

"Yes, Mami, please!" Ina always became very quiet when she did not join Dieter in his crying spell, looking from one to the other and wondering.

They heard steps on the staircase coming up.

"Tante Gmeiner is back," mother said. She lifted her index finger in front of her lips and looked at all three of us with this gesture meaning, "I don't want any comments, please."

"Hello, oh, we are having lunch," Tante Gmeiner said as she came in the door. She was tall and slim, her full breasts fitting tightly into a stylish country dress that came up high on her neck. She never relaxed her face while speaking. Her speech seemed like her bosom: compressed and more elegant than necessary. Maybe that came from dealing with the spoilt daughters of high

269

society who had been her life. I did not take to her manner and the little ones did even less.

"What's new in town?" mother asked her.

"I got my letter mailed. Surprisingly, the Post Office was open. They said nothing has come in from anywhere. They think the troops won't let anything through. There are no more vehicles to take mail, anyway. The shooting we heard last night came from the North they said. The Americans are supposed to be moving pretty fast."

"You want to eat with us? I'll make another slice of bread," Mother offered.

"No, thank you, I'd rather rest for a while. That walk really made me tired. I did not sleep well last night, again, my cramps, they hurt so much ..."

I shut my ears. I did not like this woman. She was always complaining and yet when we kids had something to complain about, she would go after us and chide us for being so "sissy." I took my mother's knife and started cutting my sister's bread. "Here you are," I said, pushing the plate in front of her. "For you, too?" I asked my brother.

"No, I want Mami to cut mine," Dieter said out from under my mother's arms, "I want my apple." He reached over and grabbed one of the quarters.

Suddenly the door flew open without warning.

"The enemy is here!"

Frau Müller stood erect and angry in the doorway, with one hand on the door handle and the other holding onto her son's hand. "Look out the window!"

We all jumped up and ran to the windows.

Those were the vehicles and the uniforms I had seen in the newsreels. American soldiers on light tanks, armored personnel carriers, followed by Jeeps. A JEEP. Finally, I get to see a real Jeep. I was excited. The soldiers looked tense. Their helmets were down over their foreheads, chinstraps tight, their fingers wrapped around the triggers of the machine guns mounted on the vehicles. Vehicle after vehicle drove by. Herr Kastinger, his wife and sister had come out onto their balcony below us. The people in the circus wagon were standing out front. The neighbors down the street were hanging out their windows.

"What do you say?" Frau Müller wanted to know. "We are occupied now," she said, "by the enemy."

"Yes, I guess that is it," Mother said. "I am so glad there is no shooting."

"Oh God, what now? What next?" Tante Gmeiner put her hands over her face and started to sob.

"Why don't they shoot?" Dieter asked me.

"There are no German soldiers here, and nobody is shooting at them, so they don't have to shoot," I explained.

"Are they afraid of shooting?"

"You bet they are afraid of shooting," Frau Müller said. Her voice was high and haughty. "They are afraid of the German Army, they have been beaten badly. What a disgrace. What humiliation."

"Frau Müller, please, don't get all excited. It is over. There is nothing we can do. It is over, everywhere. It has been obvious for a while," Mother said.

"But what about the 'Wunderwaffe' the Führer has promised us?" Frau Müller countered.

"That has been promised for a long time, too. Where is it? Where are they hiding it? And if they pull it out now they will kill more of us than of them. This is all insane. It must stop."

"They are waving. Look, the soldiers are waving!" Dieter said pointing out the window. He still had tears on his cheeks, running down over his chin.

The gypsy girl from the circus wagon and her mother were waving at the soldiers. The soldiers were waving back. This group was all smiles and not so tense as the first few units. The column was moving slowly. Now it was all Jeeps with four soldiers in each of them. Battle gear loaded high around them and the machine gun mounted in the center with one of the rear riders at the ready. It looked very threatening but then when they waved it did look rather friendly. The Enemy. Different uniforms, different vehicles, different weapons, different helmets. *"Still people these soldiers, just like the Germans, just like my Dad riding through Russia, waving,"* I thought, *"The tables have turned, what is going to happen to him now?"*

271

There were heavier guns, trucks full of waving soldiers and then the street was empty again. Everything looked the way it had looked before.

"Well, what do you say?" Herr Kastinger looked up from his balcony to our window. "I guess we are occupied. Glad they didn't shoot. Don't look too threatening, except for those guns."

"They are the *Enemy*," Frau Müller said, "We must not forget that." She took her little blonde son and walked back through the door to her room across the hall. Her husband had been missing in action on the Russian front for two years. Quietly, people had been treating her like a widow.

I sat down and started eating my slice of sugared bread. The soldiers were heading in the direction of the gun noises we had heard last night. I was confused. *Who was where, going, coming?* I remembered the band of Hungarian soldiers, clad partly in German uniforms, with SS insignia, marching into the direction the Americans had come from today. *Had they met? Had they fought? Had they hidden?* I shuddered. I remembered the dead soldier up in the woods. *Was he better off than the others who had marched on? Were they prisoners now? Had they been shot because of their belonging to the bad SS?* I had heard people say that many soldiers were forced to join the SS, tattoo and all. The Germans deployed these units to scare the enemy troops. The SS units had a bad reputation. They were said to be fierce and merciless fighters. The unit I had seen march through here had looked neither fierce nor merciless.

MILKRUN BY BOAT

"May I go up to the meadow with Miro?"

"Well, when are you going for the milk today?"

"Afterwards, when I come back."

"I think it would be a better idea to go now, and then play with Miro when you come back. Then you can stay out till dinner time."

"Yeah, I'll go now."

I went upstairs to get the milk pitcher, which was big enough to hold our daily ration, three quarters of a liter, one-quarter liter for each child in the household.

"Mama, its nice today, can I take the boat? Herr Kastinger said I could, any time I wanted to."

"Isn't that too far for this little boat? You know it does not steer well."

"If I can take Dieter along, he can help me keep it straight. I showed him the other day, and he can do it."

"Well, if you think you want to, go ahead, but are you sure it's not too far?"

"It takes me 20 minutes to get there by bicycle and I have one steep hill where I have to get off and push, and I have to go around the whole bay. You can see the place where the store is straight across the water from here, see?"

"So how long do you think it will take you?"

"We'll be back in an hour or so, I think."

"Be sure to keep the life jacket on your brother, you know, he cannot swim!"

"Yes, Mama, I'll see that he keeps it on. I'll watch."

I ran down the little crooked driveway swinging the metal milk jug in a big circle with my outstretched arm.

"Dieter come, we are going to get the milk by boat. You have to help me steer. Come on."

I stopped at the street and waited for my brother to catch up with me. He seemed excited about going with me in the boat.

"We are going to go all the way across the lake to the milk store over there," I pointed with the arm with the milk jug across the bay to the left. "It's not as far as by bicycle," I added, squinting at the distance.

We cleared the road together and went through the little gate to where the boat was tied to the pier.

"Mr. Kastinger made this boat himself, he told me," I explained to my brother, "he used only three boards so there would not be many cracks for the water to come in."

"But there are cracks on the bottom," my brother retorted pointing to the seams where side and bottom boards came together.

"Yes, but they have to be there, that's where the corners are. They are sealed with tar, the black smelly stuff they put on roads. That makes the cracks watertight."

"Then how come there is water in the boat?" my brother observed correctly.

"Well, some water comes through the boards, they are very thin, but only when they dry out beforehand. Come on, get in and bring your life jacket."

I had untied the boat and was holding it close to the pier so my brother could step in. There were no seats in the narrow boat, just two blocks to sit on and a rather crude, handmade paddle. I threw in two small boards, which we had used as supplementary oars a few days ago.

"Do you remember how we did this the other day, Dieter? You sit in front to keep the front end of the boat in the water and I'll paddle from the very back. If I don't go straight, you have to push us straight with the board. Remember? Let's go."

I lodged the paddle against the pier and gave us a good shove. The boat turned almost a full turn, immediately. I sat down on the little cross brace at the very end and started to paddle to point the boat towards our destination. I maneuvered the boat past the neighbor's pier and through some reeds and then we were out on the lake.

"Dieter, look there ... where that big tree stands next to the cottage ... can you see it?"

"Yes, I see it," Dieter said, "with the yellow bush next to it?"

"Yeah, exactly. That is where we have to go. The nose of the boat has to point at that tree all the time. Otherwise we will be off course and it'll take us longer."

Every stroke of the paddle made the boat move to one side or the other. The flat bottom, which had a thin strip of wood nailed to it for a keel did not help to hold the direction at all. Dieter sat in the front, his feet up in the tip of the boat, his hands holding on to the paddleboards, hanging over the sides. He looked very grown up going out on the water with his brother.

We kept moving through the water at a fair speed. Every so often, I put my index finger straight down in the water to measure our actual speed. I thought I could do better and then pushed harder with the paddle, keeping the boat more on a straight course. The pier behind us looked very small already. But the tree and the cottage in front of us did not appear any closer yet. There was no wind and the surface of the lake was smooth.

"Look behind us Dieter, at the wake, we are zigzagging a little but not much, you are doing a good job!"

When we came to the shallow area with the sandy bottom, the water looked turquoise and we could see some shells on the bottom in between the swaying patches of sea grass. A school of little fish darted under the boat.

"Look Peter, the fish!" Dieter leaned over to get a better look and the boat leaned with him.

"Watch it, Dieter, stay in the middle. If we turn over and fall into the water, we will be very cold!" I said and put in a few more really hard and long paddle strokes, which made the boat glide smoothly over the transparent liquid body of water.

I looked at my brother straight ahead of me, who was concentrating on the tree on the far-off shore so seriously, trying very hard to keep us on course. I liked my brother, most of the time. When he was whiney and crying for his Mami or his Daddy, he was not much fun.

I wished I had my aunt's rowboat which was two times as long and three times as wide but moved along fast and quietly, responding to the slightest movement of the oars. It had a sleek body, made by professional boat builders at this lake, with a keel that cut the water like a knife and made the boat actually hard to turn once it was going fast.

We came across a patch of dark green seaweed just barely reaching up to the surface. As we glided over it Dieter kept looking for fish but could not spot any. He was very careful this time to keep the boat in balance.

"Can you see how big the people in front of the milk shop look? We'll be there really soon."

"Let's do just like in a race," I said, "Dieter, get on your knees so you can reach out better, and snuggle all the way up front."

"That's good. Now watch the tree. Every time the boat does not point at it and we go off to one side, you paddle hard on that side to set us straight again. We tried this the other day and you did really well.

"Yes," Dieter said. "We went fast—but then I splashed you." He turned around and looked at me and laughed. "You were mad at me."

"Just watch it! If you paddle deep and pull the board out smoothly, you won't splash."

Dieter actually caught a few deviations and corrected us but the pace got too fast and he could not keep up.

"Peter, you are pushing much harder on this side, and not so hard on the other. See, we are going too far over there!" He pointed to the left.

We let up and then sped up again, the boat turned, we straightened it out, it turned again, and we corrected again. We went back and forth, from side to side. When we looked up we were almost there.

The boat coasted onto the gravel bottom with a slow, crunching sound. We stepped out. I handed Dieter the milk pitcher, pulled the boat up and tied it to a tree stump.

We walked up through the grass to the store and got in line. I took the ration cards out of the pitcher, one for each of us and one for our sister.

"Hello, three please..." I said to the big friendly woman who ladled milk out of a gigantic vat. She wiped her hands on her white apron, reached for her hole punch and our cards, punched one hole in each, and handed them back with a smile.

"You brought a friend today, on the bicycle?" She cocked her head and smiled questioningly at me, while she measured three quarter liter ladles into the pitcher.

"No, we came with Herrn Kastinger's paddle boat. This is my brother... this one," I said as I held up my brother's ration card.

"Oh, my" she said, "the boat he built himself? That's no boat to come across the lake in, boys, you better be careful going back, stay along the shore, just in case. See you tomorrow." Then she greeted the woman in line behind us.

"How does she know about our boat?" Dieter asked when we were outside.

"I think she's related to Mrs. Kastinger or something. Don't know why she thinks it's not safe."

"Last one by the boat is a pig!" I suddenly shouted and ran down the hill. Dieter followed but couldn't catch up.

"No fair," he said, pouting. "You always do that to me without telling me beforehand. Next time I won't even run anymore." He underlined this statement with a defiant nod of the head.

"Look Peter, there is water in the boat!" He pointed at the end still sticking into the water.

"It looks a lot more than it really is, with the boat tilting down as it is. Let's pull it out and empty it out."

We both had to pull with all our strength to get it up on dry land, slipping it first over the pebbles and then over the moist grass.

"Come on this side, Dieter. You lift there and then let it go." We managed to roll it over and it landed with a big thud. For the first time we could see the underside fully exposed. The board was soaked and swollen from the water.

"What happened here?" Dieter asked, pointing to several deep gouges.

"Somebody probably hit a rock landing on the shore. That really scrapes the wood."

In several spots along the seam between the bottom and the sides the tar had come out halfway.

"See these fibers and the tar" I ran my hand over the rough bottom board along the 'keel' and the edges. "That's why we don't go any faster. It's keeping the boat from gliding smoothly in the water."

I was not sure whether my brother had understood. I knew about resistance because my uncle had shown me the smooth shellacked bottom boards on my aunt's boat and had explained how such a fine surface avoided friction and made the boat faster. I liked to know how things worked and why. My brother really did not seem to care one way or another. He barely listened to my elaborate explanations.

"Let's turn it back over. Grab there. One, two, NOW!"

"Ouch, OUCH" my brother yelled out and drew his hand up in the air away from the boat, "A splinter—take it out!"

He held his arm towards me and looked away, "Take it out quick, it hurts!"

I took my brother's hand and found the splinter right away. It was lodged deeply into the pad of the middle finger with a frazzled end showing. I squeezed his finger hard, the same way I do to myself to numb the pain, pinched the wood between my fingernails and pulled it out slowly. My brother's hand twitched but I held on firmly until I was done.

"Ouch, that hurt, is it gone?" His voice came from behind. "Does it bleed?"

"No, it's fine. You'll live. Suck on it for a while, that'll clean it out."

"Thanks. But I won't touch that dumb boat anymore." He kicked the side of the boat, "Splinterboat-Splinterboat," he laughed.

"Now, let's go home. I want to go into the woods with Miro still before dinner. Mama said I could go."

"Can I come—I paddled well, didn't I?" Dieter pleaded in his nicest voice.

"No, not today. We are going to look for guns. You would be scared. You're too little for that."

"No I'm not. I'll tell Mama you are going to look for guns if you won't let me come."

"I'll leave you here, then you can't tell her anything, you ratfink."

"I'm not a ratfink and I'm coming with you." He jumped into the boat. It moved a little ways down the slope. I pushed hard to get it all the way into the water.

"Move all the way to the end, Dietz, I'll push us off and jump in, watch out!" I took two big steps, the last one aimed at a rock sticking out of the water. I hit it and pushed the boat free and jumped in, pulling myself with my arms. The boat rocked and took on a little water over the edge but we were clear of the bottom and ready to go.

"The milk!" Dieter shouted and pointed at the pitcher standing on the grass where we had turned the boat over. Waiting for my reaction to this mishap he sat quietly at his end of the boat. I thought, I better not blame him because he had come along just for the ride and to paddle, to help me out, really.

"*Biçka de matrina*" I cursed in Miro's words. I did not know what the words meant. But they sounded bad, especially combined with the wicked face Miro always made when he said them.

I took my place at the stern, turned the boat around slowly and headed for the beach again.

"Can you get out and get it, please. You are lighter, so we can get the boat back out again easier."

I nestled the pitcher into the stern end of the boat. Actually, it could also have been the bow because the boat's two ends were identical. Since it was the end I was sitting at and paddling from, I called it the stern.

I pushed the boat back into deeper water.

One hour later, we were way out on the lake, about an even distance between home and the milk store. The skies had turned dark, a gusty wind drove nasty little waves at our little craft, which refused to stay on course, regardless of how we maneuvered it.

"I am scared," Dieter said, "we'll never make it back to our house."

"Oh, come on, I've been out in worse weather and always made it home fine."

"But feel the wind and look at the clouds, back there," Dieter pointed towards the north end of the lake where one of the big mountains was almost totally obscured by dark rain clouds. On top of the gray clouds there was a big white thunderhead traveling in our direction.

I thought of the sailor who had drowned just a few weeks back. "He should have known better," Mr. Kastinger had said, "once those clouds come in from the north, you got to head in fast."

"Let's make a go for it, and paddle as fast as we can. Will you help me, Dietzi?" My voice was firm and challenging.

"I am tired and wet, and I am cold. I want to be home."

"Well, the better we do the faster we will be there, yes? I will be careful not to splash you, but with the dumb waves and the wind blowing so hard, it just sprays everywhere. Look at me," I said, "I am just as wet as you are."

"What side do you want me to paddle on?" Dieter said making his little snout of resignation.

"What do you like better? The right keeps you looking away from the wind and if you pull hard, we'll stay fairly straight," I said. "We need to aim for the church, then the wind will drive us closer to home."

"Fine, let's go." Dieter got up on his knees and pulled the board he was using for a paddle along the right side of the boat as strong as he could with his short arms.

"That's good. We'll be ashore in half an hour." I sat at the rear end and paddled furiously. My arms and hands were beginning to hurt. I never thought it would take us that long and that it would be so hard. I was glad my brother was wearing the life vest. I did not like the looks of the weather at all. I had watched these storms before and they were pretty wild at times.

"Hey, Dieter, can you give us an extra pull to straighten us out, I don't have enough power from here against the wind."

"My knees are hurting, I don't care where we land." Dieter flopped back and sat down on one of the little blocks to keep him from sitting in the water at the bottom of the boat.

"Dieter, you are very brave. You did really well, look how far we got, we are a lot closer. Do you see up front where the water looks calmer? That's where we need to go, there we are protected from the wind, at least a little bit, and we'll move better and straighter."

"But I cannot paddle any more. Look at this blister!" He held out his water soaked hand, palm up. There was a big red blotch with the skin coming off.

I felt badly for my little brother. "Here, wrap this around your hand." I slowly pulled the dirty handkerchief off my right hand. "Ouch, look at this!" I said as I uncovered my own blister, "I've had this for a while."

"We are drifting, Peter!" Dieter shouted in anguish. "Let's turn it to the church again." He grabbed his board, adjusted the handkerchief so it would cover his blister and pulled furiously to right the boat. That was when the board-paddle snapped. It bent slowly exposing all the fibers in the wood, swollen with the water and a nice light color in contrast to the weathered surface.

"Oh shit" I yelled and put my paddle down in the boat. Can you use it the other way?"

"What other way?" Dieter asked looking at the angled board held up in the air, water dripping on him and into the boat.

"So it will bend back before it breaks all the way."

Dieter tried carefully but the wood was too far-gone. The fibers stretched in the other direction and the angle reversed itself.

"Listen, I know what we will do. Can you paddle with the big paddle for a while? We have to get out of this wind fast. I'll paddle with the board." I started switching places with Dieter and we almost capsized the boat.

"Hey, watch out!" We both crouched down, holding on to the sides, stabilizing the narrow boat again. When I came up front, I started bending the board back and forth until it finally broke in two. I kneeled down in the bow and with one piece in each hand, I started to make long strong strokes on either side of the boat with as much power as I could still muster.

"We are moving fast, you are good!" Dieter shouted from the back over the sound of the wind and the slapping of the waves. I was stretching my body up high and then plunged the two hands with the boards deep into the water alongside the boat, crouched down I pulled them backwards, adjusting the pull to get some directional correction and then pulled the boards out of the water behind me, starting another cycle.

"Just give us a little more push, Dieter," I said, "See, we are coming closer to the calm water." I continued to work in a fury, determined to get us out of the strong wind, fast.

After another hour of paddling, stroking and frustration, we finally drifted close to shore, about a mile from our house.

"I want to get off, I'll walk home. You can take the boat," Dieter said.

I headed for the one unfenced lot close by. Nobody had built anything on it yet. Heavy railroad ties kept the waves from eroding the shoreline. The tall grass behind them looked solid and earthy, even if it was moving with the ill wind that had caused us so much trouble.

"Let's switch, I can maneuver better with the paddle," I said dropping my wooden fins into the boat and reaching for the paddle which my brother handed me.

"Can you take the milk, please? I don't want to spill it at the last minute.

"Yes, I can." Dieter was happy at the prospect of having firm soil under his feet again.

"Thanks for your rowing, you were a big help, Dietz. I'll take you with me to the circus next time we go. You want to?"

"Yeah I want to, but the circus people won't let me go. They want only you big boys because you can hold down the rope." There was the pout again.

"They'll let you come, if you just stay out of the way." I tried to sound re-assuring, although my voice trailed off with fatigue.

"Watch for the shore, now, don't let me hit it too hard," I said as I turned the rear of the boat towards the ties.

"Now you can jump off—hold on, though, otherwise you'll push the boat off and you'll end up in the water like last time!" I had the paddle stuck in the gravel bottom, holding the boat in place against the shore. Dieter stepped off.

There was a bone-piercing scream as one of his legs disappeared behind the railroad ties. I pushed the boat closer, jumped into the water and stepped up to my brother.

"What is the matter, Dieter? Did something bite you?"

"No—ouuuh—- I'm stuck, I'm hurt—it hurts so much..." and he burst into more tears.

I sat on the tie and reached down behind it to where my brother's leg was. The water had washed out a big hollow but the grass on top covered it and that is where Dieter had stepped.

I moved over onto the firm grass and started pulling my brother up.

"Ouch, be careful, it hurts so much" Dieter was shivering with pain and tears. When his knee appeared, I knew why.

Something sharp had scraped the skin off my brother's shin and knee, all the way to the bone, which looked white and threatening under the trickling blood.

"Oh God, Dieter, how did you manage this? It looks awful! Does it hurt very much? Can you walk?"

"No" he screamed through his tears and his anger, "Get Mama!"

"It'll take me fifteen minutes to get there, it'll be a good half hour before I will be back—I can carry you—let me tie up the boat first.

The boat had begun to drift out. I jumped in the water, grabbed the rope and pulled it ashore. I tied the rope around one of the ties and reached for the milk.

"Can you hold the milk while I am carrying you?"

"No, I don't want to."

"But we cannot leave it here, Dieter."

"But my hands hurt too much, dumb boat, dumb lake, dumb weather, dumb hole—ouch, get me home."

"Where is the hanky I gave you?"

"I had it on my blister when I got out of the boat."

I looked around and found it. It did not look like the sterile gauze bandage they had shown me in first aid training in school, but it would keep the blood from running.

"Let me put this on, Dieter, it will make the wound feel better. It is cool and wet." I bent down to the leg that my brother was holding, my hands clutched around the thigh just above the knee where the scrape began.

"Can you move the leg?" I asked. The wound looked so deep and final that I had doubts about my brothers knee functioning. Guilt crawled in over my sympathy for the pain. What would my mother say? Why did we have to go for the milk in the boat? But the weather had looked fine when we left.

"I don't want to try, it hurts so much." Tears were streaming down his face. "I'll never go in that boat again," he sobbed.

I dipped the handkerchief into the water, rinsed out the grass and sand it had collected when it had fallen off my brother's hand, and very softly moved it closer to the part of the wound at the knee where the most blood was coming from.

"Careful, you'll hurt me more!" Dieter cried.

"I'll be as gentle as I can be, the cold will feel good."

Dieter jerked with fear and pain when the wet hanky finally touched but then he felt the soothing coolness and he grabbed my hand. "Let's go home, please."

My mother went pale when she saw the wound. She had not brought her emergency medical supplies. She needed some iodine, for starters, at least. Maybe the Kastingers had some.

Their box with emergency medical supplies yielded a bottle of iodine tincture, a few rolls of bandages and one crinkled tube of salve looking like it could be used on an open wound. My mother also found a small roll of gauze, which on the inside of the roll looked cleaner than the bandages. She did her best in dressing the scraped knee and shin with salve, gauze and bandage. My brother was cringing and crying in his pain. We all stood around and told him how brave he was and how quickly his wound would be healing under his mother's good care. He did not look as if that was any comfort to him.

"Where is the doctor in town, Herr Kastinger?" my mother asked.

"We had a good one up in Attersee, he was drafted and we have not seen him since. I don't think there is anybody left in his office. I have not heard anything about the nurse who worked with him there."

"Where could we go to get this wound looked at? It is very deep and I am afraid it might infect."

"Well, there is a hospital in Vöklabruck, they have staff, I reckon, but it might have been bombed, we don't know. I can ask around. But how would you get there anyway? It's a long way. The bus is not running anymore."

"If I can use the rest of your salve and the bandages, I will try to keep it clean, as well as I can. Let's hope for the best."

Very soon my mother's worst fears came true. The wound was badly infected, puss was oozing out from under the bandage. Dieter could not bend his leg at all and he was in constant pain. My mother was getting desperate. Something had to be done quickly. How could she get Dieter to the hospital?

The daughter of the circus couple had connected with the liberators. There was one GI who came to visit her regularly. During one of his visits he saw my brother hobbling around the front of the house. He asked what happened to him. I scraped together my few words of English and tried "bad fall, bad wound!"

"He needs to see a doctor!" came back. I understood 'see' and 'doctor.'

I gestured "No doctor, doctor in Army, gone."

Our new friend now started mimicking my simple way of speaking. Pointing at himself he said "My army, doctor good, doctor here," pointing towards town. "I take" and pointed at my brother.

I was excited about the fact that my brother might get help but also that I had carried on some sort of conversation in English and we both apparently had understood what had been said. Now I needed to involve my mother.

"Mother," I said to the soldier, and pointed towards the house.

"Okay, get your mother, we go with the Jeep." Again, he pointed as he spoke, first to the house then to the Jeep parked down by the street.

I ran into the house and found mother. She was not as excited as I was about this interaction with the 'enemy.' It might have had something to do with how this soldier had come to be near the house.

"If he would get to see a doctor, that would be wonderful. Let's give it a try." She grabbed her purse and followed me downstairs and outside.

"I am Frank," the soldier said, "We go see the doctor with your little boy—what's his name?" pointing at Dieter. "Name?" he repeated.

"Dieter," I said slowly.

"Dieter" he repeated. It did sound a little different the way he said it. He picked up my brother and started towards the Jeep. When he passed the circus trailer, he explained to the girl who had been wondering what he was doing. She was not happy that he was leaving but he assured her that he would be back soon. He lifted my brother onto the bench in the back of the Jeep and, looking at my mother, pointed to the passenger seat. Then he turned around and looked at me. I wanted nothing more than getting to ride in a Jeep. He must have seen the wanton eagerness in my face because he smiled and motioned me next to my brother.

The 'doctor's office' was in a private house which had a big Red Cross flag hanging out front. There were also several signs in English that I did not have time to decipher. The soldier led us in, and talked with the nurse who guarded the door to the doctor.

"Ten minutes," he said, holding up his ten fingers. "You sit."

We all sat down, Dieter made a face because he could not move his leg without hurting. The soldier had waved at us, smiled, and gone back outside. My mother looked unsure about what to do, but she did not want to leave our post.

The nurse had disappeared into the other room and when she came back out, she left the door open and beckoned us in. My mother took Dieter's hand and entered. I looked at the nurse, checking nonverbally if I could go in too. She smiled and nodded.

The doctor was young. He was wearing a white coat over his uniform. He greeted us with a friendly face and, pointing to Dieter's leg, reached out for his hand. Dieter was not too sure about what would happen and held on to mother's hand at the same time.

"I have to take this bandage off. I will be very careful not to hurt you." He took some blunt-ended scissors and cut the bandage open. Between the salve and the puss,

286

there was nothing to make it stick to the wound. Dieter was still holding on to mother's hand.

The doctor shook his head. "Very bad. Bad infection! I am glad you came, this could turn into a very nasty wound." He looked at my mother to see if she had understood. She nodded "Bad? Yes!"

"There is good news, very good news!" he said as he carefully swabbed the wound with cotton soaked in some liquid. Apparently, it did not hurt because my brother held still.

"This is an American invention, very new: Penicillin!" He held up a jar with a yellowish salve in it. "It's a miracle drug. It cures infections very quickly. You will see. It healed many wounded soldiers already!"

The bandage he put over the salve was bright white and had sticky tape on top to hold it in place.

"Come back in three days!" He held up three fingers and repeated "three days! Here!"

My mother thanked him profusely, offered him money, which he refused.

"A present from America," he said and smiled.

When we stepped outside, our soldier friend Frank was standing there smoking a cigarette.

"Ah, good bandage!" he said, looking at Dieter. "You happy?" Dieter was confused by all the words he did not understand, but he smiled back. "Frank will take you home, no walking with this bad leg!" he said and walked across the street where the Jeep was parked.

I don't know what made me happier, the fact that my brother's wound was taken care of by the doctor or that I had two rides in an American Army Jeep!

CLOSE CALLS

When the circus people had pulled up at the Kastingers shortly after we had moved in they brought with them three horses. The bigger horse was light brown, gentle, and enjoyed being handled. The other two were ponies with a darker brown coat and bushy blond manes and tails. They were rather temperamental, jumping and kicking without provocation. We kids were told to stay away from them. Herr Kastinger had agreed that they could graze on the meadow next to the house and along the road. Today we boys had decided we were going to ride the bigger horse.

"You ride him first!" Miro said, "The circus people ride him all the time, easy horse, is little, too."

I was not so sure. I had always wanted to ride a horse. That was why I seriously considered joining the horse-riding branch of the Hitler Youth. So far I had never sat on a horse.

"What if I fall off? There is no saddle to hold on to."

"Look at the back, it is wide, is easy to sit on. Hold on to the mane, that is what Herr Igor does." Miro really wanted me to go first.

"Herr Igor is a circus rider, of course he can ride this horse!" I said. "I'll do it. Come help me. Dieter, you feed him some grass, so he will stand still. Just hold it up to him like I showed you—flat hand, remember?"

Dieter picked a handful of long grasses and weeds. "Careful Peter, Mama said we must stay away from the horses, remember? But I won't tell."

"Yeah, it is a smaller horse, not like the real big ones, but still, how do I get up on him without stirrups?" I asked Miro and the other two kids watching.

"I help you. You stand on my back, or no, you stand on my hands, so, you see?" Miro interlaced his fingers in front of him and walked up to the horse. The horse moved away a few steps and continued to graze.

Dieter carefully moved towards the horse. The horse lifted its head and started grabbing the grasses Dieter offered. Miro held his hands tightly together and I put one foot into his stirrup-hands, pushed off with the other foot and swung it over the horse's back. Miro pushed up a little with his hands to get me centered on the back of the horse. As soon as I settled on the wide brown back, Miro swung around and slapped the horse on its flank. "GO!" he yelled.

The horse spooked, kicked up both hind legs and started galloping down the meadow towards the road.

I dived for the mane, grabbing it with both hands. With every leap the horse took, my seating became more lopsided. Halfway down the hill I was barely hanging on.

"Peter, watch it!" my little brother stood frozen with fear, clutching the leftover weeds in his one hand, staring at the horse and its slipping rider.

Miro was laughing and slapping his thighs.

I was trying to decide whether to hold on for dear life or to let go and fall. Before I reached a conclusion I lost my grip on the coarse hair of the mane and slipped sideways off the horse. I rolled over in the soft grass and the horse went on without stepping on me.

For a while I lay there wondering why the horse had taken off so suddenly after letting me mount without any fuss. Miro and Dieter came running down the hill.

"Are you hurt? Did it hit you?" Dieter asked in panic.

"I am fine," I said and sat up, "that was a short ride."

"You look like jockey in race," Miro continued to laugh.

"Miro hit the horse, then it jumped, it was scared!" Dieter piped in.

"Oh, you did? You dumb ass, I should have known better than to trust you!" I was getting angry. "If you do anything like that ever again, I'll beat you up good."

"It was just for fun, Peter, nothing happened." Miro stopped laughing. "You held on for a long time!"

"Hey, boys, come here!" Herr Igor had come around the front of the house.

I got up.

"You're in trouble!" Dieter said.

"Ah, shut up," Miro said.

I felt a little wobbly from the fall. I wondered if Herr Igor had seen the ride. I did not know what his reaction would be.

The three of us walked through the tall grass towards Herr Igor. The two spectators were heading in the other direction.

"Good day, Herr Igor," I said and Miro just mumbled something.

"Were you fooling with the horses?" Herr Igor asked with a grin on his face.

"I was feeding the big one. He likes weeds," Dieter said quickly before anyone else could respond, showing the greens he still had left in his hand.

"Peter was trying to ride him, but he fell off." Miro gave me away.

"What happened?" Herr Igor had a serious look on his face.

"Miro scared him and he started running down the hill..." I started.

"Miro hit the horse's butt. It scared the horse. It made him jump," Dieter added.

Herr Igor turned to Miro. "I have told you several times already, Miro, I do not want you to hit the horses at all, do you understand? This is very dangerous play and Peter could have been hurt. Just leave the horses alone!"

He turned to me, "If you want to ride, I will show you, I will help you and you will learn. Do not do it alone. It is too dangerous. The horses get spooked easily. There are some tricks. I will show you. Please no more trying by yourself! Promise?"

I nodded and said "Yes." I felt embarrassed by the circus owner's concern and felt very happy about his offer to teach me to ride. Finally, someone would show me. My father had promised, but so far, we never had been around horses together.

"Thank you, Herr Igor!" I said, "I am sorry we did this, I was really scared, I was afraid the horse would step on me after I slipped off."

"Horses are very careful not to step on people. Sometimes they cannot help it though. It is by accident only when they do." Herr Igor did not sound upset any more.

"What I came to ask was that I need another boy to hold down the tightrope over at the Army Swim Club for the performance this afternoon." Herr Igor said. "Peter, you want to come?"

"Oh yes, thank you!"

I had said 'yes' quicker than any other time before in my life. Several older boys had been going with the circus people to the performances to help.

"We'll be leaving at three," Herr Igor said, "the truck will come by here at the wagon, I am counting on you!" and he pointed a finger at me.

"I am going to tell my mother right now!" I said.

I walked through the hallway towards the stairs when I heard my mother's voice mixed with crying from the Kastingers' living room. I stopped.

"He just left. He went out the back," I heard my mother say.

I wanted to enter the room and find out what was going on. Something in my mother's voice kept me from doing so. I stopped outside the door and listened.

"Shall we go after him?" somebody said.

"No, please, no, what for..." my mother said. I heard sobbing.

"Please calm down Frau Lisl. Tell us what happened. That will help you." I identified Frau Kastinger's voice.

"After lunch, the kids went out to play. I laid down for a nap. Just for a few minutes, to stretch out, to rest, you know," mother said. "A little later, the door opened, I was dozing, I thought it was one of the children, I did not look up, they come and go all the time, then somebody touched my hand ..." her voice broke and she started to cry again.

I could hear somebody moving about, the wooden floorboards creaked under the loads of Frau Kastinger and her daughter. I had not heard anybody else speak, so far.

"I opened my eyes, and saw—I saw this soldier, American soldier, I pulled my hand back, I was so afraid, I wanted to scream—but I couldn't, you know how it is in dreams, you want to scream and you open your mouth and nothing comes out—can I have more water, please, Frau Kastinger?"

There was more shuffling about, then the sounds of my mother swallowing.

"Relax, Frau Lisl," the other women's voice said.

"Yes, you need to calm down, Lieschen, everything will be all right!"

That women is in there too, I thought, she has to be into everything. It was Frau Gmeiner's voice I had just heard.

"I am trying, I am trying but I am so upset. Imagine, a strange soldier at my bedside. In my room ..." my mother said a little calmer.

"How did he get in here, I wonder, everybody was around, I was sitting out in the garden and you ..." Frau Gmeiner's voice again.

"I was in the kitchen, my husband was out on the balcony and then he went up back to check on the hogs. He must have come in upstairs through the barn, or just sneaked by here while we were not looking ... but Gus would have seen him come up the walkway. Well with the gypsy girl having soldier visitors all the time, we pay no attention any more, it is a disgrace, who do they think we are ..." Frau Kastinger was in good form.

"Mother, please do not start on this again ... " I heard the Kastinger's daughter cut in.

"Oh, hush, what do you know!" Frau Kastinger retorted.

"Let Lieschen tell her story," Frau Gmeiner said.

I was not quite sure about this, from what I had heard so far they probably would not let me be in there, so I decided to keep my post by the slightly open door. As long as nobody would come in, I was safe. Herr Kastinger was in the stable, nobody else comes through here normally.

"I said 'Go away' and pointed to the door. 'Please' I said." My mother was speaking again.

"He smiled, and he said 'Sorry, no deutsch.' He kept talking to me in English, I think he said I should not be afraid. He gestured he wants to talk. I kept saying "No, No. Please go away—I will scream if you do not go away. He did not care ... or he did not understand. He sat down at the edge of the bed ..." it sounded like my mother was overcome by emotion again.

"I moved away from him, I had the covers pulled up all the way, I was so scared ... I still could not scream. All I could do was talk quietly, sort of automatically ... I hoped for you to show up, that would have helped ... but you did not come ..." my mother was silent for a while.

"I knew you were taking a nap, I was reading in the garden" Frau Gmeiner said.

"Oh, I know, I just hoped for something, somebody to come and end this ... he said I will give me money and lots of chocolate, I said I was married and had three children ... Okay he said, okay, I give you money and chocolate, just let me look, just let me see, and he pointed, oh, he pointed ... don't these people have any shame ... they told us the Russian soldiers behave like animals .. but the Americans, I thought the Americans wouldn't be like them ... look, he kept saying, only look, money ... I said 'No, never' and it came out louder this time, and it startled him, I said the kids will come back any minute, so he said chocolate for the kids ... I cannot believe I understood all this, he did not speak any German at all, just hands and English, but he still sat there ... the bed was shaking I was trembling so much .. I was cold and hot and trembling ..." her voice was shaking badly. I was getting angry myself, I had never heard my mother in such despair, in such frustration, I was afraid to listen to the end of the story. But I had to. I wondered how much they would tell me later.

My mother blew her nose and there were noises from the other two women but I could not hear what they said.

"Then I begged, can you imagine, I begged, with my hands folded in front of my face, I begged him to go away. Please, I said 'please' in English, I remember. I said I was a wife and a mother, and my husband was far away. Please, I said, go and find a young girl friend, I said 'girl friend" in English, I don't believe it, but I did, and he said yes, girl friend and he pointed at me. 'Not me, gypsy girl, other girl, away' I said but he pulled out his wallet and reached for money, that is when I found my voice and the 'no' came out so loud that he startled ... he got up, shook his head, no, no money, no kiss, no look, no girl friend ... he shrugged his shoulders, winked at me and walked out the door ..."

"Can you imagine, such impertinence, but that is the enemy, and now we are defeated, we have to live with this scum ... this scum will rule us and the world ... I do not want to live like this ... what has this world come to ... barbarians ..." Frau Gmeiner was on one of her trips. I for once felt in step with her, I shared her anger, her despair.

What is going to become of us? What? Who will protect us, who will show us the way? Then I remembered the soldier who had taken us to the doctor, and the doctor who had treated Dieter and my mother so nicely, polite and helpful. They both had behaved like decent human beings. So they are not all bad, I thought.

My mother was crying again, softly, with a few louder sobs in between.

"Drink a glass of this Schnaps, Frau Liesl, it will pick you up. You need strength, come on." Frau Kastinger was talking. I heard the sound of cabinet doors and glasses. *That will put her under, she never touches a drop. Especially the way she feels now.*

I imagined myself entering the room while the soldier was at my mother's bedside. What would I have done? I had no weapons ... was the soldier armed? They all run around with guns in their belts. I could have fetched Herr Kastinger ... or shouted for help. Shouting for help seemed silly ... what was going on? What—- I was totally confused now.

I leaned against the wall in the hallway and closed my eyes for a moment. Poor mother. What next. In her own bedroom. Surrounded by people, in the middle of the day? What next? Is this the "LIBERATION" the new radio station is talking about? There were all kinds of jokes going around. Liberation meant being freed from watches, jewelry, family treasures, and antiques, anything they wanted. Good things, gaudy things, depending on the individual soldier's taste ... give, give, we are the victors, and we won the war. You Nazis lost. Lost good. As far as I knew, most Austrians never did like the Nazis.

I suddenly panicked. I needed to meet the circus truck at three. What time was it now? I had been listening for a long time. I had to ask my mother if I could go. In her present state she might not be willing to let me go. She might not want me to go help perform for the American soldiers. But I really wanted to go. I had never seen the circus people perform on the tightrope and I had never been within an 'Off Limits' place where only American soldiers could go. Those were regular places like movie theaters, hotels, and schools taken over by the US military and declared 'off limits' to civilians. You had to be working there or have a special pass to enter. The Swim Club was at the flat end of the lake, where I had been in school, about an hour's drive away.

I had to make a decision quickly. Time was running out. I did not want to take a chance, I did not want to miss out on this adventure. I went looking for my brother. I found him by the stable, watching Herr Kastinger fixing a gate on the pigsty.

"Good Day, Herr Kastinger," I said, "Can you tell me what time it is, please?"

Herr Kastinger straightened his back with a sigh. "What are you up to, Peter? Let me see ..." he lifted up his right shoulder, reached into his little belt pocket with his index finger and thumb and pulled out his big silver pocket watch and squinted at it, sideways. "Going on three, it looks like."

I had a flash of my grandfather, the gesture of reaching for the pocket watch was the same. "How many minutes till three?" I asked.

"Oh, about six or so, it looks like," Herr Kastinger said, raising his eyebrows, "What is going on at three?"

"Herr Igor asked me to go along to the Swim Club in Seewalchen where they perform for the soldiers. I have to help holding down the tightrope," I said.

"Ah, that sounds interesting, haven't seen them on the tightrope. They say they are pretty good. I'd never go up that high, trust me!" Herr Kastinger said.

"Dieter, will you tell Mama, please, that I went with Herr Igor. We will be back by eight, or so," I pleaded with my little brother.

"Why don't you tell her yourself, why should I tell her?" Dieter asked.

"It is late. The truck is leaving at three. Mama is talking to Frau Kastinger and the others. You can do it for me, please! I have to run." I did not wait for an answer, turned and started down the stairs to the living quarters and through the main hallway. My mother had just come out of the Kastingers' door, followed by Frau Gmeiner. I ran right into them.

"Hello Mama, I have been looking for you," I said. I noticed her pale face color and the disorderly hair. "Are you all right? You look like you were sick?"

"I had a little scare, I'll tell you about it later," my mother said. "What did you need from me? Where are you running to?"

"Herr Igor asked me to go help at the performance today. They are one helper short and they are leaving at three. Can I go?" My eyes were wide open and tense in anticipation of the answer.

"Just today? I guess it would be all right."

"Thank you, Mama," I said. I turned quickly to avoid any further discussion.

"Are you going on that old truck? Please be careful. Sit down and don't hang out over the side, it is dangerous. With all those army trucks driving everywhere. When will you be back?" she asked.

"I think eight at the latest, the show is at five, we have to pack up stuff after," I said. "Bye!" I waved and ran out the front door.

I knew the other five boys on the bed of the truck. They all lived around the area. But we were not really friends. Talking was almost impossible, there was too much noise between the engine of the truck and the rattle as it bounced over the road full of potholes. I sat on a roll of canvas with my back to the cab, holding on to one of the sides.

We passed the milk place, and after a while, we came up on Aunt Martha's house. I was straining to see if I could detect any signs of the new refugees who had replaced us instead of her kids in her beautiful house.

"Hey, Peter, didn't you go to the castle school before you moved up our way?" one of the boys asked.

"Yes, I did. Why?" I said.

"Somebody said these guys from Vienna were a bunch of weirdoes, that's why. What were they up to? Have they all gone home to live with the Russians in Vienna?" A couple of the other boys laughed.

"Some of them made it home just before the Russians moved in; their parents came to pick them up. Quite a few were stranded, they had not heard from their parents when I left. They did not know what to do. I guess the school took care of them. Before that, I was not there that long, just a couple of months, I guess they were pretty weird. I came from Linz, it was different there.

"Did you do a lot of Hitler Youth things? Shoot and march, play war?" Rudi asked.

The truck bumped through a particularly bad pothole, I did not hear the whole question. "What did you say?"

"How about Nazi Youth things?"

"Not much, it was all toned down, falling apart. We had a couple of Beebe guns and used them around the park. Shot at birds but nobody could really shoot. I was the only one who could hit the targets. My father had shown me how to aim." I felt proud, because I had been surprised at my success there. "There was no marching, just to and from meals. The Group Leader was away most of the time, visiting his parents. His stand-ins were pretty mellow."

"Have you heard from your father yet?" one of the other boys asked.

"No. Don't even know where he ended up fighting. Last letter we received was dated February 22 from Darmstadt. He was heading out to the West front. That is all we know." I fell quiet.

"My Dad is in a camp with the British. They caught him, he was trying to walk home. We just got a card. We hope they'll let him out soon. He was just a soldier. No officer or anything." Rudi seemed happy with the news.

None of the others had word from their fathers.

"My mother is taking it pretty hard. My dad's last letter is from January. We do not know where from. He was in Russia.

I moved closer to Rudi, the engine noise had gotten louder.

"What are we doing at the performance, tell me, please. I have never been there. You hold the tightrope?" I asked.

"They have two poles there with a little platform on each, pretty high, and the tightrope goes from one to the other. There are ropes going out to the sides, tied to the main rope. We hold on to the ends of these so the tightrope does not bounce or sway. They do not have a safety net."

"Is it very scary?" I asked.

"I don't think so, for them."

"I wouldn't go up there for anything," Kurt yelled from the other side. "They use these long balance bars, with weights at the ends, that makes tightrope walking more stable, I believe."

"When they clown around, Igor falls and catches himself with his hands on the rope, it looks realistic and scary, but I think, they are so used to that, it does not scare them," one of the other boys said.

We stopped at the gate. Herr Igor explained who we were to the guard and they waved us on. One of the guards saluted us boys in the back. The guards looked very official: they had their helmets on, with *MP* in big white letters painted on them, and arm bands with the same letters. Their belts and their shoulder straps were white. They carried rifles with white leather straps. I noticed that they were all chewing gum.

"Maybe we'll get some chewing gum?" I asked Rudi.

"Most of these soldiers are not very friendly. I do not know why. Maybe they have orders not to be friendly with us."

"I got some gum last time from a soldier," Kurt said. "He just offered it to me."

"If we have extra time, we can scrounge around and see what we can find. They leave a lot of stuff around," the other boy said.

"But we are not allowed to do that. Herr Igor said that the guards told him."

"Never mind what they say, nobody stopped us, did they?" Rudi said. "Do you smoke?" he asked me.

"No, why?" I was surprised.

"I don't either, but I pick up the cigarette butts and sell the tobacco to our neighbor. He is desperate for smokes. There are plenty of good long butts around here," Rudi said.

"I've seen people pick them up along the road, when the soldiers flick them out of their trucks or Jeeps, when they are still burning these people just keep smoking them. Seems pretty sick to me," I said.

"It is an ugly habit. Look at the smokers' fingers. They are all yellow from the nicotine. Watch them suck on the short butts, yuck," Kurt said, mimicking sucking on a cigarette end between the clenched index finger and thumb.

"Smokers pay an awful lot of money to get their hands on cigarettes. My mother used to sell our rations at black market prices to our relatives and friends, or we would trade them for food ration coupons. My father sent his cigarettes from the army, so we had even more to trade." Those were good deals for us.

The truck was bouncing slowly on the narrow road through the park by the lake. There were soldiers all over, with shirts off, some in swim trunks, sitting and laying in the sun. Some seemed to recognize the truck and waved to Herr Igor and the women in the cab.

We stopped right next to where the tightrope was set up. The poles and the tightrope were standing on a large meadow facing the lake. A wide band of sand separated the meadow from the water. I had never been in here before. We had done all our swimming in this lake at Aunt Martha's house at what seemed now a long time ago.

"Peter, you will be on that rope over there. Be sure to keep it taut all the time and do not move while someone is on the tightrope. Just keep it taut, watch what your partner is doing at the opposite side, try it out with him before," Herr Igor said. "Who is in this spot here?" he asked the boys.

"I am," Kurt said. "I'll practice with Peter."

A couple of the circus people were there already. The costumes and some gear were stored in a small tent on the meadow. One of the younger men was setting up a phonograph on a box outside of the tent. A couple of loudspeakers hung on the poles. After a few scratches sounding like small explosions, an Austrian march, typical circus fare, erupted from the speakers.

"We'll start in half an hour. They will announce it over the loudspeakers. Don't go too far away from the place here. They do not like you to be loose on the grounds," Herr Igor said to the boys.

"I'll show you around," Kurt said in a low voice to me. "We'll go to the bathroom," he shouted to Herr Igor.

We walked uphill, away from the lake, towards a low wooden building that housed the locker rooms. The ground was sprinkled with gum wrappers, cellophane with red tear strips from cigarette packs, and other papers I did not recognize. I was aware of every piece on the ground, though, analyzing it for its potential of containing something edible.

I felt uneasy with so many 'enemy' soldiers around me. A few weeks ago this army still had dropped bombs on my country, the soldiers had shot at the retreating German soldiers. Now we were 'friends' all of a sudden? I tried to read the expressions on their faces: Some ignored us, some looked without much interest, and a few seemed to wonder who these boys were, in civilian clothes, obviously Austrians and not staff in this place. So they waved or said "Hi" with a strange little move of the right hand, an upside down wave, and smiled.

Under a deserted lawn chair, Kurt spotted a small open package of something. Instinctively he darted in and picked it up. There were two small cookies left in the torn wax paper.

"Have one," Kurt said to me. We swallowed them in one bite.

One of the soldiers nearby had watched us. He reached into his pocket and pulled out a big package of chewing gum. He took out two sticks and held them out to us with a big grin on his face.

"Here, for you, from America!" he said.

"Danke!" "Thank you!" I remembered some English from school. I had understood what the soldier had said. I had been picking up words here and there all along. But I was not sure of the pronunciation. Some of the words I had heard did not sound at all like what I had heard from my English teacher.

Kurt smiled at me and I smiled at Kurt. "We are lucky today, it seems," Kurt said. "I'll tell you what, let's split up—you take this row here and I take the next one, yes?"

He pointed at the next two rows of beach chairs reaching as far as the bushes at the end of the property. "Then we can double back through two other rows and still make it in time for the performance. Keep listening for the announcement. You cannot miss it, Igor's speakers make a hellish noise." With that statement Kurt casually walked in behind the next row of chairs.

I did the same in the next row down. My heart was beating up to my neck. *'What if they throw me out?'* I thought. There were not many soldiers in these chairs. Rarely one was sitting there, smoking a cigarette, staring into the sky. Another one was reading a comic book. Then I saw a flash in the grass. A can. A can full of anything was a treasure. I looked around if anybody was watching me. No. Kurt was a little ahead of me, bending down to pick up something. I went to the can. It was buried in the ground. *"Why would anybody do that?"* I asked myself while I bent down. The top was flush with the surface. I scraped away some soil with my finger to get at the round slick metal. Finally I wiggled the can loose and pulled it out. It was empty. Somebody had stomped it into the ground after eating whatever had been in it. I felt as empty as the can. My food fantasy had been shattered. Dirty soil in an empty can, and an ugly scar in the lawn to boot. I moved on.

By the time I turned into the second row to make my way back, I was a seasoned scavenger. I did not get my hopes up until I had something edible in my fingers. There was an occasional cracker, even a piece of chocolate left in the foil wrapper. Piles of cigarette butts, but I did not touch these. I did not know any desperate smokers.

The few soldiers I came across did not talk. They were older than I had expected. All of them looked tired and acted tired. I thought about my father. He would be tired, too. And these men had been fighting grueling battles up to only a few weeks ago.

How long had it been since the Allies had landed in France? Not even a year. If these soldiers were part of the units that had come to Europe that way, then they had gone through hell ever since. No wonder they were tired. The war was over. Won for them, they could rest. We lost. My father was on the losing side. What had happened to him? Had he been face to face with one of these soldiers here? Had they been throwing hand grenades at each other, or shot each other with carbines, automatic rifles, and machine guns— father shooting at father in the name of their respective countries?

What country? All of a sudden I realized I lived in Austria again. But my father had fought for Germany. The Third Reich. And I was going to be one of the lucky heirs to the Empire Hitler was going to build. All I had inherited today were scraps from GI K-Rations, half-eaten by the "enemy"—now the WINNERS—at least in Europe. In the Pacific, the war was still going on. Americans were still fighting the Japanese. Maybe the Japanese had Hitler's *Wunderwaffe* and the tide would turn again?

No more turning tides. It had been confusing enough. The refugees had been moving north, some German troops had been moving north. Then the American troops had come in from the North. Who was moving which way? Had they missed each other somewhere? Endless columns of men and machines moving, moving, moving—where to? Victory? Defeat? Obscurity? Into the black holes of prison camps or refugee camps?

How would my father come home? From where? Would he come home? There were no guarantees. Were these unfilled beach chairs for the American soldiers who had not made it across France, Belgium, Germany ...who had not made it into this old-fashioned swimming facility by an old-fashioned Austrian mountain lake? Where did the bullets stop them? Before the Rhine, after the Rhine—where is the little cross that marks the end of their journey?

The static crackling out of Igor's two small speakers brought me back to my task on hand. I saw Kurt already heading towards the poles. I followed him, with my eyes still on the ground, searching for the unexpected treasure. But none was to be found today.

"Why don't you take that side, Peter," Kurt said and pointed at one end of the rope we had been practicing with earlier.

"Sure," I said and moved into position. From where I stood I could see the entrance to the little wardrobe tent.

Herr Igor was talking to a soldier, who nodded and then took the microphone.

I made out a few words of the English, actually American English, introduction but not the sentences. It must have been funny, because the soldiers, who were already sitting on the grass and the ones coming from all directions to see what was going on, were laughing and applauding.

The impromptu announcer was obviously having fun. He went on and on, until—I could tell from the intonation—he worked up to a special announcement. "The one and only ... incomparable ... Miss Carmen ..."

Carmen, the gypsy girl came running out of the tent, more beautiful than I had ever seen her before: She wore a swimsuit-like costume in a shiny silver color, a little mantilla of the same color over it and silver slippers with laces coming up over her calves. Her pitch-black hair was crowned with a small silver tiara. Two white bands hung down from the back end of the tiara. The soldiers went wild. I had never heard an audience whistle, leave alone perform a whistle concert, eardrum piercing and shrill, lasting for a long time. Carmen was dancing back and forth under the rope, making little curtsies in all directions. She flung her mantilla this way and that way, sent kisses to the soldiers with both hands, thanking them for the applause and appreciation.

"Better get used to this sight before you get hold of that rope, Peter." I was startled. Kurt had come around quietly to deliver a little warning to me.

"If you watch her on the tight rope you will forget," he said. "You must concentrate on the rope, keeping it taut, nothing else, otherwise there is trouble. Bye!" Kurt smiled and disappeared into the crowd to go back to his own position across from me. The other boys all stood in their places already.

The announcer was back in between the static crackle. This time he brought out the mother, Mrs. Igor. She was not as slim and lithe as her daughter but she received the same amount of applause. Her costume was turquoise in color and lacked the glitter. It was toned down with a little tutu. I could see that she was wearing heavy make-up; she looked nothing like this when she sat in front of the wagon at home. I was astonished at the transformation the two women had undergone.

Mother and daughter continued to wave and curtsy to the soldiers until the applause started to wane.

While everybody's attention was on the women, Herr Igor had climbed to the top of the tower next to the tent. He had pulled up the long balance beam after himself and laid it down in front of him. He was standing on the small platform when the announcer drew attention to him. He bowed briefly in all directions, acknowledging the applause and the yells that greeted him, picked up the balance beam and ran across the whole length of the tightrope. Loud applause greeted him, once he arrived at the other end.

I was surprised at how much movement there was in the rope when Herr Igor crossed it for the first time. Together with Kurt, I had to be very sensitive to the motion in order to keep the rope from swinging and bouncing. I imagined what would happen if I pulled too hard and moved the tightrope right under Herr Igor's foot. Would he slip and fall? I decided to let these thoughts go and concentrate on stability.

One of the helpers had put on some Spanish music. Without looking to the sides, from the uproar in the soldiers' applause and vocals, I guessed that the women must have been getting into the act. I quickly checked the poles—yes, Carmen was climbing up one and her mother the other. They did their bowing and curtsying, there was a crescendo of whistles and then Herr Igor raised his arms and asked for silence.

"We ask you, please to be absolutely quiet during our performance because we will need to concentrate very much on keeping the balance in this difficult act," Herr Igor said in German and then waited for the soldier at the microphone to translate. "Thank you!" he said afterwards in English and bowed in several directions.

A scratchy record started to play music from the opera "Carmen" on the phonograph. The loudspeakers, which had been on one too many a trip, were adding their own dimension of scratchiness—but everybody's attention was now on the acrobats getting ready for their act.

The soldiers were very quiet. Except for an occasional metallic flick of a Zippo lighter there were no sounds coming from the audience.

Herr Igor started with another run across the rope. This time he did some kind of a dance step. The women did the same, first the mother, then the daughter, only somewhat more gracefully.

Kurt and I were leaning backwards to use our bodies' weight to keep the rope from swinging too much. Again, I was amazed at how much motion there was between the towers, the tightrope and the stabilizing ropes.

Somehow, the overall mood did not fit with this performance. I was not sure why I thought that way. Finally, it dawned on me. The last time I had seen a tightrope act was with my grandfather in Vienna. In a cabaret theater, an indoor arena, the darkness lit up with colorful spotlights, which made the costumes of the acrobats sparkle brightly. My grandfather, my "Little Opapa," had had a life-long weakness for the cabaret, magicians, talking dogs, counting horses, acrobats, dancers, and he had taken me to see performances several times. When the cabaret finally closed because the acrobats were off performing for the German soldiers, my grandfather was very upset.

I wondered about my grandparents. All four of them had stayed in Vienna. They said we were too old to run away, run where anyway, they'd be conquered all the same, so why not be conquered at home? I wondered how the fierce fighting by the defenders of Vienna and the invading Russian army had affected the city. I had seen what American bombs had done to Vienna long before there was any actual fighting. All over the city, whole blocks were badly damaged or destroyed. All that was left of my grandfather's favorite cabaret was a big gaping hole between two damaged houses. *What does it all look like now? Would I see my grandparents again?*

Applause, shrill whistling and shouting jarred me out of my daydream. Up on the platform the performers bowed and thanked the soldiers. Herr Igor announced the intermission. He came down and told us boys we could let go of the ropes now.

The day had faded into darkness. I had noticed that here at the lake it never got really, really dark. There always was a glow on the water and in the sky, a magic light coming from the stars. I stood there looking out over the lake, it felt peaceful but there still was so much war in the air. My mother—all of a sudden I remembered what I had overheard this afternoon. Would she be over it? Would she still be in shock? Would she talk to me about it?

"Want to walk around a bit? See if we can find a few butts and maybe something to eat?" Kurt was ready to go in search of goodies again.

We strolled off and ended up in front of the main building of the facility. One corner was lit up brightly and crowded with soldiers.

"Let's check it out," Kurt said, heading for the crowd.

"We are not supposed to go there, Kurt, Herr Igor ..."

"Never mind Herr Igor, the soldiers will tell us if they don't want us there."

The old refreshment stand was adorned with a big sign saying "Snack Bar" in big clumsy letters. The soldiers were buying cans of Coca Cola, candy bars, little packages of cookies, coffee, and 'hot dogs,' a Frankfurter sausage put into a very soft roll into which the soldiers squeezed blobs of yellow mustard and a red sauce that looked like made from tomatoes. They were all having a good time, laughing and joking in the line. One of the soldiers, after he had his turn at the counter, abruptly turned towards us and as we prepared to run, he yelled "catch" and hurled one little package at Kurt and one at me. We both caught them—they were *Mars* candy bars. So far, we had only seen the empty wrappers, now we had the real thing in our hands. We both said "Thank you" at the same time, "danke" on top of it and the soldier said "dankescheen" with a grin on his face.

There was an announcement for the soldiers to return to their seats, the performance would continue in five minutes. We ran to our positions, candy bars hidden in our pockets. I was thinking about how to make the best use of mine. I had to bring some of it home to my brother and sister. *Should I eat my part—how much was my part: half, one third, one quarter? Should my mother or Frau Gmeiner even get a piece, too? If I cut this small bar into five pieces, nobody will get anything but a tiny piece. Maybe I should eat the whole bar by myself, after all, I had come over here, I had worked, and I had been given this gift. Actually, I deserved it. But then I could not tell anybody— but it was such an exciting story, how this soldier had thrown the candy at us without warning. He must have seen us standing there and seen the hunger in our eyes; maybe he had children at home? I had to tell, which meant I had to share. I would let my mother decide how.*

Kurt was again at the rope across from me. He was hitting his pocket with his hand and smiling. He was as happy about our treasure as I was. Herr Igor came by, reminded us of how to control the ropes, and instructed us on what to pick up at the end of the performance.

"Just bring all the stuff to the truck, don't hang around here, we need to leave right away, they want us out of here before the soldiers start to leave. If you are left behind, you are in big trouble. They probably put you in their jail for the night. So better be at the truck."

We held the ropes and we watched them all come out again, one by one, the pretty princess last, greeted by a whistle concert that was louder than the first. Whistling was bad manners in Austria, but why would these soldiers care about Austrian manners.

There were a couple of daring acts by Mr. Igor and his wife. Mr. Igor put a chair in the middle of the rope. It sat there with only two legs when he climbed on top of it, and finally made a handstand on the backrest. In the next act they ran towards each other and pretended to keep falling off the rope, one right, and one left, catching themselves with their hands, swinging back up, balancing again and continuing. It was very funny to look at but it must have been very strenuous because they both were breathing heavily when they arrived at the opposite platforms. Roaring applause thanked them and then the soldiers called for the princess. I realized then that outside of Mr. Igor's wife and the princess there were no women on these

307

premises. They must have felt very special or very awkward. One could not tell from their posed smiles. The princess now did a number on a trapeze suspended from one of the towers. She really would not have to do anything, I thought, every time she moved and smiled, the soldiers went wild.

Mr. Igor thanked everybody, especially the soldiers for all their applause and cheering, he said they were happy and honored to be able to perform in front of such a good audience. The soldiers shouted "more, more .." until they got another number by the princess and the Mrs. After that the lights went out, we scrambled to pick up the loose pieces we were assigned and ran for the truck.

The ride through the darkness along the lake was pretty. There were some lights along the water and some across the lake on the other shore reflecting a line of light all the way back to us. I had never experienced this since we had come up here. First there was absolute darkness because of the air raids and then I never got to ride around after dark. I took it all in and hoped for another trip with the performers soon.

My mother was waiting up and already a little worried.

"Where were you so long? I kept looking for Mr. Igor's truck. Was the performance that long?"

"Yes, the soldiers went crazy and wanted more all the time. They really liked the women."

My mother took a deep breath and sat up straight. I remembered what had happened earlier today and wanted to swallow my remark. Too late.

"So they did? Do you know that an American soldier broke into our room this afternoon and wanted to kiss me?"

"What happened?"

"I told him if he would come any closer he would hear the loudest scream he'd ever heard. Then I told him to leave. After a while he did. But I was in shock."

"I sensed something was wrong when I asked you if I could go with the circus people. Can you do anything, tell the police or something?"

"No, they don't care. I would not know how to describe this man anyway. No use. I guess we lost the war. That is what happens when you do. Please, I do not want you to talk about this to any of your friends here, understood?"

"Yes, of course, Mama. Look what I got!"

"Chocolate. How did you manage that? You did not steal it, did you?"

"No, I would not steal anything. A soldier gave them to us. One to Kurt and one to me. He said 'Catch' and threw them at us. How are we going to divide it? I couldn't decide by myself."

"Why did you not eat it right there?"

"Because I wanted to share it with all of you!"

"That is very sweet of you. But I tell you what. We'll cut it in half, you take half and then Dietz and Ina get a half of the half."

"How about you?"

I really do not need any. It's such a treat for you kids, enjoy it. Soon we will have plenty of chocolate again."

"Do you really think so? I do not believe it, not that soon."

"We will see."

WHAT'S UP AT HOME?

"Frau Heller, how are you? How are the girls? Where do you live?" I beamed at the 'house-mother' from the Castle school. My family had gone on an excursion to Seewalchen, the town with the castle. An enterprising truck owner had offered a ride for a fare and had collected a few riders. My mother was doing errands and I was visiting some of the places I knew from my days in the castle school.

"Peter, how good to see you! You know, the girls have been asking about you, they still talk about you carrying them down to the shelter when we had that bad raid, remember?" she said and put an arm around my shoulder.

"Sure do. It was a humdinger night, such a surprise around here. The planes never had come down so low.

They were strafing rather than dropping bombs, nasty crazies."

"We are fine, still living in the Schloss, but I don't think they will want us much longer."

"How come? The owners couldn't fill it all up anyway."

"Well, I think the Americans want to put some soldiers in there, a command post or something," Frau Heller said with a frown. "Have you heard anything from Linz? Or your father?"

"No. No idea what is going on. Mother is getting nervous. She wants to know if the house is still there. There was some fighting, but we do not know where." I was wondering myself. *Where would we go next? How would we meet up with my father? With my grandparents? Are they alive?*

"I want to go and look." Frau Heller said.

"The trains aren't running at all. Are there any buses?"

"No, but I have been listening around for a ride with a truck. The Amis don't want anybody on the road though. Nobody wants to drive and they don't know if there is any gas anywhere. What a time this is."

"How about going by bicycle? How long would it take?" I had that funny feeling in the pit of my stomach that signaled adventure.

"Sure! What an idea, Peter! Do you want to come?" Frau Heller was ready.

"How far is it?" I asked.

"The train takes about two and a half hours. That is with the long stop in Attnang-Puchheim. Five, six hours, maybe? What do you think?" she asked.

"I don't know. It seems like a long way. The train just goes and goes. Most of the way is flat, so it wouldn't be that hard. Do you think the roads are all open?"

"I've heard they are. The Amis run their convoys back and forth. I would have to get somebody to watch the girls. I want to stay only one day, rest up and come back." She was looking out over the lake from where we were standing outside the little grocery store. "The last raids were bad. They said Urfahr and the area around the steel works got it the worst. Our apartment is in Urfahr."

"Let's go soon. I'm sure my mother will let me go." I was ready to run home.

"Oh, please give her my regards, and tell her I would be happy to have you protect me. I wouldn't want to do it alone. Too many soldiers and too many men released from prisons out there." She smiled.

I blushed. I had liked this woman very much from the moment I had met her at the Castle. My feelings became even stronger when I found out that she had known my father a long time ago. I liked her smiling face, her blonde hair, tied back in a bun with some of the loose hair framing her face and softening it, and her strong body, always upright and always in motion. I liked the way she related to her two little girls, loving and firm at the same time. She always wore happy clothes, white blouses that showed off her small round breasts, and brightly colored skirts, not too long, so her good legs were free to move her about.

"I sure would like to go. I'll ask my mother today." I was determined to find out about our house and I was flattered by the woman's trust. It would be an adventure. I had never gone across country on my bike except for the one short tour with my father. But that was when we were rained out and had to stop after the first hour. In Linz I had been all around town on my bicycle. I biked to middle school, forty-five minutes each way, clear across town. I had been up and down this side of the lake. Five hours straight sounded doable to me.

We met in the village square at 5:30 in the morning. There was mist coming up from the lake, spreading through the village and into my bones.

"It is cold with this fog here, let's go and warm up!"

Frau Heller stood by her bicycle. She looked younger than the 35 years she had lived, with the last five not much fun at all. She had on tight slacks and a sweater over a short-sleeved blouse. Her sturdy shoes would help to push those pedals for all the hours ahead.

I felt comfortable in her company. She was woman, mother, adult, strong and determined, loving and warm.

"Off we go. Do you want to put any of your stuff in my rucksack?" she asked. She had two small saddlebags strapped over the luggage rack and a small rucksack clamped on top.

"No, thanks, I strapped mine on good," I said, "it all fit fine. Mother wanted me to take too much."

When we reached the outskirts of the village, we followed the road along the small river draining the lake. Soon the road climbed away from the riverbed. We pedaled hard but in the end we had to get off and push the bikes for a while.

"Are you still cold?" Frau Heller asked.

"No, this hill was enough to warm me up. Look over there, the sun is just about to come up over the mountain."

"I'm glad we started early, it will be hot enough later. In another five minutes we'll be heading downhill." She pointed up ahead to where the road disappeared in the trees.

My mother was roughly the same age as this woman, I thought, but she would never do this sort of thing. She looked awkward on a bicycle. One could tell that she was uncomfortable. Frau Heller was zooming down the hill in front of me. I loved long stretches of gentle downhill coasting, with soft curves, so you did not have to break at all, just letting your body cut through the air.

I bent down over my handlebars to cut down on the wind resistance. I picked up speed right away and soon passed Frau Heller.

"Away we go!" I shouted and waved back with my right hand.

The valley had been carved by glaciers millions of years ago. It was flat and wide, full of green meadows and fields with gently sloped hills at the sides where the glacier had to let go of some of the gravel and soil when it melted.

The road went straight and flat, past the farms, crisscrossing the railroad line several times and bridging the river where it meandered from side to side in the valley.

It was peaceful here. We rode side by side, moving along with even strokes at a good speed. There was a lot of road ahead of us. I had figured the total distance in kilometers from Herr Kastinger's old road map. At ten to

312

fifteen kilometers per hour, we would make it in six or so hours, barring any delays, detours or flat tires.

"Look at the steam above the horses there," I pointed ahead to the right. "These Haflingers look so strong."

"Yes, they are beautiful horses. He is lucky the army didn't take these away from him. He must have a big farm. Lots of wheat."

The farmer was walking behind the two heavy draw horses with long white manes, pulling a harrow, smoothing out the freshly plowed soil. The bodies of the animals were giving off steam, which looked all white against the pale blue sky in the weak morning sun.

"Looks like a painting, doesn't it?" I always looked for paintings. My father had done some watercolors while in Russia. Purple and green skies with a few trees along the horizon, rather depressing, he had said, for hours and hours the scenery would not change at all. My father had a knack to catch moods like that.

"What are you thinking?" Frau Heller asked, "Your face looks so serious."

"Oh, I just remembered my father's watercolors. I wish I could paint like him. When he comes back, he will teach me. I like to paint, but I don't know how to use colors. It always comes out yucky."

"I am sure you are doing fine, Peter. Remember the drawings you made for Erika and Helga? They looked very nice to me. You probably have the same talent your father has."

"I hope so. I want to." I said with a sigh. I turned my head to take another look at the farmer and his horses.

"Doesn't feel like we have had a war here, does it?" Frau Heller took a deep breath of the fresh morning air.

"Do you think we will see a lot of destruction along the way?" I asked.

"The station in Attnang-Puchheim is totally demolished, but you saw that when you took the train to get supplies for the school, didn't you?"

"Yes, that was very scary. I came through the day after the raid. It was one big mess, awful. Tracks sticking up in the air, pieces of freight cars all over the place, locomotives bent so you couldn't tell front and back. It looked like some big bad child had stomped around a model railroad setup."

"It will take a long time to fix all this. A very long time. Lots of work. Lots of money." Frau Heller said, shaking her head.

They rode in silence for a while. The only noise was the straining and screeching of the two bicycle chains. A church steeple up on the horizon signaled the conquest of the first village on the way.

This is where I thought the fighting had taken place the night we had heard the bellowing of artillery and the machine gun fire. At first it sounded like a thunderstorm. But then it became clear that it was the war approaching. The noise had come from this village, I thought. But it did not look disturbed in any way. A few people were up and about. We bid them a good morning, they answered with a friendly wave of the hand, and the common greeting here in the country *Grüß Gott,* may God greet you.

"Where are you going?" one old man asked.

"Linz" we both answered.

"My, that's a long way, on the bicycle. Better watch out. This is not a good time to be on the road. Too many army trucks. Good luck, anyway."

We passed a cart full of fresh dung, steaming and smelly. The horse trotted slowly, the man walked alongside, holding the bridle.

"Grüß Gott" he said.

"Good load you have there." I taunted him.

"It goes on the cabbage field, makes the cabbages grow big heads," the farmer shouted after us, laughing.

Here, life was undisturbed. I suspected that Linz was different. Many places were probably different. That is why my father had insisted that we move to the country. My *father. Where was he? What was he doing? Was he on his way home?* I had seen some German soldiers coming through on foot. They had torn their insignia off the uniforms, so they would look like civilians or at least no longer beholden to the *Führer.* It really was not a very good cover. Most of them had looked hungry and scared, with the horror of the last days of fighting in their faces. Mostly they had been young boys and old men drafted at the last minute into the *Volkssturm*, the People's Army, who had not gone very far from home to fight.

"What do you think your father will do when he comes home?" It felt as if Frau Heller had guessed my thoughts.

"Mama was talking about a photo studio. He has won many prizes at photo contests. And everybody loves the way he does portraits because they never look posed—people look the way they really look or they do what they are doing ..."

"Yes, I know. That is how I met your father. He stopped us on the street and asked if he could take our picture: My husband, the babies and me, we were just out for a stroll."

"He always embarrassed us by asking strangers, but they did not seem to mind. My mother did not like it at all when he did that."

"Why? We thought it was fun and the pictures came out so well. He came to the house and brought us prints and enlargements, you know, we live in Urfahr ..."

"Yes, you mentioned that, that's where his photo club had its lab. Papa took me there several times. I loved it. I remember the red light and the counting and the waiting for the images to develop."

"Well, it sounds as if you could be a big help in the studio, you already know some of the tricks of the trade."

Frau Heller smiled at me and I could feel the hope and warmth in her soul and body for my father and for me. I could also sense the little cold worm creeping up from her stomach. She had to fight not to let it mar her smile, because it was an ugly worm. *"What if this man does not make it, what if he does not come back? What will this boy do, what will we all do without our men? Who knows who will return?"*

"On his last leave Papa said that soon it will be possible to take pictures in color with a regular camera, just with different film. Did you see the movie they made in color? My dad took my mother. It was called *Baron von Münchhausen,* I think. I could not go because it was for adults only."

I was very excited. The idea of working with my father rather than watching him do things always filled me with such joy. I was impatient to get started.

We had come to the top of a ridge. The talking and thinking had made us forget about the strain of pedaling up the slight incline. The stretch in front of us looked like it was going downhill for a while.

On the shady side of the big wooded hill, the air was still cool. Coasting downhill we went faster and faster and our eyes started to water from the wind.

"I wish it would go like this all the way to Linz," I shouted to Frau Heller over my shoulder, "We would be there in no time."

"This is fun, isn't it?" She yelled back and pedaled a few strokes so she could catch up with me.

I looked over at her. She was smiling and her cheeks were rosy and her blouse was flying in the wind. I felt good with her as my companion for this adventure. Frau Heller was only a few years younger than my mother was but she seemed so much freer. Here I was going across the countryside with this woman, for hours, through a territory torn by war with unknown destruction and unknown scars. The only way I had gone this stretch before was by train. Although we must have come this way when we had visited Aunt Martha by car. Of course, I did not remember the road.

"After this hill it seems to be easier to ride on the flat, don't you think so?" Frau Heller was coasting, pedaling lightly to maintain the speed.

"Yes, I hope we don't get any headwind; that is something I really hate. Sometimes when I go fetch our milk by bike, there is an open stretch, where the headwind can feel worse than going uphill. Sometimes it is so bad, I have to get off the bicycle and push it."

"Where do you go for the milk?" Frau Heller asked.

"The little store by the boat dock in Litzelberg."

"Isn't that pretty far from where you live?"

"Yes, it takes not quite half an hour if I go fast."

"Do you go every day?"

"Yes, I have to. We only get three quarters of a liter a day for the three of us. My sister needs it the most, I

316

think. Occasionally we all walk, when it is sunny and nice, but it takes too long. My sister is too little to walk all the way and too heavy to be carried. My brother does not like to walk. He runs and then he gets tired and cranky."

"Do you see what I see?" I said, using the phrase from the children's game.

"What is it?" Frau Heller asked, scanning the horizon. "I cannot see anything special."

"Over there," I pointed, "see the top of the chimney?"

"Oh, yes! You have good eyes, it must be the paper mill in Lenzing."

"Why was that plant not bombed?" I asked.

"It probably was but they did not hit the chimney. We'll see when we ride by. I think we can see the plant from the road," Frau Heller said.

For a while, we pedaled on in silence. The road was flat and empty, lined by big old trees.

I spotted the Jeep first. It was coming at us. It moved slowly, with its lights on and a big red flag flying from its right fender. The soldier riding next to the driver gestured to us, with a smile and no words. It looked like "clear the road" to me.

"Do you think he wants us off the road?" I asked Frau Heller.

"It sure looks like it—oh, look what's coming behind him!" she answered and got off her bicycle. Then she pushed it into the field next to the road.

I followed suit but not without noticing the graceful way this woman had disentangled herself from the bicycle. I looked ahead and saw what she had referred to: a gigantic truck had come around the bend in the road, from behind the trees, another one following it in its tracks. I had never seen a truck this big. It filled the country road from side to side, the tires alone were higher than I was and as wide as three or four regular truck tires put together. The top scraped the branches of the trees along the road. From my second story window at home I probably would not be able to see over the canvas top. The engine roared like that of a tank—that was the only comparison I could think of.

"Have you ever seen anything this big?" I shouted to Frau Heller who was standing right next to me.

The driver of the first truck waved to us with a big grin on his face as the truck rumbled by. He seemed as high up as on top of a hay wagon. I waved back. I was totally in awe of the big monster made of steel and rubber.

The weight of these trucks wreaked havoc with whatever was left of the roads after the abuse they had taken from tanks and other caterpillar treaded vehicles before them. The blacktop was all broken up and the tires started to sink into the roadbed proper, with pieces of asphalt popping out in different directions.

I leaned over to Frau Heller's ear. "My father told me that he saw some dirt roads in Russia where the tanks had dug in the turns so deep that you could not see the cars going through afterwards! If we have a few more tanks coming through here, that turn up there might become that way."

"It is awful how it breaks up the road, there will be nothing left for us to ride on ...!" she said loudly towards my ear.

I felt her presence and a closeness that was intensified by us being the only humans on foot aside from the machines making up this giant snake. I also noticed the way she avoided looking at the soldiers in the cabs. The GI's already had a reputation for hooting and whistling at every female they passed. Frau Heller's fresh looks did not go unnoticed here either but these engines were so loud that any appreciation had to be communicated by gestures only. There had been faces, waves, and even invitations. She had ignored them all.

"This is really bumpy now!" I said, leading the way after the convoy had passed. We stayed on the narrow strip of dust between what was left of the pavement and the grass growing out of the drainage ditch.

"You really have to watch for these bits of asphalt the trucks shot all over." Frau Heller's voice came from close behind. "I almost fell just a little way back."

They met another convoy not long after the first one. This time there were regular trucks, the high clearance trucks with the letters GMC on the grill I had seen all along. I still could not understand why there was so much space between the front fenders and the wheels.

"You know, I have been drawing cars and trucks all through the war, these look so strange to me. Look at them from the side!" I pointed to the abnormality. "Just like those square fenders on the Jeeps. There must be some reason."

We were standing on the inside of a turn in the road, in the shade of a few trees, watching the trucks go by. Tank treads or whatever had massacred this turn also. There was nothing left of the road surface but dirt, with large holes filled with water from the last rain. The trucks slowed down, and most drivers shifted down before they bumped through that stretch, one after another.

"Look at him, he's trying to be smart!" I pointed to a truck that had gone off the road into the grass to avoid the bad stretch. We watched him struggle to make it back on. The field was wet and the tires spun out digging themselves into the soil.

"Oh ..." Frau Heller grabbed my arm, "We should pick it up!" A carton had bounced off one of the trucks and was lying right in the tracks. One end had cracked open and showed the shiny sides of tin cans.

"I am sure it is food," she said, "all those cans, it must be food, we could eat for days!"

I pushed my bicycle towards her and motioned her to hold it, "You think they would let us have it?"

"No, Peter, don't..."

The front wheels of the next truck had come very close to the carton, the double rear tires had gone right over it and crushed it wide open. The cans emerged bent into different shapes, none had burst open and revealed its contents though.

I was ready to dart in before the next truck could do more damage but Frau Heller held me back. "It is too dangerous, Peter, they move pretty fast and from where they sit, they cannot see that box—or you!"

We stood there in silence, watching as the cans were flattened and pushed into the soil by truck after truck, soon gone and invisible. At the end, only some scraps of the cardboard were flapping from the mud.

"What do you think it was?" I asked, sounding hungry and sad.

"I don't think the cans ever broke open, the ground is so soft ..."

"We can dig them up when the convoy is gone by ...," I said and my face lit up. "We would be able to reach the treasure after all."

"Forget it, I, it looks soft, but these trucks weigh tons, they compact that soil, you wouldn't be able to dig into it." Frau Heller looked at me and smiled, "I wish we could salvage them, they could be full of chicken or salmon—oh, let's pretend they were full of spinach or those white soft things they eat ... aren't you glad we don't have to ..."

I was not convinced yet. "I have my pocket knife. It would be worth a try ..."

"Let's get on with our trip, we'll never get there today if we keep dawdling like this. We'll eat our lunch at the next nice spot, yes?" Frau Heller sounded motherly and yet firm.

"This feels like going uphill, but it is perfectly flat, isn't it?" I was again leaning low over my handlebars to give the wind less to push against.

Frau Heller was struggling the same way. We were out on the open highway cutting through what was called the *Welser Heide,* a big plain stretching west from the outskirts of Linz. At least our destination seemed within reach.

"Just two more hours, I believe, if we do not run into any more obstacles."

Both of us felt tired. The lack of real food over the past few months had taken its toll.

"Maybe we need another snack break, I have some smoked meat left and some of that good cheese from Seewalchen which you like so much. That will pick us up."

"I want to get home, I am anxious to see what we will find—or what we will not find," I added, after I had felt a sudden twang in my stomach. "But I do need something to drink. Let's find a place in the shade—up there it looks like some trees?"

"I believe we can go that far before we run out of steam completely, we are so much closer now. We must

320

not get discouraged." Frau Heller said, pedaling harder to gain speed.

We shared a couple of slices of famers' bread and Frau Heller's meat and cheese. We drank water out of our canteens. Somewhat refreshed we took off again.

After another hour the scenery and some buildings began to look familiar. There was the little butcher shop where my mother used to buy our meat. It looked closed. I stopped at the next small intersection with a big sigh. "Here I am, here I turn off."

"We made it! How far is it from here to your house?"

"Up the hill and then a few short streets! I cannot believe it!"

"Just a little farther for me, into town and across the Danube. I hope the bridge is open. I have your address and the little map you drew me, I think I can find you. I will be back day after tomorrow, as early as I can make it."

We shook hands and said our good-byes.

I pushed my bike up the hill towards my old elementary school. I had been tempted to walk into the grocery store at the foot of the hill and look for familiar faces. I decided I was too excited and needed to find out about our house first.

I followed my old way from school through the park with the old wild pear trees, in between the new butcher shop and the bakery, I turned the corner at the little milk store and headed straight towards the house. So far, I had not noticed any damage that had not been there when I had left. There was the old hump in the road again, I had to wait until I was on top of it before I could see my house. It was there. Unchanged. Undamaged. Incredibly relieved I coasted closer.

The front door was open, and so were the bedroom windows upstairs. I did not see anybody in the garden. I leaned my bike against the front wall, stepped up to the door and knocked. Waiting for an answer, I could smell food. A woman, about the age and height of my mother appeared in the doorway from the kitchen. She looked at me, smiled and said "Hello?"

"I am the son of the owner of this house ..." I really did not know how to phrase my position without offending, without intruding...

"Oh, please come in. You must be Frau Slonek's son, let me think, Peter ... is that right?"

"Yes, I am Peter Slonek," I said.

"I am so glad to see you, you are all right, aren't you?" she had put her hand on my arm as if to check for damages. "Everybody fine in your family?"

"Yes, we made it through. But we have not heard from my father yet." I was anxious to start my own questioning. What were these people doing in my house?

"Well, it is too early; there is no mail, still. He will either come himself or you will get some news, I am sure. Where was he last?" she talked fast but warmly, with her eyes never leaving mine.

"Darmstadt. Heading for the Western front," I said. "Not very far to go, I guess," I added as an afterthought.

"Come on in, please, sit down in the living room. Let me explain about us—but first, can I get you something to drink, to eat? How did you get here?"

"By bicycle, from Attersee. We started early this morning. My friend went to Urfahr, to check on her apartment."

"You must be exhausted—and hungry. Let me see what I have. What do you like to drink? I have only a little milk left, is water all right? Sit down and rest. I'll be back right away." She hurried off into the kitchen.

I sat down on my father's big easy chair with the ottoman. My legs deserved a rest. I looked around. Everything looked the same.

How long has it been since I left? I asked myself. It seemed such a long time. *Are we coming back here? Soon, I hope. Will these people stay with us? How many of them are there? She said 'we,' didn't she?*

It was dark in here. The curtains were drawn. I was used to having the back door open into the garden. Maybe they don't use this room.

"I did not even introduce myself. This all came too quickly. I am Anni Schreiber." She sat a tray with a glass of water and a plate with two big pieces of coffee cake down on the small round table next to the easy chair. She wiped her hands on her apron and extended her hand.

I stood up and shook her hand. "Pleased to meet you, Frau Schreiber."

"Oh, you are such a gentleman. Sit down please. After all your bicycle riding. Such a brave young man. Now, the coffee cake is all I have for now, but dinner is almost ready, you will have dinner with us, won't you?"

"Thank you, Frau Schreiber, yes ..." I hesitated, thinking of where else I could go. I had assumed I would be in the house alone.

"Where are you staying overnight? You are staying overnight, aren't you?—You cannot go back by bicycle right away? You will stay here, it is YOUR house, no?" The woman seemed as confused about the situation I was.

"Yes, I had planned to stay here—if it was still standing," I said, picking up the water to hide my nervousness.

"Well, it is standing and you certainly will stay here. Now that that is settled, let me tell you how we got here, why we are in your house ..." Frau Schreiber sat down in the other easy chair.

I drank half the water to quench my thirst, noticing a chemical taste, and put it down. I was anxious to have a bite of the cake since I had not had anything to eat since the snack break before Wels.

"Eat Peter, please, I make a big sheet of this cake every week, the kids like it, my husband Rudy would rather have meat, but you know how that goes—there is no meat. I hope you like cake. It has Streusel on top. Anyway, Frau Baumgartner, the lady your mother gave your house keys to, just in case, you know, somebody must have the keys, otherwise they break down the door, she, Frau Baumgartner said we should move over here to protect your house—it is safer when there is somebody in it—there were so many people roaming around right after the American troops came. They opened the jails, you know, they let out everybody. It was supposed to be only the political prisoners, but they let out everybody. These people wandered around and broke into all the empty houses and took what they needed."

I felt comfortable with this woman. I did not know what it was, but my initial reaction of her being an intruder had gone away very quickly. I was wondering about her accent. She was Austrian all right, but where from? Sometimes she even sounded very German, some inflections definitely were not Austrian at all.

"The five of us had two rooms over there in the bachelor apartments, they were made for men living alone, just to sleep in, nothing else, now they are all full of families, refugees ... but we were lucky to get that, yes, we have been on the go for quite a while, ever since that bad night they burned down Dresden. We were lucky, we survived. I took the children down to the river and put wet comforters over them, it was so hot from the fires, ashes falling constantly, and the planes were still dropping bombs, firebombs, napalm I think they call it, can you imagine—women and children, thousands of them dead ..., twenty thousand, thirty thousand dead, burnt alive in one night."

Frau Schreiber's voice had changed when she started to describe that night. She had tears rolling down her cheeks, she sat up erect as if she were looking for someone to accuse, someone to put on trial for what she had seen with her own eyes.

"All we had left were the clothes on our backs. Everything else was gone, burnt, even our suitcases we had taken to the shelter, burnt to ashes. We went as soon as we could and found a train to Austria. Luckily, I have relatives in *Krummnussbaum*, where I grew up. They let us stay there. When the Russian army came closer and closer, we decided to pack up again and move here to Linz, where my husband was working for the Steel Works. He had been sent home from the German Army in Russia because of his training. They needed him to work here in the factory, I do not know what he did there. He designed vending machines before the war. That's not what they were making here, as you know.

I was overwhelmed by the tale of horror. It brought back memories of other stories I had heard, of the many hours spent in shelters, of the narrow escapes, of days and days of watching people with all their belongings in

bags on their backs or on small handcarts, p
drawn, very tired old people, some with dirty b
some on crutches, streaming by, without a destin
the run from what they had experienced ...

"He is a very special man, he is a very special
technician, they needed him for God knows what," Frau
Schreiber continued.

"So I should be grateful I have him. Most women are
without their men, very few men have come home yet, and
nobody knows where anybody is. It is such chaos."

I had finally dared to eat a piece of cake. It felt
strange being offered food by a stranger on one of my
family's plates. I recognized my mother's old white china.

I had been so intent on listening and so full of my
own emotions, I did not know how to respond to this
woman. I was sure she had told the story many times
before, but it could not be told often enough. Why all this
killing? Has everyone gone insane? Will the killing end
now?

"I don't know where my children are, they should be
back by now. We have three: two boys and a girl. They are
probably playing out behind the apartments, that's where
all their friends play. Tell me about your family, where is
everybody now? You said Attersee? I do not know where
that is."

"Yes, we ended up in a farm house outside of
Attersee. Very kind people, they had to take in three
families, one from Berlin, one from Yugoslavia, and us. A
gypsy circus wagon full of people is parked in their front
yard. The five of us live in the farmer's bedroom upstairs."

"Five? I thought you were three kids, I saw the photos
here in the house," Frau Schreiber interrupted.

"Yes, there are only three of us, my brother Dieter, my
sister Ina and myself, but we took in, my mother took in,
this woman from Berlin, she was bombed out a long time
ago."

"You don't like her, do you?" Frau Schreiber said.

"Oh, she is fine, I guess, but she always gets involved
in our affairs. She used to run a girls' boarding house, she
thinks she is still doing that, correcting us and ordering

us around." My voice trailed off with the unpleasant memory.

I heard footsteps from the hallway.

"Mutti?" a girl's voice called.

"I am in here, we have a visitor," Frau Schreiber said.

The girl came in slowly. She was younger than me, tall, and her blond hair ended in two short braids. She moved close to her mother right away and looked at me curiously.

"This is Peter Slonek, who lives here," the mother said. "He came by bicycle from Attersee to check on the house."

"Do we have to move out?" the girl asked.

"Why don't you first say hello, before you ask any questions," the mother said.

"Hello Peter," the girl said because she had been told to.

"Her name is Isolde," the mother added.

"Hello Isolde," I said and smiled. I wanted her to be at ease. I was not here to push them out. When we all come back, we'll see what to do.

"Her older brother is Helmut and her younger brother is Helge," the mother said, putting an arm around the girl's waist. "Where are they? Do you know?"

"Last I saw them they were playing over by the Metzgers," she said, her eyes still on Peter.

"Could you go and find them and tell them to come home, please. I would like them to meet Peter," Frau Schreiber said.

"Is Peter staying with us?" she asked and twisted out of her mother's arm.

"He is having dinner with us and he is staying overnight," she said. "Are you riding back tomorrow or when?" she asked Peter.

"Frau Heller, my friend who came with me, will come by here the day after tomorrow in the morning. That is when we want to start on our way back."

Isolde left as soon as I had finished. I remembered her big eyes and her little round nose. Her accent was really German. A real German family, I thought, Helmut, Helge and Isolde. In Austria only Nazis gave their kids

Germanic names, taken from the old sagas and promoted by Hitler's propaganda 'to keep the Germanic heritage alive.'

"The cake was very good, thank you," I said.

"The water is horrible, isn't it? The Americans put chlorine in it and who knows what else. They say it would not be safe to drink without it. Too many bodies not buried properly. I do not know how we came to that, it is God awful," Frau Schreiber said. "This war, I do not know what it was for. This fool Hitler thought he could conquer the world. One country cannot fight them all and win. Any fool should know that. The help he had, really was no help."

"Boys, behave, please," Frau Schreiber shouted as they came running in, the older one first, the little one behind.

"This is Peter—do you recognize him from the pictures we saw?" she asked.

"I do," the older one said. "Hello."

"I don't," the younger one said and laughed.

I got up and shook Helmut's hand and then Helge's. "Hello."

There was an awkward pause. I had realized that I had not shaken hands with Isolde and was trying to think of a way to make good on it. She had come in behind the boys, proud of her successful errand.

"You did not shake hands with me," she said and walked up to me with her hand out.

"I am sorry," I said and took her hand. "Hello, formally now, I am pleased to meet you," mocking a formal tone of voice.

We both laughed. I was embarrassed. Isolde seemed embarrassed, too. She pulled her hand back quickly.

"You kids keep Peter entertained, I have to finish dinner before Father comes home. Peter can bring his rucksack in, he will sleep in the room right down here. Helmut, can you please check if there are any of our things in there. Peter, take your bicycle to the back of the house so it will not be stolen. We have to be careful here. If you want to wash up, go ahead, use the bathroom here or upstairs, you know where we are! You can find a towel where you used to keep them." Frau Schreiber thought of everything.

I was glad to be in a functioning household again. Not these cramped quarters. I was going to tell my mother to move back here right away.

"Thank you, Helmut," I said. Helmut had brought in my rucksack off the bicycle.

"It is pretty heavy. How long did it take you?" Helmut asked.

"Six hours, not counting the rest stops. We ran into a lot of army traffic on the narrow roads off Attnang. They drove big trucks, bigger than I had ever seen. We had to pull off the road and wait them out. One of them lost a couple of boxes with cans. I wanted to get them but it was too dangerous. The other trucks just smashed them into the ground, it was awful to watch," I said.

They all stood around me, looking. I was the tallest.

"How old are you?" I asked Helmut.

"I'll be eleven in September, and you?"

"What day in September?" I asked with surprise, "my birthday is in September, on the sixteenth!"

"Mine is on the sixth," Helmut said.

"That's pretty close. I am two years older than you, maybe we can celebrate together," I said. "Let me put my bicycle away."

We all went outside and around the house. I looked down into the garden. They had not done anything there. Somehow, I was glad. It was my father's design and my and my mother's work to keep it up. The fruit trees had grown and the shrubs looked immense.

"I will be nine years old," Isolde said looking me straight in the eyes.

"Wow! Nine years. And how old is your brother?" I asked.

"He is only five-and-a-half," she said.

When we went back to the front, I pointed at the badly repaired, frying pan size hole in the wall of the apartment building across the street. "We were sitting at lunch during an air raid, we did not hear any planes, and all of a sudden this crazy plane came very low and fired his gun—this was the only hit we could find, it exploded in the basement and made a mess. We were scared. It could have been us. From then on, we always went into the shelter in the basement right away when there was an alarm.

"Did mother tell you about the firebombing in Dresden?" Helmut asked.

"Yes, she did tell me. That is why you are here," I said.

"We first went to our grandmother's house in Krummnussbaum in Lower Austria but then the Russians came there. So Vati wanted us to come up here" Isolde spoke up.

I was amused at their accent and their use of *Vati* and *Mutti*. I had heard it before but Austrians did not use these terms.

"Tell me, who lives next to us and down the row? Do you know?" I asked.

"The neighbors are new. They just got put in there before the war was over. Frau Horn and her son are in the next one. The Metzgers are gone, but all their stuff is still in there. A doctor is living there." Helmut seemed to be up to date.

"I have to see Frau Horn and Friedl," I said, "Do you think they are home now?"

"They are always home, everybody is always home. There is no place to go," Helmut said. He sounded very mature and resigned.

"Let's go over there, can we?" I was already heading along the houses to the Horn's door. I rang the doorbell. After a while Frau Horn opened the door. She jumped out and hugged me. "How good to see you, Peter! Where is your mother?"

"Still in Attersee. I just came down by bicycle to see how things are. We could not stand it any longer, not knowing," I was all excited to see a familiar face. "How are you? Have you heard from Uncle Turl?"

All of a sudden, her smile was gone. I felt a pain in my gut. *'I should have kept my mouth shut,'* I thought.

"No, the last we heard, he was in Stalingrad. That was a long time ago. But, of course, nobody has heard from anybody in Russia," Frau Horn said, comforting herself.

"How is Friedl?" I asked about her son.

"He is fine, growing like a weed, even without food. Now tell me, what is your mother doing? Have you heard from your father? Are you coming back, soon?" She put her arm around me and stood next to me.

"Papa's last letter was from February. Nothing since then. I think we will come back, he does not know where we are anyway. It is no fun out there, we are living in one room. I'll tell Mama to come back. Do you get any food?" I asked.

"Well, we get our rations, mostly. There is a lot of trading going on around here, you know, people grow things, they have chickens, rabbits—do you still have cigarettes? They are worth gold. For cigarettes you can get anything you want. American cigarettes are worth even more." She laughed. "I stopped. I couldn't afford it any more. Remember I smoked a lot?"

Frau Schreiber called from the other end. "Dinner is ready, Vati is home."

"When are you going back? You came all alone on the bicycle? Your mother would let you do that?" Frau Horn sounded horrified.

"No, I came with a friend, a woman who lives in Urfahr. We are going back together, day after tomorrow."

"Then you can see Friedl tomorrow. He's over with his friend. I want to ask you more questions, too. How did you make it through the end, all right? Dieter and Ina? Tell me tomorrow. The Schreibers will take good care of you, they are nice people. Bye. I am so glad you all are fine." I could see little tears rolling down her cheeks. She closed the door quickly.

"This is our Vati!" Frau Schreiber proudly introduced her husband.

I shook hands with him, "Pleased to meet you, Herr Schreiber."

"We are so glad you came, we were wondering how we could get in touch with your mother. Nobody knew where she went. Frau Baumgartner said, she did not even know when she left here. It was still up in the air."

330

"The relatives did not want us, so my mother kept looking. Finally the relocation people assigned us a place. That is where we are now," I said.

"I have to tell you some things for your mother after dinner. Let's eat now. I am hungry," Herr Schreiber said.

I did not know what to make of this man. He was friendly and warm. He looked a little odd with large lips and rosy round cheekbones over hollow cheeks full of beard stubbles. His voice was raspy and he smelled of smoke. He was wearing strong old-fashioned glasses with round steel rims.

We sat down around the old round table in the living room. The familiar china, the familiar silverware and glasses. I felt torn between resenting these strangers using all our things and my compassion for the family who had lost everything they had in one dreadful night.

With the father present, the specific German accent was more prevalent than before.

"You sound very different from most other Germans I have talked with. Where does your accent come from?"

"Saxony" was the answer. Of course, I could have figured that out myself. Dresden is one of the major cities in the province of Saxony. I even thought that our Christmas shipment from the Erzgebirge had come from somewhere in Saxony

I noticed that even Frau Schreiber pronounced many of her words in that dialect. Well, she had lived there for most of her adult life.

The father's presence also stirred up memories for me. It had been a long time since I had been eating a meal with my father present. After a few hours of knowing this family, I felt protected and cared for. I thought of letting them stay in the house when we come back. It would be fun to have them for company. I would suggest this to my mother.

"You must stay here when we come back. There is enough room for all of us," I said out loud.

"No, we have to leave this to you. We promised Frau Baumgartner that we would move out as soon as your mother comes back," Frau Schreiber said.

"We can send Frau Gmeiner on her way, there is one room," I said.

"It is very nice of you, Peter, to invite us, to even think that we could live together, but I think it will be better if we move back to the apartments," Herr Schreiber said, "there are too many of us."

"Oh, I think it would be fun ..." all three of the Schreiber children said at the same time, and I nodded.

"Please, that is not for you to decide," their father said. That ended the discussion. Herr Schreiber asked me to come with him to sit in the easy chairs. He lit a cigarette. His cheeks became even more hollow when he drew in the smoke.

"Peter, let me tell you what we did when we moved in here. I want you to pay close attention and tell all of this to your mother as soon as you return to her. I think my wife has told you why we moved over here. Frau Baumgartner wanted somebody to be in the house because so many empty houses were broken into and vandalized by some of the people who were released from jail, or by foreign forced laborers who wanted to get revenge. There were bands of them roaming around for a while. Some of them demanded to search houses to see if the occupants had been Nazis.

"I decided to look at everything in the house that could show that your parents were Nazi friendly or even active. The neighbors told us you weren't but we wanted to make sure. I found your *Adler* magazines, I found a "*Mein Kampf*," I found several other books with swastikas on the cover in the bookshelf—and I burnt them all. I hope your mother is not going to be upset about that. I did not make a list of all the items, who knows, somebody might find the list, you see?"

I had listened intently. I tried to remember what else could be there, but I could not think of anything.

"Thank you for doing that, I think it is all right. It could have saved our other belongings. My father really did not like the Nazis. He did not even want me to go to the Hitler Youth meetings. We had a lot of trouble about that, they came and took me with them, several times," I said.

"Oh, what about a flag? I could not find your flag. Everybody had a flag, no?" Herr Schreiber said.

"My father hated that flag business. We never had a big one, only the little paper ones for the window when we absolutely had to, and he burnt those right after," I said. I remembered listening to my father and mother arguing. My mother was afraid we would have trouble with the party officials. They came around and threatened people who did not display flags properly.

Helmut and I traded war stories for a while. The younger ones were listening in, off and on, or adding their own comments when they thought something important had been left out.

"Time to go to bed," Frau Schreiber finally announced.

"Where do you all sleep?" I asked the children.

"I'll show you," Helge the youngest said and took my hand. He pulled me upstairs.

"Helmut and I sleep in your room, here!" he opened the door and gestured with his free hand.

I did not notice any changes but my memory was vague. We had shifted the furniture around so many times because of heating and the raids, and my brother's crying spells. But this was the room that my brother and I had been given when we moved into the house. I remembered sitting up there by the only window and reading or watching my mother tending the plants in the garden.

"Come on!" Helge said, "I'll show you where my parents sleep, next."

We entered the master bedroom. It jolted my memory back to that lunch before my father left for the army. *Soon we'll hear from him. I wonder what he will think of the Schreibers? I believe they would get along fine, Herr Schreiber seems like a man Papa would like.* The dark burgundy table had reminded me. We had used it when eating upstairs in the winter since it was the only heated room.

"Isolde sleeps over here, alone," Helge said, moving to the study. "Look at her Waldi, the doggie she brought from home."

"It was with me in the raid, it covered my face," Isolde said. She picked it up and showed it to me. It looked like it had been white once and furry. Now it was more gray and shabby looking. Its big glass eyes were still shiny and looked alive. "Want to pet him?" she said and held the doggie out towards me. I took the stuffed animal and gave it a real cuddle against my chest.

"Good doggie," I said. "You are a brave doggie, not afraid of the fire!"

We all laughed. Isolde took the dog back and put him down on the bed. I caught her looking at me very seriously.

After saying good night to everybody, I found myself in the current guest room, where Frau Gmeiner had lived before we moved to the lake. The furniture was still arranged the way she had put it. I thought I could still smell her perfume. I shuddered. *"I wonder how long she is going to be with us."* I thought, *"Berlin was taken by the Russians, she couldn't go there."*

It had been months since I had been in this house. I had missed it. This was home. Not the Castle, not Aunt Martha's, not the Kastingers. I pulled the familiar old comforter up high and went to sleep instantly.

Frau Heller rang the doorbell a little after ten on the morning after our rest day. She introduced herself to Frau Schreiber who asked her in.

"Can I make you something before you take off?" Frau Schreiber asked. "We are so glad we met Peter. Thank you for making this trip with him!"

When I came in from the garden and saw Frau Heller, I was shocked. This woman did not look like the woman who had said *Auf Wiedersehen* to me two days ago, a short distance from here.

"Frau Heller, hello, what did you find?" I asked but I really was afraid to hear the answer. Frau Heller was pale and her eyes were hollow and red as if she had cried. Her bright blue cotton dress did not help her appearance at all.

"Hello, Peter. I see you have new friends. How nice. My apartment is gone, most all of it. The building had a direct hit, which ripped open one whole side. The neighbors put what was left of my furniture into the corner of one remaining room, but it was not closed off, so people could see into it. They helped themselves to whatever they needed. There is not much left. I locked it up with friends." She stared into space with dead eyes when she was finished.

I was angry and speechless. I ran up to her and hugged her. "I am sorry," I said, "that is not what we came for, is it?"

"Well, yes, that is what we came for, we wanted to find out. I did not expect that, though. One never expects it for oneself, but nobody is exempt, I guess. We will have to start all over, that is if my husband makes it home. Who knows." She shook her head, sighed deeply and pulled out a handkerchief from a pocket in her skirt to wipe away some tears.

"I do know how you must feel," Frau Schreiber said. "We lost everything in Dresden, in one night, I am sorry it had to happen to you. We are glad we are alive, all of us. One becomes very modest in this war, or whatever is left of it. I will make you some coffee. My husband traded some off a fellow at work, good coffee, real beans." Frau Schreiber went to the kitchen without waiting for an answer.

"No, thank you, we should be going, we have a long way to pedal before we will be home ..." Frau Heller realized she was not heard and stopped. "Peter, are you ready for the trip? How do your legs feel? Are they sore? Mine still hurt a little on the first day."

Now her voice sounded the way I remembered. It was hard for me to get used to her looks. I had an imaginary flashback of arriving at the house here and finding it destroyed—or just damaged—how would I have felt? I would have had to stay with strangers somewhere in the apartments, or Frau Baumgartner would have taken me in ... nothing left of their dream. How would I have told my mother?

Frau Heller will have to tell her girls. Maybe they are little enough not to understand fully. They have lived in different places for a while, maybe they don't remember 'home' at all.

"My legs felt stiff, when I got up, but then it sort of went away. I forgot about it, running around," I said.

Frau Schreiber came in with a cup and placed it in front of Frau Heller. "There you are, it will give you energy for the trip! Would you like a piece of cake? I packed some for you and Peter, anyway. Do you take sugar or milk? You are in luck if you do, because I happen to have both today."

"No, thank you, black is fine. Such a treat, it smells wonderful, I had almost forgotten the power of the aroma. Thank you so much."

Frau Schreiber went back to the kitchen and brought out a carefully wrapped package. "Here are a few provisions for your trip. There is bread and a little sausage and cheese. I put the coffee cake into an extra bag so it does not taste like sausage. You did fill your canteen, Peter? I hope you will have enough, because it will be a long ride. Looks like you will have good weather."

Helmut had brought my bicycle up front. I put the food package into my rucksack, strapped it on the back of my bike. It was time to say goodbye. I had come to like this family in the few hours I had spent with them. I was looking forward to the time when I would come back and we could all be together. We shook hands, Frau Schreiber gave me a hug, wishing us a safe journey.

The kids waved to us as long as we could see them, and Frau Heller and I waved back. We were on our way. The lake seemed farther away now that we had gone the whole distance once already.

"Let's hope there is no headwind on that long flat part," Frau Heller said.

"Yes, we could do without it," I answered and took the lead down the big hill onto the main highway leading us out of town.

4. THE RETURN

FROM THE LAKE BACK TO TOWN

The rumors persisted that the Russians wanted more of Austria than they already occupied. We heard about ongoing negotiations between the four Allied powers currently occupying Austria. People were nervous, especially the ones living in areas bordering on Russian-occupied territory. Linz was firmly in the hands of the US Army, so everybody said. My mother was convinced that that was true and wanted to return to our house as soon as possible. There was still time to clean up the garden and plant some winter vegetables. We could harvest our own without having to scrounge through the woods.

Larger cities still had problems with food supplies. Out where we were, away from population centers, we could always get the occasional slab of butter, or a piece of meat when a farmer had his slaughter day. Mother consulted with Tante Gmeiner. They agreed that having the old space back and the garden would help more and be more comfortable than remaining here.

"Herr Kastinger, I am thinking of taking the kids and our friend back to town. I want to get things ready for when my husband is coming home. I think he would like to find us in the house, rather than having to track us down here."

"Well, I think you are right. But you know what they say about the Russians, they have not stopped moving. You think you will be safe? We'd be happy to have you stay a while longer. You are good people, haven't made any trouble."

"Thank you so much, Herr Kastinger, it is very kind of you to say that. We appreciate so much that we could stay here, in your bedroom, too. It is a good room."

"Yeah, couldn't say it isn't. We sure like it. The view from up there is better yet than from the balcony in the downstairs living room. It is. Suit yourselves; let me know what you are going to do. How will you get back?"

"I thought I would look for someone to take the big suitcases with a car or a truck, and we would go with the bus and then the train from Seewalchen."

"Wish you luck there, them buses don't run all the time. Depends on them getting fuel, the Amis don't give them fuel all the time. With the kids you cannot walk. Peter can take his bicycle to the train but you got to have a transport. I'll ask around if you don't mind."

"Oh, I cannot thank you enough, Herr Kastinger, you are an angel. If you do hear ..."

"We'll work something out, Frau Slonek, don't you worry."

"Thank you!"

"Found you a truck, will take you, all of you, all the way to town, to Linz. We'll have to find some butter and some meat besides the fare, but he'll get you there, safe. I know the fellow driving it. As long as the truck don't break down or he run out of gas, you'll be there, back home, just like you wanted. I was right about them buses, most of the time they don't run at all. The trains, I hear, when they go, are full up to the roofs with people. Don't want you and your kids and your friend travel like that!"

"Oh, Herr Kastinger, how did you manage that? I cannot believe it! Thank you, so much, Thank you!" My mother went to the man and grabbed his hand and shook it with both of hers.

"Never mind how, just worked out, asking around. He goes to Linz about once a week, depending on how many people want to go."

One week later the truck stopped in front of the Kastinger house. We lifted our suitcases and my bicycle on the open flatbed. There was a load of people already on board. It would be crowded up there. Tante Gmeiner took one look and I could see her hair stand up.

"How, how can I ..."

The driver, a modest and friendly man, must have noticed her reaction, too.

"You, lady, come and sit in the cab with me. You'll keep warm there.

"Really, do you mean ..."

"Yes, yes, it is alright. Just make sure your friends here watch your bags, why don't you," and he pointed at me, "take care of this grandma's bags till you all get off? She is going the same place you are? Agreed?"

I nodded and took her large travel bag and put it on the truck. "Your big suitcase is already on, isn't it?"

"Yes, thank you!" she said with the friendliest face I had seen on her in months. "Thank you, Peter."

I helped mother lift my sister on the truck bed, and then gave Dieter a helping push to get on. The driver helped my mother after she had handed him the money for the fare. Herr Kastinger had taken care of the two packages, one with butter and the other with smoked pork, as the driver's incentive, which would be on the Black Market in Linz by tonight.

"Let's go!" the driver said, "One more stop in Seewalchen, two more people, then we are off for good. You people let me know when you have to go, just knock on the window here, and I'll see what I can do. Just try to do it all at once, don't want to stop all the time."

The Kastingers stood there and lined up next to them was Miro and his parents and the woman from Berlin and her son. Over by the circus wagon, mother and daughter were having breakfast outside with an American soldier who looked like he had spent the night there. They all looked over when the truck started up and waved. The Kastingers and their housemates waved too.

Slowly the truck coasted down the driveway and entered the road. As we were leaving all these people who had shared these scary weeks with us, I became sad. We had a house to go to, these people had nowhere to go, nowhere to call home, and owned no more than they had in their small rooms here. We would never know what would become of them. There was no way for us to keep in touch. Except for the Kastingers. We could visit them and show my father where we had lived while hiding from the bombs.

The whole group kept waving, Miro was running after the truck flailing his arms. He had been a good companion, I had learned a lot from him. I wished now

339

that I could take him with me. The truck went around the first curve in the road and we were out of sight. I settled down next to Tante Gmeiner's suitcase and looked at the scenery. This was my milk run route, where I had ridden my bicycle most days of the week. How easily this old truck made it up the hill where I had to struggle so hard. We passed the milk store, following the road along the lake.

"Watch for Aunt Martha's house, it will come up pretty soon!" my mother pointed towards the lake on the right.

A few minutes later, it did come up. I could see the red berries on the mountain ash trees by the gate. A few white things were dangling on the laundry line. Probably the old butter wrappings to be used to cover her canning jars with. *Good old Aunt Martha, her life does not seem to change, regardless of what is going on around her.* I wondered if I would have been happier with her than at the Kastingers? I didn't think so. Too many rules, too much gloom. Up there I had been free and exposed to adventures I had never even dreamed of before. Most probably we would have never known that part of the lakefront.

The truck rattled on, everybody's hair was blowing in the wind, except for the women's who had tied scarves around their heads. We looked like a band of guerillas running from some unknown enemy.

We passed the resort where the girls' school had been. I wondered if they were still there or if they had connected with their parents before everything fell apart. What about Elspeth, my short-lived 'girlfriend'—I had walked with her, arm in arm, for a few turns, one night. But what a memory that had become. The messages passed between us by Ollie, the threat from "big bad Frank," the dream of going back.

There was the Castle, up on the hillside, all hidden behind the tall trees in the park except for one of the towers. It seemed ages ago that I had been a resident there although it was only a few months ago, when I left this wild bunch of city boys. They had accepted me after I had played along with their crude life, a way that went against every grain in my body. The truck headed through

340

the village run by a mayor whose daughter I had admired. Oh, he probably was not mayor any more. There had been a change in the system since I had left the school. However Annemarie, his daughter would be older and even more beautiful. As I was thinking this, my eyes kept searching the streets we were passing, maybe I would be so lucky and see her by chance, walking her big woolly Chow with the blue tongue. I felt my face blushing as I remembered the thrill of the shy glances we had exchanged in class. One day, I would come back and find her.

The truck pulled off to the side and stopped next to an elderly couple. The driver jumped out of the cab, greeted them and helped them to get their luggage and themselves aboard. We all had to squeeze a little tighter together and rearrange some of the bags to make enough room for them to sit down. They had brought a blanket, which they wrapped around themselves to protect them from the wind.

"Everybody alright up there?" the driver asked us. "Pretty tight, is it? But that'll keep you warm all the way. Snuggle up, it'll be nice and cozy. Out on the highway now I'll be able to go faster, so hold on and duck out of the wind. Off we go!"

Tante Gmeiner turned her head and looked through the back window of the cab. She smiled. What a blessing, I thought. Back here she would have died and while she was dying, she would have complained all the way. I would have considered jumping ship. Thank God for the driver and his good heart.

"That's where Frau Heller and I went with the bicycle," I shouted to my mother over the rattling of the truck and the wind noises. She quickly raised her head to look and nodded to me with an appreciative smile, but ducked back down, with her arms wrapped around the bundle that was my sister. Dieter sat next to her, leaning up against her, looking sleepy. I made a face at him; he made one back and smiled.

A few times we were signaled off the road by Military Police to let an Army convoy pass. Those trucks looked every bit as large as they had when I had come through by bicycle. The soldiers driving or riding waved to us on the truck as they passed. I no longer thought it odd that all of them were chewing gum and smoking cigarettes.

It did not take long before we pulled into Wels and stopped. There were ruins all around. Probably misses from the raids on the *Luftwaffe* airport and the big freight train yard and switching station. A few people got off, said goodbye, and the truck took off again. "Hey, this is where Ina was born!" I called to my mother. She nodded and said something to my sister I could not hear. Ina poked her head out of the blanket and looked around. I waved at her. She laughed and crawled back under the covers. My mother looked serious and sad. I wondered if she was thinking of the time she had met my father in this town when he was laid up with a troop transport. I felt sorry for her, sorry for all of us with a missing family member, traveling on an open truck like refugees.

Now it was not much farther to Linz. I remembered that flat stretch where we had almost run out of steam coming in on the bikes. The wind was blowing harder on these flats, there was nothing to slow it down.

After a while, the truck turned off the main road. It was where I had separated from my cycling companion a few weeks ago. The truck drove up to the development where we lived. Tante Gmeiner obviously had given the driver directions. The extra packages of goodies had earned us the privilege of being dropped off in front of the house. With all our luggage and nobody to help us we could not have made it very far on foot. The familiar streets and shops looked strange, although they were the same. It would take a few days or weeks to get back into our neighborhood, absorbing the changes, reconnecting with old friends and meeting the new people who had moved in while we were gone.

The truck stopped in front of our house. It looked empty and deserted. My mother and I got off slowly, straightening our shaken-up bodies. We lifted Dieter and Ina down, collected our luggage, thanked the driver, waved to the remaining people on the truck and stood there, in front of the house, with the suitcases and packages and the bicycle on the ground next to us. My mother looked for the key.

"Peter, Peter you are here!" It was Isolde, the Schreiber's daughter I had met on my visit. She came running across the square. "I'll tell my mother you are here." She turned and ran back, all excited.

My mother unlocked the door and we all went in. The place was spotless. The smell of baking was in the air and there was a bunch of flowers on the little table in the hall. The Schreibers must have gotten our message about coming back.

"Well, that is a nice welcome ..." my mother said.

"You deserve a nice welcome in this nice house!" It was Frau Schreiber knocking on the open door. "Welcome Frau Slonek, back in your home! I am Anni Schreiber, we had the privilege to live here while you were gone. I am sure Peter told you all about it."

"Yes, he did. I am pleased to meet you, but I thought you would stay here, with us?"

"No, we could not do that, it is your house, we got our two rooms back over there. That is fine with us."

"Oh, I want you to meet Frau Gmeiner from Berlin who has been staying with us, and this is Dieter and Ina. Peter you know."

"Yes, I do. Well, I am happy to meet you all," she said, shaking hands with Frau Gmeiner. "You probably were bombed out in Berlin?

"Yes, lost everything but what I had in the shelter with me."

"I know, we were in the firebombing of Dresden. We survived. Thirty thousand others did not. It was awful. But you know, I don't have to tell you."

"Yes, unfortunately I do know but I guess Berlin was not as bad as Dresden. That is beyond comprehension for anybody who was not there. What cruelty!"

"We do not want to talk about this now, though. These are my children Helmut, Isolde and Helge." They had lined up behind her and were looking at all those newcomers. Everybody smiled and shook hands with my mother and Tante Gmeiner. They said hello to Dieter and Ina.

"I baked you a simple cake ..."

"You shouldn't have, Frau Schreiber, we all don't have extra ..."

"Don't mention it. It is just flour, yeast and a streusel topping. We make it every weekend as a treat. Enjoy it while it is fresh!"

"Well, thank you so much, also for the flowers, they look lovely, and they smell good, combined with the baking smell ... "

"The flowers are from your garden, most of them came up by themselves. We did everything to encourage them. You did a nice job of laying out the garden, we really enjoyed it."

"That was my husband, he had been planning it for a long time."

"I'll let you go now, you must be tired from the trip and wanting to get settled in. Look around, I hope we have put everything in the proper place again, we can sit down tomorrow and talk some more. If you cannot find anything, please send one of the children and we will find it for you. My kids are outside, they'll know where to find me. Welcome, again, I am so glad we met now!" Frau Schreiber cocked her head slightly, flashed her biggest smile and shook my mother's hand again. "Good bye for now!"

"Good bye, Frau Schreiber, and thank you so much for taking such good care of the house. I don't know how to thank you—we really have to talk about you moving in with us."

"It was our pleasure. We are fine where we are. Thank you. Goodbye for now."

LIFE WITH THE SCHREIBERS

When I went see my old friend August, he was not home. His mother told me that he was now an apprentice in a carpenter's shop. He was at work all day. I visited with him one night after he had come home. He was covered with sawdust and very tired. There was no way we could continue our routine of spending afternoons and evenings together. He promised me though that he would hold on to our expedition plans. He was already earning a little money and he said he would save some of it.

When my mother had planned our return to Linz, I had thought I could slip back into my old life around the old house. Without August it did not feel like the same place. The two of us had established a life of our own around this neighborhood. Now he was no longer available, a sawdust-covered shadow. I felt deserted, forlorn until I started seeing more of Helmut, the oldest of the Schreiber children. The first project we tackled together was to build a new 'home' for us since I had lost the one out in the fields to a landscaped garden. We considered a walled-off corner by the fence or a hideout in the shrubs, which had grown considerably.

"How about a digging a bunker in the sandbox?" I proposed to Helmut.

"What do you mean? Where do you want to dig? Your mother will never allow it!"

"My brother and my sister hardly play in it any more. They could play with us in the bunker, some of the time. I'll ask my mother when she comes home."

It took lengthy negotiations and many changes to my plans until my mother agreed. There was one condition however, if she did not approve of the result, we would have to restore everything to the way it was before we started.

Helmut and I went to work. The sandbox was three by three meters with 40-centimeter high wooden boards enclosing it.

"If we dig out half the size of the sandbox, we end up with a bunker 1½ meters by 3 meters. Is that large enough to play, you think?"

"How deep do we have to go so we can stand up?" Helmut asked.

"We will put the roof across the top of the boards. That gives us 40 centimeters we do not have to dig. Another meter or so would do it I think."

"Where are we going to put all the dirt we dig up? We cannot put it on the lawn around the sandbox. Your mother would not like that."

"I think, first of all we have to get rid of the sand. Then the first load of the excavated dirt we will put on the half of the sandbox we are not digging. Some of the next load we'll save for piling on the roof, and the rest we will distribute in the garden. We can use the wheel barrow."

"That's a pretty clever plan but it sounds like a lot of digging and shoveling."

It was a lot of digging and shoveling. The top layers were fill from the construction and deeper down we found nice yellow loam. There were many problems along the way. Part of one wall caved in and had to be shored up, the boards lost their footing when the dirt was dug away, my mother made us store the extra dirt in the shrubs quite a distance away. She was not comfortable with our digging so deep but I convinced her that it would be safe.

My stash of leftover building materials came in handy for constructing the roof. After we piled dirt on it, we had a unique underground 'living' space. A square hole at one end provided an entry and enough light. We put a board on each of the longer edges for benches. At the other end I built a stove, using a large US Army graham cracker tin dug in sideways. We added a small hole at the far end and connected it to a stove pipe leading outside. The top of the tin became a cooking surface; on the inside, we built the cooking fires. Our favorite dish was potato pancakes made from raw potatoes and a little flour and salt.

All the children in the neighborhood wanted to visit with us to experience life in the underground bunker and taste the pancakes. We had some gatherings but mostly Helmut and I used this space for private conversations and plotting of excursions and pranks.

I really enjoyed Helmut's company. He was younger but loads of fun. He was always on the go, full of ideas, and a good sport. With him, I spent time with his parents and became very familiar with them. His father was special. He worked hard all day but when he came home, he always had time to spend with us. He could fix anything. He showed me how to re-sole shoes. He had a smithy at work where he had made a stand for the shoes to be slipped on upside down for the repair. He made a candleholder with a special foot, a square piece of iron, cut in four strips but leaving the ends connected, then heated and blunted into a spiral. In the fall, when we kids started collecting leftover grains on the surrounding fields, he constructed a full-functioning, hand-driven grain mill. It delivered 'whole wheat' flour and cereal from the spelt for our two families, a welcome addition to our sparse diet. I did not particularly care for the sharp ends of the spelt which had escaped the teeth of the mill and found their way into the cereal and my teeth, but I was too hungry to be picky about I was going to eat.

Our mothers traded recipes on how to make cakes out of dried beans and false whipping cream from skim milk. Every weekend Frau Schreiber used our oven to bake her streusel cake. She shared enough of it so we all could have a piece.

Helmut's father was an avid stamp and coin collector. His big collections had been stored in a safe location and were spared the meltdown caused by the firebombing of their city. These albums were the only valuables they had been able to rescue. They were his pride and joy. He would sit in the evenings leafing through the stamp books, rearranging some stamps, sorting in new ones he had bought, and adjusting others that had slipped from their perch behind cellophane strips. Occasionally he would come back from a swap meet and proudly show us his latest acquisition. With every stamp, there was a story, either about the person pictured on the stamp and his or her reign, their place in history, or about an historic event that we needed to learn about. Father Schreiber, as his wife called him, was extremely knowledgeable about history, especially the local history of Saxony, his home state in Germany. He told us many stories about the dukes and their wives, their fortunes and their wars, their castles and conquests. He knew when they had issued this stamp and for what reason, who had been the artist engraving the likeness of the potentate on the stamp. He could point out the smallest flaw in a printing plate, which made the stamp more valuable.

While he was telling us these good stories, he would pull out a small tin box, which had a built-in mechanism for rolling cigarettes. First, he would slip a cigarette paper next to the little canvas cradle, then he'd fill the cradle with coarse tobacco, pat it down with one finger, and then close the cover of the box slowly. There was a special sound to this whole operation. The squeak of the box when it was opened putting the mechanism into operating mode, the rustle of the tobacco and the paper, the spittle for licking the glued edge of the paper, finally the crunching sound of forcing the box closed, compressing the tobacco into the slim shape that emerged from the slot in its cover.

Herr Schreiber then sat back, took out his matches and lit the new cigarette. There was a slight hissing sound when the flame hit the leftover spittle on the seam. His big lips clenched the end, avoiding the loose tobacco pieces spilling from the cigarette.

"When you smoke, you look like a clown, Rudy," his wife would comment almost every time he took that first puff with gusto and satisfaction. Helmut and I just watched and enjoyed the smell of the sweet tobacco. However, my mother did not like that smell on my clothes when I came home.

"You should be in the other room when Herr Schreiber smokes!"

"Mama, he is teaching us about the stamps, it is very interesting!"

"What could be interesting about stamps...?"

"Some of them are very old and very valuable, they tell a lot about history and Herr Schreiber knows history. Actually, he knows it better than my history teacher at school does. Did you know that Saxony—where they speak the funny dialect—had its own money? One of their dukes became King of Poland, and famous china comes from a town in Saxony—Meissen."

"Well, I did not know you were learning so much from the stamps. That is very good. I hope you are nice to Herr Schreiber and thank him properly when he teaches you."

"Yes, we do. Helmut knows a lot of this already, too. Herr Schreiber wants us to start our own stamp collection. He will give us some of his duplicates so we can start."

"Isn't that a very expensive hobby?"

348

"No Mama, there are a many stamps that are worth very little. I can collect the stamps off the letters we get. I can wash the stamps off your old postcards and envelopes for my collection. Herr Schreiber said he would show us how to make our own albums. He is so nice. Papa will like him."

Stamp collecting developed into a passion for me. Later when it demanded some investment, I financed my purchases with money I made smuggling American cigarettes to my uncle in Vienna. A friend of mine in school lived next to an American Army camp. He bought cigarettes at a very low price from the soldiers and sold them to me for a good profit. That price however was still way below that of the Black Market in the Russian zone. My uncle was willing to pay top price, I took the risk of carrying them across the *Demarcation Line*, as they called the borders between the occupation zones. Luckily, the Russians never caught me. My stamp collection grew quickly, helped by a big boost from finding an envelope full of stamps my father apparently had accumulated over the years.

The sandbox bunker remained our favorite hangout. We ate our lunches in there, we cooked and we made plans.

"Isolde's birthday is coming up soon, isn't it?"

"Yes, next week. My mother is going to bake a special cake," Helmut said, smacking his lips. He loved good food as much as I did. Unfortunately there was very little of it.

"Shall we have a party for her in the bunker?"

"Good idea, she'll like that. She likes you!"

"She is just a little girl, she is so young. I like her, too."

My life outside the bunker was very much concentrated on my bicycle. It was actually my father's but I was tall enough to ride it. I could do tricks with it, slide around corners, stop just centimeters short of a wall or take it on one of the small dirt paths around the buildings. I gave rides to my brother on the frame just behind the handlebars, with him sitting sideways and holding on in front. Isolde had begged me to do the same with her. She was bigger than my brother. Her head came up to below my chin. I noticed the fresh smell of her hair the first time she rode with me. She was pleased with our rides up and down the street. I felt like a gentleman. I liked the idea of putting on a little party for her.

I had decorated the bunker with copies of the insignia of the different US Army units stationed around us. They were round and colorful, depicting animal heads, geometric patterns, lightning bolts—it had been a challenge to draw and color them all exactly as they showed on Army vehicles or the soldiers' uniforms. I was proud of the results. I did not think that Isolde was much into Army insignia. What could I use for decorations? I knew there was a little stand of pine trees not too far from us. I wanted to collect a few branches to make the loam walls of the bunker look festive. I snuck away on my bicycle when my mother was off shopping. She did not approve of lengthy excursions by myself other than to school. I found the woods and cut several branches, tied them to my carrier and headed home. Of course, my mother caught me as I came around the corner towards our house.

"What's that? It isn't Christmas time, is it?"

"Helmut and I want to have a birthday party for Isolde in the bunker. These branches are for decorations."

"Well, well, very nice. A party for your little girl friend, huh?"

"She is not my girl friend, she is much too young. She is Helmut's sister and we want to surprise her."

The 'party' was a great success. I gave Isolde a little bunch of flowers from our garden. Helmut made her a paper hat. We let some of the smaller children into the bunker until it was full to capacity, made potato pancakes on our stove for all of us and served tea with them. As a Thank You, I received a shy little kiss from Isolde. I was happy.

"Peter, come quickly, I have to tell you something!" Helmut ran by our door to the bunker. When I joined him, he was still out of breath. "Frau Fessl, our neighbor, you know, the one with the Army boyfriend, she came over this morning to talk with my mother. She had on a pair of Lederhosen, I don't know where she had them from,

maybe they are her husband's, and she was lau
put her hands inside the front flap. 'Look at
isn't it cute?' and she wiggled her hands aroun

"That's it?"

"Yes! Don't you think it is exciting—all the hair in there, imagine!"

Helmut and I had taken to exploring some of the secrets of life, mostly those connected to sex. When we had time alone in the evening, we pulled out my parents' encyclopedia and looked up the newest word we had come across. We sat there, huddled together under the lamp in the dark room, sweaty with excitement about the unknown, the imagined and the need-to-know. Helmut asked me to re-read most of what we found, as we moved from reference to reference without really coming up with any great revelations. Just pronouncing the words, saying them aloud was enough to give us thrills. Armed with this knowledge we would fan out into our worlds the next day and report to each other later what we had heard from the adults or seen, who had disappeared behind what door and where did we catch a glimpse of female flesh normally hidden to us. With all the odd people that the circumstances had tumbled together in this big apartment building, now so far from its original purpose of housing only single men, the possibility for all kinds of wild things to happen was unlimited. We kept a close watch and we were listening carefully. The occasional shouting match overheard through an open window brought us new words to be investigated and prepared us–unbeknownst to us–for some of life's realities our parents had managed to shield us from so far. Lights left on carelessly after dark with open curtains provided us with a few more insights not meant for us. We discussed all of this in the bunker, away from adult supervision and questioning.

"My father wants to go home," Helmut said one day looking very serious.

"What? Where is home?" I felt a deep hollow creeping into my body. I did not want them to leave.

"His roots are in Saxony. Dresden is his hometown."

"The place is in shambles, it is run by the Russians, and nothing is happening there. You can't just leave here.

How would you even get there? There are no trains, no buses between the different zones." Germany was divided into four Allied occupation zones, just like Austria.

"My father found out there is a transport train going to East Germany for refugees who want to return. It is being put together and it is supposed to leave in a few weeks."

"Do you want to go to Dresden? Does your mother want to go to Dresden? Your apartment is gone, charred, and so is everything you owned. Why would you want to do this? Your mother is Austrian, which means her family can stay in Austria. They want to get rid of the foreigners, the foreign workers the Germans brought in here, and all the refugees who fled from the Russian troops. Your family is good, they want you to stay here. I want you to stay here!"

I could not believe what I had just heard. Maybe Helmut's father was just playing with the idea but he could not be serious. Here things were slowly looking up, especially in the Western zones. What we heard from the Russian zones was horrible. The soldiers were still taking women, people were disappearing, the Russian soldiers were demolishing the quarters where they lived, and they dismantled private businesses and factories and shipped all the goods and machinery to Russia. Why would anybody in his or her right mind move into such a chaotic and hostile environment? Why?

Father Schreiber was determined. His roots in Saxony were too deep. He would never feel truly at home here in Austria. He wanted to be there when they were rebuilding his homeland. He wanted to participate in the rebuilding. He wanted to rejoin his fellow Saxons who had stayed behind and were suffering for it now. He had no illusions about what they would find. He had his skills and his family. His wife had adapted to her new homeland more or less and she was fine with her husband's decision. The children were torn. They knew what they had here and they had no idea what was in store for them there.

It was a very sad gray day when we took them to the freight train yard. That was where their special train would leave. Several of their friends from the apartment house had made the trip to see them off. All of them were puzzled over their decision to 'repatriate.' Nobody had heard anything good from the Russian occupied territories.

The train did not look very inviting. There were only freight cars, boxcars with sliding doors in the center. We called them cattle cars. They did not look very clean. The floors were covered with straw for warmth and cushioning. People had brought blankets and heavy coats. It was late in the year. The weather was turning cold. The trip could last several days, depending on oncoming traffic on single tracks, repairs to existing tracks, and availability of locomotives and coal. Over a year after the end of the war, those were still the most certain uncertainties. Why travel if you did not have to travel at all?

We stood around and said very little. The Schreibers had settled their sparse belongings into one end of the car and were talking with their fellow travelers. There seemed too many of them, too many wanting to go where they had come from. Their longing for home must be stronger than for safety in the West. Although many of these people had been in refugee camps or living in cramped quarters, I thought, they still would be better off staying right here.

There was commotion and loud shouting from the front end of the train. It sounded like they were getting ready to take off. There were puffs of smoke coming from the locomotive. A slight drizzle came from the gray clouds. Austria was crying ...

The Schreibers all came down from the car and there was lots of hugging and crying. They made the rounds of all the well-wishers. We were the last to say our goodbyes. I was overwhelmed with grief. This was my second family, which had become my anchor in these shifting seas. It even had a father whom I cherished, whom I could trust and who had given me so much in knowledge and confidence. Frau Schreiber was another mother to me, strong and cheerful, always ready to help, who had taken me under her wings, adding me to her brood. What would I do without all of them? Helmut who had shared my days of excitement and wonder, his sister who had helped me with getting more comfortable with flirty girls, and their little brother Helge, who was always ready with a joke in spite of his young age. We all were part of one family and now we were being torn apart like everything else. Isn't there anything that can last?

The steam whistle blew a few toots. Somebody called "All aboard" walking along the train. People climbed up. I held on to every one of them as long as I could. I did not know who was the hardest to let go. Another one of my worlds was falling apart.

The train slowly started to move. Every boxcar door was full of teary, waving people being carried off into a future I could not imagine. When the train disappeared around a curve, we, the left behind, the bereaved, slowly started to walk towards home. The rain had stopped but my tears kept falling for a lot longer.

NEW NEIGHBORS—ANOTHER NEW LIFE

When Victor and his parents moved in four houses down, I did not like him at first: He spoke with a German accent, he had kinky reddish hair, and he was always pale.

But after the Schreibers left, I started spending time with Victor. He was one year older and that gave me status with the smaller kids.

"Let's go take the bikes," I said, "and ride around the big field."

The 'big field' started right behind the apartment building across the street from my house and sloped down into a little valley. There was another slope up on the other side with some small gardens with tool sheds and a big ugly tenement development on the horizon, quite a ways beyond the gardens. In the other direction the big field went on and on, first just raw land, dirt and weeds, and then planted with potatoes, corn, and wheat, all the way to the big farmhouse, which peeked out from behind some trees at the far end.

"We'll go along the fence here, that is the smoother path." After six years in this area, I knew every path and every inch of soil within a radius of about two to three miles.

We went slowly on the hard-packed loam along the backyards of the houses, avoiding eroded gullies and big patches of weeds.

"Hey, what's that?" Victor had dropped his bike and was running down one of the gullies. I followed instantly. If Victor got excited, it must be good.

"It's a cable," Victor said, "three-phase, probably army telephone," he added with the wisdom of the elder.

"Let's check where it goes," I said and picked up the smooth black cable. I followed its path the way I had seen the soldiers do when they were laying wires. I crouched down and started running slowly through the weeds and the various dips in the ground, the cable sliding smoothly through my open hand, fingers up, so I would track it without losing it.

"There is a whole reel of it, look here Victor!" I shouted back.

"We will take it home today, before anybody else can take it,"

Victor said, "Let's check the other end, quick."

We went back up the hill. The cable took us close to the fence by the houses and ran along there for a long time towards the big street. Suddenly it ended. There was a clean cut without any splicing.

"Must have been training or something," I said, but in my head I was calculating how long this piece could be.

"How long do you think it is, Victor?"

"From here to where it leaves the fence is almost 10—20—30 meters, another ten down to the spool and I don't know how much on the spool." Victor was very methodical about his estimate.

"Let's take it home and lay it out in the garden? Shall we roll it up from this side or shall we put it all on the spool?" I asked.

"All on the spool, then we can roll the whole spool home and we don't have to carry it. It's too heavy anyway."

We had a hard time heaving the spool through the rough terrain up to the path. From there on it was easy to roll up along the rest of the cable.

"Let's hide the bikes and go. We should pass through the apartment house before everybody comes home from work. Herr Diehl or somebody might take it away from us. It's worth some money, I am sure," Victor said, acting very adult.

We pushed the reel in front of us, one on either side. The ground was flat and smooth, so traveling was easy.

"You know what," I yelled all of a sudden, stopping wherever I was when I had this momentous thought, "we can use this for a telephone line between your house and mine—just for us!"

"Yes, that would be great, we can talk at night and it won't cost anything."

We looked at each other triumphantly. This was an excellent and unexpected booty for such a short outing.

"Peter watch—the spool—oh no ..." Victor's voice trailed off as the spool rolled off into the bushes and stopped only at the foot of a small hill. "We better watch this telephone cable of ours before we lose it. I wouldn't want to push it up here from all the way down there," Victor said, pointing to the lowest point of the big field.

"Last year in Physics I had to draw a plan of the electrical wiring in our house, with switches and outlets and all. Did you do that too?" I asked Victor. I smiled because I remembered the big 'Sehr gut' I had earned on the drawing and Herr Professor Witzinger had praised my clean lines and use of color.

"With Witzi? Oh yeah, we did that. I did not like it. Too much trouble. I don't like to draw, anyway."

"Where do we get the telephones? Do you have one?" Victor asked.

"No, I don't. But I have a pair of earphones from my uncle, would they work?" I cocked my head in thought.

"I'll ask my Dad tonight when he comes home. He knows."

Victor's Dad had not been drafted into the armed services. He had stayed home and now was working somewhere dressed in a suit and tie every day. I thought my Dad would know about telephones, too. But he had not come home from the war yet.

"Do you think my Dad will come home soon?" I asked.

"Every day somebody shows up, you never know. Was he in Russia?"

"At first, yes, but last he was in a hospital in Germany, in Darmstadt, recuperating from Malaria. From what he wrote we think he was ordered into the final battles along the French border.

"How come he had Malaria? Was he in the Africa Corps? With Rommel?" Victor asked with some intensity. He smelled a good story. There were lots of good stories from the fronts. The best of them came from the Russian and the African fronts.

"No, he caught it in Russia. Around Kiev. There are some big swamps there, along the Dnieper River. He had a relapse, an attack, on leave, once. It was awful. He was walking in the garden. All of a sudden he started to shake like crazy, and then he collapsed. My mother and I had a hard time dragging him back into the house."

"How long did the relapse last?" Victor asked.

"Just one day. He took lots of quinine pills, tiny little yellow pills, very bitter, even your fingers tasted bitter for a long time after you touched them!" I was not comfortable with the memory. It had hurt me to see my father weak and helpless. Now I did not even know where he was.

"You know, it depends on who took him prisoner. The Americans let most of theirs go already. They call them POW's—it stands for Prisoners of War. I hope he did not end up with the French. People say they have been the meanest—after the Russians. But he also could have met up with a British unit. They have a reputation of being civil. He'll be here soon." Victor watched for my reaction and let it be at that. There was so much uncertainty.

"Can Victor play?" I asked. Victor's older sister Helene was standing in the door, smiling.

"Hello Peter!" she said with her funny lisp. "He's upstairs, I'll ask mother. Come on in." She closed the door behind me and went up the stairs.

"*She talks funny but she smells good,*" I thought as I watched her disappear around the corner of the staircase.

Helene was a little taller than I was, about three years older, teenage lanky with long limbs, disorderly long dark hair around an oval face with big eyes and full lips. Her lips were as loose as her limbs and sometimes got into the way of her words. Then the words came out a little wet but always very soft. I liked that somehow. It had a motherly quality to it.

Victor also had two younger sisters, one year apart, the babies of the family, who were six and seven years old. I could hear them playing in the living room downstairs.

Victor appeared on the staircase. "Want to play with the train set?"

"Oh, that would be fun," I said, "Where do we set it up?"

"It's already set up in the bedroom upstairs, out of the way of the girls." Victor led the way up.

I was excited. My parents never had had enough money for an electric train set. I had two windup locomotives, one steam and one electric, and several passenger cars and a few freight cars. Every Christmas and birthday, I got another car or more tracks. Victor had a large double loop layout with a crossover in the middle, all electric, with automatic switches and a big control board. He had many other expensive toys and so did his siblings. The house was nicely furnished, the parents spoke in a hush and very politely. I thought my father would approve of the whole family.

"I want to build a freight yard with three tracks under the bed," Victor said, "Do you want to help me?"

"Yes, where are the tracks?"

We added and rearranged for a while, concentrating quietly.

"No trains running today?" Helene peeked in the door.

"Oh, leave us alone!" Victor said. "We are working on a new layout."

"Can I come and watch when you are ready?" Helene asked, ignoring the rejection.

"Yeah, why not, we'll be ready in a minute. Peter, which train do you want to control?" Victor asked.

"Can I have the Blue Lightening?" This was my absolute favorite. A sleek three-car express passenger train, built for fast intercity traffic. It was midnight blue and had little people sitting at little tables in the dining section.

"Sure. Why don't you set it up at the main station? I'll take the freight train, I want to try out the new yard."

Helene handed me the box with my dream train. I had been looking at this train again and again in my old *Maerklin* catalogs for several years.

"Thank you," I said to her and started to unpack.

Helene went to the opposite side of the oval and rearranged one of the freight trains.

"Leave it alone!" Victor shouted at her, "It's mine and you know it."

"I am just putting it on the tracks for you, so you can drive it to the yard," Helene said. She crouched down, with her legs apart. Her dress got in the way of her arm when she arranged the cars and she casually pulled it up over her knees.

My eyes went wide open: Helene was not wearing panties under her dress. Her position offered the best possible view of what I had thought about often since my doctor-playing days. When I caught myself staring, I turned my attention back to my train. I checked the alignment of the wheels on the tracks, moving the whole train back and forth lightly with my hand.

"Never push the engine backwards, that ruins the motor, please," Victor admonished me. "Let's make them move! You go first."

I looked around. I was right in front of the control panel. I turned the dial slowly, the train engines started to hum first and then the little wheels started turning. I concentrated very hard to make the miniature train look just like a real one picking up speed. I let it go around, slowed down at the station in front of Helene, which pulled my glance again to the magic view.

"I'll stop here," I said. Under the pretense of watching my favorite train, I could enjoy viewing Helene's bared secret.

Helene looked at me with a big grin. I locked eyes with her and blushed. It occurred to me that she might be aware of what she was showing. Confused I turned back to the controls.

"Shall I move your train to Victor's yard?" I asked her.

Last winter I had had another intimate look. I had been sleighing a lot on the little hill behind the apartment house. There were always a dozen or so kids from the neighborhood. We raced, did tricks on our sleds, threw snowballs, rolled in the snow and froze, but we always had loads of fun until it was time to go home.

A repatriated poor family from Southern Tyrol had moved into a house a few blocks away some time ago. There were nine children, seven girls and two boys. They were all short and stocky, poorly dressed and spoke with the strange singsong dialect of their region.

They all knew how to have fun. I loved to play with them, especially the girls. The older ones always looked out for the younger ones, lifting them up, wiping their noses, and helping them make it up the hill after the downhill run.

Bertha, the second oldest girl was in the same class as I. She was solid and friendly, not very bright but warm. I liked her. Maybe I felt a little bit sorry for her because she had come to school barefoot long after everybody else had been putting on shoes in the fall, and her dresses were mended, and her books were kind of torn and dog-eared. The signs of a home where there was no special place and care for books.

I could not understand why my father had told me over and over that I should not have anything to do with this family. But my father always had strange reasons for everything. He did not have to know who I was sledding with during the day.

"Let's tie the sleighs together, come on!" somebody shouted and everybody scurried up the hill, pulling their sleighs behind them. On top we lined up, one after another. They asked me to be in the lead. There was an argument about who would be the last one in line. Because of the skidding back and forth, that was the most fun position and everybody wanted to be there.

"Why doesn't Karla go now and Andy can go the next run. We'll do another and then another anyway." I tried to settle the argument in the back. Andy agreed to wait it out and took the next to last spot now.

"Push off—one, two, three—- go, go, go!"

Everybody's feet were pushing off on the snow, getting the sleds to move. As soon as we had gained some momentum, I started to steer into some flat turns.

Everybody screamed with pleasure as the sleigh wound its way down the hill.

I looked back to see how everybody was doing. Bertha was behind me with her younger sister riding in front of her. They were cuddled together, leaning back and holding on to one another. Bertha's sister's legs were wide apart and stretched out. Under her dress she wore long wool socks with big holes, darned crudely, held up by rubber bands above her knees, and nothing. I looked again. There it was, again. The most secret place of the female body. Almost in plain view. I did not dare to look very long but I felt a strange feeling spreading through my body. Curiosity. Longing for the unknown, ever since my first experience as the doctor in the bushes.

"Hey, Peter watch out!" Karla shouted from the back. We were headed for the deep snow where we did not want to be. I dug in my left heel and we started to turn quickly. Too quickly. The sleigh chain could not follow smoothly. The third sleigh skidded far out, caught on an icy ledge and toppled over spilling its two riders into the snow. The rest of the sleds followed in a wild tumble. Only Bertha and I continued down, all the way.

"Fine steering!" I heard from the pile of bodies amidst the laughter and the screams of delight.

Without much cleaning off we all headed back up for a repeat.

"My turn in the back now," Andy yelled so everybody could hear.

I let somebody else take the lead. I put my sleigh again in front of Bertha's.

"I am going to ride backwards this time," I said, and sat myself looking uphill. "This way I never know when there is a bump. It's a total surprise. It's fun."

But my real motivation on this run was to check out my discovery a little better. I was lucky. Bertha positioned her sister in front of herself again. Bertha smiled at me. *She is far from where she grew up and now people are making fun of her accent and the way she dresses* I thought as I was looking at her. I felt sorry for her predicament.

The chain of sleighs started moving. The girls leaned back and the vista opened up. The colors of rosy to red, the lips, the folds, the mystery, the darkness, the rays of light breaking in, maybe a snowflake melting on the warmth of the skin? Yes, there was moisture and there was a beckoning, which I did not understand. There was this longing to touch, to be close, and to be taken in whole. My body was alive and vibrant, I felt the cold air, the clean breaths of wind, the smell of the snow, and my eyes were full of the glitter of the icy crystals in the afternoon sun.

We all ran up the hill again. I breathed more fully in my awareness of beauty and life. We thought up another way of going downhill, and then another and another, until darkness slowly replaced the laughter on the hill.

I leaned my sleigh against the wall next to the door, wiped the runners with my mitts and went inside.

"It's about time you came home. You must be frozen stiff! Do you know how cold it is?"

"You said 'before it gets dark' and it's just getting dark outside. The cold felt good, the snow was fast, we had lots of fun. What is the temperature?"

"Go look. Last time I looked, it was 12 Celsius below," my mother said moving some pots around on the stove.

I went to the kitchen window to peek at the outside thermometer.

"It's almost fifteen now. It did not feel that cold."

"What's for dinner?" I asked my mother lifting lids at the same time. My body absorbed the warmth of the hot food and the little coal-burning stove, which was attached to the electric range. "Hum, looks like vegetable soup, my favorite kind. Thanks, Mama. Are they all from the garden still?"

"Yes, all except the potatoes. The carrots and parsnips are keeping really well in the sand in the cellar. I am glad Papa built the bins, it's so easy to keep everything in order this way."

"Can I go sleighing tomorrow again, please, Mama?"

"If you go and do your homework right now and finish it before dinner, yes. I will look at it and I will ask you some questions later. The kids are playing upstairs, so you go to the living room. It is warm in there and you will be alone until dinner."

"Fine. Thanks." I gave her a kiss on the cheek. Mother. Woman. She looked nice and young in her flannel house dress with the white apron, just a little tired from all the housework.

FATHER'S BEST FRIEND

"How was school today?" my mother asked.

"Boring, it's the same stuff as last year only without books," I said. Since the previous school year was cut short by the end of the war chaos we had to start over with the same curriculum. I put my heavy school satchel on the floor in the hall.

"How about homework?"

"Another 'description of a picture' for Stundner, my *favorite* teacher, a page of fraction problems, and a topographical map of South America. I wonder why they let us go home at all," I said. "It is 2:30 now and I have not eaten any lunch. When do I get to play? I also want to read some more in the book about the dog in Alaska, the one from the library."

"You will have time for it all, come I'll make you some potato pancakes and there is fresh Kohlrabi from the garden," my mother said. I did not hear much sympathy for my complaint.

"Can I eat outside?" I asked.

"No, everything is set up in the living room but the door is wide open, you are almost sitting outside."

I followed my mother into the kitchen. I liked to watch her cook. I also liked to cook myself. She always had let me do little tasks and I got very good at them. I could make all kinds of dough and cookies from her handwritten recipes or the cookbook. I could clean and cut vegetables, make paper-thin crepes, watch things cooking and frying. I was an expert in turning the heavy electric burners on our kitchen stove on and off at exactly the right time. The burners heated up and cooled down very slowly, and I could time it so that the burner was at the right temperature when the pot went on and could turn it off so that no electricity was wasted after the pot was taken off.

"You can fry the potato pancakes while I heat up the kohlrabi. The oil is in the cabinet under the window."

I poured sunflower oil into the frying pan on the hot burner. The greenish oil started to smoke right away. When I put the potato dough in, it started to sizzle and there was that strong peculiar smell of sunflower oil. I liked it. I turned the heat down a little.

"I had a visitor this morning. Rudi Müller, your father's best friend from Vienna."

I felt uneasy right away. There was a peculiar way my mother sounded, that made me suspicious. Something was up. "Yes, what about him?" I asked.

"His wife Helga and their two daughters are stranded up in the *Mühlviertel*, which is now in the Russian Zone. They live the same way we did in Attersee, one room in a farmhouse. He is hiding out here and trying to find a place for all of them in the American Zone. He wants to get them out. He is afraid for them, he wants them to come over here as quickly as possible. He asked if they could stay with us for a while."

"Why is he afraid of the Russians? He is from Vienna, was he in the army?"

"He was a Nazi. He took over a Pretzel factory from a Jewish family who left—I do not know the story, it is fishy, your father never talked about it. So he got out of serving in the military, producing food was classified as 'supporting the war effort.' He was 'needed at home.'"

"One of those. Do you like him?" I asked.

"Not really, he fixed Papa up with this girl after he had started dating me, I was furious."

"Is that her in the photo in the box that is all crumpled up?"

"Yes, that is her. I still get angry thinking about it."

"What did you do?"

"I told your father it would be all over if he ever saw her again," my mother said.

I could hear the hurt in her voice.

"After we got married we did not see much of Rudi. Only once in a while. We were invited to his wedding. When we moved to Linz we lost contact altogether."

"So, why does he think he can come here?" I asked.

"Peter, he is your father's good friend. They have no place to go. They lost everything they had."

"So did the Jewish family he took the factory from. That was a Nazi trick. They told us about that scheme in school."

"No, they got money and they got out. At least that is what he told us. It was early after the Germans marched in. Your pancakes are burning," my mother pointed at the smoke raising from the pan.

"See, you distracted me," I said and lifted the pan off the burner. I turned the pancakes one by one and put them back. They were sort of dark on the bottom side but still edible.

"I believe that if the Russians would catch him, he would go to prison. Or to some camp in Siberia, wherever they take people now," my mother said. "Helga, his wife is rather nice, and they have two girls, Hedda, who is two years younger than you, and Herlinde, she is another two years behind her sister."

"Where would you put them?" I asked.

"The big bedroom upstairs. They'd fit fine. Just like we did."

"We finally just got rid of Tante Gmeiner. I do not want anybody else like her in the house. She was mean and interfering. When Papa comes back we want the whole house to ourselves, don't we?" I said.

"Papa also would like us to take care of his friends, our friends. There will be a solution, somehow."

"Look, Tante Gmeiner came to us for two weeks. How long did she stay? Almost a year? Or longer than a year? Will we ever live alone again? As soon as she was gone, you took in that woman, the Chaplain's girl friend."

"They pay, and we need the money, and we are getting extra food, and he took you on the pheasant hunt—it is not such a bad deal, is it?" my mother's voice was shaky.

365

She was doing what she thought best for us, best by her conscience, best for her children, best to keep this all together until her husband, my father would come back. She needed her husband back, she needed him to make decisions, to talk things over, to share responsibilities, the way it was meant to be in a marriage. She could not even ask him in letters any more, getting his approval afterwards at least. He was gone, floating out there in the void, with millions of others—alive? Dead? She did not feel his aliveness any more. She felt alone, drained and dead herself, keeping going for us, for the children's sake.

"A priest is not supposed to have a girl friend anyway," I said.

"He is not a priest, he is a chaplain. They call him a *Minister* in America, they can get married. He is not Catholic."

"Well, is he married in America? Then he should not have a girl friend either." I was confused. "Frau Weiss over at the apartments has an American soldier for a boyfriend, and she is married. What if her husband comes home and finds Johnny with her? I hope he does not bring his gun home."

"Peter, I know this is all very confusing, these are horrible times, but they will become better, soon, they have to. Everybody does what they think is right. They are responsible for themselves only. We all have to do our best. Come and eat your lunch now." She stood next to me and put her arm around me. "I'll sit with you."

I carried my plate to the living room and sat down at the table so I could look through the open French doors into the garden. My mother sat down next to me. The garden was an extension of the house to us. My father had made sure that it would be that way. He had insisted that the landscapers would not follow the plan of planting rosebushes in front of the terrace. He wanted to be able to go out the door, onto the terrace and onto the lawn. No flower beds, no shrubs creating artificial barriers. I could see all the way down to the very end of our garden where the compost pile sat in the corner against the fence.

"So will you take them in?" I asked.

"We are the only people they know in the Western Sectors. There is no more assigned sharing of living space, so if they leave the farmers up there, they are without a roof over their head," my mother said. She seemed deep in thought.

I looked at my mother. She had become very thin. Her skin was pale in spite of the many hours she spent working in the garden. Her face showed the sorrow and the worry she was living with. Her thin hair seemed to have become thinner. She tied it back in a big bun, but it would never stay up. She had talked about cutting it shorter. It was unusual for her to sit and not do anything. Her hands were restless.

"No matter what he did, I don't want him to be dragged away by the Russians. I feel sorry for her and the kids. They have to start a whole new life. Remember how it was when I was looking for a place for us? You cannot imagine how I felt when all these relatives, who had plenty of space and food, said no to me. For their own reasons."

"Oh Mama, I saw you cry, I saw how sad you were when you came back from your trips. You were not just tired," I said.

"Well, there was more to it than tears. The coldness, the harshness of the people out there, who lived in the country, away from the bombs, away from the war, really. They left us here, searching, exposed as if we had brought this on ourselves. Maybe we did. But had we stayed in Vienna it would have been worse. We still don't know about your grandparents, your uncles and aunts, the whole clan. Anyway, that is why I feel sorry for Uncle Rudi and his family, and that is why I do not want to turn them away." She looked at me awaiting my reaction.

"Can you make them promise that they will move out when Papa comes back?" I asked.

"I am sure they are decent enough to respect our life when the time comes. When Uncle Rudi gets a job they can start looking for a place."

"But there aren't any places. There are less apartments than before. So many are destroyed. People are returning from where the war had taken them. They told us in school there is no way to predict when there will be enough apartments for all the people."

"We are doing our share to help. We were taken care of when we needed it, weren't we?" my mother said.

"Yes, the Kastingers were extremely nice, they gave us their own bedroom, food and comfort. They did not have to do that," I said. "I liked the meadows, the woods and the lake."

My sister started crying upstairs.

"Oh, oh—Ina is up, I hope she does not wake Dieter. He was really tired today. I want him to sleep a little longer. Then he won't be as cranky tonight. I'll get her." My mother got up and went upstairs.

I picked up my plate and went outside. I sat on the steps in front of the door and finished my lunch there.

My mother's constant fear of not having enough money to survive until her husband came back, combined with her almost addictive desire to help other people brought us a steady flow of varied characters renting our "formal dining room" as it was called on the original house plans. I could not remember it ever being used as a dining room. Instead it became the guest room where my grandparents or any other of our guests slept. Having a bed downstairs was handy also when one of us children was sick because we could be kept close for care and supervision.

The first ever outside stranger to occupy this room had been *'Tante Gmeiner'* the woman from Berlin, who had connected with us through my friend Hans' mother. Shortly after we had come back from the evacuation at the Lake she returned to a transition camp in Germany. My siblings and I were very glad not to be subjected to her interference in our upbringing any longer.

Through an acquaintance of hers, the tall, gray-haired German "publisher" and his young male assistant found their way to us. They would appear for one or two days on their way from Germany—or going back there—stay over night in the living room, do *business* in the city during the day and evening and then depart again. They were friendly, paid what my mother asked, hardly ever engaged in conversation, and never carried any books or other

printed material. I observed them in awe, neve̲
them, and tried to fit them into one of the adve̲
stories I had read.

Then there was a young blonde woman who came to
visit her fiancé who shared a room with two other men in
the apartments across from us. She rented the family
'guest room' to have a place to visit with her man in
private. She chatted with my mother while he was at work,
they discovered a few acquaintances they had in common;
overall she was a pleasant breeze in the house. The only
reason I remember her and her fiancé at all is because
they came back a few months later and wanted to borrow
two of my father's yacht design books. These books were
bound in exquisite navy blue linen and were full of
intricate foldout engineering drawings and photographs of
elegant sailing boats. I loved them and looked at them
quite often, because they gave me a glimpse into another
world, a world that my father was familiar with, or at least
I thought so since my father had attended the engineering
college and had sailed, kayaked and canoed all through
his younger years. My mother, in her innocence and
naiveté, handed the books over without hesitation,
without making it clear that she wanted them back. Of
course, we never saw the man or the books again. Every
time I looked at our bookshelf and saw the hole these big
books had left there welled up a pain in my heart that
never got soothed again.

Many others of my father's special possessions, like
his fine drawing tools, art supplies and more books were
traded for food or clothing. How would we tell my father
where his treasures had gone to when he came back? I felt
responsible for letting them go without protest—without
registering their ownership in a clear way. I felt guilty
eating the food and wearing the clothes my mother had
gained in these deals.

Our next tenant was connected with an US Army
Chaplain with the rank of a Captain. He had a full head of
pitch-black hair and bushy eyebrows to match them. He
talked a mile a minute and his crisply ironed uniform
showed in certain places that he could lose a few pounds.
He showed up one day and inquired if he could rent a

room for his girl friend, a very serious and well-educated Austrian lady. My mother was torn, since it was still not in good taste to associate with the 'enemy' in such intimate ways, and she thought she had spotted a wedding band on the Captain's hand. However, the length of the stay and the rent he offered, including the promise of some extra rations for her children made her circumvent the moral qualms. So, for a few weeks there was an Army Jeep parked outside our house almost every night, properly marked with a black cross, denoting the driver's profession.

The woman turned out to be levels above the standard war bride of the moment and never stopped to explain to my mother why she was in this affair. The Captain and his lady friend were always happy and laughing. In his jovial manner, he was an excellent provider. He brought boxes and boxes of food, some for his own cooking and lots for us. He took me on a pheasant hunt through my old hunting grounds behind the apartments, and showed me how to use a shotgun. This one had a stock on it and the recoil was not as bad as with the German carbine I had fired. The birdshot was probably being propelled by a lesser amount of powder than the combat projectile. I was fascinated but I felt awful about shooting at a bird. As many times as I had roamed these fields with my bow and arrow, with the intent to hunt down a bird or a rabbit, I never had thought my actions all the way through to the end when I would have to kill the animal. I remembered how sad I had felt after shooting the bird at the Castle school. I could not do it again. It was terrible for me to watch the Captain shoot these beautiful birds right out of the sky as they were fluttering away. He downed four the first afternoon. By the time the Captain had plucked, cleaned and roasted them, I had reconciled with the fact that in order to eat an animal one has to kill it first.

Next in line for the guest room was a very German-Prussian couple. They had lived across the way, in the singles complex, as a temporary solution, and Mrs. Manko had used my mother's oven for her baking, in return for a piece of the finished product. When they had to leave their quarters over there, they moved in with us. They were both heavy and jolly, totally in contrast to their story. They had to leave their ancestral lands in East Prussia over night, taking only what they could carry. They told of quite an odyssey, which finally brought them to Linz, Austria, without being killed, without freezing or starving to death or being picked up and dragged to some labor camp. Their cooking always looked and smelled extra good, in spite of the meager supplies available. They always shared more than just a taste, much to my pleasure. Mr. Manko who was huge in height and girth, with a red shiny bald top, was very concerned that I would develop into a valuable, honest young man with full integrity. When he found out about my interest in books, he gave me a thick volume of collected novellas by well-known German and Austrian authors. He wrote–in beautifully even-shaped old German handwriting- almost a whole page dedication into the book, the longest and most meaningful I had ever received. It spoke of the beauty and inspirational power of words, the importance of literature and reading. There were encouraging words to me to continue my interest in books and even to attempt writing myself. After a few weeks they went on their way to find a new home somewhere in Germany, but first they would have to stay in one of the many refugee camps.

In the meantime, another distant friend of the family from Vienna had appeared on the scene. He had been a career officer first in the Austrian and then in the German Army. He apparently had a "clean vest" as it was called at the time, he had done his time in a British POW camp and then been released. His wife and daughter were still at one of the mountain lakes where they had fled to from Vienna. Their home was in Vienna, but, as so many others in the same predicament, they had no intentions to move into the Russian occupation zone. Uncle Totila, as he became known to us, was earning his living as an advertising salesman for a company in Linz. Since he was living alone in town in a tiny bachelor flat, my mother had taken pity on him and decided to invite him for dinner every Thursday night. He was very attentive to my mother, in his officer-gentleman way: He always brought her little presents or flowers, bowed and kissed her hand when he greeted her. He also held her chair when she sat down, which I had never seen done before. My mother was embarrassed by all this attention but also enjoyed it because she had not had any of it for a long time. Uncle Totila had a very low, sonorous voice, which he employed to tell long anecdotes about his family or military life. I was relieved that the question of him moving in with us never came up, but eventually his mother ended up staying with us.

She had lived in Prague during the war but now she had been on the run for months. She was way over eighty years old, very well taken care of and always dressed well. She would not dare to come to breakfast without being freshly bathed, her hair and face done perfectly, and wearing a nice dress. Her presence again was a serious infringement on my and my siblings' freedom. She could not tolerate any running, any noise, and any lively discussion at meals. During her lengthy naps there had to be absolute silence in the house. She also loved to give advice to my mother on how to be stricter with us children. She was a Czech-Austrian re-issue of Tante Gmeiner to me. She thought we needed to be tamed and made into *good* little kids. She was always ready to tell us what we were doing wrong, which did not endear her to us. She also had some good stories to tell of her past, her young years as a society girl in Vienna and Prague, opening balls and dancing the nights away. She had been embarked on a career as an actress but developed pigment problems with the skin on her face and arms. The big brown patches contrasting with her very white skin could not be covered up by makeup and she had to let go of her dream. This fate had caused some bitterness to creep into her life, which now, at her advanced age, was directed at her surroundings. But she was utterly grateful for having found us, becoming her "home" and family.

One day when I came home from school, my mother motioned me to be quiet and pointed at "Grandma Totila's" room. Earlier in the day, coming home from a short shopping trip my mother had found her bent over the ironing board, lifeless. Grandma had had a stroke and had left this world without a struggle. My mother asked me if I wanted to see her to say goodbye. I nodded. My mother opened the door to the guest room slowly. There she was, paler than before and motionless, eyes closed, laid out on the bed, dead. It was the first time I experienced the death of a person with a relationship to the family. This was different from the dead soldier in the woods. This was a peaceful death at the end of a long life. I was quite surprised when I heard Uncle Totila's explosion of grief when he came to see his dead mother. He sobbed uncontrolled for a long time. I wondered how I would react to my own mother's death. It would be an awful experience but I convinced myself that it would not happen for a long, long time.

Less than a week after my conversation with my mother about the Müller's they arrived, four people with all their belongings in two suitcases. The whole house needed to be rearranged to accommodate them. They would take over the master bedroom upstairs and I would be in the small bedroom next to them, where I had weathered my scarlet fever quarantine. My mother would sleep downstairs in the living room sharing her bed with Ina, and Dieter was moved into the guest room with the connecting door to mother's quarters wide open. Only when there were 'guests' he was relegated to a make-shift bed on the floor next to my mother's couch.

Uncle Rudi was jovial, always joking, always smiling. Aunt Helga wore low cut Dirndl dresses, laughed loudly and heartily at her husband's and my jokes and took good care of her daughters. The girls were quiet. They mostly played with Dieter and Ina or stayed upstairs with their parents.

Our two families became very enmeshed. We cooked together, ate together, and out of that, certain rituals developed.

"I don't believe how many dishes we have again," I said. My permanent assignment was drying the dishes after meals. Aunt Helga was the one who washed them. She and my mother shared the cooking, with me helping by harvesting and cleaning vegetables from the garden. The younger children only did little chores around setting and clearing the table.

VISIT TO THE RUSSIAN ZONE

I watched my mother walking down the path along the garden. I felt a slight tremor going through my body when she passed the spot where I had seen my father collapse, when he started the malaria relapse. I would never forget that image.

Mama called me to follow her and turned into the bed where the carrots grew. She bent the greens slightly to the side so she could choose the bigger carrots before pulling them. I had joined her and I was close to the tall, bright green carrot tops. I could smell them after they had been crushed by pulling the carrots out of the ground. They smelled a little like parsley, but not as strongly, maybe a little sweeter. When my mother had a handful of beautiful orange carrots, she carried them by their tops down towards the little concrete basin my father had installed halfway in between all the vegetable beds. It had a water line running to it, which meant we did not have to carry heavy watering cans from the spigot by the house. Hoses were hard to come by and made from such inferior material that they did not last very long. The water in the basin warmed up in the sun before we used it for watering the garden. My father had read somewhere in one of our gardening books that cold tap water was bad for plants.

After my mother had rinsed off the carrots, she twisted off the greens, handed them to me, and asked me to take them down to the compost pile.

"Don't you think the grandparents would enjoy these fresh carrots?" I asked, knowing that my mother was concerned about them being hungry. The stories we heard about Russian-occupied Vienna were not very encouraging.

"I would like to go see them," I said.

"You know there are no trains or buses."

"There are private trucks taking people, like the one we came home on, maybe I can find one, please Mama, let me do that," I begged.

"See if you can find out something, but I am not in favor of it. It is too dangerous—how do you know what these trucks smuggle, or who even runs them?" My

374

mother had a very negative attitude about such an adventure.

A few weeks later I had made a connection.

"Mama, can I go to Vienna with Herr Rischka? He is taking Uncle Rudi's truck down there again next week. You told me I could look for a way to get there. I want to see Omi and Little Opapa, and Musch Omi and Big Opapa. I want to see if they are all right."

"You cannot go, it is not safe."

"But we have not heard from them, and they have nothing to eat. I could take some food."

"We did hear from them. They were all in the basement under the store, three stories down under the Wild delicatessen, where they age the Swiss cheese."

"Did they sit with the Emmenthaler wheels?" I asked.

"I do not know, but the main thing is, they were safe," mother replied somewhat sternly.

"There was some really heavy street fighting going on in the city, wasn't there? And shelling by heavy artillery."

"They said, the SS tried to destroy the city before they gave it up. They set fire to St. Stephen's, can you imagine, they wanted to blow it up."

"What happened?" I asked.

"I think the Russians moved in too fast. The Germans did not have enough time. How did we get on this, I don't want to talk about it. I need some potatoes for the soup," she said, "could you get me two or three from the cellar, please?"

"Mama, please let me go! Herr Rischka just went there two weeks ago, everything went fine. He came back. All his passengers came back. He'll let me ride for free. He has a permit for the truck. They let him through without any problem," I was pleading.

"How do you know everything went smoothly?"

"He told me. Uncle Rudi said it too. I have my new ID card—it has my name in Russian on it, in Russian letters."

"Cyrillic, Papa wrote us about that when he was still in Russia. He started to learn before he got sick. Go get the potatoes now. Otherwise, they won't be done by lunchtime. They need to cook for a while." She made an abrupt move as if to tear herself from my request, the conversation, and the memory. She went through the door from the kitchen to the hallway into the living room.

I went down to the basement, singing. I used to be afraid to go down there by myself when we first moved in and I had kept up the habit of making noise. I really did not know why—to scare whoever could be down there? Or to warn them? I picked the potatoes out of the bin and went back up.

"There are quite a few left, where did we get them?" I asked my mother.

"Uncle Rudi brought them from one of his trips. A whole rucksack full from some farmer. I don't know what he traded for them."

"Will you ask Uncle Rudi when he comes home about the Vienna trip? Please! Herr Rischka is just staying three days, then I'll be back and we'll know about all the relatives in Vienna." I was not going to give up. I wanted to make this trip, I wanted to see my grandparents and hear how they had fared during the last few weeks of the fighting. I also wanted to see the Russian soldiers and I wanted to see how badly damaged Vienna was.

"I will ask Uncle Rudi and see what he says," my mother said finally, with some resignation in her voice. "Isn't Herr Rischka from Romania? There are so many stories about people disappearing at the border of the Russian zone. The Russians just take people and nobody hears from them again. I am worried about you. I don't want to lose you. Imagine Papa comes home and you are gone. I would have to tell him I let you go to the Russian zone and you did not come back."

"Mama, the people they take are men, ex-soldiers, or Nazis ..."

"People they think were Nazis—and that could be anybody. They do not seem to care. Off to Siberia. Do you want to end up in a labor camp in Siberia?" my mother interrupted me.

"Mama, they do not take children. I am still a child!" I said.

"You are fourteen now, and you are tall, who knows? Don't argue with me, please. I need you here, I'd go insane if anything would happen to you. Do you know how lucky we were to get through all this together, the only one missing Papa? Do you remember when Ina was in the hospital, Dieter with Tante Martha in Linz, you in the school in Seewalchen and I was looking for temporary quarters for us, all over the place? Bombs every day, everywhere, they could have hit you, Ina, Dieter, me—any one of us, and what about the others? I cannot even think about that again, it makes me sick. Let's stay together until Papa comes home, then things should be calmed down and safer, I hope."

"But the grandparents are most probably starving and I could bring them some food. I asked Herr Rischka if he would take a package for them, but he said he couldn't. He has too much already, and no time to deliver. He said 'you come with me and you bring food to your grandmother. I bring you safe.' I imitated Herr Rischka's accent.

"I know, Peter. I feel terrible for them. I am worried also about my sister Martha and her two children. We have no word from them at all. Uncle Fritz was in Czechoslovakia. I wonder what camp he is in."

Herr Rischka's truck was in pretty good shape. The canvas top over the flat bed was slightly weathered but it did not have any holes in it. I walked up to the rear end to climb aboard. An older woman helped me up. I thanked her, turned around and waved to my mother. Then I looked for a place to sit. All the good spots against the cab and the sideboards were taken. I plunked down my rucksack and my two bags in the middle of the truck bed and sat down, using my baggage as a backrest. I looked around. The other passengers were mostly women. A couple of men who looked like tired soldiers going home. I was the youngest.

"Where are you going?" the woman who had helped me, asked.

"I am bringing some food to my grandparents. We have not heard from them. All we know is that they are alive."

"Were they in Vienna the whole time, during the fighting?" the woman asked.

"Yes, in the very end they hid in a cellar, in a very old house, three stories down," I answered.

"I am looking for my sister. She and her two little kids live in Floridsdorf. I have not heard from her. I hope to find her alive. There were some very bad air raids towards the end. Floridsdorf they always hit because of the locomotive factory. I pray she is alive."

"Everybody ready? Everybody paid up?" Herr Rischka had appeared at the rear. "You owe, I know," he said to one of the men. You'll pay me in Vienna. Good. We are ready. You want this closed or open? There is enough of a draft, even with the flap closed. Now everybody, listen up. First stop is the border to the Russian Zone in Enns. If you have not seen any Russian soldiers, don't panic. They all look like warriors. Kirghizians mostly, last time I went through. With rifles slung over their shoulders. Don't let them scare you. Just show them ID card—everybody have an ID card?" He looked around and collected a nod from all the passengers, one by one. "Trouble for you, trouble for me, big trouble for me, no ID card. Got to have your name in Russian, that's all they look for. Ready to go? Let's go." He closed the canvas flap at the rear of the truck bed and soon thereafter we heard the engine starting up, felt the vibration and the motion. We were off.

A couple of people tried to talk but the rattle of the truck and the flapping of the canvas top made it impossible to understand anything. I felt for my ID card in the outside pocket of my rucksack. It was there. Four pages with my photograph and the Austrian double-headed eagle on the front. Name, address and birth date and place in German, English, French, and Russian, the Russian entries in Cyrillic. The word was that most of the Russian soldiers couldn't even read. They were mostly young men from the Steppes and the mountains of Central Asia. Now they occupied Vienna, Lower Austria, the Burgenland, and the northern half of Upper Austria. The Americans, the British and the French had divided the rest of Austria into three parts.

After not quite an hour, the truck came to a halt. We heard foreign sounding words. I picked up a few words in English.

"That must be the Americans," I said.

"We could be at the border already, it's the American side," one of the women said.

The man sitting closest to the back, looked through the opening in the canvas. "Yes, we are in Enns. The American guards are checking the truck papers, I guess," he said.

"If it is like in Linz when you go across the Danube, the Americans don't check your papers, only when you come back," somebody said.

"And then they spray you with DDT so you don't bring any Russian lice with you," another woman said. Everybody laughed.

The truck started moving again. It stopped not very long after. This time the voices were louder and I did not understand anything. Must be the Russians. Soon Herr Rischka opened the back flaps. Then he let down the gate. That's when the Russian soldier came around. He looked very much like a Mongolian.

"*Raus!*" he said in German and motioned the passengers off the truck with his rifle.

"He wants everybody off so they can search the truck," Herr Rischka said.

"Do we take the bags with us?" the woman next to me said.

Herr Rischka pointed to a suitcase on the truck, motioning it off, looking at the soldier.

"Njet—nix" he said, shaking his head.

We all got off and were motioned towards a shed next to the road.

"Do you have your ID cards with you?" Herr Rischka asked. "Better take them, they'll check you in the shed.

There was a group of Russians standing in front of the shed. Two of them were close to the lowered gates, blocking the road. The others were smoking and looking over the women who had just come off the truck. There was no other vehicle in sight other than the military truck behind the shed, with a big red star on it. One of the smokers pointed to the door on the shed.

"Dawai," he said and waved us on.

The passengers from the truck shuffled, nobody wanted to go first it seemed, until one of the men was sort of pushed into the front. He went through the open door first. A soldier appeared from inside and barred the door with his rifle behind the man who had just entered.

"We look like a small herd of sheep," I thought, *"better not get shorn, though,"* I added in my mind. After quite some time the soldier admitted the women next in line to the shed. The man came from behind the shed and walked towards the truck.

"Njet, Njet" one of the soldiers yelled and motioned him to the other side, indicating with a gesture for him to stay put there.

I compared these soldiers with the ones I had seen at the checkpoint on the bridge in Linz. These had dirty uniforms and acted a lot harsher than the guards on the bridge who wore fancy dress uniforms with red epaulets and gold insignia. The soldiers here were plain. Their uniforms looked like they had worn them in combat including their boots. What a contrast to the Americans: They presented quite a different picture: clean uniforms with creases pressed into them, boots shined, and an easygoing manner most of the time.

In the meantime two soldiers searched the truck rather thoroughly. After a while they seemed to be satisfied that there were no hidden people and no contraband—whatever they considered contraband. They called the people who had gone through the shed to come and pick their luggage off the truck. Each piece had to be opened and inspected. Nobody knew what they were looking for but rumor had it that they took whatever they needed or what pleased them. It could be a wristwatch or food, if it was *karascho* -good- it disappeared into their pockets. No argument, no recourse.

One of the men emerged from the shed pale and accompanied by a soldier. They went to the truck and the man got his bags, not for inspection but to take with him. *"Kommandantura"* was the word, headquarters, officers, more checking.

Herr Rischka pointed at the man, looking at the soldier and shaking his head.

"*Papiera njet karascho -kommandantura*" the soldier said, pronouncing the words slowly..

"If you are not back by the time we are done here, we cannot wait, sorry," Herr Rischka said, "I am lucky they haven't blamed me, not yet. Here, take your money, somebody will give you a lift from here, just ask. Good luck if we don't see you!"

The other passengers both in front and in back of the shed stood in awe. One of the women looked like she was going to intercede, but before she could say or do anything, Herr Rischka had motioned her back into the line, making unmistakable signs for her to shut up. I felt this old knot in the stomach and with it the urge to go to the bathroom. There was none in sight. There was no communication other than by sign language and a few words. With the Americans there was always somebody who could speak enough English to make a conversation possible. I felt frustrated and I was trembling. Over two hours had passed since we first stopped here. Now we were all done. One of the soldiers opened the gate and waved us through.

It was pitch dark when we entered Vienna. Peeking out from behind the canvas I had not recognized any landmarks so far. The roads along the way had been a mess. Detours around bomb craters, stretches of road all worn out from heavy tank traffic, troop convoys we had to stop for—we were all sore from sitting on the hard planks for so many hours. At a brief rest stop Herr Rischka had laid out his general route through Vienna and asked everybody to tell him where they wanted to get off.

A few people had wanted to get off in the suburbs already.

"*Schwarzenbergplatz* is next stop," Herr Rischka announced, as he closed the back flap, "but now it is called *Platz* of the Red Army. Don't be confused. Peter, that's you. Do you know where you are going?"

"Yes, from the *Platz* I know," I answered. "It's just a few streets up."

The truck stopped, Herr Rischka opened the flap again and helped me slinging my bags down.

"Same spot, three days from now, about noon, I'll pick you up again. Don't miss me—no trains, no buses, I'll be back in few weeks only, no way to get in touch. Who does not show up, left behind. Good luck!" He waved and drove off.

There was dead silence and not a single light except for a few stars in the sky. I let my eyes adjust to the dark. Nothing looked familiar. *Maybe Herr Rischka had dropped me off at the wrong place?* I panicked. I could see the outline of a tank in the middle of the *Platz. A leftover from the fighting or a Russian patrol?* No engine noises, no movement. I thought about the big rucksack with the potatoes and the two heavy bags with the rest of the food I had brought. I did not want to go far out of the way, my load was too heavy to carry far.

Where am I on this darned Platz? There should be big apartment buildings over there, but I cannot see any. Where is the fountain in the center? The fountain, famous for its light show with the dancing waters, where was it?

Do they have a curfew? We had one in the American Zone the first few months, but the Russians are stricter. What if they find me here? Will they take my stuff away? Arrest me?

Just as the thought had entered my mind, I heard voices coming from the opposite side of the open space. Commands, boots marching on the cobble stones in step. I froze. The only object I could make out from where I stood -other than the silhouette of the tank- was something like a wooden fence. I remembered having seen it lit up by the headlights when the truck pulled away. I made my plan while listening to the footsteps. I would go over to the fence, move along it until I found some buildings. Then look for a slight grade uphill—South—well where was South? I looked up at the sky. No big dipper. No way to find the North Star.

The voices and the footsteps moved away. I was relieved. I picked up my rucksack, heaved it over my shoulders and grabbed the other bags, one on each side.

I hope it's not far, I thought as I felt the weight pulling my body down. When I reached the fence I saw the big pile of rubble—all that was left of the four-story apartment building. The one next to it was still standing, it was set back somewhat, I recognized the columns flanking the entrance. It used to house an embassy, it always had a foreign flag flying outside. Now I thought I knew where I was. *There should be streetcar tracks running close by, the D-line, I'll check.* I put down my bags. I walked away from the buildings to where I suspected the tracks. *There they are!* I breathed a sigh of relief.

As I walked, I began to see more houses and then the trees on the other side of the street where the park around the fountain should be. I had never experienced such impenetrable darkness. It was so dark I had forgotten to be afraid of the dark. I laughed at the thought.

I put the bags down again, shifted the straps so they would cut my shoulders in another area, and continued. I could feel the incline now, which reassured me that I was walking in the right direction. So far, I had not recognized another building. The opposite of the street seemed right. That is where the alley starts along the wall of the Belvedere. I could barely see the outlines of trees. Two more streets and I should be there. Finally, I saw the sign: *Wohllebengasse.* "Street of the Good Life,' an appropriate name, my grandmother always had shown style.

After a few more minutes of confusion and disorientation caused by some gaping holes in the row of apartment buildings, I stood in front of the gigantic wrought iron gate with the number seven. I had no key. Therefore, I had to ring the concierge. *What if the bell does not work?* The old concierge–if he is still there- lived too far inside the building to hear any knocking out here. There were no direct bells to the apartments.

Ringing out the concierge had always involved a whole ritual. There were unasked questions like "Why do you not have a key?" or "What are you doing out so late?" and last but not least, "What time is it?," because that determines the amount of *Sperrgeld*, the obligatory tip for the late night service. I knew my grandmother would take care of it all in the morning, but still I hesitated to ring the bell. Finally I did. I was shocked at the shrill tone reverberating through the large marbled hall behind the gate. My finger jumped back from the button. Then I waited.

Just when I decided to ring again, a light came on in the concierge's loge and soon thereafter the old man appeared on the stairs. I remembered his name, *Herr Gumpelmayer*, he had been there as long as my grandmother had lived there, forever. Before he put the key into the lock, Herr Gumpelmayer looked through the glass to see who was out there. When he recognized me, he opened the heavy gate.

"Well, look who we have here, the young Mr. Slonek. Hello, Good Evening. So we both survived. Good. Let me help you with the bags."

"Thank you! Good Evening, *Herr Gumpelmayer*. How are you? Sorry to bother you so late, but the truck just let me off at the Platz. I hardly found my way, it looks so different and it is so dark."

"Yes, the street lights are still out and the spots on the monument they turn off at ten."

"What monument?"

"By the fountain, the big arch with the Russian soldier, you did not see it?

"No, I was way down by the Reisebüro side, where the big building is missing ..."

"Oh well, without lights, and not knowing, it would be hard to see." Herr *Gumpelmayer* had carried the one bag up the first flight of stairs. He put it down in front of his daytime watch post, the concierge's loge.

"Sorry, Herr Slonek, the elevator does not work. Nobody to fix it. No parts."

"Well, I'll manage. I will leave one bag here and fetch it on a second run. My grandmother is going to take care of the Sperrgeld in the morning, sorry, I only have US zone money." It was the first time I was confronted with the fact that Austria now had four different types of currency, one for each of the occupation zones, US, Russian, French, and British.

"Oh, don't you worry. Get up there. Your grandmother will be happy to see you, I bet. Good night. No lights on the stairway either, can you manage in the dark? I'll leave my lights on, at least you have a little bit of light. Be careful, yes? See you in the morning." He shut the door behind himself and waved through the glass enclosure.

Quite a change from the grouchy silent man I remembered.

I was exhausted but close to home. Only six flights of stairs away from embracing my grandparents, from delivering the precious nourishment and from bed. The journey, the tension, the excitement, the fear, and the heavy load I was carrying had eaten away at my youthful strength.

This apartment building was very 'vornehm'- fancy. Marble, wrought iron, elaborate patterns in the enclosure of the elevator and the handrails, the elevator itself paneled in fine woods, normally illuminated by small crystal glass fixtures. Right now, the only part of the fanciness I noticed was the height of the individual stories. The stairs wound around and around, two landings for each floor. At the second one, I put down my bags and continued with the rucksack alone. I was out of breath.

I felt around the doorframe for the doorbell. I could not find it where I remembered it. Up here, the concierge's skimpy light did not have any power left. I started knocking at the door. Instantly I could hear my grandmother's voice and the flopping of her old house slippers. *She must have waited up, so she got our note. Thank God, otherwise she might have had a stroke if she opens the door and sees me here,* raced through my mind.

"Peterle, my Peterle," she said over and over again, pulled me inside the doorway, giving me and my Rucksack a long hug. She smothered me with kisses. Tears ran down her cheeks. My eyes started to tear up, too.

I felt a strong sensation of being alive, of having survived, and holding my tiny, fragile grandmother in my arms, finally relieved of my fear that harm had come to her. She was thinner than I had ever seen her.

"I left two more bags downstairs," I said as I slipped the rucksack off my shoulders. My grandmother tried to help but she was overwhelmed by the weight.

"How could you carry all this? How far did you have to walk? How did you find your way?" she bombarded me with questions as had been her habit all along.

"I'll get the bags so nobody will trip over them in the dark," I said. "Do you have a flashlight, maybe? Herr

Gumpelmayer left his light on but it does not shine all the way up. It is very dark out there."

"Yes, Opapa has a flashlight, but the batteries are very weak already, let me get it."

"Where is Opapa?" I asked.

"Oh, he is snoring in his bed, he wanted to wait up but he fell asleep in his chair about an hour ago. We were not sure how you would get here, how everything would work out. I was so worried. Did the Russians give you any trouble at the border?"

"No, not really, it just took a long time," I said. I did not tell her about the man kept back. They would never let me go again, if I told. "Let me get the bags."

"Are you hungry? When did you leave Linz?" Omi said and pushed me into a chair. "We'll unpack in the morning when Opapa is up, yes?"

"You have to tell me about the fighting, was it awful?" I asked.

We traded stories for another hour until my eyes would not stay open any longer.

"You get your couch bed here, as always. Good night, my dear Peterle! Thank you so much, I am so happy you came!" She smothered me with another round of kisses and embraces and finally let me go.

The next day I took half of the provisions to the other grandparents. Their bodies also showed the lack of proper nourishment. They were thin and pale. My aunt and her two children, who lived with them, looked a little better but also appeared alarmingly thin. I was shocked to see with my own eyes what the curtailed food supplies had done to these people. They all were ecstatic to see me and hear that we had survived well. They appreciated the few supplies I had brought with me. My aunt had not heard anything about her husband. His last posting was to Czechoslovakia. She was beginning to worry about his fate. I was glad that I had insisted on making this trip and bring at least a little food to help out.

On my way back to the other grandparents, I took a little detour through the center of town. I was astounded by the amount of damage that had occurred since my last visit. Building after building had been reduced to rubble.

Slow moving crews of elderly people were at work in many of the ruins cleaning bricks and stacking them for re-use. Most of the people I encountered in the street looked ashen and lifeless. St. Stephens Cathedral was gutted and roofless and looked very sad with the black smoke scars around the windows.

The three days passed very quickly. I felt like a time traveler. What I saw and experienced was nothing like anything I had experienced ever before. After long and very tearful goodbyes, my Omi and my little Opapa waved as the truck left with me on my way back to Linz.

GOING TO THE MOVIES

"We are going to the movies today," Mr. Krenn, my homeroom teacher who had survived the purge of teachers who had been linked to the Nazi Party announced without warning.

The class reacted with pleasure-sounds associated with any mention of non-direct-learning activities. Mr. Krenn did not hush us as he would do normally. He just continued in his habitual matter-of-fact tone.

"The American Military Government has decreed that every high school student is required to see the documentary films that were made when the Allied troops liberated the Concentration Camps throughout the German Reich and the Occupied Territories."

All the noises in the classroom immediately went on hold. The KZ's–*Konzentrationslager*-, as the Concentration Camps were called in German, had a presence in everybody's mind since the end of the war when news about them spread rapidly, but they were still not talked about freely. They were one of the subjects that had not been mentioned in the course of instruction since school reconvened. Neither teachers nor parents knew what to say about them other than how horrible and how inconceivable it was for human beings to inflict such outrageous atrocities to other human beings.

"This will be a lesson in history which you will not forget for the rest of your lives," Mr. Krenn continued, "I attended a screening of the films for teachers the other day ..."

After a pause during which he did not look at anybody in the class, he said, "I cannot tell you what we saw, you have to see for yourself. I think it is a good decision by the Americans to make you see what went on here in our country, in Germany, and in many of the German-occupied countries. These pictures tell a horrible truth."

I had never had Mr. Krenn in one of my classes until this year. Now he was my homeroom teacher. He was a rather quiet man who never showed any excitement, not even during the disciplinary actions he had to carry out with my rowdier classmates. Today he showed a different face. He was visibly shaken and moved.

"We are scheduled for the ten o'clock screening. It will be at the Museum Theater so we shall leave here in about ten minutes. Take a quick break, please be quiet in the hall so you don't disturb the other classes and then line up here by the door."

We trotted up towards the center of town, other classes ahead of us and others behind us.

As the classes entered the theater and filled row after row, there was considerable noise from much talking and some nervous joking in anticipation of what was to come. Finally, all the seats were taken and the lights went out. We could hear the projector starting its whirly sound, the light beam caught the dust particles in the air and the screen lit up with the title sequence. Over the scratchy music track we were informed that this documentary was made by the war correspondents who had accompanied the Allied Troops who had first come upon the concentration camps and freed the inmates. Then there was a map of Central Europe showing the locations of the camps. There was one very close to Lake Attersee and one between Linz and Vienna, near the town of Mauthausen. I had heard the name mentioned because some of the criminal inmates from there had plundered houses near Linz after they went free. The names of the other camps were familiar also because I had heard them mentioned in conversations. Word of mouth had traveled quickly after the end of the war. Everybody we knew was horrified by what they had heard. Some people did not believe the stories, others admitted to have heard whispered allegations earlier on.

When the actual pictures started appearing on the screen, absolute quiet befell the theater. My hands grabbed the armrests tightly. I forgot to breathe. I had never seen pictures like this: Walking skeletons shuffling along, lifeless, without expressions on their faces other than the accusing hollow eyes of starvation. Oversized heads on emaciated bodies. Some others making an attempt at smiling and waving. Many of them looked like they did not comprehend what had happened. The idea of being free and allowed to live was overwhelming and more than they could take in. There were interviews with inmates who had arrived at the camp not so long ago, who were still in better shape. Some of them had been forced to work on the "*Sonderkommandos*"—the crews that had been feeding the bodies into the crematoriums. They had kept track of the numbers of human beings passing through their hands. I shut my eyes and ears in disbelief. There were the pictures of wooden carts stacked full with bodies, skeletons covered with skin, no more. There were fire pits still smoldering with the remains of burning bodies—the meticulously constructed rows of brick ovens could not handle the steady flow of bodies from the gas chambers—so the camp commanders had ordered fire pits to be dug to take care of the overflow. The narrator explained how the camp functioned. There was a devilish master plan in place. The whole process was organized to the last detail. It started with the arrival of the long trains with locked freight cars full of starving, weather-exposed prisoners. As the prisoners came off the train they were being robbed of their last belongings, their clothes, sometimes even their children, before being divided into two columns. One was for the older people, who were destined for the gas chambers and the other one for the younger people, who were fit to perform slave labor, going to the barracks. A wrought iron gate at one of the camps spelled out the motto: *Arbeit macht frei!* Work is liberating!

The worst came when the camera focused on the huge piles of bodies, skeletons heaped high near the ovens and the pits where they were to be cremated. I was in a cold sweat, openly crying. All around me in the dark, I heard people sobbing and blowing their noses. *Did my parents know about all this? Was my father, as a soldier in the German army, part of this? He could not be. How could anybody be? How could anybody be part of this outrageous cruelty, this inhuman behavior, day in, day out without throwing themselves into the ovens or running away or turning against the butchers who designed this death machine?*

But here were pictures of the uniformed guards standing by the barracks, guarded by American soldiers, some with numb expressions, others looking defiant as if they expected the tide to turn quickly again.

The film showed another camp, the gates, the railroad spurs leading into it, the barracks and the barbed wire fences around it all, dotted with watchtowers. Above all, hundreds of people milling about in a daze, walking, shuffling slowly, or sitting against the barrack walls, hardly able to keep their upper bodies from falling. Many too weak to even get up, still in their bunk beds, where they had been packed so tightly that at night, they had to turn all at once, because there was not enough individual space. The horror tale went on and on. Without much explanation, the pictures spoke eloquently of the crime committed on humanity.

When the lights came back on, we all filed slowly out of the theater, and marched back towards the school. There was no talking. Even the class clown had nothing to say. "Think about it all and tell your parents what you saw," the teacher said and dismissed us for the day.

I went home on the bus. It was almost empty since regular school had not let out yet and the adults were still at work. The images kept coming back in my mind: arms and legs, with the bones visible, ribcages covered only with skin, lifeless bodies, piled high, bottomless eye sockets, black, with just the tiniest glimmer of life left in the hidden eyeballs, staring straight into the camera

...unbelieving, expressionless, not even asking for help or food, just staring and not believing ...

My mother noticed the difference in my mood immediately.

"What happened in school today? Why are you home so early?"

"We saw a film and they sent us home early."

"What kind of film? The old cartoon about the country mouse visiting the city mouse? Not again?"

"No, it was about the KZ's. When the American and the Russian troops found the camps, they took movies of what they found. You could never imagine what they found!"

"Well, there have been some pretty awful stories, and we know what kind of people were kept there, we heard what they did when they came out—they robbed and they plundered and they stole ..."

"No, Mama, these were pictures of the extermination camps, Auschwitz for one, where they gassed thousands of Jews every day ..."

"Every day? How could they do that? What would they do with that many bodies?" My mother's voice became less stable and assured.

"It was very organized, disgustingly well organized, the film explained the whole process. I saw the bodies, I saw the gas chambers, I saw the ovens, I saw the fire pits ... I saw the people who survived ..." my eyes started to tear up and I turned away from my mother. "I do not want to talk about it, not now, maybe later."

"Why did they have to show this to you? Isn't there enough death and enough pain and enough destruction?"

"The American Military Government said that every high school student must see this film. So that we cannot say it was not true or not so many or not any other silly excuse. There is no excuse. It was totally awful to see what the Nazis have done!"

"Let's leave it at that. Come, have some lunch."

"No, thank you, I cannot eat with all that on my mind."

"You have to eat, Peter, you are growing and there is not that much anyway!"

"Not now, maybe tonight. I'll go and do my homework upstairs."

TROUBLE IN SCHOOL

"Milk was two thirty, Frau Humer eight Schillings ..."

"That is the baker lady?" Uncle Rudi asked.

"Yes," my mother said, "fourteen Schillings for the butcher ..."

I sat at the top of the stairs and listened to my mother doing the budget with Uncle Rudi as they did every night before going to bed. Uncle Rudi had suggested it to my mother since she had been worried about her finances. With communications cut off with my father, she had no help and advice. The money paid by the New Austrian Republic until my father would come home—or be declared dead—was not enough to live on for the four of us. Reserves had been used up a long time ago.

"When are they going to finish," I thought. I had some personal business with my mother alone and so far, I had not had the courage to bring it up. I heard Uncle Rudi's wife walking around in the bedroom behind me. *"I hope she does not come out and ask me what I am doing here. I am really not interested in the budget or anything else these two have to discuss. It is always the same, too many bills and not enough income."* I did not like to hear it, my mother sounded so desperate and hopeless. Uncle Rudi kept saying that it was important to know where the money went.

"Well, we are ahead so far, this month," Uncle Rudi said. I could hear the big budget book sliding around on the dining table. That book was from Uncle Otto's things, when we had received his belongings packed in suitcases and boxes. The budget book had red covers made of laminated cardboard and thick glossy pages of tinted accounting sheets. I had looked through it several times and felt the smoothness of the paper with my hands. It was quite different from the paper in my school note books, which was coarse and hairy so the pencil and pens points would rip little holes in it when you were not careful enough ..."

School—the thought ripped through my intestines the way air bubbles raise up in a drink when you blow into it through a straw. My mother had to sign another "Ungenügend," another F on my latest composition test. I held on tight to the banister to ease my pain. The voices downstairs no longer reached my brain. It was occupied with an image of my German teacher's pudgy stature, the stare of his beady eyes, the shine of his green-blue tweed suit that he wore three times a week, and the only half-hidden smile on his face when he cut me or any other one of his targets down. Herr Stundner was one of the few teachers left over from the war staff. Many others had been dismissed for their true or imagined involvement with the Nazi doctrine. *"Why did he have to survive this purge?"* I thought, *"The one man I hate. How did he survive? Why was he not drafted to begin with?"* He was young and looked healthy. Maybe he was too short and too heavy? An army rifle slung over his shoulder would probably drag on the ground. I shook in disgust thinking of the man. He must have lied to the authorities. And a lie was what had started our feud.

The day had lodged itself in my memory forever. I had not done my homework, a written description of yet another picture, this teacher's favorite assignment. The old German woodcut showed a farmer behind a plow drawn by two huge horses across a field. I hated these assignments. They were so lacking in challenge, nothing to think about, just translating what you saw into words. I did the opposite whenever I was reading. The words in the books I was reading would create fabulous scenes, better than the ones I had seen in the movies. Jungles with luscious foliage full of exotic animals and the sounds they made, the glaring deserts of the Llano Estacado from my Indian stories...

I had read Tom Sawyer's Adventures instead of describing the farmer's stance and the size of the horses' haunches, and the children grouped around a tree in the background. When Herr Stundner had asked the class -as he always did- who had not done the homework, I had ducked and not raised my hand. A few minutes later I had been asked to read my description. I had stood up as required, but I was not holding my notebook in my hands to read—instead I stared at the teacher and my head felt as if I had stuck it into an oven. I had blushed a crimson red with the embarrassment.

"Well," the teacher said, cocking his head in anticipation of an answer, "what did you write, Slonek?"

"I did not write ...," I said, and I wanted to continue saying that I had forgotten my notebook but my mouth went dry with the heat from my head. "I did not do the assignment. I forgot," I finally managed to hiss at the teacher. After that I sat down.

"We are not finished, Slonek. Would you please stand?" the teacher said. His voice was edgy and cutting. "You do not like to do these, do you? Well, by tomorrow, you will do this assignment and the next three pictures following in the book. Is that clear?"

"Yes," I said. Another wave of crimson crawled up to my hairline and then across my scalp.

"Furthermore, I am putting you down for an 'F' as if you had failed the last test. You can work that off during the remainder of the year. I do not like lying. I will not be lied to, not for any reason." He turned his head slowly away from me towards the other side of the classroom. "Mayer," he said, "read your description to the class."

"Ja, Herr Professor," Mayer said, stood up and droned, "In the foreground we see a farmer ..."

"He looks just like a little Herr Stundner," I thought, "just as pudgy, the same little pig eyes ... I hate this class." I sat down. My hands were sweaty and my body was shaking.

From that day on, I could not do anything right for this teacher. We were together at least two hours a day since he also taught English. That made going to school an ordeal.

There was another teacher, Herr Professor Meixner, who taught mathematics and art. The art class consisted mostly of inventing a series of little creatures that would live on one large sheet of No. 2 drawing paper. I delighted in these fantasy characters and their underground dwellings.

"Just because you draw well, you will not get a better grade in mathematics," the teacher kept saying. I was not sure what that meant because I never assumed that my talents in the arts would help me in calculating fractions. However, I managed to make up for my failures at the math tests by passing oral examinations.

My main interest was and remained reading. I checked out books from the school library, which -after being closed for a long period of political cleansing- was open again. I borrowed books from neighbors and friends, and I read through all the volumes on my parents' bookshelves. Whatever presented itself, I read: Adventure, history, novels, youth and adult fiction. While pretending to do homework I had my current book out, ready to be hidden under the schoolbooks. Many evenings my mother would catch me reading by a flashlight under the covers in my bed. My grades did not reflect my general knowledge but my performance in school, which was dismal.

Sometime during this period my mother had decided not to wait for my father's return but to find a career for herself to support us. Her first choice was the love of her youth: the medical profession. One career open and of interest to her was midwifery. She signed up for the three-year certification program. The hitch was, it was a residential program. Who would take care of her children while she was gone? My mother's youngest sister, Aunt Trude, lived in Vienna. Her husband, a physician, had been drafted into the German army and had returned from the war unharmed. A few weeks later the Russians had taken him away, 'to help his countrymen in a hospital.' After that there was no communication from him and not a word about his whereabouts. My mother asked her if she would be willing to move into our house and take care of the three of us until her husband came home. Aunt Trude, who had a daughter younger than my sister, grabbed the chance of leaving the Russian Zone for the American one.

"You don't know how much I appreciate this," my mother told her sister. "But I do not see any other way out of this dilemma."

"What about Peter? You mentioned that he is having trouble with his learning." Aunt Trude sounded unsure. "I am afraid I might not be able to handle him, and from what you have been telling me, he is getting rather strong headed.

LIVING WITH THE OBERBAURATS

My mother had been struggling with this situation and had called on family and friends to help her with converting me into an ambitious student. Some advocated learning a trade rather than force me to continue to be tortured in middle school. The only venue I was inclined to follow was fine woodworking and maybe garden design. Then an adventurous, distant uncle, who was making money in the newly launched plastics industry, had offered to invest into my future. An old friend and political ally of his, a retired civil engineer and his wife were now supplementing their pension by taking in several students during the school year. The *Oberbaurat* whose career had been building roads and railroads in the Balkans under the last Austrian Emperor, and his wife, housed, fed and supervised these students. It had turned out that they had space for one more in the current year. One week after the uncle offered the generous deal, I moved into this nest of learning, which happened to be in the same building in town as our good Dr. Thier who had taken care of me during my two long illnesses.

After having lived there for almost the whole school year, I still entered the cool and dark hallways of this massive apartment building with a sense of defiance. I climbed the four flights of stairs, taking two steps at a time. I pulled myself around the corners on the banisters and I was proud of my fluid movements. I did not like this house.

"Why am I living here? We have a house in this town, I have a family—and now I have been living with these strangers rather than at home where I belong. These people are old and weird, they are drinking Turkish coffee and they are passing out leaflets about somebody called Luddendorf. Yes, I had not been doing my homework

occasionally, and I was close to failing in three subjects, but I could have pulled through, I know. That was not reason enough to deport me, to exclude me from the family. When Papa comes home, he will change all that. He will help me with the homework, not just yell at me to do it. And we will be doing fun things together, too, not only chores."

I rang the doorbell. Anton came to the door. He was a farmer's son, about my age, very serious about his studies of architecture. I liked him the best out of the three other boarders.

"Hey, Peter. Are you looking forward to blood sausage day? It's as good as ever!" He grinned.

Tuesday was blood sausage day at this household. *Frau Oberbaurat's* menu was very rigid. There was one dish for each day of the week, regardless of weather, season or taste. I like good, fresh blood sausage very much. What passed in this house under the same label was unacceptable. It tasted like sawdust and it behaved like sawdust. The longer you kept it in your mouth, the more it became—sawdust. Except that it was black.

I had talked to Karl, the oldest of the students here, some time ago. I thought I could take him into my confidence.

"I cannot swallow this blood sausage. It grows in your mouth, doesn't it?"

"Yes, we talked to her last year, but she will not go to another butcher or drop it from the menu. It is awful. You know what I do?"

"No, tell me?"

"If you promise not to tell anybody else. You promise?"

"I promise," I said solemnly, anything to get out of this one.

"See, I bring this little paper bag with me every Tuesday," Karl said and pulled out a neatly folded paper bag," and when I am alone here in the dining room I fill it with the blood sausage off my plate and put it into my pocket. Later on, I flush it down the toilet. It works every time." Karl was proud of his scheme.

He probably uses this trick for other foods as well, I thought, because I knew Karl was a fussy eater. "I'll do the same from now on, otherwise I'll throw up. And she insists on a large portion, she will not let me take less or nothing at all."

"I know, Peter, don't feel bad. That is the way she is. She wants us fed well."

"Just like with the bathing?" I asked, "She wants us bathed well."

"Well, I don't know. That is another story. I've told her that I always rinse myself off with cold water after the bath but she insists that she has to do it." Karl had a little grin on his face.

"She does not believe we do the cold water rinse by ourselves, she says. I feel uncomfortable with the old woman hosing me down. She takes her time, too. I don't mind the cold water, but I do mind the stares."

"Is she looking?"

"She is looking all right. It doesn't hurt, does it?" Karl said.

"Yes, but it is ...." I couldn't think of a proper word to describe my feelings about the strong, heavy-bodied old lady, with the deep voice and the birdlike features, full of wrinkles through which her basic kindness sometimes shone, in spite of her harsh demeanor.

"The old man is probably withered away by now. She wants to see some young flesh. Maybe that's why they have students in the house? What do you think?" Karl's eyes were wide with excitement over this new thought.

"As long as she doesn't touch anything, I guess I am fine," I continued, "but I feel embarrassed standing there, naked in front of her ..."

"Maybe she would like to help us masturbate?" Karl said in a low voice. "We should ask her."

We both laughed, self-conscious and awkward.

I was glad Karl had said the word, I looked towards him for guidance, but him being the oldest and the only one who had been in this household the year before, I was not sure how close we could be. I could hold out the longest against him in chess, so I felt somewhat assured in my own standing. In addition, it seemed that Karl took my opinions seriously, not like those spouted by some kid without thought.

The door opened and *Frau Oberbaurat* appeared.

"Peter, your aunt just called, she wants you to come out to the house tomorrow afternoon."

"Did she say why?" I asked back.

"No, your mother is still in the hospital, maybe she needs some help. How about some more sausage and sauerkraut?" she said and headed for the serving spoon.

"No, thank you, I am stuffed already," both Karl and I said.

"Please, do not use the word 'stuffed.' It is impolite. If you have to indicate that you have eaten enough, say so, or say you are no longer hungry. Not 'stuffed.' Sausages are stuffed. Do you want to be taken for a sausage?"

"No, thank you." We both answered, again in tune. This sort of dialogue was not new, of course. Both *Oberbaurats* loved to impart their views on manners on us. Sometimes they even added little bits of wisdom of the world for good measure.

"Good. I hope you will remember." *Frau Oberbaurat* said. "But you really should eat some more. Look there is half the bowl left and Toni is the only one who hasn't eaten yet. He should be here any minute now, unless he is dawdling in the streets again," she continued, looking at the big old grandfather clock ticking away between the two windows of the dining room. "He is such a baby."

HOME FOR THE NEWS

I decided to take the 2:30 train of the *Eferdinger Bahn* rather than the old forty-five minute walk out to the house, which I had done far too long already. This way it only took me five minutes to the downtown station, ten minutes on the old train, and twenty minutes up the hill and over to the edge of the development to our house.

"What's up this time?" I scanned through the whole spectrum of known mischief in response to the call "home." Mother had been hospitalized with a serious case of pneumonia and I had not had a chance to visit her yet. In school I had done well thanks to the *Oberbaurat's* strict supervision of my study habits, and the teachers were

behaving for a change, no hostility, no accusations of lying or studying for the wrong teacher, and no flunked tests.

"It must be something new then." I shook in disgust. These adults had such devious ways to confront me with their objection to my behavior. Nobody ever came out straight and said what they meant. And there were never any suggestions on how to alleviate the problem other than by studying harder, more intense, or by being 'good' or 'responsible.'

The train rattled and squeaked to a stop. *This stop or the next?* I considered quickly. It was the same distance to the house from either station, but the walks home were different. One led by my old school. That would be the next stop. Just when the train started to pull out of the station I decided to get off here and walk by the big old farmhouse. It reminded me of the visit I had paid there with my father at what seemed a very long time ago.

I jumped off the train only as it started to move again, swinging off the handles next to the steps and landing safely on the gravel path lining the rails within the little station.

The bars on the big railroad crossing were down. I loved the shaking of the earth caused by the approaching and passing train. I closed my eyes and listened for it with the soles of my feet. I had read in one of the *Karl May* books that American Indians put an ear to the ground or the rails to listen for approaching horses or trains. My feet were now listening to the 'iron horse' heading towards the main railway station.

The train carried a different kind of Americana: Jeeps, trucks, and tanks. And lots of containers. Ammunition? Food? Bombs? Car after car ticked by on the rails and after the last one, the bars opened slowly. It was the old conductor's wife at the controls today. I knew her well by sight from the days when I had walked to school this way every day. She was tired and worn out. There had been too many trains in her lifetime, too many pedestrians complaining about the blocking of the way, too many school kids trying to climb over the bars, asking for an accident to happen.

I crossed the rails, one long step per rail. That was my game. *Where do all these Jeeps, tanks, and trucks go?* Sometimes they went west, sometimes they went east; if they all went in one direction, it would make sense. This way it did not. I decided conclusively that it did not make sense to ship the same items in opposite directions. Many things did not make sense to me in this time.

Before I started up the hill, I passed the entrance to the old farmhouse. It was built in the traditional style for the province of Upper Austria. The main entrance was wide enough for a wagon. It went into a square courtyard through and under the two-story living quarters finished in brick and mortar. The two other wings of the quadrangle had brick walls only for the first floor, which housed the stables for the livestock, the second floor was built of wood, with a thatched roof all around. The fourth side was made of wood and mostly open to the inside court. It housed wagons and farm equipment. An outside ramp lead to the second floor above the stables, where hay and grains were stored.

Before we had moved into our new house, my father had taken me on a walk to explore the neighborhood. When we had come by the farmhouse, my father had entered the courtyard. I was scared then. First, we had not been invited in and second, most farmers had big dogs and I was very afraid of dogs. My father had shielded me from the dog when it appeared and we had a nice chat with the farmer himself who told us what parts of his property he had kept and what he would plant on these fields.

I thought of the gentleness of the old man, with his gnarled hands holding the long drooping pipe, the strength in his voice and the love of the land, which sang through his sentences. He was not in agreement with all the construction going on around him, nor with the money he had received for his fields, but he conceded that the town had to grow and he was at the edge of it—therefore it was he who had to make space. He could still make a living off the fields that remained in his possession and the easier load was welcome since he had known that his sons would be drafted into the army within months of the sale.

I had climbed the hill to the plateau where all the new houses stood. I entered the lower sling of the big "S" formed by the road, which would take me to my house. I looked right and left, I knew all the fences and yards, all the houses and their occupants. On the right here I had fetched lettuce and cabbage seedlings, and coming up on the left was the house of the woman who had a male rabbit suitable to mate with our gray chinchilla. My friend and I had taken her over there for this purpose. When we came home, my mother had asked whether we had watched the rabbits. 'Of course,' we had said with a grin, but it had happened very fast and had not looked romantic at all, as I had expected. The act was noisy and almost hostile. Creating new life should happen more gently. But it was fun. When I told the story to my friends, we always had a good laugh.

The last stretch into our cul-de-sac was the part of the walk I dreaded most. It still housed the big old bulldog, always watching for passers-by. Today I tiptoed along in the hope not to awaken the beast. I was lucky. There was no sight of it. And no sound. But the feeling of fear alone made those last hundred or so yards a torture.

"Anybody home?" It was strange for me to knock at the door of my own house that did not feel like my home any more.

"Peter, is that you? I am in the basement, in the laundry room. I'll be up in a minute." My aunt's voice came from downstairs.

Through the window in the living room I could see my sister in the sandbox, which had been restored from my play-bunker-home back to a proper sandbox. Ina was propping up her little doll on the corner seat and talking to her friend. The faces of the two little girls were serious. I thought about that. I could remember my sister only as mostly serious or crying.

"There you are!—Are you hungry? Can you stay for dinner?" my aunt had come up behind me. I turned and gave her a quick kiss on both cheeks. She dried her hands on her white apron. Her round face was red from rubbing and wringing the large laundry pieces and from the hot water in the big laundry tub.

"Yeah, I can stay. *Frau Oberbaurat* is not expecting me. I don't want anything now, though, thanks. What's new?" The last words were fishing for the reason of my summons. It could not be bad because I could not sense any clouds around.

"Dieter will be home any minute now, so let's go into the other room. I want to tell you something, just between you and me."

"This whole house is a mess," I thought to myself when I entered the old 'dining' room that had housed all our boarders. I recalled that this was where we had put up our first Christmas tree after moving in. Now it was a full bed that filled it. I remembered Grandma Totila lying on this bed, dead.

On the opposite wall stood my sister's little bed next to a dresser. So my brother is sleeping on the bed here? Maybe the Müller's had taken over the "boys" room upstairs. That would be mean. They had started out in only one room.

"What's so secret, that we have to come in here for?" I asked.

My aunt had taken off the apron, folded it neatly besides her on the bed, and then had smoothed her dress. She stretched out her arm and begged me to sit next to her.

The cold, waxy figure of the dead old woman swam through my imagination. I sat down next to my aunt.

"You know that your Grosse Opapa has been corresponding with the Red Cross people about Uncle Fritz, Uncle Leo, your father, and two of his cousins."

"Yes," I said, quickly scanning my priority list. Whom would I miss the least? Uncle Fritz always told wonderful jokes, Uncle Leo came back and then the Russians took him away, he was alive for sure, the cousins I really did not know...

"Opapa sent us a letter yesterday. It was about your father. He is not coming back."

My aunt put her arm over my shoulders and pulled me up to her soft supple body.

"I took your grandfather's letter to your mother in the hospital, yesterday. She said she had known in her heart for a long time. I am sorry, Peter. It will be all right."

Nothing will be all right! I wanted to shout but no sound came out of my throat. Tears streamed down my cheeks. "When?"

"When what?" my aunt asked, sitting up straight and letting her arm come off my shoulders.

"When was he killed? And where?" my voice cracked. I pulled out my handkerchief, wiped off my tears, and blew my nose.

"On the third of March, near a small town Southwest of Aachen. It is in Belgium. Opapa found it on the map. It's something with 'Henry,' I do not remember the full name."

"His last letter to Mama was from February 22, wasn't it?" I asked but I knew anyway. My mother and I had read this letter so many times. We had looked at it and analyzed it for clues. It did not yield any more than that he was moving towards the front. Together with all the others from the hospital who could walk.

"Do you have the letter?" I asked my aunt.

"From the Red Cross?"

"Yes. What else does it say?" I was impatient.

"Opapa still has it. You know how he is."

I got up and stood in front of the window. I was looking into the garden. I remembered how my father had made the architect change the standard plan and there was much grief but he did get the changes. He always wanted things different and practical. It had to make sense, common sense and not convoluted sense.

"Who will plan the garden? Who will take us camping? Who will build the house on the hill? Who will take pictures? Who? WHO? TELL ME WHO?"

"What?" my aunt asked.

I threw up my arms and started to cry loudly. "How do we know? It's a mistake! Can't it be a mistake? So many men have come home after they were pronounced dead. It's too soon. Everything is still a mess. No?"

"Opapa said it was very clear. It had the name of the person who has his personal belongings, his watch and his wallet."

I looked at my aunt. Was she about to say more? Did she know more? *I am sure she is thinking about her husband.* He had been taken prisoner by the British and held in a camp. After being discharged properly, he had walked for two weeks to get home to Vienna. He had knocked on her door one day. He had looked thin and weak, with long hair, some of it already gray, and his face unshaven, but he was home. Safe and alive.

A few mornings later, two Russian soldiers came to their door. "You Doctor, you help your people. We need doctor, come." He had taken his instrument bag, his hat and coat and they had left. That was almost a year ago and she had not heard a word from him. The *Kommandantura* said they have been investigating but cannot find a trail. *Will he ever come back?*

"I don't want to stay for dinner, thank you. Did you tell Dieter and Ina?"

"No, not yet, we wanted you to know first. You should go and visit your mother, soon. She is waiting for you."

"Yes, I know but with the dumb visiting hours ..." I remembered the battle with the nurse on the floor to let me come in after visiting hours. They were so stupid, clinging to minute instructions in the middle of all this confusion.

I headed for the door leading to the hallway. "I am going back. I really want to see the letter. Have Opapa send it to us. I will go and see Mama tomorrow. I will take off from school. If you talk to her before, tell her please."

"Why had my mother not wanted to tell me herself? Why? It was a matter between us, between her, the wife, and me, the son, flesh and blood of them both. Nobody should come between us. I loved my aunt. Nevertheless, she was a stranger. Still is, and always would be. My mother's little kid sister. Now she had become the bringer of bad news."

Uncle Rudi stood in the hallway and Tante Helga on the stairs right behind him. Their faces were serious. They had been waiting for me to come out. "Poor boy," my uncle said, and there was a noise from the woman. The man stretched out his hand to me. I took it very briefly, looking away and never stopping my walk. They were just more strangers. This man was alive. He had avoided the draft, dishonestly. Now he was alive and living in our house. My father was dead, gone, vanished.

See you on the weekend, probably," I said before I closed the outside door behind me.

I heard my sister call out my name from the garden. I turned and waved to her over the fence. I did not stop. For the first time in over five years, I walked right past the house with the bulldog without even the slightest awareness of its existence.

I passed August's house, my first friend after moving here. The only one I could really talk to, the one who was coming with me on the expedition to the Oasis in the Libyan Desert. Should I go in and tell him? *"My father is dead. Killed in Action. Defending what? Killed by whom? Why? Why? Why him? He wanted to come back to us. Badly."* I remembered my father's tears when he had left the first time, and the last time.

When was it that I had seen him last? It had been the surprise visit when my father had arrived on Christmas Eve together with all our presents and the Christmas tree. He had sat under the tree when we all came in for the opening of the gifts.

At the end of the street, I hesitated briefly while making the decision on how to go back to my quarters. I could catch the train back, the same way I had come. It was late enough for the commuter buses to run. That would even be faster. However, I was not ready to face any people. The whole world would see in my face that I was alone, that I had been robbed of my father by this stupid war.

I would walk. It would turn dark before I would arrive back where I lived. Where I lived—without a family, with an artificial father, an artificial mother, with artificial brothers, already separated brutally from the warm foursome we had been, which did not exist any more.

In the weak light of the setting sun, the brightly colored bubbles burst one by one.

406

The photo studio my father would open on his own. In the faint red light I would be watching the images emerging in the developer; I would help keeping the right amount of the different photo papers on hand; I would learn all about photography, maybe even study it.

The advertising agency was my mother's favorite idea, with my father designing logos and brochures, helping talented artisans sell their products. I would get to visit the potter's studio and the weaver's, maybe even the design furniture store, owned by the beautiful woman who was on many photos my father had taken.

I would learn the crafts my father admired so much. I would master them all so I could create the works others had not created yet.

His talents would work well with a gallery, an interior design studio, or designing garden furniture, stylish and functional, durable and made from smooth hardwoods.

My mother was not artistic. She and I could not do this alone. Even with my father's notebooks full of ideas and drawings, his collection of magazine clippings, his books, and his tools. It was all gone. These ideas would not materialize without the man who created them.

I felt as if I were hanging, suspended in midair, uncomfortably, without a way down to the ground. Who? Where? What could I lean on, rely on? There was nothing, nobody. Everybody was rebuilding their own life from the chaos: The uncle with plastics making good money, loving it, but also loving the old ways that had brought on the war. Politics did not make sense to me. Everybody fighting everybody else with the same weapons. With the help of God. Who's God? What God?

Alone. I was alone. Like here on this street. The railroad tracks on the right, the little gardens with the weekend shelters on the left. The city lay ahead of me, much of it in ruins. Looking around I did not see anybody. Tears were coming up again. Death made me remember death.

Here on this road I had watched a prisoner trying to escape from a work gang repairing the ruined rails. He had jumped across the railroad tracks in front of a train, climbed the fence to the road, and had run for cover in the little gardens on the other side of the street. The train had not been long enough for him to get a good lead on his pursuers. Three of them came running from behind the last car. They were in uniform, rifles held high. As soon as the guards had climbed the fence, they spread out on the road. I went down for cover by the fence towards the railroad tracks. They started to yell to the invisible fugitive to come out and give up.

"Wo? Wo?" asked the one closest to me, pointing into the gardens. I shrugged my shoulders. The guards did not speak German. From the few words I heard when they talked to each other, they sounded like Hungarians. One of them started to shoot. The others joined. I watched in horror as they fired round after round wildly into the gardens. The shots rang aloud in the noon air. A few of them hit the sheds. I recoiled at the sound of splintering wood and shattering metal.

Suddenly there was a yell from the guard farthest up the road. He must have seen movement in the shrubbery. He pointed and they all fired into the same bushes. Then there was this animal scream, from the man I had seen running earlier. The figure in the striped prison outfit jumped up high, ran a few steps, then threw up his arms as he was hit by another shot and fell screaming between the flowers and the shrubs. The guards ran towards him, each firing more shots.

When they came back to the road a few minutes later two of them were dragging the man in the prison clothes between them, their arms hooked under his, his legs limp and his head dangling on one side. I could not move from my spot. I was leaning against the fence and felt like throwing up. Sadness, anger, compassion for the man who had run, and fear mixed together with the sickness in my stomach, and the smell of the gunpowder, creating one great turmoil in my head.

They came straight at me. The prisoner was bleeding from several wounds, his head wobbling without life. The two soldiers had a hard time keeping him upright. The third soldier was carrying all three rifles. He kept hitting the dead man with his rifle, as if he could awaken him. I will never forget the sound of the rifle butt hitting that lifeless body. The guards' faces were serious but mixed with a little triumphant smile hidden in their features.

I looked at the dead man's face. The cheekbones stood out, the cheeks were hollow and gray, covered with a few days growth of beard, the lifeless eyes looking upward, showing a lot of white. I turned away and ran. I kept running for a long time until I was out of breath—and out of reach. I never told anybody about this experience, but I cried for the dead man whenever his face crossed my memory.

It was dark now, my eyes still full of tears, for which one of the dead men? I had not played this movie for a long time, but now it had played as clear as ever. It was hurting as much as the first time. Man killing man. Why? To what avail? Could one hate another human being enough to kill him or her?

I wondered how my father had died. Rifle fire? Bombs? Mines? Machine gun? Strafing? Or man-to-man combat? I had seen it all in the newsreels. Anonymous gray figures falling, disintegrating in explosions. Fire and smoke, bodies of men and beasts and buildings, dead forests, dead cannons and tanks. Smiling victors, smoking cigarettes, waving to children and women. Rallies, speeches, flags. Noise, noise, noise.

A train went by on one of the few tracks rebuilt by those prisoners after the final raid of the war.

I came up on the first houses; soon I walked on what looked like a city street. Fifteen more minutes. I was tired and worn out inside.

Again, I entered this building, this non-home of mine and climbed its four tall floors. I rang the bell. I could hear "Baby" bouncing down the hallway.

"There you are! We just started a new tournament. You can still join."

He was talking about our nightly chess rounds under the supervision of *Herr Oberbaurat* who was an excellent player and instructor.

"I think I will. Let me wash my hands quickly." I turned towards the bathroom in the hall. I wanted to check my face for traces of tears.

"Did you eat dinner at home?" *Frau Oberbaurat* was standing in the middle of the big kitchen ironing away at a pile of her husband's shirts. She used a wet rag under the iron, so the creases would come out easier.

"Yes, thank you," I lied.

"Why did they want you at home? Everything going well out there?" she asked. Her husband sat in the corner by the little table and looked up from his book, waiting for my answer.

No matter what I say, it will be hard, I thought and felt the tears coming up again.

"We received official word that my father was killed in action. The Red Cross sent a letter to my Grandfather."

"We all knew that, didn't we? If you had not heard anything from him that long ... "she said without looking up from the shirt, the steam hissing from under the hot iron.

Herr Oberbaurat said, "That is sad," nodded a few times and made his little pointed mouth, which he did only when he thought hard.

I looked through the door where the others were playing chess. Maybe they would be more sympathetic towards my pain that felt worse now. I wanted to scream— *"we already knew that"*—NO WE DID NOT ALREADY KNOW THAT, WE KNEW THAT HE WAS A GOOD FATHER AND THAT WE WANTED HIM BACK. BUT SOMEBODY STOLE HIM. SOMEBODY WHO DOES NOT CARE ABOUT FATHERS AND CHILDREN AND WIVES AND LOVE AND LIFE, SENT HIM OFF THIS WORLD, BRUTALLY, WITHOUT ASKING ANYBODY, HIM AND HUNDREDS OF THOUSANDS OF OTHERS, MILLIONS OF OTHERS—*"We already knew that"*—NO, NOBODY ALREADY KNEW THAT. UNCLE OTTO HAD BEEN BLOWN TO BITS TWO YEARS EARLIER SOMEWHERE IN RUSSIA, ONE MORNING BEFORE HE EVEN WOKE UP. DO YOU KNOW HOW MY GRANDMOTHER IS FEELING? TWO SONS DEAD. ALL SHE HAD. TWO SONS. AND THOSE ARE ONLY TWO, TWO OUT OF SO MANY MILLIONS—DO YOU KNOW HOW MANY MOTHERS THERE ARE, CRYING, MOURNING FOR THE UNFINISHED LIVES OF THEIR CHILDREN, AND HOW MANY WIVES ARE CRYING FOR THEIR UNFINISHED LOVES?

"We already knew that"—Life must go on.

I went to wash my hands and then moved slowly to the study. I asked Werner to set up a board. "Let's play one. The winner plays their winner." I pointed to the other two.

"I am very sorry about your father," Werner said, looking straight at me with eyes full of genuine feeling. He held out his hand and took mine firmly. I closed my eyes for a moment, and then opened them again. I said "Thank you, Werner," trying to put *Frau Oberbaurat's* insensitivity out of my mind.

Werner now held out his two fists, one containing a white and the other a black pawn, "your choice."

I tapped on the left fist. Werner turned it over and opened it: White.

We turned the board so the white figures were in front of me. I immediately made the first move, part of a standard opening. Werner responded swiftly with the black knight, I advanced my pawn, came out with the bishop and finally with another pawn.

We opted for an early trade of bishops. When I took Werner's man off the board, I sat him down very gently on the side. "You will be back and alive for the next game, don't worry!" I said quietly.

"What?" Werner asked without looking up, intent on his next move.

"Nothing."

I easily found room 208 on the second floor of the hospital. What I did not find was my mother. The three women in the room did not know anything about her. They all had moved in today. I felt my heart stop.

The floor nurse consulted her records and directed me to the ground floor, room 48. My mother had been transferred there. When I entered that room, I was overwhelmed. It was a hall, not a room. It was huge, with high windows letting in so much of the afternoon sun that one had the feeling of being outdoors. After my eyes had adjusted from the darkness in the hallways, I quickly spotted my mother in a bed in the center of this fleet of beds.

I made my way past at least a dozen other patients, nodding at them as I passed. The ones without visitors nodded back and looked at me with curiosity, maybe trying to guess whom I was there to see.

I walked erect and self-conscious. I still had not caught my mother's eye. I wanted to drop my anchor; I wanted to stop drifting between those white ships with their passengers headed for who knows where.

My mother was sitting up in her bed, a fragile figure propped up by two huge white pillows, which stuck out at either side of her head just like the starched headgear of the Sisters of the Holy Cross who ran this place.

"You look like one of the sisters, Mama," I said to her instead of a greeting, imitating the 'wings' with my hands alongside my head.

She smiled and slowly stretched out one of her arms. "I am so glad you could come. Thank you." I bent down for the hug and a kiss on each cheek.

"Aunt Trude told me that they don't allow flowers in the hospital, so you'll get a nice bouquet when you come out." I felt I had to apologize for not bringing any flowers.

"When will you get out?" I asked.

"Oh, they don't know yet. They keep hearing noises in my chest, and they will not let me go until those noises have cleared up." Her voice was a few notches weaker than usual. She sounded as frail as she looked. Nevertheless, she smiled in an effort to look like she was recovering.

"Come on, please tell me, let's talk about Papa!" I thought as I started to choke, partly from the reality of the loss of my father surfacing again and partly because she looked so sick and weak, and so far from recovery. She had another six months to go before finishing the midwifery course, then three months of internship in a maternity ward. There was no way she could finish in this condition. She could hardly keep herself in the world, how could she help others to slip into it? New babies need strength in the mothers to deliver them and strength in the world to receive them. This mother did not look like she could deliver that assistance.

"How is everything working out at the Oberbaurats? How is the food?" she asked putting her hand on mine.

"Oh, it's food. The menu has not changed. I cannot believe she cooks the same meals every week. Could you do that?" I asked, shaking my head slightly to show my impatience and annoyance.

"No, it would be boring. I'd have to invent something new every once in a while," my mother said. Talking brought some color into her face. She looked better already. The bright sunshine throughout the hall helped, too.

We chatted on for a while about her treatments, about the hospital food, about the sisters, and about who had come to visit.

There was the sound of a bell out in the hallway.

"Visiting hours are over ... visiting hours are over. All visitors please leave the building, immediately." The nun ringing her bell shouting the announcement was serious. It sounded so brutal to me, so not in concert with healing, this loud demand for separation of patients and their visitors. She came through the main door and looked around. Swinging her bell one more time and nodding at the visitors who slowly got up and obediently started to move.

"Now I have to leave, and she has not said one word about Papa. I cannot believe it! What can I say? I am going to cry. Maybe we should cry together, maybe that would help. I am not going to start it. She is sick and weak. Maybe she doesn't want to think about it, and for sure not talk about it."

I held her hand, moving away slowly, letting it slip out of mine.

"Aunt Trude told you?" She had waited until the separation.

I felt the lava of pain coming up out of my core—*"I don't want to cry now, it does not help!"* I nodded. "What are we going to do?"

"I thought about it a lot. I will tell you next time."

"*Frau Oberbaurat* didn't even say she was sorry when I told her about Papa, can you imagine?" I saw a change in her face but she did not speak.

"When will you come back?"

"Visiting hours ...." the nun and the bell reappeared.

"I'll take off early from school, if they let me, on Thursday. I could not leave earlier today. The visiting hours are only from one to three. I will try again to make it here in time. Yes?"

"Thank you. Thank you for coming. I wanted to see you. You look well. Goodbye." She blew me a kiss.

All her movements look so tired, I thought. *I wonder how sick she really is*. Musch Omi, her mother, had died of complications with her lungs.

Please do not let her die—please she cannot leave us, too. Please Mama, get well, please.

I turned one more time at the door and waved. Her eyes were still on me. I walked quickly down the long hallway and out into the open. The huge park surrounding the hospital was bathed in the afternoon light. I looked down the alley of magnificent old chestnut trees who had withstood so many more years than I had. The sun outlined their big five-fingered leaves. However, the light shining through them did not reach the inside of me.

The "next time," when we would talk about my mother's plans for the future, never happened. She became weaker and she was in no condition to discuss my father's death and our future. All was on hold for now.

In school my grades were looking up. I had found out how easy it was for me to study if I applied myself. Every day I finished my homework quickly after eating lunch, I let the Oberbaurats query me in all subjects and check my written work and then I was free to do as I pleased. On hot sunny days, I would go to a public pool or to a quiet arm of the Danube to swim, on rainy days I would read or go to a movie. When the school year finished, I moved back to my real home. It was good to have the garden, my brother, my sister, and whoever was left of my old friends back. It did not have the same feel, though. I had been cut away and the wound did not want to heal. My mother recovered slowly and eased back into her training program. We had a few more short and neutral visits. I was not looking forward to going back to the Oberbaurats in the fall.

That threat was hanging over me like a cloud all summer until at the last minute my uncle in Graz came to the rescue. I was to start school there in the fall, as a resident in the *Marieninstitut*, a Catholic boarding school run by Marianist brothers. My uncle would pay for room and board. I had no concept of what to expect. It sounded very scary and controlled. Could it be worse than being rinsed off with cold water by an old woman at the weekly bath? Would there be worse things to eat than sawdust blood sausage once a week? Would they lock me in for good and drag me to Holy Mass every Sunday? Graz was a very long train ride from Linz—how long I did not know for sure yet. Visiting home during school holidays would certainly be difficult.

On the positive side were my three cousins–should I get to see them more than just before moving into the school- because we had had lots of fun together on visits and vacations. I liked their mother, too. My uncle however was known as very cold and strict—and very Catholic.

Life, as I had known it, was over. It was up to me to shape my future within the constraints of my new environment, which I assumed, had a few characteristics in common with the school in the Castle. Regimentation would be Catholic not Nazi inspired. Instead of the friendly housemother, Frau Haller, there would be nuns, study hall, free time and nights would be under the supervision of the Marianist Brothers. I was not so sure about my uncle's powers over all this. My guess was that the local family council had—without coming up with an acceptable plan—self destructed. If I did not cause any trouble, I had a chance to sail on my own, pretty much.

Would I miss the 'family'? There had not been much of it recently. My mother locked up in the hospital, my siblings and myself playing family with surrogate 'mothers.' Before that, the four of us living with other people at some place other than our home or with strangers in our house who had been more or less embroiled in our family life. My father had been absent for many years now, first alive, communicating with us through letters and short visits, and now dead, an inspirational ghost only, former lover and maker of rules.

Did I really want to remain as part of this unit, bound by blood alone? Or was it time for the cell to divide, with me the first part breaking off into a new universe? The thoughts were too vague, too esoteric at this point. I needed to experience the change in order to come to a conclusion.

When the time came, I packed up my clothes, my favorite books, my water color set and some brushes, colored pencils, and a few family photographs. Where and how would I live? *Marieninstitut* does not sound very homey.

Nobody was available to take me to the train station. My mother was in class, my aunt could not be expected to deal with both my siblings and her own little daughter on public transportation, so it was me. Me, I guessed, would be it from now on.

Acknowledgements

Many people have been there for me throughout the years of writing. My children and other family, friends, therapists—too many to mention all here by name. But some have been very consistent in reminding me at every opportunity (every chance they had) of my duty to finish this book. Foremost among those are my dear old friends Hans-Jürgen and Elfi Döpel and lately Cotton Fite.

Several people were kind (brave?) enough to take it on themselves to read through the complete manuscript and offer their invaluable comments—Caroll Shreeve, Elizabeth Sailer, Bob and Liz Crow, Anne Berenberg, my wife Marcia Heeter, and last but not least, Helen Gallagher who offered constant encouragement and became my guiding spirit in completing the project.

To all of them I offer my gratitude and sincere Thank You's for not giving up on me. You made me do it!

About the Author

Peter Slonek grew up in Austria during and after WWII. His early interest in books and the theater inspired him to write his own stories. He received a scholarship to study Journalism in the US for one year. Back in Austria he wrote essays, poetry and stories for young adult magazines. For several years he worked as an editor at the U.S. Information Agency where he created the Austrian Fulbright Alumni Magazine. He immigrated to the US at age thirty where he continued his writing and published several short stories and essays in English. He is still steeped in both cultures which give his writing a special flavor. This memoir is his first full length book.